Obtaining PRC Approvals

for Foreign Investment Enterprises and Infrastructure Projects

Second Edition

INSERT

法
ASIA LAW & PRACTICE
A EUROMONEY COMPANY

ADDENDUM

The following legislation is an addition to Legislation Appendix 2 and follows the "Industries, Products and Technologies Currently Particularly Encouraged by the State for Development Catalogue" (pp. 247-257).

Obtaining PRC Approvals

for Foreign Investment Enterprises and Infrastructure Projects

Second Edition

General Editor

Clark T. RANDT, Jr.

Contributors

Don H. BENNETT
Patty P.Y. CHAN
Laurence C. FRANKLIN
David FU
Mark J. HARTY
LIU Chu
Randall PEERENBOOM
Edward L. TURNER III
Shirley XU
Ariel Lu YE
Xiaowei YE
Wei-Min ZHANG

法
ASIA LAW & PRACTICE
A EUROMONEY COMPANY

Published by
Asia Law & Practice
Euromoney Publications (Jersey) Limited
5/F. Printing House
6 Duddell Street
Central, Hong Kong

Managing Director: Patrick M. Dransfield
Managing Editor: Benedict Rogers
Editor: J. Roger Decavele
Production Manager: Esther Li

ISBN: 962-936-066-7

Printed in Hong Kong

CONTENTS

LEGISLATION APPENDICES

ABOUT THE CONTRIBUTORS

Clark T. RANDT, Jr. – General Editor

Clark T. Randt, Jr. is a Partner at Shearman & Sterling and is resident in the firm's Hong Kong office, from where, in addition to specializing in foreign investment, infrastructure projects, mergers and acquisitions and private equity fund transactions in the Asia-Pacific Region, he leads the firm's substantial China practice. He has practised law as a member of the New York bar since 1976 and has lived in Asia for more than 20 years, in cities like Beijing, Hong Kong and Tokyo. He has been travelling to China on business for more than 25 years and in a wide range of foreign investment projects in China he has represented clients, including many top Fortune 100 and European companies. Mr. Randt led the legal teams in the first three New York Stock Exchange listings of securities by China-related companies. He is currently acting on behalf of the People's Government of Guangdong Province in connection with the privatization of the Dongshen Water Supply Company, which supplies 75% of Hong Kong's water, and the restructuring of the Guangdong Enterprises Group of companies. In 1996, Mr. Randt also became a member of the Hong Kong Bar and the Hong Kong Law Society.

Mr. Randt first visited China on business in 1974 as the representative of the National Council for United States-China Trade. From 1982 until 1984, he served as Commercial Attaché and First Secretary at the American Embassy in Beijing. He was awarded a Distinguished Service Silver Medal by the US Secretary of Commerce Malcolm Baldrige.

Mr Randt received a Juris Doctor degree from the University of Michigan Law School in 1975 and attended Harvard Law School from 1973 to 1974, where he was awarded an East Asian Legal Studies Travelling Fellowship to China. Mr. Randt also holds a Diploma in the Law of the People's Republic of China from the University of East Asia, Macau awarded in 1989. He received a BA from Yale University in 1968. He is fluent in Mandarin Chinese.

Mr. Randt is a former Governor and First Vice President of the American Chamber of Commerce in Hong Kong and Chairman of its China Commercial Relations Committee. He is routinely selected as a leading China practice lawyer by *Asia Law* and is listed in *Who's Who in American Law* and *Who's Who in Hong Kong*. He has spoken frequently and published numerous articles concerning business and law in China, including the chapter on "The Approval and Registration Process" in *The Life and Death of a Joint Venture in China*. He is a member of the American Bar Association, the International Bar Association, the American Society of International Law, the New York State Bar Association and the Inter-Pacific Bar Association.

Founded in 1873 and one of the world's leading international law firms with over 700 lawyers, **Shearman and Sterling** has a multinational presence in Asia, with offices in Beijing, Hong Kong, Singapore and Tokyo. The firm was among the first international law firms to be active in China, commencing with its representation of the Ministry of Coal in 1979 and was also among the first international firms approved by China's Ministry of Justice to establish an office in Beijing. The firm services its significant China practice with bilingual lawyers specializing in China transactions from its Hong Kong and Beijing offices.

Don H. BENNETT

Don H. Bennett is an Associate in Shearman & Sterling's Hong Kong office. He has been involved in project finance, and mergers and acquisitions transactions which have mainly focused on power project investment in China and the Philippines. Mr. Bennett has lived and worked in Taiwan and Hong Kong for over five years and is a fluent Mandarin speaker.

Mr. Bennett received a dual BA from the University of Hawaii at Manoa in 1993, a Juris Doctor degree from the William S. Richardson School of Law in 1997 and an LLM from the University of Hong Kong School of Law in 1998. Mr Bennett is admitted to the bar in New York and Hawaii.

Patty P.Y. CHAN

Patty P.Y. Chan is an Associate in Vivien Chan & Co., Hong Kong. She obtained her law degree from the University of Hong Kong. She was admitted to practise as a solicitor in Hong Kong in 1991 and in England and Wales in 1995. Miss Chan practises in various fields of law but specialises in the field of real property law. She is the head of the Conveyancing Department of her current firm and is responsible for handling all Hong Kong and PRC conveyancing and tenancy matters as well as commercial matters in the firm. Miss Chan also served as a part-time lecturer and tutor in law in the Vocational Training Council and City University of Hong Kong during her early years of practice.

Vivien Chan & Co. was one of the first foreign law firms to be given formal approval by the PRC, Ministry of Justice in 1993 to set up an office in Beijing. Ms Vivien Chan started the firm's China's practice in 1989. Vivien Chan & Co. advises multinational corporations and Hong Kong companies on investment and tax issues and intellectual property rights protection in China. The firm regularly represented many of the leading commercial, financial, service and industrial companies in the region, as well as numerous "Fortune 500" companies as their appointed regional counsel.

The firm's China practice is known for their experience in government relations. To attain clients' objectives, and to achieve success within the bureaucracy in China, the firm has established relations with government departments and their responsible officers at various levels. With such network, the firm is therefore able to advise clients on up-to-date laws (consisting often of notices and ad hoc regulations which remain unpublished or generally unavailable to members of the public) and policies of the day to readily assess how representation should be submitted to secure respective approvals.

Laurence C. FRANKLIN

Laurence C. Franklin is Adjunct Associate Professor in the Department of Finance at the Hong Kong University of Science & Technology (HKUST). He teaches about investment in China in the MBA Program and in the Kellogg-HKUST Executive MBA Program. In addition to numerous China advisory engagements, Professor Franklin has been involved in the successful completion of more than 45 equity and debt transactions in China, either as an investment banker, commercial banker or attorney.

Professor Franklin holds M.B.A. and Juris Doctor degrees from Stanford, and is qualified as a Certified Public Accountant. He is admitted to practice in California, Illinois and Florida, as well as before the United States Supreme Court.

In addition to his work at HKUST, Professor Franklin has taught in the MBA Programs at Stanford University, the University of Chicago, the University of Southern California, and the China-Europe International Business School (CEIBS) in Shanghai and Beijing.

David FU

David Fu is an associate in Shearman & Sterling's Beijing Office. He works primarily on China-related direct investment projects, mergers and acquisitions deals and securities transactions. Mr. Fu has extensive experience in telecommunications and Internet projects. Since joining Shearman & Sterling in October 1995, he has focused on the structuring of investments by international telecommunications corporations in the construction and operation of telecommunications networks. Prior to joining the firm, Mr. Fu served as a legal advisor to Shanghai Science & Technology Investment Co., Ltd., a shareholder of China United Telecommunications Corporation ("China Unicom"). He actively participated in negotiations with U.S., Australian and Singaporean telecommunications corporations concerning the establishment of Sino-foreign joint ventures to invest in GSM and VSAT networks in several major cities in China.

Mr. Fu received an LLM from Columbia University School of Law in 1998. He received a Master of Law from Shanghai Institute of Foreign Trade, School of Law in 1993 and a BA from Anhui Institute of Education in 1990. Mr. Fu is a native speaker of Mandarin and is fluent in written and spoken English. Mr. Fu is admitted to the bar in New York.

Mark J. HARTY

Mark J. Harty, Asian Counsel, is an attorney in Shearman & Sterling's Hong Kong office. He was previously the resident attorney in charge of Shearman & Sterling's Beijing and Taipei Offices, and has also worked in the firm's New York office. He graduated from Harvard Law School in 1982 and has lived and worked in Asia for more than 14 years. Mr. Harty has broad experience in corporate, securities and international finance.

LIU Chu

Professor Liu Chu is Senior China Counsel to Shearman & Sterling. He has extensive experience in drafting Chinese foreign investment regulations, negotiating treaties and conventions on behalf of the PRC Government, and in examining and approving foreign investment contracts submitted to the PRC's Ministry of Foreign Trade and Economic Cooperation (MOFTEC).

From 1982 to 1988, Professor Liu served as Deputy Director, Department of Treaties and Law at MOFTEC in the PRC. In that capacity, he acted as the chief drafter of the PRC regulations governing joint ventures, wholly foreign-owned enterprises, Sino-foreign cooperative enterprises and foreign economic contracts. Professor Liu also assumed primary responsibility for reviewing and approving the contracts for prominent joint ventures in China.

Professor Liu led the PRC delegation which negotiated the Treaties on Mutual Promotion and Protection of Investment between China and the United States, the USSR, Canada, Australia, Poland and other countries; the Geneva Convention on Agency in International Sales of Goods; the Hague Convention on Applicable Law of Contracts in International Sales of Goods; the UNIDROIT Convention on International Leasing; and the United Nations' Code of Conduct for Transnational Corporations.

The author of numerous articles, in Chinese and English, on foreign investment in China, Professor Liu has taught at Harvard University, the Georgetown University Law Center, the University of Hawaii at Manoa, the University of Minnesota, the University of Melbourne, Australia and the University of California at Los Angeles (UCLA) School of Law. He is currently a visiting professor at the University of Southern California.

Professor Liu is also a member of the Chinese Bar. He is fluent in English, Mandarin, Shanghainese and Cantonese.

Randall PEERENBOOM

Randall Peerenboom obtained a B.A. in Philosophy, M.A. in Chinese Religion and Ph.D in Philosophy before obtaining a Juris Doctor degree from Columbia Law School. He has written several books and numerous articles on Chinese law and philosophy. From 1994 to 1998, he practised law with Freshfields in Beijing. He is currently teaching Chinese law at the University of California at Los Angeles Law School. In addition to advising on various aspects of foreign investment in China, he often serves as an expert witness on PRC legal issues and is Of Counsel at Yiwen Law Firm, a PRC firm specializing in foreign investment and litigation.

Edward L. TURNER III

Edward L. Turner III is Shearman & Sterling Managing Partner – Asia. Prior to relocating to Hong Kong in early 1994, Mr. Turner practised in the firm's New York and San Francisco offices, where his active practice areas included joint ventures and related financing transactions in the coal, oil and steel industries, and for manufacturing companies in various industries. Since coming to Asia, Mr. Turner has worked on numerous China direct investment transactions, involving both equity and debt financing for industrial and infrastructure projects. Mr. Turner's current practice focuses on financings and joint ventures including project development and project finance. Several project sponsors and financial institutions are among the clients Mr. Turner currently represents in the development, non-recourse financing and construction of electric power plants in China.

Mr. Turner obtained a BA from Vanderbilt University in 1966, studied at Harvard University on an Interim Study Programme, gained a Corning Glass Travelling Fellowship (International Business) in 1967 and obtained a Juris Doctor degree from Vanderbilt Law School in 1970. Mr. Turner is admitted to the Bar in California, New York and Hong Kong.

Shirley XU

Shirley (Xueli) Xu, a partner with Yi Wen Law Firm, graduated from Beijing University in 1987 with joint Bachelor of Laws and Bachelor of Arts degrees. She obtained an LLM from the University of Virginia School of Law in 1996 and was admitted to the Bar of the State of New York in the same year. Before joining Yi Wen in May 1999, she worked for a well established PRC law firm and two major international law firms in Beijing for more than seven years. Fluent in English, she specializes in general corporate matters, foreign investment, technology licensing and transfer, as well as China aspects of project finance and international trade.

The **Yi Wen Law Firm** (formerly known as Zhou & Liu) was founded as a partnership in Beijing in 1994. It currently consists of 14 lawyers. In addition to general corporate matters, the firm specializes in four main areas: foreign investment (including project finance; the establishment of joint ventures, wholly foreign owned enterprises, holding companies and representative offices; corporate restructuring; mergers and acquisitions; foreign trade; and technology transfers); securities; real estate and arbitration and litigation. Yi Wen and its partners have acted as lead counsel for a number of major multinational companies and/or their subsidiaries. They are able to provide legal services in Chinese, English or Japanese depending on client needs.

Ariel Lu YE

Ariel Lu Ye is a registered foreign lawyer in the China Group of Clifford Chance in Hong Kong and speaks frequently on Chinese law. She has extensive experience in commercial disputes resolution including commercial arbitration and litigation before Chinese and international arbitration institutions and Chinese courts.
Ariel received her undergraduate law degree from Peking University and her two graduate law degrees from the Chinese Academy of Social Science and Harvard Law School. She is qualified to practise law in both China and New York, U.S. and is fluent in Mandarin and English.

Ariel joined Clifford Chance, Hong Kong office in December 1995. Before that she worked in a Chinese state-owned law firm for 5 years (1986-1991) in Beijing, China and worked for a private owned China law firm (as a founding partner) for two years (1991-1993) in Beijing, China.

In November 1998, in recognition of her expertise in disputes resolution, Ariel was appointed as an Arbitrator of the Beijing Arbitration Commission in November 1998.

Clifford Chance is a leading multi-jurisdictional law firm with offices in 26 major business and financial centres world-wide and over 2000 lawyers representing 30 nationalities. On January 1, 2000 Clifford Chance will merge with US firm Rogers & Wells and German firm Pünder, Volhard, Weber & Axster to form the world's largest global law firm. Clifford Chance established its presence in Asia over 20 years ago. With offices in Hong Kong, Shanghai, Singapore, Tokyo, Bangkok, Hanoi and Ho Chi Minh City, Clifford Chance provides an unrivalled breadth and depth of experience across the region.

Xiaowei YE

Xiaowei Ye, a consultant to Shearman & Sterling's China practice group resident in the firm's Beijing office, is a qualified lawyer in the United States, being a member of both the District of Columbia and the Pennsylvania Bars. Ms. Ye is a native of Beijing, graduated from Georgetown College with a BA and obtained her Juris Doctor degree from Georgetown University Law Center. She has more than ten years of experience with China in the areas of investment, international trade and government relations.

Wei-Min ZHANG

Wei-Min Zhang is an Australian lawyer and a junior associate of Clifford Chance Hong Kong office. He is a native Mandarin speaker and is fluent in Cantonese. He has experience in general PRC commercial work and has been involved in various China-related projects including joint venture projects, power projects, restructurings and acquisitions.

ABBREVIATIONS

The following abbreviations are used in this book:

BOOT	Build-Own-Operate-Transfer
BOT	Build-Operate-Transfer
CDMA	Code Division Multiple Access
CIETAC	China International Economic and Trade Arbitration Commission
CIN	Computer Information Networks
CIRC	China Insurance Regulatory Commission
CJV	Sino-foreign Cooperative Joint Venture
COFTEC	Commission of Foreign Trade and Economic Cooperation
DGT	Directorate General of Telecommunications
DIC	Department of International Cooperation
EJV	Sino-foreign Equity Joint Venture
EPC	Equipment, Procurement and Construction
FERC	Foreign Investment Enterprise Foreign Exchange Registration Certificate
FFI	Foreign Financial Institution
FIE	Foreign Investment Enterprise
ICBC	Industrial and Commercial Bank of China
ISDN	Integrated Services Digital Network
ITICs	International Trust and Investment Corporations
JVFTE	Sino-foreign Joint Venture Foreign Trade Enterprise
MII	Ministry of Information Industry
MOC	Ministry of Communications
MOEP	Ministry of Electric Power
MOFTEC	Ministry of Foreign Trade and Economic Cooperation (established in 1993; successor of the Ministry of Foreign Economic Relations and Trade or "MOFERT")
MPI	Ministry of Power Industry
MPT	Ministry of Posts and Telecommunications
MW	Megawatts

PBOC	People's Bank of China
PRC	People's Republic of China
PTA	Post and Telecommunications Administration
RMB	Renminbi
SAFE	State Administration of Foreign Exchange (before October 1, 1996 translated as "State Administration of Exchange Control")
SAIC	State Administration of Industry and Commerce
SDB	State Development Bank
SDPC	State Development and Planning Commission (succeeded the State Planning Commission ("SPC") in 1998)
SETC	State Economic and Trade Commission
SEZ	Special Economic Zone
SRRC	State Radio Regulatory Commission
TAE	Technologically Advanced Enterprise
VSAT	Very Small Aperture Terminal
WFOE	Wholly Foreign-owned Enterprise

INTRODUCTION

As China faces the new millennium, many dramatic changes have occurred since the publication of the first edition of this book in March 1996, not the least of which is the significant streamlining and reform of the Chinese government bureaucracy itself. As dramatic as these changes have been, they pale in comparison to the winds of change that promise to sweep China's regulatory and economic landscape as a result of China's impending entry into the WTO regime and consequent adoption of significant economic reform measures directly impacting foreign investment and trade. Commercial sectors traditionally closed to foreign investors will be open to them. Certain commercial activities, once the exclusive preserve of China's trading companies, will also be opening up to foreign participation.

This Second Edition addresses the changes that have occurred and those that are anticipated in respect of obtaining the critical PRC government approvals for foreign investment enterprises and infrastructure projects. Not only have all the chapters been revised and updated to address new legislation but a new chapter on toll road projects and an expanded Legislation Appendix including some of the most recent measures, have been added.

The focus of this edition, however, remains the same: what approvals does my project in China require from whom and how do I obtain them? The authors, all leading experts in their respective fields, have tried to answer not only these basic but not simple questions, but also to suggest helpful strategies and to provide helpful insights into the thinking of the examination and approval authorities at the local and central levels. What are the parameters by which authorities examine prospective projects? What are the problems they have encountered and what are the bureaucratic sensitivities? What are the grey areas and, moreover, lest we be guilty of - as a client once put it - "confusing law with reality", what is the common practice?

Each chapter deals with a significant form of investment or specially regulated sector or infrastructure project type, each with their unique regulatory and approval issues.

We hope that you find this new edition as helpful and informative as we intend it to be and wish to thank our unfailingly encouraging and ever-patient managing editor and editor, Benedict Rogers and J. Roger Decavele.

Clark T. Randt, Jr.
Shearman & Sterling Hong Kong
December 1999

SECTION I:

ESTABLISHING FOREIGN INVESTMENT ENTERPRISES

CHAPTER 1

APPROVALS FOR ESTABLISHING A JOINT VENTURE

Clark T. Randt, Jr., Partner
Shearman & Sterling, Hong Kong

In China, prospective foreign investors may choose between two distinct joint venture investment vehicles:

- the equity joint venture ("EJV") and
- the cooperative enterprise, alternatively referred to as a cooperative joint venture or as a contractual joint venture ("CJV").

EJVs are established under the *PRC, Sino-foreign Equity Joint Venture Law*[1] (the Joint Venture Law) and supplemented by the PRC, *Sino-foreign Equity Joint Venture Law Implementing Regulations*[2] (the Joint Venture Implementing Regulations). CJVs are established under the *PRC, Sino-foreign Cooperative Joint Venture Law*[3] (the Cooperative Enterprise Law) and supplemented by the *PRC, Sino-foreign Cooperative Joint Venture Law Implementing Regulations*[4] (the Cooperative Enterprise Implementing Regulations). Both EJVs and CJVs are further subject to numerous notices and circulars, many affecting foreign-invested enterprises (FIEs) generally.[5]

For government approval purposes, both types of joint venture are treated almost identically.[6] The approval authority is delegated by the State Council to the State Development and Planning Commission ("SDPC") of the People's Republic of China ("PRC") and in the PRC's Ministry of Foreign Trade and Economic Cooperation (MOFTEC) in Beijing. Under certain specified conditions, this authority may be delegated by SDPC and MOFTEC to analogous local organs in the provinces, autonomous regions and municipalities directly under the control of the central government and, in some cases, further down the bureaucratic chain to the corresponding government organs at the smaller municipality and county levels. The conditions on this devolution of approval authority with respect to an EJV are twofold:

- the "total amount of investment" is within the limit set by the State Council and the source of capital of the Chinese participants has been ascertained; and
- no additional allocations of raw materials by the State are required, and the national balance of fuel, power, transportation and foreign trade export quotas is not affected.[7]

---

1. Adopted on July 1, 1979 by the National People's Congress and amended on the basis of the *National People's Congress, Revision of the PRC, Sino-foreign Equity Joint Venture Law* of April 4, 1990.
2. Promulgated on September 20, 1983 and thereafter amended and supplemented.
3. Approved by the National People's Congress on April 13, 1988.
4. Approved by the State Council on August 7, 1995.
5. Such as the *Questions Concerning Further Strengthening the Administration of the Examination, Approval and Registration of Foreign Investment Enterprises Circular Notice* adopted by the State Administration of Industry and Commerce and MOFTEC, November 3, 1994. See **Legislation Appendices**.
6. Joint Venture Implementing Regulations, Article 8 and Cooperative Enterprise Implementing Regulations, Article 5.
7. Joint Venture Implementing Regulations, Article 8.

There are five conditions for local approval of a CJV which are fundamentally similar to those for an EJV. They are:

- where the total investment in the CJV is within the limits subject to examination and approval by a department or local people's government authorized by the State Council;
- where the CJV is self-financing and does not need the State to contribute to the balance of its construction and production conditions;
- where it is not necessary for the CJV to obtain an export quota and/or licence issued by the relevant State department in charge of the export of products;
- where it is necessary to obtain an export quota and/or licence but where the consent of the relevant State departments in charge has been obtained prior to submission of the project proposal; and
- in other circumstances in which the establishment of a CJV is subject to examination and approval by a department or local people's government authorized by the State Council as stipulated in applicable laws and statutory regulations.[8]

As a general matter, SDPC and its lower level designees are charged with reviewing the Project Proposal and Feasibility Study (about which more later) to ensure that a project is appropriate for the industry and region, is not contrary to the relevant economic plan for such industry and region, is not redundant and does not violate "the comprehensive balance of the State", an ambiguous parameter discussed in more detail later. MOFTEC and its lower level designees, on the other hand, through their Departments of Foreign Investment Administration and their Departments of Treaties and Law, review the Joint Venture Contract and related Articles of Association of the proposed new joint venture company to check for compliance.

In the case of either an EJV or CJV, one of the problems is that the threshold amount of "total investment" above which the project must be examined and approved by SDPC and MOFTEC in Beijing is not entirely transparent as it is not clearly delineated in a public document or regulation but is, instead, apparently considered by the Chinese Government to be an internal administrative matter subject only to confidential, internal documents, although the current thresholds set forth in Table 2: Approval Thresholds (see "Approval Jurisdiction" below) are freely disclosed by most foreign investment officials to those who ask.

Confusion over the appropriate level of examination and approval authority is aggravated by the chorus of local municipal and provincial officials who, despite a confidential internal warning circular jointly commissioned by the SDPC's predecessor commission, the State Planning Commission and MOFTEC, exhorting local examination and approval authorities to be more careful in their examination and approval work in respect of foreign investment enterprises in China, confidently declare that

8. Cooperative Enterprise Implementing Regulations, Article 6.

"We can approve your joint venture locally without bothering with the central government in Beijing."

In many cases, experience has shown, this claim is simply incorrect, thus putting the prospective foreign investor in an awkward and difficult position.

As discussed below, the promulgation of a new notice in this regard, although well-intended, has, regrettably, further clouded the picture.[9] Additional uncertainty is added by China's apparently imminent entry into the World Trade Organization. An official from China's National People's Legislative Affairs Commission was recently quoted as saying that the Chinese laws governing joint venture "will likely be merged to eliminate the different treatment of foreign investors. We'll adopt principles familiar to foreign businesses and principles adopted by the international community."[10]

Project Priority

The first enquiries a prospective foreign joint venture investor should make are:

- what is the appropriate examination and approval authority in China? (see "Approval Jurisdiction" below); and
- is the industrial type or other category of the proposed joint venture (unless expressly indicated to the contrary, each reference to "joint venture" includes both EJVs and CJVs) a category that is either encouraged, permitted, restricted or prohibited altogether by the Chinese Government?

In respect of project priorities, Table 1 (below) sets out general lists promulgated by the SDPC, State Economic and Trade Commission and MOFTEC of the types of investment which fall into each of the four categories, except the "Permitted" Category.[11] The Permitted Category contains all foreign investment project types not specifically encouraged, restricted or prohibited. The State Council has published an updated, expanded and more detailed breakdown of the four categories in the *Foreign Investment Industrial Guidance Catalogue*[12] (see **Legislation Appendices**).

9. *Notice Regarding Relevant Issues in Reporting for the Record to MOFTEC Foreign Investment Enterprises under the Encouraged Category Examined and Approved by Local Authorities Themselves,* promulgated by MOFTEC on October 15, 1999. See **Legislation Appendices**.

10. "NPC Prepares Laws for Entry into Trade Body," Vivien Pik-Kwan Chan, *South China Morning Post*, November 21, 1999, p.5.

11. Directing of Foreign Investment Tentative Provisions (see **Legislation Appendices**), promulgated by the SDPC, the State Economic Commission and MOFTEC on June 20, 1995.

12. Adopted the State Council on December 29, 1997 with effect on January 1, 1998.

Table 1: Joint Venture Project Categories

Project Category	Types of Investment
I. ENCOURAGED	1. Projects which involve new agricultural technology, comprehensive development of agriculture and construction of industries in energy, transport and important raw materials; 2. Projects which involve new and high technology or advanced technology, or which involve new equipment or new materials capable of improving product quality and efficiency, capable of saving energy and raw materials, or capable of improving the technological and economic efficiency of enterprises or projects which produce new equipment or new materials to satisfy market demands where there is a shortage of supply in China; 3. Projects which satisfy international market demands and are capable of upgrading product quality, opening up new markets, increasing sales of products for exports and expanding exports; 4. Projects which involve new technology and/or new equipment involving comprehensive utilization of natural resources and renewable resources and prevention and control of environmental pollution; 5. Projects which are capable of taking advantage of human and natural resources in central and western China and are in compliance with the State industry policies of China; and 6. Any other projects which are encouraged by the State laws and statutory regulations of China.
II. PERMITTED	All others not listed above or below.
III. RESTRICTED	1. Projects involving technology which has already been developed in China or which has already been introduced into China and where production capability has already been able to satisfy domestic market demands; 2. Projects in industries in which the State seeks to attract foreign investment on a trial basis or projects in industries which have exclusive selling rights within China; 3. Projects involving exploration or exploitation of rare or valuable mineral deposits;

	4. Projects involving industries where State uniform planning is required; and 5. Any other projects which are restricted by State laws and statutory regulations of China.
IV. PROHIBITED	1. Projects which endanger the national security or harm the public interest; 2. Projects which pollute or damage the environment, harm natural resources or pose threats to human health; 3. Projects which utilize large tracts of farm land, are harmful to the protection and development of land resources, or endanger the security of military installations and their effective use; 4. Projects which utilize production techniques or technology indigenous to China; and 5. Any other projects which are prohibited under the State laws and statutory regulations of China.

The Restricted Category is further sub-divided into two sub-categories of projects: Restricted A and Restricted B.[13] The approval authority for Projects falling within the Restricted A category cannot be delegated below the level of the relevant provincial, autonomous region or municipality subject to direct central government control.[14] The Production of aspirin or paracetamol or the establishment of foreign-invested gas stations or taxi services are examples of this category.[15] Restricted B projects have the added requirement that their project proposals must also be examined and approved by the department or departments in charge of the relevant industry.[16] For example, automobile and motorcycle assembly projects and projects to manufacture engines therefor would require the approval of the State Machine Industry Bureau.[17]

If the joint venture does not require resources from the central government and does not require special licenses to operate (see above), then the examination and approval authority will be determined by the total amount of investment set out in Table 2: Approval Thresholds (see "Approval Jurisdiction" below).

13. Directing of Foreign Investment Tentative Procedures, Article 10.

14. Id.

15. *Foreign Investment Industrial Guidance Catalogue*, Category A(6)(2) and (7)(1) and (2).

16. Directing of Foreign Investment, Article 10.

17. *Foreign Investment Industrial Guidance Catalogue*, Category B(8)(1) and (2).

Approval Jurisdiction

Approval jurisdiction is one of the most controversial and difficult issues facing prospective foreign investors in China, especially when the total investment is in excess of US$30 million. Table 2 below outlines the current approval thresholds for total investment amounts governing approval jurisdiction. "Total Investment" under the Joint Venture Law is a term of art referring to the sum of both registered capital and debt. "Registered Capital" is a concept akin to paid-in capital.

The Directing of Foreign Investment Tentative Provisions (see **Legislation Appendices**) state that:

"Examination and approval authority personnel who abuse their powers of office, practice favouritism, neglect their duties or grant approval beyond their jurisdiction shall have administrative sanctions imposed. When the case is serious enough to constitute a crime, criminal liability shall be pursued in accordance with the law."[18]

However, certain large municipalities, provinces, autonomous regions, minority areas and Special Economic Zones (SEZs) still insist that they have special power to approve projects in excess of US$30 million and actually refuse the requests of prudent foreign investors to report the projects up to the higher authorities in Beijing, usually out of concern that the central authorities may not share their enthusiasm for a project or may like the project but want it in another location and, at a minimum, will take a long time to respond.

In fact, for a brief while, in certain areas of Guangdong Province, the local branches of the State Administrative of Industry and Commerce, in a bold self-initiated reform, were registering joint ventures without any planning or investment authority approvals. MOFTEC, once news of this novel practice reached Beijing, quickly had this practice stopped.

In some cases, the capital base of the joint venture will be strong enough to support leasing land, plant and equipment, thereby legitimately keeping such land, plant and equipment out of the total investment calculation and, therefore, more likely to result in a total investment below US$30 million. In other cases, a single project is split into two or more joint ventures, each of which has a total investment of below US$30 million. The legitimacy and likelihood of success of this latter tactic depends on the ability to partition one project into several joint ventures. A dramatic example of this approach is a number of toll road projects which are split into numerous joint ventures, each covering a US$29.9 million section of the highway. (See Chapter 10: **Toll Roads Approvals: Where the Rubber Meets The Road**). Some of the factors which will determine the feasibility of such an approach are whether each resulting venture has its own buildings and separate lines of equipment with different products.

---

18. Directing of Foreign Investment Tentative Provisions (see **Legislation Appendices**), Article 14.

Table 2: Approval Thresholds*

Total Investment Expressed in Millions of US Dollars	Joint Venture Location	Approval Authority
$100 and above	PRC	State Council
$30 and above	PRC	SDPC and Central MOFTEC in Beijing
Under $30	All provinces, autonomous regions and municipalities directly under Beijing, SEZs	Local provincial, autonomous region, municipal and zone authorities through the local Development and Planning Commission and COFTEC
Under $10	Other PRC localities, townships, counties.	Local provincial and municipal Development and Planning Commissions and COFTEC.

* Note discussion of approval authority with respect to Encouraged Projects below.

Another common but flawed ploy is to split a joint venture into several successive stages, each of which is below US$30 million. Accordingly, a joint venture is locally approved for a first stage of US$29.9 million with an unspecified second stage to come. The joint venture then receives a second local approval for an increase in capital of, say, another US$29.9 million. This is clearly contrary to the law. The approval threshold is based on the aggregate amount of total investment and, therefore, when the proposal to increase the total investment is made, MOFTEC approval should be sought. In fact, MOFTEC expressly ruled on this issue in 1987 in its *Ministry of Foreign Economic Relations and Trade, Legal Questions Raised During the Course of Operating a Sino-foreign Joint Venture Enterprises Notice* (the "Joint Venture Notice") stating that:

"An approved Sino-foreign joint equity enterprise which needs to increase investment for the purposes of production and operations shall, if the sum of the increased investment and the total amount of the original investment exceeds the limits of authority of the original examination and approval organ, and if the additional investment is part of the same project, submit an agreement to increase investment together with the original document of approval to the Ministry of Foreign Economic Relations and Trade for examination and approval."

Some Chinese parties and local approval authorities have cited the conditional language in the Joint Venture Notice, that "if the additional investment is part of the same project", to argue that if the additional investment is for a different "project" under the roof of the same joint venture, the requirement for MOFTEC approval does not apply. Allegedly, several projects can be lumped under one joint venture. MOFTEC officials have confirmed that this interpretation is not correct.

Another excuse for not seeking central government approval on some large projects is that they are "non-productive" projects, such as toll roads, subways or water treatment plants and, accordingly, can be approved by local authorities. While a discussion with a MOFTEC official in this regard revealed that this might be a grey area, prudence and the comfort of potential lenders or investors would indicate that Beijing approval is the preferred route.

The recent appearance of a MOFTEC Notice apparently indicating that, provided a proposed foreign investment project is (i) in the Encouraged Category, and (ii) is "not subject to the comprehensive balance of the State", such projects may be approved in excess of US$30 million at the provincial, autonomous region and directly administered municipality level has added further confusion.[19] The local approval authority need only file with MOFTEC the (i) Feasibility Study Report approval document, (ii) the approval document for the Joint Venture Contract and Articles of Association summarizing the principal terms thereof, and (iii) the local COFTEC's explanation with respect to the project not being subject to the "comprehensive balance of the State".[20] If MOFTEC does not raise any objection with one month from the receipt thereof, the local COFTEC may issue a Certificate of Approval.[21] Discussions with MOFTEC officials reveal that, despite its promulgation, the Notice will not be implemented until additional implementing regulations can be promulgated. One of the issues requiring elaboration and clarification is the meaning of the particularly opaque reference to "the comprehensive balance of the State".

While some Chinese officials believe this reference is similar to the "balance" described in Article 8 of the Joint Venture Implementing Regulations referring to required allocations of strategic raw materials such as "fuel, power, transportation and foreign trade export quotas", others, apparently, have a different view.

In any event, when the local authorities currently refuse to refer a joint venture with a total investment in excess of US$30 million to Beijing, but instead cause the local government to issue an Approval Certificate for the full amount of the total investment, is the foreign investor at risk? According to the author's experience and various experienced Chinese lawyers, probably not much, provided that external bank or debt financing or a private placement or initial public offering ("IPO") involving the Joint Venture is not contemplated, on the grounds that, vis-à-vis the foreign party, if the Approval Certificate is sufficient on its face and properly chopped, it is sufficient for the foreign party which is under no obligation to second guess the local Chinese approval authorities.

---

19. *Notice Regarding Relevant Issues in Reporting for the Record to MOFTEC Foreign Investment Enterprises under the Encouraged Category Examined and Approved by Local Authorities Themselves,* promulgated by MOFTEC on October 15, 1999, paragraph 1.

20. Id., paragraph 3.

21. Id., paragraph 5.

However, the local examination and approval authority has overstepped its authority and could be the subject of sanctions. In addition, failure to secure approvals at the proper level will make it difficult to secure the sort of comprehensive PRC legal opinion that is required by financial institutions in connection with financing exercises. One MOFTEC official, when asked about this issue, gave the discomforting response that MOFTEC would respond, if anyone asked, that such a Joint Venture Contract was invalid and void from the beginning for want of proper approval. Despite this, there are no current reports of any foreign investor suffering as a result of such non-conforming approvals, but caution is recommended.

In one case, where a joint venture with a total investment in excess of US$30 million was approved locally on the theory that it contained several "projects" under one roof, the joint venture, in order to obtain a "clean" Chinese legal opinion on its establishment as a prerequisite to securing international financing, was forced to ask the local Commission on Foreign Trade and Economic Cooperation (COFTEC) to submit the papers to MOFTEC in Beijing for approval. MOFTEC responded by acknowledging receipt of the documents and admonishing the local COFTEC to more strictly abide by the law and not to exceed its authority again.

Approval Process

Assuming that the proposed joint venture investment does not fall under the Prohibited or Restrictive Categories and that the appropriate level of approval authority has been identified, the joint venture investors can begin the approval process. Chart 1 below outlines the various stages of a joint venture project's development at which approvals are required and the procedures and documents necessary at each stage.

When considering the various approval stages for a project and strategies for obtaining the requisite approvals, two things are important to keep in mind. First, the approval process itself is a response to the internal needs of an elaborate Chinese Government bureaucracy charged with guiding planned economic development. While China has certainly moved in the direction of a market economy, albeit a socialist market economy, in respect of the foreign investment sector, the old command economy is still to some degree in place. As noted above, China's entry into the WTO is expected over time to have a significant impact on this process. To some extent, this would appear to reflect the reluctance of China's leadership to loosen their control over foreign investment, presumably both because of the significant size of these capital inflows and the potential for economic problems flowing from such inflows including inflation and domestic competition and the perceived need for industrial rationalization. Accordingly, the State and local Development and Planning Commissions continue to play a critical role in determining whether a given project is suitable in the context of existing economic plans.

Chart 1: Approval Stages

The procedures and documents required to set up equity joint ventures or cooperative joint ventures in the PRC are summarized as follows. It should be noted that the procedures may differ according to geographic region of the PRC and that what follows is only a general guideline.

	Procedures	Document
	Foreign Party / **Chinese Party**	
1.	Parties sign a Letter of Intent, Memorandum of Understanding, a Preliminary Agreement	Letter of Intent/Preliminary Agreement/ Memorandum of Understanding.
2.	PRC Party prepares a Project Proposal Report (Note 1)	
3.	MOFTEC or COFTEC (Note 3) and State or local Development and Planning Commission approve the Project Proposal Report (Note 1	
4.	PRC Party and Foreign Party jointly prepare a Feasibility Study Report for the project which is then submitted to the State or local Development and Planning Commission and MOFTEC or COFTEC for approval (Note 1)	
5.	Relevant government authorities (Note 2) consulte	
6.	State or local Development and Planning Commission an MOFTEC or COFTEC approves the Feasibility Study Report (Note 1)	Approval of State or local Development and Planning Commission and MOFTEC or COFTEC of the Project Proposal Report
7.	PRC Party and Foreign Party negotiate and sign a Joint Venture Contract and Articles of Association for the Joint Venture Company and submit them to MOFTEC or COFTEC for approval	Joint Venture Contract, Articles of Association for the Joint Venture Company.
8.	MOFTEC or COFTEC approves the Joint Venture Contract and the Articles of Association and the establishment of the Joint Venture Company	Approval Document in respect of the Joint Venture Contract and Articles of Association and Approval Certificate confirming the approval of the joint venture.
9.	Business License is issued to the Joint Venture Company by the relevant branch of State Administration Bureau of Industry and Commerce	Business Licence.

(1) The Project Proposal Report in Step 2 and the Feasibility Study Report referred to in Step 4 may be submitted at the same time. Step 3 and 6 may take place at the same time. Step 3 and 6 may take place at the same time.

(2) For instance, for property development, government departments including by the City Planning Bureau, the Land Administration Bureau and the Construction Commission will be consulted (see Chapter 8: **Approvals for Establishing Real Estate Development and Management Operations**).

(3) COFTEC, depending on the amount of total investment (see discussion above), has been delegated approval authority by MOFTEC (formerly known as the Ministry of Foreign Economic Relations and Trade).

The Chinese foreign investment approval system was not originally intended to be transparent to foreigners. Ensuring the acquisition of all appropriate PRC central and local approvals was primarily the responsibility of the Chinese parties to any given foreign investment transaction. The increasing requirements for bank or public financing of projects in China have necessitated that foreign investors and their advisors become intimately familiar with, aware of and, to the extent possible, involved in the approval process even though foreign investors in projects with Chinese partners have no independent standing to approach a central or local Chinese approval authority and are expected to work with and through their Chinese partners. Even in the case of a wholly foreign-owned enterprise ("WFOE") (see Chapter 2: **Approvals for Establishing a Wholly Foreign-owned Enterprise**), the foreign investor is expected to work with its assigned Chinese "department-in-charge" in this regard.

As a holdover from when State plans and guidelines were apparently considered by China's bureaucracy as strictly "internal" matters to be kept from foreigners, and from the mandarin reflex to relegate the handling of foreigners to specially designated and trained units, recent experience indicates that when, as occasionally happens, a Chinese party refuses to take up a particular concern of a prospective investor with the approval authorities or, worse, when the message received from the approval authority through the Chinese party is so detailed and self-serving as to be suspect, it can be difficult for the foreign investor to secure an audience directly with the concerned approval authority.

Law firms and consultants active in China can be helpful in arranging for such meetings as they may have contacts at the various approval agencies with whom they can communicate directly. If the proposed joint venture is large or has some unique or particularly complicated aspect to it, the potential foreign investor is well advised to pay a courtesy call on the examination and approval authorities, particularly the relevant Development and Planning Commission, during the initial stage of the project to introduce the project to such officials. These officials may be in a position to help later when problems arise. If the investor waits until there are problems before recognizing the examination and approval authority, he is far less likely to be well-received. If the joint venture requires SDPC and central MOFTEC approval, the local authorities should nevertheless not be ignored either as foreign investment projects are normally "reported up" to Beijing by the local officials. Such visits will assist the potential investor in identifying the actual officials within the appropriate agency who are responsible for their project.

Letter of approval and project proposal

The first step in the approval process (see "Chart 1: Approval Stages" above) is always the signing of a non-binding Preliminary Agreement variously referred to as a "Letter of Intent", "Memorandum of Understanding" or even just a "Minutes of Meeting". Under relevant Chinese foreign investment law,[22] such preliminary documents are however not binding, and, as a commercial matter, an investor should be careful not to commit or appear to commit to something he is not firmly committed to do. These Preliminary Agreements typically contain a description of the proposed project, an estimate of the total amount of investment required so that the appropriate level of examination and approval authority can be engaged, the proposed allocation for equity interests and a general undertaking by each of the parties to jointly investigate the opportunity at their own expense and, perhaps, to jointly prepare a preliminary Feasibility Study. Often, such Preliminary Agreements also include a general description of what the respective parties intend to contribute to the joint venture and a confidentiality covenant to protect any information exchanged. "No-shop" provisions effective for a specific period of time after the signing of the Preliminary Agreement are also common in Preliminary Agreements. Such Preliminary Agreements, however, can be much more detailed like the heads of agreement setting forth principal areas of agreement. An investor can walk away from a project if the Feasibility Study or their own further investigation later reveals it not to be suitable, but it can be extremely difficult to change a fundamental term and continue with a project if the Chinese side is strongly opposed.

The basic bureaucratic purpose served by such a Preliminary Agreement is that it is attached to a form of Project Proposal prepared by the Chinese party which generally identifies the parties, the purpose of the joint venture, the proposed amounts of total investment and registered capital, generally what each of the parties is expected to contribute, the proposed allocation of equity and any unique or unusual provisions. In other words, generally it identifies what is required in the basic Preliminary Agreement. The Project Proposal and the executed Preliminary Agreement are then submitted to the appropriate level of the Development and Planning Commission (see "Approval Jurisdiction" above) and COFTEC as evidence that a foreign company is interested in the project described in the Preliminary Agreement and in the Project Proposal. One danger is that the Project Proposal, which can be more detailed than the Preliminary Agreement, contains terms to which the foreign investor has not and would not agree. In order to obviate any possible later misunderstandings with the approval authorities and to ensure that a foreign investor understands clearly what it is that is being approved, a copy of this Chinese language Project Proposal should be requested from the Chinese party for review and agreement prior to its submission. Sometimes, Chinese parties submit a Project Proposal for the project they wish to have as opposed to any upon which the particular foreign investor might agree. This may not come out until later when the approval authorities reject the non-conforming Feasibility Study and Joint Venture Contract, after the expenditure of significant time and money on the part of the prospective foreign investor.

22. Joint Venture Law and Cooperative Enterprise Law.

In a not isolated case, a large company was shocked to discover at the Feasibility Study stage that the relevant Project Proposal contained a 30% export quota requirement, which had not been mentioned to them by the Chinese party.

A foreign partner to the joint venture should ask the intended Chinese partner to see a copy of the document they intend to submit as a Project Proposal. If they will not show it, the foreign investor may have grounds to be suspicious. If, however, a foreign investor obtains a satisfactory copy of the Project Proposal but is concerned that the prospective Chinese partner will amend it prior to submission, finding another Chinese partner may be a consideration. At a minimum, if there is any "drop-dead" issue which is a concern, the prospective foreign investor should try to address it directly in the Preliminary Agreement thereby making it difficult for the Chinese partner to advance an inconsistent term which has not been agreed upon.

Preliminary approval

Within 20 to 30 days, of submission of an executed Preliminary Agreement together with a Project Proposal, a preliminary approval (*lixiang*) is issued by the relevant Development and Planning Commission and COFTEC or MOFTEC, as the case may be (see "Approval Jurisdiction" above). Again, the prospective foreign investor should ask to see the original copy of the preliminary approval in Chinese, bearing the seals, or "chops", of the relevant approval authorities to see precisely what principal terms have been approved.

The approval work at this stage, as at the Feasibility Study stage (see "Feasibility Study" below), is primarily for the Development and Planning Commission at the relevant level (see "Approval Jurisdiction" above) to decide whether the proposed project is appropriate for China by being:

- not something China already has too many of or does not want;
- in accordance with the State's economic plans at the various levels; and
- appropriate for the specific location proposed; for instance, heavy industrial or "smokestack" industries probably would not be approved in and around Beijing Municipality.

If "high technology" is involved such as advanced imaging or laser technology, the State Science and Technology Commission might become involved to determine whether the technology to be employed in the joint venture is appropriate for China or whether China has already developed or imported similar technology. For example, for this reason, China has prohibited additional television cathode-ray tube manufacturing joint ventures.

Feasibility study

The next step in the joint venture approval process is the joint preparation and submission of a Feasibility Study Report to the relevant approval authorities, which is also sometimes referred to as a "Preliminary Feasibility Study" at this stage, pending possible comments from the relevant approval authorities. The contents of a Feasibility Study for a joint venture are set out in the **Appendices**.

The principal approval authority focus in connection with the Feasibility Study appears to be:

- the description of the joint venture's specific scope and scale of business;
- whether the project's material and supply requirements can be met locally;
- whether the local infrastructure in terms of utilities, can support the project;
- the proposed market and demand for the joint venture's products; and
- ensuring that the joint venture can achieve a foreign exchange "balance", (a balance between its proposed sources of foreign exchange, such as exports, with its uses, such as purchasing imported components and paying the salaries of foreign technicians).

The Development and Planning Commission will disseminate the Feasibility Study to all the Chinese agencies concerned with, or impacted by, the project from the local power, labour and environmental bureaus to water, construction and transportation units. Each unit then reviews the Feasibility Study and sends it back to the Development and Planning Commission together with its written opinion on the Feasibility Study. For instance, in one actual case, the local Power Bureau responded:

"We see no problem in delivering the amount of electric power required by this proposed project."

A classic mistake is to treat the Feasibility Study as an "Approvability Study". The Feasibility Study functions as the foreign investor's contract with the local government. Accordingly, if the amount of power the factory will consume has been underestimated, a foreign investor could be in the position of one foreign investor in Guangdong's Pearl River Delta who arrived at his factory on what he assumed to be a working day to find it closed down for lack of power. This story has been repeated throughout China. If the Feasibility Study indicates a greater quantity of some strategic raw material is required than is actually available, then a basis exists on which to assert a complaint with at least some chance of receiving the additional quantities. If instead, the quantity of such raw material needed has been underestimated, the local officials may be hard put to help.

The Feasibility Study is usually returned within a month to 45 days, although Shanghai purports to provide a 15-day turnaround. If the joint venture requires central government approval, and the Feasibility Study is submitted to the SDPC in Beijing, the approval process could easily take months or, in some cases, even more than a year. This is particularly true in those cases where the total investment is more than US$100 million and where an additional final approval from the State Council is required (see "Approval Jurisdiction" and "Table 2: Approval Thresholds" above).

scope of business

The section of the Feasibility Study describing the joint venture's Scope of Business should be carefully drafted as it will be repeated in the Joint Venture Contract, the Articles of Association (see "Joint Venture Contract and Articles of Association" below) and, again, in the joint venture' Business Licence. In China, broad business scopes, such as "for any lawful purpose", are not permitted. Moreover, business scopes are strictly construed. A joint venture hotel in Beijing which wanted to add an ancillary taxi service had to amend its Joint Venture Contract and Articles of Association and receive further government approval for the amendments prior to providing the additional service. Therefore, if not carefully worded, additional approvals may be required to expand product lines.

resources from central government

If the project requires resources that can only be supplied from the central government or is part of a system controlled by the central government such as railroads or the national highway grid, central government approval will be required and the local Development and Planning Commission and COFTEC should report the Feasibility Study up to SDPC and MOFTEC for their review and approval.

foreign exchange balancing

With respect to ensuring a foreign exchange balance for the joint venture, China's approval authorities still sometimes instinctively attempt to impose an export quota on the products of the joint venture, often in the 20% and 30% range, even in cases where the project targets the domestic China market and even though the days of foreign exchange scarcity, at least with respect to permitted current account transactions, appear to be gone. There is no legal requirement to agree to any specific export quota.

There have been cases where foreign investors have accepted export quotas in their Feasibility Studies and Joint Venture Contracts and have not fulfilled them when, as is frequently the case, all of the joint venture's production is sold domestically in China. No penalties or reprimands for such failures have been reported although there is a risk that the annual review by the State General Administration for Foreign Exchange Control ("SAFE") of Joint Venture Contracts for compliance in this respect may prompt SAFE to deprive such joint venture from access to the foreign exchange settlements system.

capital structure

The proposed capital structure of the joint venture as described in the Feasibility Study and again, later, in the Joint Venture Contract, must comply with the *Sino-foreign Equity Joint*

Venture Ratio of Registered Capital to Total Investment Tentative Provisions[23] and *Capital Contribution by all Parties to Sino-foreign Equity Joint Ventures Several Provisions*[24] to be eligible for approval. While both regulations stipulate that they apply only to EJVs, in fact, by analogy these regulations are routinely applied to CJVs as well . The amount of debt a joint venture is permitted to incur as a percentage of its total investment is limited as shown in Table 3 below. This regulation was enacted after a large hotel project was approved in Shanghai with a capital structure comprised of 1% equity and 99% debt.

Under the latter regulation, time limits have been imposed for each party to a joint venture to make their capital contributions in cash or in kind to the registered capital of the joint venture. These time limits are outlined below in Table 4 and Table 5. Over time, the Chinese authorities have seen that capital "commitments" have not always translated into actual capital contributions, hence the imposition of more rigid time requirements. Failure to make timely contributions will result in financial penalties in the nature of default interest and, eventually, a cancellation of the joint venture's Business Licence.

Table 3: Required Debt/Equity Ratio

Total Investment	Percentage Debt Permitted
US$3 million or under	30%
Between US$3 million and US$10 million	50%
Between US$10 million and US$30 million	60%
Greater than US$30 million	70%

Table 4: Capital Contribution Schedule Requirements for EJVs

Capital Contribution by Parties	Time Limit
In one lump sum	Within six months of issue of Business Licence
In instalments	First instalment of not less than 15% due within three months of the issuance of business licence. Schedule for following instalments according to total amount of registered capital (see Table 5)

23. Promulgated by the State Administration for Industry and Commerce ("SAIC") on March 1, 1987.

24. Approved by the State Council on December 30, 1987 and effective on March 1, 1988.

Table 5: Time Limits for Further Instalments

Total Amount of Registered Capital	Time Limit for Total Contributions (After Issuance of JV Business Licence)
US$500,000 or under	One year
US$500,000 to US$1 million	One and a half years
US$1 million to US$3 million	Two years
US$3 million to US$10 million	Three years
Above US$10 million	Subject to approval of relevant government authority on a case-by-case basis

In the most common joint venture situation, the Chinese party contributes land, plant and some equipment, while the foreign investor contributes cash with which to upgrade the facility. While a foreign investor normally pays his subscribed capital contribution in instalments as described above, the Chinese party, as a practical matter because of their indivisible nature, must contribute its assets all at once soon after the joint venture's business license is issued. Prior to September, 1997, despite the fact that at the commencement of the joint venture, the Chinese party had usually contributed 100% of its subscribed capital and the foreign investor perhaps as little as 15%, no distinction was made between this early imbalance and the final equity apportionment in respect of the right to receive dividends and vote. This arrangement struck Chinese parties as unfair.

Accordingly, certain supplementary regulations affecting only EJV's were promulgated that, absent special approval from the original examination and approval authority, require the parties to synchronize their contributions.[25] If the contributions are not pro rata, profit distribution will be distributed based on the ratio of actual amounts invested as opposed to amounts committed but not paid-in. In addition, during the period before an investor's subscribed capital is fully paid-in, "the investor will not be entitled to have decision-making powers in respect of the enterprise".[26] Anecdotal evidence suggests that to date this rather impractical penalty apparently has been used mostly for its in terrorem effect. These regulations do not apply to CJV's.

Another method of dealing with foreign investors who do not meet their required capital contribution payment schedules has been developed by the SAIC which, in joint ventures where capital contributions are to be made in instalments, has begun the practice of issuing

25. *<Capital Contributions by the Parties to Sino-Foreign Equity Joint Ventures Several Provisions> Supplementary Provisions* approved by State Council September 2, 1992 and promulgated by MOFTEC and SAIC on September 29, 1997, paragraph 2.

26. Id.

such joint ventures temporary business licenses that expire on the due date for the next instalment.

valuation of contributions

Valuation of contributions in kind has long been a source of contentious debate during Joint Venture Contract negotiations (see "Joint Venture Contract and Articles of Association" below). It has been reported that some Chinese factory managers are so delighted to be part of a Sino-foreign joint venture and enjoy the presumably higher salary levels and increases in benefits, that they have been willing to contribute Chinese State assets at below their fair market value. Also, it has been reported that some foreigners have contributed machinery and equipment at inflated prices. As a result, two regulations have been promulgated to address these problems. First, the State-owned Property Bureau under the Ministry of Finance has issued a regulation requiring that Chinese State enterprise assets to be contributed to a joint venture must have a valuation performed by State-designated Chinese appraisers.[27] Second, the Ministry of Finance and the China Import and Export Commodity Inspection Bureau have jointly promulgated a regulation requiring that any contribution in kind by a foreign party be appraised by the China Import and Export Commodity Inspection Bureau upon arrival in China.[28] Accordingly, a foreign party contributing machinery and equipment may find its valuation reduced if it fails to substantiate the stipulated value of such contributions in the Joint Venture Contract and, therefore, may be required to "top-up" its contribution with cash to prevent its percentage interest in the joint venture from being decreased.

An additional related problem arises when a Chinese State enterprise purports to contribute land in China to the joint venture for its use. Diligent research of the Land-Use Certificate and the associated Land Transfer Contract should be performed to ascertain that the land in question is not "allocated land" which has been given free to the Chinese enterprise by the State for its specific use. This land cannot be properly transferred or sold and a Land-Use Certificate issued in the joint venture's name without the payment of a significant "conversion fee", which may become a liability of the new joint venture. Additionally, a prospective foreign investor should examine the underlying land grant contract for possible restrictions on the use of the land.

Joint venture contract and articles of association

While the Preliminary Feasibility Study is being reviewed and approved, the joint venture parties are usually working to complete negotiation of the Joint Venture Contract, the related Articles of Association and any required ancillary contracts to be attached for submission to

27. *Administration of State Asset Valuation Procedures* promulgated by the State Council on November 16, 1991.

28. *Administration of the Appraisal of Assets Invested by Foreign Investors Procedures*, promulgated by the State Administration for Import and Export Commodities and the Ministry of Finance on March 18, 1994.

the approval authorities. The Joint Venture Contract should set forth the detailed understanding among the joint venture partners and is often supplemented by:

- a Technology License Contract;
- a Technical Assistance Contract;
- a Trademark Licence Contract; and
- various supply and distribution agreements.

legal requirements

The Joint Venture Contract and Articles of Association both must meet the legal requirements for content as set out in the Joint Venture Law and the Cooperative Enterprise Law and their respective Implementing Regulations. Once the Joint Venture Contract and Articles of Association have been agreed upon and executed, they should be submitted to the local COFTEC together with a copy of:

- the Feasibility Study;
- the Preliminary Project Approval;
- certificates of incorporation and a bank's letter of creditworthiness with respect to the joint venture parties; and
- a list of the names and nationalities of the initial Board of Directors.

Local COFTECs should approve or reject the application within 90 days for an EJV and within 45 days for a CJV.[29]

In practice, the approval authorities sometimes respond with questions which work to restart the time period running again or, if appropriate, the documents may be sent up to MOFTEC in Beijing. At this stage of the approval process, assuming that the Feasibility Study has been already approved by the SDPC or the local Development and Planning Commission, the Foreign Investment Administration and the Treaties and Law Department of COFTEC and MOFTEC are the key agencies involved in approving the Joint Venture Contract and Articles of Association. Often, COFTEC or MOFTEC will respond with specific drafting revisions which they require to be incorporated before giving their approval. If technology transfer is an important part of the proposed venture, then the Technology Import Bureau of COFTEC or MOFTEC (and, in some cases, the Ministry of Science and Technology) will be involved as well. During this process the Chinese partner and, hopefully, the foreign partner should be engaged in a dialogue with the examination and approval authorities. If a proposed project is not going to be approved, the foreign partner should be aware of it long before the final submission of documents. For a project to be rejected outright at this stage is, however, extremely rare.

29. Joint Venture Implementing Regulations, Article 12 and Cooperative Enterprise Law, Article 5.

It should be noted that, if the foreign partner is relying on a substantive understanding in a joint venture transaction, such understanding or agreement should ideally be clearly set forth in one of the documents sent to COFTEC and, if required, MOFTEC for their approval. Not infrequently, parties to a Chinese joint venture will suggest that certain contentious issues be resolved in sideletters which are not submitted to COFTEC or MOFTEC. If these sideletters can be viewed as amending or supplementing the terms and conditions of the Feasibility Study, Joint Venture Contract or Articles of Association in some fundamental way, they are likely to be deemed unenforceable for want of proper approval. One such case involved a sideletter purporting to condition the obligation of the foreign investor to make investments subject to the foreign investor obtaining satisfactory debt financing. Without receiving COFTEC or MOFTEC approval, such sideletter was without legal effect and no defense to the foreign investor seeking to avoid his contribution obligations under the Joint Venture Contract.

Company Registration

Once the Approval Certificate has been approved, the joint venture parties have one month in which to submit the Approval Certificate together with an application to the local branch of the SAIC which will, usually within two-to-four weeks of receipt of the Approval Certificate,[30] issue a Business Licence for the joint venture. This date of issuance of the Business Licence is, under Chinese law, the date on which the joint venture is deemed to have been established. A nominal registration fee based on the aggregate registered capital of the joint venture is required to be paid.[31]

Approval Strategies

During the joint venture approval process, if and to the extent possible, it is a definite advantage to have direct contact with the relevant Chinese approval authorities. This helps prevent the miscommunications and misunderstandings that often occur when the comments of the relevant approval authorities are relayed by and filtered through the Chinese partner and helps prevent surprises at a later date. Occasionally, in important transactions, the approval authorities will participate directly in the Joint Venture Contract negotiations. This is helpful in flushing out the concerns of the approval authorities at an earlier stage of the negotiations. In any event, these discussions should be had in advance of the formal submission of the final joint venture application documents.

In cases where central government approvals are also required, some companies have found it helpful to informally advise SDPC and MOFTEC about the project prior to its being reported up, both to alert SDPC and MOFTEC and to see if either SDPC or MOFTEC is likely to raise

30. Cooperative Enterprise Law, Article 6.

31. *Standards of Registration Fees to be Paid by Joint Ventures Using Chinese and Foreign Investment Provisional Regulations* promulgated by the SAIC on February 2, 1982.

any objections or comments at a later date. Working the system simultaneously from both the bottom and the top is a time-tested method of doing business in China and the process of securing joint venture approvals is no exception.

Conclusion

After identifying the priority of a proposed joint venture project (see "Project Priority" above), a prospective foreign investor should quickly identify the appropriate level of approval and examination authority required (local or national) (see "Approval Jurisdiction" above) and seek from the Chinese partner to be introduced to, and be included in, a continuing dialogue with them as the project develops and before tough issues and problems arise. If the Chinese partner or, worse, the local government insists for whatever reason that the SDPC and MOFTEC in Beijing should not be involved, even though the total investment amount would appear to require central government approval, the risks of proceeding should be weighed carefully. In any event, a thorough knowledge of the approval process and a developed sensitivity to the bureaucratic dynamics and possible friction between various levels of examination and approval authorities are invaluable assets in achieving a properly approved and successful joint venture in China.

Summary Checklist

1. Before beginning the approval process a prospective joint venture investor must identify the permissibility and priority of the proposed project by referring to the project categories in the *Foreign Investment Industrial Guidance Catalogue* (see Table 1: Joint Venture Project Categories and the **Appendices**).
2. The relevant Chinese examination and approval authorities must next be identified by:
   - identifying the "total amount of investment" required by the proposed project (see Table 2: Approval Thresholds);
   - assessing the need, if any, for resources under the control of the central government; and
   - examining specific industry regulations or policies such as automotive, telecommunications or pharmaceutical.
3. The approval process begins with the preparation and negotiation of a Letter of Intent or Memorandum of Understanding between the parties to the joint venture. The foreign party should be careful not to commit to, or imply a commitment to, more than it is willing to deliver, while including express caveats as appropriate.
4. A copy of the Project Proposal should be obtained from the prospective Chinese party for examination and confirmation prior to its submission to the Chinese examination and approval authority, to ensure that the project being proposed conforms to what the foreign party has in mind.
5. A copy of the preliminary approval (*lixiang*) document should be requested from the prospective Chinese partner to see what precisely has been approved.
6. Introductions to the local and, if applicable, central approval authorities from the prospective Chinese partner should be requested in order to commence a dialogue with them which can prove useful when difficulties arise. If the Chinese partner refuses to make such introductions, ask your professional advisors for help.
7. The risks and possible risk-reduction strategies of proceeding with a project which appears to require central government approvals but which the local government refuses to report up must be assessed.
8. A detailed and realistic Feasibility Study should be prepared remembering that it functions after approval as your "contract" with the local and, if applicable, central governments in terms of allocating strategic resources.
9. The Scope of Business description in the Feasibility Study, Joint Venture Contract and Articles of Association should be carefully considered as it will strictly define the Business Licence and the parameters of the joint venture's business.

10. A detailed Joint Venture Contract and Articles of Association should be prepared. Remember the cardinal rule: if it is ambiguous, the foreign investor loses. Also, an investor should try to "preview" any novel or controversial provisions with the examination and approval authorities to avoid unhappy surprises. Slipping ambiguous provisions past the approval authorities can backfire if difficulties arise later.
11. Sideletters purporting to modify the Joint Venture Contract or Articles of Association should not be relied upon. If not approved (usually the reason for them being sideletters) they are not enforceable.
12. The foreign partner should work closely with the Chinese partner and the examination and approval authorities to try to find a way of reaching their desired and often different objectives. Patience and persistence are required.
13. Any ancillary approvals required to conduct the business contemplated in the joint venture documents or to receive any advantageous treatment upon which the foreign investor is relying should be in place before the obligation to make any capital contributions to the joint venture arises.

CHAPTER 2

APPROVALS FOR ESTABLISHING A WHOLLY FOREIGN-OWNED ENTERPRISE

Randall Peerenboom, Professor, **UCLA School of Law** *&*
Shirley Xu, Partner, **Yi Wen Law Firm, Beijing**

The first issue faced by a foreign investor committed to setting up operations in China is the choice of the investment vehicle. The three standard vehicles for foreign direct investment are:

- equity joint ventures ("EJVs");
- cooperative joint ventures ("CJVs"); and
- wholly foreign-owned enterprises ("WFOEs").[1]

To date, EJVs have been the most popular structure, although foreign investors have recently shown a preference for WFOEs. According to MOFTEC, while 54% of the foreign invested enterprises approved in the first eight months of 1997 were either EJVs or CJVs, a full 45% were WFOEs, with the number of WFOEs actually exceeding the number of EJVs.[2] This represented a 26.65% increase in the number of WFOEs over 1996.[3]

The reasons for this trend are several, including:

- growing if begrudging acceptance of WFOEs by the PRC government and approval authorities;
- elimination of discriminatory treatment of WFOEs under PRC regulations;
- competition for foreign investment by local governments, resulting in greater flexibility with respect to the approval requirements for WFOEs;
- investor dissatisfaction with joint ventures ("JVs"); and
- increased investor sophistication in doing business in China such that it is no longer necessary to rely on local partners.

The PRC government undoubtedly continues to prefer that foreign investors establish JVs rather than WFOEs. This is evident from various restrictions being imposed on WFOEs: the restrictive approval requirements that set a high export quota for WFOEs; the need for foreign investors to introduce advanced technology; and the express prohibitions on the establishment of WFOEs in a number of industries.

---

1. Foreign entities may also establish holding companies (also referred to as foreign investment companies or umbrella companies), which may be either joint ventures or WFOEs (see Chapter 3 – **Approvals for Establishing a Holding Company**). In addition, foreign investors may invest in PRC companies by acquiring an equity interest in or assets of a PRC company, acquiring B shares in PRC companies listed on China's exchanges, shares in PRC companies listed overseas, or shares in red chip companies (companies incorporated and listed abroad but that own PRC assets), or by participating in foreign investment enterprises limited by shares. Foreign entities may also invest indirectly in China through representative offices, technology licensing, countertrade, and various other contractual relations. China's ongoing efforts to reform State-owned enterprises may provide additional channels for investment.

2. MOFTEC Bulletin, October 25, 1997, p. 12. In total, there were 13,089 EJVs, CJVs and WFOEs: 5751 EJVs, 1392 CJVs, and 5946 WFOEs. There were also two foreign invested companies limited by shares. In comparison, there were 9772 EJVs, 2245 CJVs and 6784 WFOEs established in the first nine months of 1996. MOFTEC Bulletin, December 25, 1996, p. 16.

3. Wei Ke, "Foreign investment up substantially in first half," *China Daily*, August 13, 1997, p. 5.

One of the primary goals of the PRC's investment policy has been to encourage the introduction of advanced technology, and more specifically to encourage the *transfer* of such technology to PRC companies badly in need of modernization. While establishment of a WFOE may result in the introduction of new technology, it will not normally result in the transfer of the technology to a PRC entity. Moreover, without an infusion of technology, many State-owned enterprises are likely to lose out in the marketplace and end up bankrupt. Indeed, the increased competition resulting from the establishment of WFOEs, fully equipped with state-of-the-art technology, will only hasten the demise of many local companies.

Its preference for JVs notwithstanding, the government has increasingly tolerated the establishment of WFOEs. Beginning in the early 1990s, the government took steps to eliminate discriminatory treatment of WFOEs under PRC laws and regulations. Most notably, the unification of tax laws in the 1991 *PRC, Income Tax Law for Enterprises with Foreign Investment and Foreign Enterprises* eliminated disparate tax treatment between WFOEs and JVs.[4]

The government's increased tolerance of WFOEs may be attributed to a variety of factors. Presumably, the government realized that foreign investors were often reluctant to transfer technology to JVs for fear of technology leakage. In fact, many investors are discouraged from setting up JVs and transferring their technology to the JV by China's excessively rigid and demanding PRC technology regulations.[5] Pressures to open the market and provide equal treatment to foreign and domestic entities in exchange for WTO access may also be contributing factors.

4. Despite the trend to treat WFOEs and JVs similarly, differences remain. As noted previously, WFOEs are subject to different establishment criteria. In addition, while many JVs may have an unlimited term *subject to approval*, WFOEs are limited to a fixed term, in most instances no longer than 50 years. See *PRC, Wholly Foreign-owned Enterprise Law Implementing Rules*, approved October 28, 1990 by the State Council, issued December 12, 1990 by MOFTEC (WFOE Implementing Rules), Article 73; *Sino-foreign Equity Joint Venture Enterprises Terms Tentative Provisions* ("Tentative Provisions"), approved September 30, 1990 by the State Council, promulgated October 20, 1990 by MOFERT (later known as MOFTEC); *Issues Related to Implementation of the <Sino-foreign Equity Joint Venture Enterprises Terms Tentative Provisions>*, promulgated June 24, 1991. Certain JVs,in particular those projects within a restricted category, must have a fixed term. See *Tentative Provisions*, Art. 3; *Direction of Foreign Investment Tentative Provisions*, Art. 9(1)). Further, if a WFOE wants to mortgage its assets to a foreign entity, approval of the approval authority is required whereas no such approval is required when a JV mortgages its assets. See WFOE Implementing Rules Art. 24; *Ministry of Foreign Economic Relations and Trade, <PRC Wholly Foreign-owned Enterprise Law, Implementing Rules> Interpretation* promulgated December 6, 1991 ("WFOE Implementing Rules Interpretation"), Art. 7. On the other hand, SAFE approval is required for a JV to provide security on behalf of third parties to foreign entities under Article 8 of the *Administration of the Provision of Security to Foreign Entities by Institutions Inside China Procedures Implementing Rules* (issued by SAFE, effective January 1, 1998). No such approval is required for WFOEs. Finally, local regulations and policies, particularly with respect to land prices and certain preferential treatment, may favor JVs over WFOEs.

5. See Randy Peerenboom, "A Missed Opportunity? China's New Contract Law Fails to Address Foreign Technology Providers' Concerns," in *China Law & Practice,* May 1999, pp.83-87.

Arguably the biggest factor, however, is the keen competition among local governments to attract foreign investment, and Beijing's decreasing ability to rein in local authorities. Local governments have been increasingly flexible in interpreting the restrictive approval requirements for WFOEs. This is due to their eagerness to expand the local tax base and generate employment opportunities for the large number of workers laid off as a result of State-owned enterprise reforms, or for those who are still on company pay-rolls but have no work to do (*xiagang*). The recent downturn in foreign direct investment due to the Southeast Asian financial crisis as well as China's uncertain and difficult domestic investment environment has increased the pressure on approval authorities to be flexible in their interpretation of WFOE approval requirements.[6]

Finally, foreign investors have gained experience directly or indirectly with JVs, and in doing business in China generally. As a result, many are more comfortable going it alone, and want to avoid the difficulties often associated with joint venturing in China.

A. Choice of Vehicle

1. *EJVs, CJVs, WFOEs*

EJVs are limited liability companies with legal person status.[7] The key distinguishing feature of an EJV is that profits are distributed and risks allocated in proportion to each party's contribution to the registered capital of the company.[8]

CJVs may be either legal persons or non-legal persons; the latter are often referred to as contractual CJVs.[9] Legal person CJVs are limited liability companies;[10] liability of non-legal

6. Trade figures for the first quarter of 1999 indicate a fall in comparison to 1998, which was already a bad year in comparison to years past. During the first quarter of 1999, contracted foreign direct investment (FDI) dropped 14.6%. Moreover, only $7.34 billion of the $8.72 billion contracted investment was actually utilized. Exports also continued to decline at a rate of 7.9%. See Jianfu Chen and Lijian Hong, "The Chinese economy: the first quarter," 2:5 *China Law Update* 1-2 (May, 1999). Although in 1998 actual paid in FDI amounted to $45.6 billion, a slight increase over 1997, the number of new FIEs approved decreased by 6%. Moreover, contracted FDI numbers were buoyed by the approval of a couple of large billion dollar plus projects such as Kodak and Krupp. It is unlikely that China will be able to rely on a steady stream of such large projects unless it provides greater market access in telecommunications and the service sector. The focus of many foreign investors has shifted from new investment to consolidation and reorganization of existing ventures. See David Murphy, "Smoke "n" mirrors: China's foreign direct investment numbers," *China Economic Quarterly*, 1999, p. 41-43.

7. *PRC, Sino-foreign Equity Joint Venture Law*, adopted on July 1, 1979 by the NPC and amended April 4, 1990 ("EJV Law"), Art. 4; *PRC Sino-foreign Equity Joint Venture Law Implementing Regulations*, promulgated September 20, 1983 by the State Council and amended by the State Council on January 15, 1986 and December 21, 1987 ("EJV Implementing Regulations"), Art. 2.

8. EJV Law Art. 4.

9. See *PRC, Sino-foreign Co-operative Joint Venture Law*, adopted April 13, 1988 by the NPC ("CJV Law"), Art. 2; *PRC, Sino-foreign Co-operative Joint Venture Law* Implementing Rules, promulgated September 4, 1995 by MOFTEC ("CJV Implementing Rules"), Art. 4 and Chapter 9 for special rules for non-legal person CJVs.

10. CJV Implementing Rules Art. 14.

person CJVs is unclear under PRC law.[11] The key differentiating features of a CJV are:

- the parties may allocate profits and losses as they choose rather than in proportion to their respective contributions to the registered capital;[12] and
- the foreign party may apply to recover its investment during the term of enterprise.[13]

In general, WFOEs are limited liability legal persons, though other liability structures are possible subject to MOFTEC approval.[14] The main feature of a WFOE is that it is wholly owned by one or more foreign investors.

2. *JVs versus WFOEs*

a. Advantages of JVs

- Certain industries are off limits to WFOEs.

  PRC regulations and policies prohibit the establishment of WFOEs in a number of industries. As a result, joint ventures may be the only choice in some cases.
- Connections.

  Many foreign investors feel the assistance of a well-connected local partner that understands China is, if not necessary, at least highly valuable in securing approval of the project and future operations. A Chinese partner may be useful in ensuring that the company obtains all available preferential treatment and support from the government, fending off government and administrative entities seeking to impose various fees on the company, and more generally interfacing with the multi-headed PRC bureaucracy.
- Assets.

  The PRC partner may have assets valuable to the foreign investor, including land use rights, equipment, factories, key raw materials, infrastructure (water, telecommunications, electricity etc.), trained staff or well-established marketing and distribution channels.
- Less capital required, risks spread.

  Foreign investors may wish to reduce their start-up costs and diversify risks by shifting some of the cost and risk to their joint venture partner(s).

---

11. See CJV Implementing Rules Art. 50, which provides that non-legal person CJVs and the parties to such CJVs shall bear civil liability in accordance with the relevant provisions of PRC civil laws; *PRC, General Principles of Civil Law*, Arts. 52-53, which set forth liabilities of the parties to a non-legal person joint enterprise or a cooperation contract but are silent on the liabilities of the enterprise itself.

12. CJV Law, Art. 2; CJV Implementing Rules, Art. 14.

13. CJV Law, Art. 22; CJV Implementing Rules, Arts. 44-45. Whether a PRC party to a CJV may also obtain early return on investment is unclear. In one case, Dalian COFTEC permitted one of the PRC parties to a three party CJV to do so. However, MOFTEC officials indicated that MOFTEC had not reached a firm decision on this issue.

14. *PRC, Wholly Foreign-Owned Enterprise Law*, adopted April 12, 1986 by the NPC ("WFOE Law"), Art. 8; WFOE Implementing Rules, Art. 19; WFOE Implementing Rules Interpretation, Art.4. In practice, most if not all foreign investors will opt for limited liability WFOEs. In fact, we are not aware of any instance where a WFOE adopts any liability structure other than a limited liability company.

CJV advantages.

CJVs have certain additional advantages over both EJVs and WFOEs. The major advantages are flexibility with respect to profit sharing and that the foreign investor may obtain return of its investment during the term of the company, in some cases before payment of income tax, although special approvals are required for the latter.[15]

b.Advantages of WFOEs

- Faster establishment.

  Negotiating a joint venture contract and ancillary agreements in China is often time-consuming, expensive and frustrating. Without a joint venture partner to deal with, preparation of the documents required for approval of a WFOE is much simpler and less expensive. Accordingly, the foreign investor is often able to establish the company and begin operations in a much shorter time period.
- Management control.

  The corporate culture and management styles of most foreign companies differ significantly from that of PRC companies. In addition, the basic goals of the parties may differ, with the foreign party interested in reducing employment and maximizing profits while the PRC side is more concerned about keeping workers employed and local officials happy. The differences in management styles, corporate culture, and fundamental goals often result in tensions, conflicts and in some cases deadlock and inability to continue operations.
- Future development.

  Foreign investors with a long term vision for the China market may be wary of provisions in PRC regulations that require certain key decisions be unanimously agreed by the parties, including increase or assignment of registered capital, dissolution of the company, and amendment of the articles.[16] Minority partners with an insignificant share in the company

15. CJV Law Implementing Rules Arts. 44-45. On the other hand, whereas PRC laws and regulations on EJVs and WFOEs expressly state that investors will be given "appropriate compensation" in case of government takings, such express assurances are absent in the laws and regulations on CJVs. See WFOE Law Art. 5; EJV Law Art. 2. It is unclear whether this was simply a legislative oversight or whether CJVs would be treated differently in practice.

16. EJV Implementing Regulations, Art. 36 (there are four items requiring unanimous agreement of the directors present at a duly convened meeting – i.e. amendment of the Articles of Association; increase or assignment of registered capital; termination or dissolution; merger); CJV Implementing Rules, Art. 29 (there are five items requiring unanimous agreement of the directors present at a duly convened meeting - i.e. amendment of the Articles of Association; increase or decrease of registered capital; dissolution; merger, division or change of structure form; and mortgage of company property). The four EJV items are subject to approval of the approval authorities as they involve amendment of the Articles of Association (EJV Implementing Regulations, Art. 17). Article 11 of the CJV Implementing Rules requires approval of the approval authorities for "significant", "major" (*zhongda*) amendments to the Articles of Association. As mortgage of company assets does not generally involve amendment of the Articles of Association, approval of the approval authorities is not required. As for WFOEs, while unanimous board approval is not required by statute for any particular action, even when there is more than one foreign investor to a WFOE, approval of the approval authorities is required for division, merger or other "significant" , "major" changes in the capital of the company as a result of other events, increase or assignment of registered capital, and mortgage or assignment of company property or rights and interests (WFOE Implementing Rules, Arts. 18, 23, 24.).

may use such provisions to thwart the foreign investor's plans to expand the company or reorganize it in line with the foreign investor's worldwide strategy. For instance, cash strapped PRC partners will often not have the capital to participate in an expansion of the company and yet, not wanting to be diluted, prohibit the foreign investor from funding the entire capital increase needed to grow the company. While parties may attempt to deal with such problems contractually, the enforceability of such contractual solutions remains untested and uncertain.[17]

- Protection of technology.

  Many foreign investors are reluctant to contribute or license technology to joint ventures for fear that the technology will end up in the wrong hands. Such fears are fuelled by horror stories where the PRC partner to the JV either directly or indirectly through affiliate companies uses misappropriated technology to compete with the JV.[18] While establishment of a WFOE alone cannot ensure that the foreign party's technology will never find its way into the wrong hands, it may reduce the risk somewhat.

- More profit.

  The potential upside of a WFOE is greater in that there is no need to share profits with a JV partner or partners.

- Benefits of JVs often illusory.

  Foreign investors are increasingly opting for WFOEs in part because the alleged benefits of having a PRC partner often turn out to be illusory. Foreign companies hoping to minimize project costs by hooking up with a PRC partner often discover that the "assets" of the

---

17. Parties anticipating restructuring abroad or the establishment of a holding company in China should include a clause providing for free transfer to affiliates, with the non-transferring party agreeing in advance in the joint venture contract to allow such transfers and to cause its appointed directors to vote in favour of the transfer. Similarly, parties may provide that in the event the board of directors determines that additional funds are needed to grow the company and one of the parties is unable or unwilling to contribute its pro rata share to the increase in registered capital, the other party shall have the right to make such contribution and the non-contributing party will agree to be diluted. Nevertheless, it remains unclear what would happen if at the time of the proposed transfer or increase one of the parties refused to consent or the directors refused to approve the board resolution, notwithstanding provisions in the contract to the contrary. Presumably, the issue would be resolved through arbitration as provided in most joint venture contracts, with the arbitration tribunal applying PRC law, the statutorily required governing law for such contracts. Even if the board decided in favour of the foreign party, the arbitration award would then need to be enforced in China, which would present difficulties. Even if a PRC court could require the parties *and their appointed directors* to consent to the transaction, the transfer or increase would require the consent of the approval authorities. The arbitration award would not be binding on the approval authorities, which are not party to the agreement. Indeed, that the transaction must be approved gives the PRC party a second bite at the apple. If a party later regretted its decision to allow transfers to an affiliate or accept dilution, the party could comply with the joint venture contract, consenting to the transaction and causing its directors to vote in favour, but then make its opposition known to the approval authorities behind the scenes. While it is not to be assumed that the approval authorities will necessarily follow the PRC party's bidding in every case, the risk that the approval authorities will side with the PRC party at least in some cases must be recognized.

18. See, e.g., Dexter Roberts, Chistopher Power, Stephanie Anderson Forest, "Cheated in China?," *Business Week*, October 6, 1997, at 142, citing the case of Borg-Warner Automative Inc. whose partner attempted to set up a rival operation and also citing the case of Kimberly-Clark's joint venture in Handan where a former manager selected by the Chinese partner set up a plant producing similar products and diverted materials from the joint venture to the new factory.

Chinese party turn out to be run down buildings and outdated equipment for which the Chinese side demands top dollar. Investors may also hope that the Chinese partner will provide invaluable connections to local officials and expertise in marketing and distribution. Again, this may prove to be wishful thinking. In fact, in some cases where disagreements have arisen between the partners as to the direction of the joint venture, the connections of the PRC party have been used to the detriment of the joint venture and the foreign investor.[19] Moreover, many foreign investors have discovered, much to their dismay, that the PRC party's marketing and distribution capabilities are actually quite limited. In many State-owned enterprises, poor marketing skills and lack of a sales and distribution network are key factors in the poor economic performance of the company.

B. Legal Framework

2. *Applicable legislation*

The establishment and operation of WFOEs in the PRC is primarily governed by three sets of legislation:

- *PRC, Wholly Foreign-owned Enterprise Law* (WFOE Law);
- *PRC, Wholly Foreign-owned Enterprise Law Implementing Rules* (WFOE Implementing Rules); and
- *Ministry of Foreign Economic Relations and Trade PRC, <Wholly Foreign-owned Enterprise Law Implementing Rules> Interpretation of Several Provisions* (WFOE Implementing Rules Interpretation).[20]

The *Foreign Investment Industrial Guidance Catalogue* also set forth a number of areas in which WFOEs are prohibited.[21] From time to time, different ministries enact regulations

19. To provide some examples, in one case a foreign general manager to a Beijing joint venture wanted to hire a personal assistant/translator from outside Beijing. The PRC partner insisted that the general manager rely on a translator provided by the PRC partner, thus ensuring that the general manager only heard and communicated to others what the PRC side thought was appropriate. At a meeting with the Beijing labour bureau to discuss the possibility of hiring the non-Beijing resident, the labour bureau official made it clear that the PRC partner had already spoken to the official's superiors and that the official's hands were tied. In another case, a foreign investor to a Shanghai joint venture company was having a hard time with its Chinese partner in the JV's daily operation and management and therefore tried to buy out the Chinese partner and convert the company from a JV into a WFOE. However, the Chinese partner and the approval authority had a close relationship. One day, the general manager of the JV, who was appointed by the foreign investor, was asked to visit the approval authority. During this visit, the approval authority warned the GM that it would not approve the establishment of the WFOE by the foreign investor and that the foreign investor must give up the buy-out plan.

20. *Supra* notes 4, 14.

21. Approved by the State Council on December 29, 1997, effective January 1, 1998, amending and revising the 1995 Catalogue promulgated by the State Development and Planning Commission, State Economic and Trade Commission and MOFTEC on June 20, 1995.

further restricting the establishment of WFOEs.[22] In addition, WFOEs are subject to other regulations that apply to all FIEs and to PRC companies more generally.

2. *Legal requirements for establishment*

The WFOE Law provided the first legal basis for the establishment of WFOEs but also stated the general requirement that such an entity "must be beneficial to the development of the Chinese national economy", and must "utilize advanced technology or equipment, or export all or a large portion of its products".[23] However, detailed implementing regulations did not emerge until the end of 1990, prior to which time specific issues were often handled with reference to the regulations and procedures governing joint ventures.

The WFOE Implementing Rules fill in many of the gaps in the WFOE Law but also restate the general approval criteria in more specific terms. In addition to facilitating the development of the Chinese economy and achieving significant economic results, the WFOE must either:

- "adopt advanced technology and equipment, engage in the development of new products, economize in the use of energy and raw materials, achieve product upgrading and replacement, or produce import substitutes"; or
- "have annual exports amounting to at least 50% of the value of its total product output for the year and achieve a foreign exchange balance or surplus".[24]

WFOEs will not be approved if the approval authorities deem them to be:

- detrimental to national sovereignty or public interest;
- threatening to national security;
- in violation of PRC laws or regulations;
- at odds with China's plans to develop the national economy; or
- likely to cause environmental pollution.[25]

The WFOE Implementing Rules expressly prohibit WFOEs in a number of areas, including:

- newspapers, publishing, broadcasting, television or films;
- domestic commerce, foreign trade or insurance;

---

22. See, e.g., *Administration of the Examination, Approval and Registration of Foreign-invested Crop Seed Enterprises Provisions*, promulgated by the Ministry of Agriculture, State Development and Planning Commission, MOFTEC, and SAIC on September 8, 1997 (prohibiting WFOEs that produce and sell crop seeds).

23. WFOE Law, Art. 3.

24. WFOE Implementing Rules, Art. 3.

25. WFOE Implementing Rules, Art. 6.

- post and telecommunications; and
- other industries as determined by the government.

The *Foreign Investment Industrial Guidance Catalogue* specifies a number of additional industries off limits to WFOEs (see **Legislation Appendices** for a detailed list).[26]

More generally, foreign investment – whether in the form of JVs, WFOEs or otherwise – is prohibited or restricted in a number of other areas, as set forth primarily in the *Foreign Investment Industrial Guidance Catalogue.*

As WFOEs do not benefit a Chinese partner through direct participation, they are held to stricter establishment criteria than JVs. As noted, a WFOE must meet either a high tech requirement or an export requirement. In practice, foreign investors have found it increasingly easy to meet these standards, particularly where the project is approved locally. Provided WFOEs are not expressly prohibited under current PRC regulations, most local authorities, eager to attract investment, will find some way to classify the project as high tech or just ignore the high-tech requirement. In this regard, the *Foreign Investment Industrial Guidance Catalogue* expressly encourages projects that save energy or resources or reduce pollution.[27] These are relatively broad standards applicable to most projects. Investors may also argue that the project will develop new products or reduce imports.

The establishment of low tech WFOEs is increasingly common. Examples of such WFOEs approved in recent years (in particular, between 1997 and 1999) in the areas of Beijing, Tianjin, Shanghai, Dalian, Harbin and Nanchang include furniture companies, liquid petroleum gas bottling companies, cosmetic companies, fruit juice processing plants, food product (frozen and non-frozen) companies, garment processing plants, gardening companies for growing flowers and companies for the production of zippers, paper, tissues, chopsticks, toothpicks, umbrellas, detergents and toys. Many of these WFOEs have a registered capital of US$70,000 to US$100,000.

26. WFOEs are prohibited not only by the WFOE Law, WFOE Implementing Rules and *Foreign Investment Industrial Guidance Catalogue* but by a number of regulations and normative documents, many issued by particular ministries. See, e.g., *MOFTEC, Directing of the Examination and Approval of Foreign Investment Enterprises Opinion* November 5, /.1996 (prohibiting WFOEs in asset valuation services, financial leasing services, operation of medical institutions, etc.); *Administration of the Examination, Approval and Registration of Foreign-invested Crop Seed Enterprises Provisions*, promulgated by the Ministry of Agriculture, State Development and Planning Commission, MOFTEC, and SAIC on September 8, 1997. In addition, government and/or ministry policy may prohibit WFOEs or make it very difficult for WFOEs to be approved in certain areas, even though the policy is not expressly set forth in any regulation. While the 1998 investment guidance catalogue reflects current policy and incorporates the limitations imposed by most of these other regulations, presumably over time new regulations and policies diverging from the current guidelines will emerge, necessitating another update to the guidelines.

27. *Foreign Investment Industrial Guidance Catalogue*, *supra* note, Art. I(16)(8-10).

Recently, investors have also found it easier to register service companies as WFOEs. Examples include the establishment of a WFOE research station to grow and develop grain, entertainment companies providing electronic games, karaoke, sauna and beauty services, commercial consulting companies and companies providing cleaning services and real estate management. WFOE service and repair centres have also been established. Again, most of these WFOEs feature a small investment, with one of them having a registered capital of only US$30,000.

Similarly, the 50% export quota requirement is also increasingly less relevant. In the past, approval authorities have often taken a hard line on exports, insisting that WFOEs meet an annual export quota, in some cases well over the 50% standard set out in the WFOE Implementing Rules.[28] Moreover, approval authorities have regularly attempted to impose an export quota on WFOEs established on the basis of the high tech requirement, even though the WFOE Implementing Rules state that a WFOE must meet *either* the 50% export quota *or* the high tech requirement.

Official pressure notwithstanding, many foreign investors have managed to avoid committing to a specific export quota in either the Feasibility Study or the Articles of Association. One strategy has been to include a vague clause that leaves ample room to manoeuvre, such as:

"The enterprise shall use exports and all other means available under PRC law to balance its foreign exchange requirements."; or
"Subject to decision by the board, the enterprise shall endeavour to export products based on market conditions and the best interests of the enterprise."

Given the downturn in foreign direct investment and the desire of approval authorities to be more accommodating, foreign investors now face less pressure from the authorities to accept specific export quotas. Some approval authorities, particularly in the more investor friendly special zones or parts of the company have ceased inquiring about exports targets all together. Moreover, both SAFE and Beijing Administration of Foreign Exchange officials have confirmed that WFOEs that fail to meet specific export quotas will not suffer any adverse consequences, and will continue to enjoy access to designated foreign exchange banks where they will be

28. In one case, Shenzhen officials tried to impose a 80% export quota on one foreign investor. Despite repeated requests by the investor's foreign lawyer, the official was unable to produce any legal basis for such a requirement.

permitted to exchange Renminbi for foreign exchange.[29] Furthermore, the Annual Inspection Report Form for the joint annual inspection of all foreign invested enterprises no longer calls for information regarding satisfaction of export quotas.[30]

3. *Approval jurisdiction*

The rules that determine whether a WFOE will be approved centrally by the State Development and Planning Commission and MOFTEC (or the State Council) or locally by their duly authorized representatives are the same as for JVs. In general, projects over US$ 30 million in total investment[31] will require State Development and Planning Commission approval of the feasibility study and MOFTEC approval of the Articles of Association, and projects over US$100 million will generally require State Council approval of the feasibility study and Articles of Association.

Foreign investors have used a variety of strategies to skirt MOFTEC. Most common perhaps is to divide the project into two or three phases. The first phase is under US$30 million. The investor then applies to increase the registered capital and total investment when phase two is ready to begin. Of course, this violates the spirit of the law if not the letter, and MOFTEC has actually issued notices barring this practice. MOFTEC's view is that any increase in total investment that raises the aggregate total investment above US$30 million must be approved by MOFTEC.

MOFTEC approval is also needed for raw materials and inputs subject to import licences or quotas. If such imports are needed, then given MOFTEC's role as the dispenser of import licences, it is advisable to have the project approved in its entirety in one phase at the MOFTEC level.

---

29. On January 13, 1995, SAFE issued the *Annual Foreign Exchange Inspection of Foreign Investment Enterprises Tentative Regulations* (the "Tentative Regulations"), which require an FIE, such as a WFOE, to apply to SAFE for a Foreign Investment Enterprise Foreign Exchange Registration Certificate ("FERC") as part of its establishment procedures. The FERC allows a WFOE to maintain a foreign exchange account and also plays a part in deciding whether it will be granted access to foreign exchange entities, in the past swap centres, as of 1996, designated foreign exchange banks. The FERC is valid for one year and renewable annually, subject to a foreign exchange inspection. Investors feared that if the WFOE failed to meet its export quota, SAFE would refuse to renew the FERC, and if the FERC was not renewed, the WFOE would be refused free access to the swap centres. Nevertheless, it would still have been possible for the WFOE to purchase or sell foreign exchange at the swap centres, but with separate approval by SAFE for each transaction. In such cases the centres might have placed limitations on the purposes for which the foreign exchange could be used, such as debt service or profit remittance. On June 20, 1996, the People's Bank of China issued the *Administration of the Settlement, Sale and Payment of Foreign Exchange Provisions* and also the *Trial Implementation of Settlement and Sale of Foreign Exchange by Banks with and to Foreign Investment Enterprises Notice*, under which FIEs were granted access to both foreign designated exchange banks and swap centres for purchase and sales of foreign exchange. This system was altered when the People's Bank of China and SAFE jointly issued the *Terminating Swap Centre Activities Notice* on October 25, 1998. As of December 1, 1998, all FIE foreign exchange business is to be handled by the banks. Investors apparently no longer worry that SAFE will refuse to renew the FERC for failure to meet an export quota.

30. SAIC officials have confirmed orally that they would not take any action against WFOEs that failed to meet an export quota set forth in their articles or incorporation documents or approvals.

31. Total investment is the maximum allowed debt plus equity (registered capital in PRC terms), and is used to demarcate the level of approval authority for foreign investment enterprises (FIEs) among various Chinese government authorities.

If no raw materials or inputs are subject to licence or quota then the foreign investor should carefully consider the risk of obtaining local approval now and then seeking MOFTEC approval if and when the total investment is increased beyond the local approval limit. In particular, investors should consider the possibility that should they need to obtain additional financing in the future, a prudent foreign lender may have concerns about the validity of the approval. In most cases, a foreign lender will lend on various conditions, one of which is that the WFOE has been duly established. If the WFOE did not obtain MOFTEC approval which it should have in the first place, it may have difficulty in securing such approval when it is required by the foreign lender for the purpose of the loan. Assuming there are legitimate reasons for dividing the project into two phases and that a reasonable amount of time passed between the first and second phase, it should be achievable.

However, were the project to be arbitrarily divided into several phases, each just under US$30 million, and were the foreign investor then to have the local approval authorities approve a series of increases within a matter of days, there could be problems, notwithstanding the adamant assurances of the local authorities to the contrary.

Although the penalties are not clearly stated under PRC law, in a worst case scenario, MOFTEC could presumably declare the approval of the project and its Business Licence invalid and cancel the legal existence of the enterprise. While this is rare in practice, MOFTEC has recently indicated that it will enforce the approval limits more strictly. Apparently MOFTEC has notified approval authorities in Tianjin that any projects approved locally that should have been approved by MOFTEC must be resubmitted to MOFTEC for approval or face possible cancellation of their Business Licence. The fear is that MOFTEC may impose new conditions on the parties, in particular, conditions which are commercially unacceptable to the foreign party.

In any case, the question of approval jurisdiction is something to keep in mind before starting the formal application process.

4. *Approval process*

a. overview of approval process

In general, the approval process involves the following steps:

- Preliminary Project Report;[32]
- Feasibility Study;

32. It is unclear under Art. 10 of the WFOE Implementing Rules what this report is. However, Art. 2 of the WFOE Implementing Rules Interpretation clearly states that this report is not a project establishment (*lixiang*) report, and the reply issued by the relevant government in respect of the report is not a project establishment approval (*lixiang pifu*). Instead, the reply only responds to the questions raised by the foreign investor in the report as to whether all the conditions (such as land, utilities and communication facilities, etc.) for the establishment of the WFOE can be satisfied.

- Articles of Association; and
- formal application process.

In the meantime, the investor will need to acquire land use rights to a site, which in most cases will involve negotiating a grant contract with the land bureau. The investor will also want to visit the local utility companies to ensure adequate supplies of utilities, meet with suppliers and purchasers, negotiate construction contracts with local and/or foreign contractors and a local design institute, arrange for environmental studies to be conducted on the site and arrange for housing for its expatriate and local employees.

b. preliminary project report

Unlike joint ventures, a WFOE has no Chinese partner to interface with the approval authorities. The foreign investor or its lawyers may directly contact the local government approval authorities, such as the local Commission of Foreign Trade and Economic Cooperation ("COFTEC"), although some jurisdictions require that the investor engage an authorized agent.[33]

The first major step in the approval process is the preparation of a project report briefly describing the project. The project report should summarize the purpose and aims of the proposed WFOE, including:

- the purpose of the company and the proposed scope and scale of operations;
- products to be manufactured;
- technology and equipment to be used;
- an estimate of export sales in terms of percentages of products;
- land requirements and area of land needed; and
- requirements for water, electricity or other forms of energy as well as other utilities.[34]

A written reply must be issued in response to the Project Report within 30 days of its submission to the relevant government authorities at the county level or above.[35] The reply should indicate, for instance, whether the conditions (such as land, water, electricity and other utilities, etc.) as stated in the project report for the establishment of the WFOE may be satisfied. Based on the issued reply, the foreign investor may then decide whether to apply for the establishment of the WFOE. If it so decides, it may take the next step for preparing a feasibility study report.

---

33. See, e.g., *Shanghai Municipality, Examination and Approval of Foreign Investment Enterprises Regulations*, issued September 2, 1996, Art. 14. Agents are required to meet the standards set forth in the *Administration of Agents for Enterprise Registration Tentative Provisions*, issued by SAIC on December 21, 1995. In practice, many agencies are affiliates of the local COFTEC or established by former COFTEC members.

34. WFOE Implementing Rules, Art. 10.

35. Id. In most cases the Project Report will be submitted to MOFTEC or COFTEC.

c. feasibility study

Although there is no need to prepare a joint venture contract for WFOEs as there is no Chinese party involved, a Feasibility Study Report and Articles of Association similar to those that would be prepared for a joint venture must be prepared.

The contents of the Feasibility Study Report are in broad outline the same as for the Project Report. However, all aspects of the project are treated in much more detail, particularly the technical and economic aspects. The Feasibility Study is basically an analysis of the project with respect to all inputs required, costs and projected revenues, and projected markets. This is intended to provide an overview of the technical and economic viability of the project. Specific areas covered include:

- business scope, scale of annual production, and expected ratio of products to be exported;
- product manufacturing and sales plans;
- total investment and registered capital;
- projections and analysis of domestic and foreign markets;
- plan for transportation and supply of natural resources;
- selection of site and method for obtaining land use rights;
- production equipment and technology;
- environmental impact assessment;
- project implementation schedule; and
- financial projections and foreign exchange balancing.

Many special economic or high tech zones around the country, in an effort to simplify the application process and encourage investment, provide standard Feasibility Study Report forms. These forms often call for only the most rudimentary information, such as:

- name and address of the investor and the WFOE;
- registered capital and total investment; and
- scope of business.

The authorities then take this information and incorporate it into a report in narrative form. In most instances, the foreign investor will want to conduct a more thorough feasibility study for its own purposes. Most investors will then want to include such information in the Feasibility Study Report, particularly if the investor anticipates unusual energy or utility needs or anything that might require approval by the various government bureaus. In theory, including such information in the Feasibility Study will ensure that the appropriate bureau has been made aware of and signed off on the investor's proposal.

The investor who relies on the simplified form supplied by the authorities should review the narrative report prepared by the authorities carefully. The narrative report will usually include certain standard or "boilerplate" clauses regarding such issues as employees, labour unions and export requirements that the investor will want deleted.[36]

d. articles of association

The Articles of Association are the constituent documents for the formation of the WFOE. They are analogous to the articles of incorporation and by-laws of a Western company, and cover such matters as:

- the name and address of the WFOE;
- its purpose and scope of operations;
- its total investment and registered capital;
- its organizational framework and the powers and duties of its officers; and
- principles governing finance, accounting, foreign exchange, labour management, duration, termination, liquidation and amendment of the Articles of Association.[37]

It should be noted that any amendment of the Articles of Association, as well as mergers, divisions, or material change in the registered capital of the company, must be approved by the approval authorities.[38]

e. submission of application documents

In addition to the Feasibility Study and Articles of Association, the following documents must be submitted together with a formal application report:

- a list of the chairman and directors on the WFOE's board of directors (along with their resumes and copies of their passports);
- a copy of the certificate of incorporation and certificate of good standing of the foreign investor;
- a letter from a reputable bank attesting to the investor's creditworthiness (some areas also require the balance sheets of the investor for the previous three years);
- the response of the approval authorities to the Project Report;
- a detailed list of the equipment and materials to be imported by the WFOE;

---

36. For example, the Feasibility Study Report prepared by the Kunshan Economic and Technology Development Zone on the basis of an application form completed by one foreign investor provided that the WFOE would export more than 20% of its products, whereas the foreign investor had merely stated in the application that it would endeavour to export as much as possible given market conditions and the best interests of the company. The report also provided for a trade union. While WFOE employees have the right to establish a union, not all do. Accordingly, many companies prefer not to mention trade unions in the feasibility study report.

37. WFOE Implementing Rules, Art. 16.

38. Id. Arts. 17, 18.

- a power of attorney on behalf of the person executing the application documents on behalf of the investor; and
- if the investor intends to contribute know-how as part of its registered capital, the investor must also provide documents such as patents to evidence the value of such know-how at the time of application.[39]

The formal application basically restates the same information included in the Project Report and Feasibility Study, and again a form is often supplied by the local approval authority requiring the following information:

- name or title, address and registered address of the foreign investor and name, nationality and position of its legal representative;
- name and address of the company;
- scope of operations, product type and production scale;
- total amount of investment in the proposed enterprise, amount of registered capital, source of capital, method of investment and term of investment;[40]
- organizational format and structure and the legal representative of the proposed enterprise;
- main types of production equipment to be used and respective age of equipment, production technology to be used, level of technology and source of supply;
- product sales direction, regions, sales channels, methods and the product sales ratio on domestic and overseas markets;
- foreign exchange income and expenditure arrangements;
- personnel framework, arrangements for employee recruitment, training, wages, welfare benefits, insurance, and labour protection;
- amount of environmental pollution likely to be caused and combative measures;
- site selection and area of land to be used;
- capital construction and capital, resources and raw materials required for production and operations and supply measures;
- progress plans for project implementation; and
- period of operation of the proposed enterprise.[41]

Upon submission of the application package, the approval authorities have 90 days to issue their decision.[42]

39. Id. Art. 11.

40. If equipment is to be used as registered capital investment, the investor must append a detailed list of the equipment, quantity and value to the application. Id. Art. 27.

41. Id. Art. 15.

42. Id. Art. 12.

f. enterprise registration

Once the WFOE has been approved and an approval certificate issued by the approval authority, the foreign investor will have to register the WFOE's legal existence with SAIC or local Administration of Industry and Commerce (AIC). To register the enterprise and obtain a Business Licence, the foreign investor must submit the following documents to the local AIC within 30 days of issuance of the Certificate of Approval:[43]

- a registration application signed by the chairman and vice chairman of the board of directors of the WFOE;
- the Project Report, Feasibility Study Report and their approvals;
- the Articles of Association and Approval Certificate from MOFTEC or COFTEC;
- certificates of creditworthiness for the foreign investor;
- a list of persons in charge of the enterprise (directors, general manager, deputy general manager) and their appointment letters; and
- the Business Licences of the foreign investor (that is, the certificate of incorporation).[44]

In addition, the WFOE will have to pay a registration fee of 0.1% of the first Rmb10 million of registered capital and 0.05% of the next Rmb90 million.[45]

SAIC or local AIC will then issue a Business Licence, usually within a few days. The WFOE's legal existence begins on the date the Business Licence is issued. The board of directors can then have its first meeting.

g. post-approval formalities

Once the WFOE obtains its Business License it will also have to take care of additional matters at the following bureaus and entities:

- register with the local foreign exchange bureau to obtain a foreign exchange certificate;
- register with customs for the importation of equipment;
- register with the local tax bureau (local tax bureau include the local state tax (*guo shui*) bureau and local tax (*di shui*) bureau) to pay enterprise income tax, business tax and other taxes;
- register with the local financial bureau;
- open a Renminbi and foreign exchange bank account at a bank of the investor's choice;

---

43. Id. Art. 13.

44. *PRC, Administration of Enterprise Legal Person Registration Implementing Rules*, effective December 1, 1988, Art. 35, as amended on December 25, 1996.

45. *Legal Person Registration Fee Standards and Their Applicable Scope Regulations*, issued by SAIC, Ministry of Finance, State Prices Bureau, effective December 1, 1988, Art. 2.

- arrange with the local utilities for water, gas, and electricity;
- arrange with the Post and Telecommunication Bureau to obtain phone lines and register faxes;
- sign a grant contract with the local land bureau;
- obtain approval from the local planning authority to begin construction (*kaigong*);
- register the company's seal and stamp with the Public Security Bureau; and
- expatriate employees will need to deal with Customs to import personal effects; the Public Security Bureau to obtain a Residence Card; and the Local Tax Bureau to register to pay personal income tax.

C. Approval Strategies

In planning the project and tailoring the documents, the foreign investor should seek to anticipate the reception the proposed venture will get from the approval authorities – pinpointing potential areas of contention in advance could save a lot of time and headaches later.

The foreign investor should, of course, keep the approval authorities informed of their plans. This will reduce the likelihood of last minute unanticipated objections. One particular area of concern is the scope of business. In most countries, companies are allowed to pursue whatever objectives the board of directors determines is in the best interests of the company, provided that in so doing the company does not violate any laws or regulations. Accordingly, it is not uncommon to include a catch-all phrase in the scope of business permitting the company to engage in any activity permitted by law. In China, however, all FIE legal persons, including WFOEs, are tightly restricted in their scope of business. The SAIC supervises all FIEs and will not allow FIEs to engage in activities outside their authorized scope of business.

The scope of business will be set forth in the Feasibility Study and Articles of Association (see "Feasibility Study and Articles of Association" above). It is important to keep in mind the long-term strategic aspirations of the project in crafting the business scope, and an FIE should try to push for as broad a scope as possible even though the approval authorities will usually try to narrow it.

Policy considerations

In addition, it is helpful to keep in mind the policy considerations that drive the approval decisions. This is true regardless of whether the project is a WFOE or a joint venture. The authorities will inevitably scrutinize the project with an eye on how it would benefit the Chinese national economy. This will particularly be the case if you go through MOFTEC rather than the local authorities. Competition for foreign investment has increased among the various localities, and approval may often be obtained from local authorities more easily and with fewer conditions.

The compatibility of a project with current State plans and priorities will typically be a key factor in the receptiveness of approval authorities. For example, a notice was issued a while back suspending the approval of new float glass plants due to the perception of market overcapacity.

On a broader level, the publication of MOFTEC's *Foreign Investment Industrial Guidance Catalogue* (see **Legislation Appendices**) provides some idea of the State's current priorities in developing the national economy. Investments in China's underdeveloped interior are particularly encouraged, although the central authorities have failed to offer any significant concessions for foreign investors in these areas.

Technologically Advanced Enterprise (TAE) Status

TAE status, which entitles a project to tax breaks and other concessions, is equivalent to that which would be obtained for a joint venture. The general eligibility requirements are:

- the project should be in an industry or pertain to a project for which foreign investment is encouraged as publicly announced by the SDPC or the relevant ministry;
- the technology, know-how and equipment adopted must be internationally advanced and have practical applicability; and
- the products produced by use of the technology are advanced when considered in comparison to the products produced using domestically available technology.[46]

Generally, TAE status is available only to FIEs that produce tangible items, although an exception can be made for high technology development ventures. Ordinary processing projects that are limited to importing machinery and equipment that are superior to domestically manufactured items in terms of functions and efficiency would not normally be confirmed as TAEs.

With respect to the first condition listed above, a foreign investor must first determine whether the proposed project bears any relation to an industry for which foreign investment is encouraged by the State. From time to time, the SDPC, in conjunction with other State agencies, issues directives specifying the industries for which foreign investment is encouraged, permitted, restricted and prohibited by the State. Currently you can refer to the *Foreign Investment Industrial Guidance Catalogue* (see **Legislation Appendices**).

Regarding the second condition, a foreign investor must assert that the technology, know-how and equipment adopted by the WFOE is internationally advanced and has practical applicability.

---

46. *Confirming and Verifying Foreign Investment Enterprises as Product Export Enterprises and Technologically Advanced Enterprises Implementing Rules*, issued by MOFTEC on December 3, 1996 and effective on January 1, 1997, Art. 4.

This is usually done in general and specific statements in each of the documents pertaining to the project including:

- the Project Report;
- the Feasibility Study; and
- the Articles of Association.

As for the third condition, the enterprise may be confirmed as a TAE if there are improvements in the quality of the products from the enterprise and the technical nature of the products when compared to the quality of the products from Chinese enterprises producing similar products.

A foreign investor may apply for confirmation of its TAE status after its commencement of business operations for six months.[47] In most cases, the examination and confirmation authority (MOFTEC or its local commissions) should decide whether to confirm or reject TAE status within 45 days of receipt of all application materials.

After the WFOE has been confirmed as a TAE, it is no longer required to conduct annual examinations, as used to be the case, unless specifically required to do so by the examination and confirmation authority. If the examination and confirmation authority considers it necessary to conduct such examination, it shall issue a 30-day notice to the WFOE, which should then provide the authority with a report detailing production, sales and the progress of technology transfer. A TAE which fails in such examination must apply for another examination after one year and if fails to do so or if it applies but fails in the examination, its TAE status will be revoked.

Technology Transfer

A foreign investor may also want to consider a technology transfer agreement between the parent and the WFOE. The advantage of a technology transfer agreement is that you can take money out of the company in the form of royalties, which are taxed on a withholding basis at the rate of 20% (or 10% if the investor's country has entered into a double taxation avoidance treaty with China). In contrast, enterprise income tax is generally 33% (30% national tax and 3% local tax). However, if the WFOE is established in an Special Economic Zone ("SEZ")[48], or in an economic and technical development zone established under the approval of the

47. Id., Art.10.

48. Currently there are five SEZs in Shenzhen, Zhuhai, Shantou, Xiamen and Hainan respectively. See *PRC, Foreign Investment Enterprise and Foreign Enterprise Income Tax Law Implementing Rules*, Art. 69.

State Council or in a coastal open city, the income tax rate is reduced to either 24% or 15%.[49] In addition, FIEs engaged in production are entitled to a two-year tax exemption and further three-year 50% tax reduction beginning from the first profitable year. TAEs are entitled to a further three-year 50% tax reduction. In light of these reductions, a technology transfer agreement may not be of much benefit for several years, but in the long run might be useful.

When establishing a WFOE outside an SEZ, an economic and technical development zone or a coastal open city, a foreign investor should, however, keep the possibility in mind that tax rules may change. Preferential tax treatment may be eliminated as China moves to level the playing field for domestic and foreign companies, in part to meet the standards for entry into the World Trade Organization, although for now, the preferential tax treatments remain.

49. If a WFOE is established in an SEZ or in an economic and technical development zone, it is entitled to a tax rate of 15%; however, if the WFOE is established in the old urban area of the city where the SEZ or the economic and technical development zone is located, or in a coastal open city, the tax rate is 24%. See *PRC, Foreign Investment Enterprises and Foreign Enterprises Income Tax Law*, Art. 7.

Summary Checklist

1. WFOEs offer the foreign investor a number of potential advantages over joint ventures including faster establishment management control, protection of technology and avoidance of the need to share profits with a Chinese partner.
2. WFOEs may not be established in certain restricted or controlled areas such as media, real estate, most infrastructure projects, full assembly of sedan cars and the management of telecommunications businesses.
3. Investors must submit a preliminary project report summarizing the purpose and aims of the proposed WFOE including the purpose of the company, the proposed scope and scale of operations, products to be manufactured, technology and equipment to be used, and the estimate of export sales in terms of percentages of products, land requirements and of land needed, and requirements for energy and other utilities.
4. Local approval authority is restricted to projects under US$30 million. This is often circumvented by the artificial division of large projects into separate stages, although doing so is of dubious legality.
5. After the receipt of the response from the relevant authority with respect to the project report, the investor must prepare a Feasibility Study report covering the purpose and aims of the project in greater detail.
6. The investor must also prepare Articles of Association analogous to the articles of incorporation and by-laws of a Western company.
7. The formal application for approval of the WFOE restates the information in the Feasibility Study and Articles of Association but also requires a number of other documents, including a list of the chairman and directors for the WFOE, letters of creditworthiness and good standing, a list of import requirements and a power of attorney.
8. Policy considerations drive approval decisions, and the compatibility of a project with current State plans and priorities will typically be a key factor in the receptiveness of approval authorities.
9. Export ratios and technology transfer are two other key considerations for the approval authorities.
10. In drafting the documents for approval, it is best to avoid boxing the WFOE into a specific export commitment, otherwise the WFOE may experience problems in gaining foreign exchange approvals later down the road.
11. The approval authorities will generally attempt to make the WFOE's permitted scope of business as narrow as possible.

12. TAE status entitles projects to tax breaks and other concessions. However, approval is dependent on the level of the technology and products produced as well as upon PRC industrial policy.

CHAPTER 3

APPROVALS FOR ESTABLISHING A HOLDING COMPANY

Laurence C. Franklin, Adjunct Associate Professor
Hong Kong University of Science & Technology, Hong Kong

The foreign investor is permitted to invest in China via a restricted number of forms of foreign investment. These forms include:

- three kinds of foreign investment enterprise (FIE): Sino-foreign equity joint ventures (EJVs), Sino-foreign cooperative joint ventures (CJVs) (see Chapter 1: **Approvals for Establishing a Joint Venture**), and wholly foreign-owned enterprises (WFOEs) (see Chapter 2: **Approvals for Establishing a Wholly Foreign-Owned Enterprise**);
- companies limited by shares (though approval is still targeted to companies intending to list) and
- representative offices (which are quite restricted in their commercial activities, principally to liaison work).

Certain preferred forms of foreign investment, such as "branches" of a foreign company (with some exceptions like banks) and FIEs which do not have a specific business objective or a production activity (such as a shell company) are generally prohibited. The *Establishment of Companies With an Investment Nature by Foreign Investors Tentative Provisions*[1] (the "Holding Company Tentative Provisions") (see **Legislation Appendices**) offer the foreign investor a new form of FIE, the holding company, which can be established either as a WFOE or an EJV.[2] A holding company is by regulation a limited liability company.[3] A holding company can be established although it has no production activity; it may merely be an investment company. However, with imagination, it can be used for much, much more. With the recent, August, 1999 liberalization of the Scope of Business activities a holding company can engage in, there is a lot of renewed interest in establishing holding companies.

Why Establish a Holding Company?

A holding company has some advantages over other forms of doing business in China. It has several disadvantages as well. Hence, the value of a holding company should be carefully assessed by a foreign investor. The principal advantages of establishing a holding company are:

- centralized coordination

  The main thrust of the Holding Company Tentative Provisions is in this area. The holding company can centralize and coordinate many functions for its investee companies, improving efficiency and cost effectiveness (see "Scope of Business" below). Significantly, since August, 1999, the holding company can take title to and sell its investee companies' goods domestically as well as outside China;

1. Promulgated by the Ministry of Foreign Trade and Economic Cooperation ("MOFTEC") on April 4, 1995 and effective from the same date.
2. Holding Company Tentative Provisions, Article 1.
3. Id.

- handling representative office functions

  A holding company can assume the representative office's functions and more. A holding company has its own Business Licence and can therefore engage in direct business activities, unlike a representative office. Moreover, it can directly employ staff and pay them their full pay in Renminbi. By contrast, representative offices must hire China nationals through a system of Foreign Enterprise Service Companies (FESCO), or similar organizations. Payments must be made in foreign exchange to FESCO, which in turn retains a substantial amount of the local employees' pay, affecting employee motivation and loyalty;

- increased Chinese presence with authorities

  For many multinationals with several small to medium-sized FIEs, often in different PRC industrial sectors and in different geographic areas, a holding company offers the opportunity to consolidate the foreign investor's profile in China and to speak with a single corporate voice to the authorities. A holding company provides a natural "country headquarters" vehicle. These foreign investors generally register their holding company in Beijing, where the holding company executives can interact with the relevant ministries and other government officials;

- increased influence with suppliers and customers

  A holding company can centralize and coordinate purchasing, information reporting, marketing, customer training and similar activities. This may lead to substantial time and cost efficiencies;

- some current advantages in foreign exchange balancing (see "Coordinating Foreign Exchange And Local Currency Balancing" below)

  As a practical matter, since a holding company has been approved at the national level, the foreign investor will have "standing" to see, and better access to, the State Administration of Foreign Exchange (SAFE) at the national level. The national SAFE office has greater authority than provincial or municipal authorities to help solve foreign exchange imbalance issues;

- potentially, self-financing operation

  The Holding Company Tentative Provisions permit the holding company to charge for its services. The potential exists for the cost of the establishment and operation of the holding company to be fully paid for by its activities. Thus, a holding company can eliminate or reduce the need for continuous head office funding to support a "country headquarters" representative office; and

- future benefits

  Some view the present advantages of a holding company as marginal. But, they seek a holding company now in anticipation of further liberalization of a holding company's activities. Specifically, if and when permitted, they may be interested in:

  - trading opportunities in its various forms (such as taking title to imported finished goods and selling them domestically, investing in trading firms). Since August, 1999

it is possible for holding companies to buy goods domestically in their own name for sale domestically or abroad;
- greater intra-group currency management powers (see "Scope of Business" below); and
- group consolidation for tax and accounting purposes.

The principal disadvantages of establishing a holding company include:

- The start up costs for a holding company are considerably higher than for a representative office, because of the time and resources required in the approval process;
- The foreign investor must contribute a minimum of US$30 million fresh capital within a two-year period, whether or not the investee companies are ready to be funded;
- The holding company may provide services to investee companies only with the unanimous consent of the Board of Directors, which may diminish the value of the holding company to some of its joint venture investee companies;
- The future potential benefits may or may not materialize – presently, the restrictions on holding companies significantly diminish the value of such entities;
- The legal status of a holding company is not clearly defined under Chinese law – the Holding Company Tentative Provisions go a long way towards clarifying the legal position, but several issues involving such areas as taxation (see "taxation" below), scope of business and dispute resolution (see "Contracts and dispute resolution" below) remain unclear; and
- The legal status of the investee companies under a holding company is defined by the Holding Company Tentative Provisions, but it is uncertain whether MOFTEC's determination of FIE status will in practice be fully supported by the other relevant authorities (for example, tax, foreign exchange control and customs) at the local, municipal and provincial levels. As holding companies have a longer history and become more familiar, this disadvantage should disappear.

Legal Framework

The Holding Company Tentative Provisions (see **Legislation Appendices**) form the legal basis for establishing a holding company. These are based on two principal laws:

- for a WFOE holding company, the *PRC, Wholly Foreign-owned Enterprise Law*[4] (the "WFOE Law"), and the *PRC, Wholly Foreign-owned Enterprise Law Implementing Regulations*;[5]

4. Promulgated on April 12, 1986.

5. Approved by the State Council on October 28, 1990, promulgated by MOFTEC on December 12, 1990 and effective from the same date.

- for a joint venture holding company, the *PRC, Sino-foreign Equity Joint Venture Law*[6] (the "Joint Venture Law"), and the *PRC, Sino-foreign Equity Joint Venture Law Implementing Regulations*.[7]

Table 1 below summarizes the advantages and disadvantages of a holding company in China.

Table 1: Advantages and Disadvantages of Establishing a Holding Company in China

Advantages	Disadvantages
• Centralized coordination of investee companies' operations • Handling representative office functions and much more • Consolidated presence in China with national authorities • Increased influence with suppliers and customers • Some current advantages in foreign exchange balancing • Potentially self-financing operation • Future potential benefits: – trading (already liberalized) – foreign exchange and local currency balancing – group consolidation for accounting and tax purposes	• High start-up cost, relative to a representative office • US$30 million in registered capital • Future potential benefits may or may not occur • Legal status of holding company still unclear for some purposes • MOFTEC's determination of legal status of the holding company's investee companies may not be fully supported by other authorities at local levels

Foreign investors with experience of these laws will find the Holding Company Tentative Provisions familiar in their approach. They are supplemented by:

- *MOFTEC, Issues Concerning the <Establishment of Companies With an Investment Nature by Foreign Investors Tentative Provisions> Explanation* (the "Explanation")[8];

6. Effective on July 1, 1979 and amended on April 4, 1990.
7. Promulgated by the State Council on September 20, 1983 and amended on January 15, 1986.
8. Promulgated by the MOFTEC on February 16, 1996.

- *MOFTEC, Directing of the Examination and approval of Foreign Investment Enterprises opinion* (the "Opinion")[9]; and
- *MOFTEC, <Establishment of Companies With an Investment Nature by Foreign Investors Tentative Provisions> Supplementary Provisions* (the "1999 Supplement")[10].

Neither the WFOE Law nor the Joint Venture Law contain provisions regarding a holding company. However, for several years MOFTEC has been interpreting these two laws in an expansive manner to permit companies to establish WFOEs or joint venture companies whose primary purpose was to hold equity interests in investee companies. It is interesting to note that China's willingness to allow WFOEs which may not "produce" anything (such as manufacturing goods) is a significant evolution in Chinese thinking; the WFOE Law specifically states that only 'productive' enterprises will be considered for approval.

Further liberalization of the Holding Company Tentative Provisions may well occur, depending on China's experience with holding companies. According to MOFTEC, the first holding company was approved in mid-1984, and to date, more than 170 holding companies (most wholly foreign-owned) have been approved, with many applications in the queue.

Legal requirements

WFOE holding company

The Holding Company Tentative Provisions provide that a foreign investor must satisfy the following MOFTEC requirements to be eligible to establish a WFOE holding company:

- have sound creditworthiness and sufficient resources for establishing and operating a holding company;
- have a minimum of US$400 million in total assets for the year prior to application;
- have established FIEs with actual paid-up registered capital contributed by the foreign investor exceeding US$10 million; and
- have obtained approval for more than three investment projects.[11]

Alternatively, the foreign investor can satisfy the following requirements:

- have sound creditworthiness and sufficient resources for establishing a holding company;
- have established at least 10 FIEs engaged in production or infrastructure construction; and

9. Promulgated by the MOFTEC on November 5, 1996.

10. Promulgated by the MOFTEC on August 24, 1999.

11. Holding Company Tentative Provisions, Article 2(1)(i).

- have established FIEs with actual paid-up registered capital contributed by the foreign investor exceeding US$30 million.[12]

joint venture holding company

To establish a joint venture holding company, MOFTEC requires that:

- the Chinese investor must have sound creditworthiness and sufficient resources for establishing a holding company;
- the Chinese investor must have at least Rmb100 million (about $12 million) in total assets;[13] and
- the foreign investor must meet the same requirements as for a WFOE holding company.

Investment

In addition, the holding company must fulfil the following investment criteria:

- the registered capital of the holding company should be at least US$30 million of fresh capital,[14] and should be fully paid up within two years from the date of issuance of the business licence;[15] and
- the foreign investor must contribute capital in freely convertible currencies; for a joint venture holding company the Chinese investor may contribute capital in Renminbi.[16]

It is interesting to note that six months prior to the issuance in April, 1995 of the Holding Company Tentative Provisions, the MOFTEC policy guidelines were more liberal:

- a "reputable and financially solid" foreign investor requirement, but no US$400 million minimum assets test;
- no minimum US$10 million foreign investor's contribution to existing FIEs;
- three or more projects approved requirement; and
- the holding company's registered capital was a minimum of US$10 million (fresh capital contribution), not US$30 million.

By Spring, 1995, MOFTEC had clearly tightened the criteria, in part because it was receiving too many applications for holding companies and in part because it saw the opportunity to increase foreign investment in China.

---

12. Id. Article 2(1)(ii).

13. Id. Article 2(2).

14. Id. Article 2(3).

15. Id. Article 4.

16. Id. Article 4. Note: The foreign investor may not for its initial holding company investment utilize Renminbi, even Renminbi dividends received from its investee companies.

Table 2 below summarizes the legal requirements for the establishment of a holding company.

Table 2: Legal Requirements[17]

Type of Holding Company	Requirements
WFOE Holding Company	either • Foreign investor's assets, minimum US$400 million in total • Foreign investor must be creditworthy and economically strong enough to establish a holding company • Foreign investor's contribution to registered capital of existing foreign-invested companies exceeds US$10 million in total • Three or more projects have been approved • Registered capital of holding company, minimum of US$30 million – fresh capital
	or • Foreign investor must be creditworthy and economically strong enough to establish a holding company • Foreign investor has invested in at least 10 existing foreign investment companies • Foreign investor's contribution to registered capital of existing foreign investment companies exceeds US$30 million in total • Registered capital of holding company, minimum of US$30 million – fresh capital
Joint Venture Holding Company	• PRC party must be creditworthy and economically strong enough to establish a holding company • PRC party's assets at least Rmb100 million in total • Foreign investor must meet the same requirements as for a WFOE holding company • Registered capital of holding company, minimum of US$30 million – fresh capital

17. Holding Company Tentative Provisions, Article 2.

MOFTEC's requirement has consistently been that the registered capital of the holding company is fresh capital. This means the registered capital, already paid up, in an existing FIE does not count towards surmounting the holding company capital hurdle.[18] This is consistent with one of MOFTEC's objectives for holding companies: "To promote and absorb more foreign investment into China". The condition of "freely convertible currencies", that is, cash, should also be noted. "In kind" contributions are not permitted, not even advanced technology. Moreover, Renminbi dividends from existing FIEs cannot be reinvested to meet the US$30 million requirement.[19] However, foreign exchange dividends can be used in this way.

The timing of the contributions to the registered capital of a holding company are not specified in the Holding Company Tentative Provisions, other than that the entire amount must be contributed within two years after the date of issuance of the business licence. If the policy applicable to ordinary FIEs is followed for holding companies, as appears to be the current practice, a holding company's board of directors will have the right to determine the timing of contributions within that two-year period.

The foreign investor's US$10 million contribution to the registered capital of existing FIEs was a new (1995) requirement. Since that contribution may have taken many forms (for example, cash, equipment, proprietary technology or patents), the requirement is US$10 million in value, not necessarily cash.

MOFTEC has, in the past, shown flexibility on the status of the three "approved" projects where there was tangible evidence that the approval process was well advanced, if not completed (for example, at least the preliminary approval stage has been passed and the Chinese investor (if any) has approval to negotiate the terms of the joint venture).

Approval Process

For a WFOE holding company (the vast majority of holding companies), the application process will begin with the relevant local MOFTEC unit; typically, this is the local Commission of Foreign Trade and Economic Cooperation (COFTEC) where the holding company is to be registered.[20] For a joint venture holding company, the first step is for the PRC partner to obtain preliminary approval to invest in the joint venture holding company. Subsequently, the holding company application process should be the same, although there will be a separate approval process which the PRC partner must follow for its investment in the holding company (see Chapter 1: **Approvals for Establishing a Joint Venture**).

---

18. With regard to the use of holding company capital, the Opinion clarifies that holding company capital can be used to pay up any unpaid registered capital in an investee company.

19. Renminbi profits from investee companies can be reinvested in the increased capital of a holding company beyond the US$30 million, however.

20. Id. Article 3.

After approval by the local COFTEC, the holding company application is sent to the Foreign Investment Bureau of MOFTEC in Beijing. All holding companies are subject to final approval by MOFTEC in Beijing. While many foreign investors have chosen to register their holding companies in Beijing (perhaps seeking to emphasize their presence to the national authorities), almost an equal number of multinationals have chosen Shanghai (perhaps where they plan to establish their country headquarters, or perhaps because of the size of the foreign exchange swap market in Shanghai). Since it is now possible to set up branches and representative offices of holding companies, the location of the "head office" of the holding company has become less critical.

As with many approval processes in China, it is important to push one's case forward at both the local (for example, municipal or provincial) and the national level. There is no single formula for success. In general, if the application has unusual elements it will make the approval process more difficult. It is important to identify who on the Chinese side will benefit from the holding company and to enlist their support for approval to establish the holding company. Support could come from the locality where the holding company will be registered, the locality where a large FIE is or will be, and/or the industry sector which will benefit from the advanced technology.

If the holding company is quickly approved by the local COFTEC, this does not in itself guarantee that approval by MOFTEC in Beijing will be smooth. On the other hand, slow COFTEC approval should not necessarily be taken as a bad sign since it may mean COFTEC is taking instructions from MOFTEC and, once COFTEC approval occurs, MOFTEC approval may follow without further delay.

After MOFTEC approval, registration with the State Administration of Industry and Commerce (SAIC) and issuance of the Business Licence should normally occur within 30 days. The Business Licence issued to the holding company will state the lines of business in which the holding company is allowed to engage.

Each FIE set up under a holding company is subject to a separate approval by the relevant approval authority.[21] It is not true that MOFTEC in Beijing must approve all FIEs set up under a holding company. However, in practice, local approving authorities which can approve an FIE within local approval limits may check with MOFTEC in Beijing (for example, to ensure the scope of business of the FIE is not inconsistent with the holding company's Scope of Business approved by MOFTEC) before issuing their approvals.

---

21. Id. Article 9.

MOFTEC says it will consider a holding company application within 90 days of its submission. In practice MOFTEC has been very cautious about allowing foreign investors to establish holding companies. Historically, the application procedure has often proven to be quite lengthy and has taken some foreign investors one year or more. MOFTEC justifies the time frame by explaining that the 90-day period only begins to run when a holding company application is deemed "complete" (in that all issues have been resolved to MOFTEC's satisfaction and the application is ready for approval). The principal reason for applications being delayed usually involves the foreign investor's seeking additional flexibility in the scope of business of the holding company.

MOFTEC says it encourages the formation of holding companies. For the four-year period from 1996 to 1999, approximately 70 holding company applications were approved.

Table 3 below summarizes the approval process for both the WFOE and joint venture holding companies.

Table 3: Approval Process

Type of Holding Company	Procedure
WFOE Holding Company	• Follows nearly the same procedure as that of a WFOE under the WFOE Law (see Chapter 2: **Approvals for Establishing a Wholly Foreign-owned Enterprise**) except MOFTEC approval needed, regardless of size. • Begins with the local unit designated by MOFTEC where the holding company will be located MOFTEC in Beijing for final approval
Joint Venture Holding Company	• Follows nearly the same procedure as that of a joint venture under the Joint Venture Law (see Chapter 2: **Approvals for Establishing a Joint Venture**) except MOFTEC approval needed, regardless of size. • PRC company's industry approval • Begins with the local unit designated by MOFTEC where the holding company will be located MOFTEC in Beijing for final approval

Documents

The documents required for submission during the approval process will be familiar to foreign investors with existing FIEs and are summarized in Table 4 below. For the format of the application, a good guide for a WFOE holding company is the WFOE Application form.

For a WFOE holding company, the application and all other documents can be submitted at one time. For a joint venture holding company this is not the case because of the approval process which the Chinese partner must follow. The process has three sequential stages of approval: preliminary approval, Feasibility Study and Joint Venture Contract approval (see Chapter 1: **Approvals for Establishing a Joint Venture**).

The Project Proposal usually states the duration of the intended project. However, the Holding Company Tentative Provisions do not specify a minimum or maximum duration for a holding company.[22] This flexibility is designed to take into account that future FIEs are expected to be established for which the approved duration is not yet known. One approach is to provide that the holding company should continue for not less than a certain amount of years and for as long as its longest-lived investee company continues to exist. Pre-1995, MOFTEC approved holding company durations of up to 70 years. Post-1995, up to 50 years is possible.

The Feasibility Study does not have to be approved by the local or State Development and Planning Commission (SDPC); only MOFTEC's approval is needed. (It should be noted that this approach is consistent with the idea that prospective holding companies should not have production activities, since it is the SDPC and its local units which are responsible for planning the inputs and outputs for production).

The requirement for a "letter of guarantee"[23] from the creditworthy parent foreign investor (whether directly or indirectly the investor in the holding company) regarding contributions of capital and technology is consistent with MOFTEC's stated objective at the beginning of the Holding Company Tentative Provisions: "to promote investment in China by foreign investors and to attract advanced foreign technology...".[24] While an explicit letter of guarantee to MOFTEC may be new, assurances of making the capital contribution and transferring technology have been common provisions required by the Chinese side in the Joint Venture Contracts establishing FIEs. This letter of guarantee is not a guarantee of all the liabilities of the holding company or of its investee companies.

22. Id. Article 8.

23. Id. Article 12.

24. Introduction to the Holding Company Tentative Provisions.

Table 4: Application Documents[25]

- Application form – (It should be noted that the application form for a WFOE holding company is the same as for a WFOE)
- Project Proposal
- Feasibility Study
- Articles of Association – (It should be noted that the scope of business wording is crucial)
- Foreign investor supporting documents:
  - credit reference from a bank regarding creditworthiness;
  - certificate of incorporation;
  - evidence of signing authority, to act and bind the investor;
  - three years' audited financial statements;
  - information about existing PRC investee companies;
  - future investment plans in China;
  - letter of guarantee regarding contribution of capital and transfer of technology;
  - other documents which MOFTEC may require

For a joint venture holding company, the Joint Venture Contract and PRC investor supporting documents will be required.

Approval Strategies

MOFTEC officials have indicated the following factors which will affect the timing and the decision to approve a holding company application:

- priority will be given to well-known multinationals with advanced technology or management expertise;
- priority will be given where the advanced technology is conducive to the upgrading of Chinese technology;
- priority will be given where the investee companies are producing or will produce a substantial proportion of products for export;
- it will be helpful if the foreign investor can show the necessity or desirability of a holding company, for example, where the production activities of the investee companies would clearly benefit from the centralized service and support activities of a holding company;
- it will be helpful if the foreign investor's existing or planned activities are perceived by the Chinese Government to contribute especially to the economic development of the country.

25. Holding Company Tentative Provisions, Article 3.

This "special contribution" may be linked to an industrial sector (for example, establishing a holding company which facilitates an industrial objective of China's national Five-Year Plan), to a "pillar" industry, or to a geographic area; and

- it will be helpful if the foreign investor can show substantial future investment plans.

Foreign investor X wanted to establish a holding company in China. A principal reason was to be able to consolidate its profits and losses for tax purposes. X had read the Holding Company Tentative Provisions and had learned from other sources that consolidation would not be permitted under any circumstances. However, X was prepared to bring China advanced technology for one of China's "pillar" industries. MOFTEC agreed to grant X special approval, on an experimental basis, for X's holding company to consolidate for tax purposes.

It is important to maintain close contact at both the local and national levels during the application process. MOFTEC is under no real obligation to approve any holding company application; some minor issue can always be found. If possible, the foreign investor should enlist the active support of the geographic and industrial units in China that will benefit from the holding company's establishment.

Scope of Business

A holding company may, after MOFTEC approval, engage in all or some of the business activities outlined below.[26] As can be seen, the Holding Company Tentative Provisions and current MOFTEC policy allow a holding company to engage in a fairly wide range of business activities, with certain limitations.

Investment[27]

Holding companies are encouraged to pursue investment opportunities in China in industry sectors and geographic areas where foreign investment is encouraged or permitted. Holding companies are encouraged to act as a centralized investor for the foreign parent's investments in China. Hence, unlike the ordinary FIE, a holding company is permitted to invest its registered capital rather than only its retained earnings.

Prior to the Holding Company Tentative Provisions, a foreign investor was allowed to transfer all, part or none of its existing investments to the holding company. There are some existing

26. Id. Article 5.

27. Id. Article 5(1).

holding companies, not engaged in production, where the holding company actually holds none of the foreign investor's equity interest in investee companies; those investments are held by one or more offshore entities of the foreign investor. The Holding Company Tentative Provisions are not clear on this point but the Explanation[28] states that the holding company should not hold less than 10% of an investee company's registered capital; a partial transfer from the offshore foreign investor to the holding company is permitted. The final paragraph of Article 6 of the Holding Company Tentative Provisions should also be noted: it states that with MOFTEC's "special approval", a holding company may provide services to companies which do not meet the investee company requirements.

Foreign investor Y wanted to establish a holding company, but did not want to change its direct overseas shareholding in its existing FIEs (it may have been concerned about obtaining consent from the Chinese investors in each FIE, or it may have been concerned about potential tax on the transfer, or about the loss of an international arbitration forum for disputes). Y knew other holding companies had not directly invested in their FIEs, and was aware that the Holding Company Tentative Provisions contained no minimum investment requirement by the holding company in its investee company. Y's application to establish a holding company was rejected by MOFTEC. MOFTEC pointed to the Explanation which requires the holding company to hold a minimum 10% interest in the FIE if such FIE is to qualify as an investee company for purposes of the Holding Company Tentative Provisions.

Provide services to its investee companies

Holding companies are permitted to provide services to its investee companies. A holding company's "investee company" is defined by the Holding Company Tentative Provisions as one directly invested by the holding company and other foreign investors where their aggregate capital contribution accounts for not less than 25% of the registered capital.[29] The Explanation further provides that the holding company must hold at least 10% of the registered capital.

A holding company may provide services to an investee company only with the unanimous approval of the FIE's Board of Directors.[30] Thus, for each service provided to each joint venture investee company, each and every PRC investor will have to agree. This condition is more onerous than for pre-1995 approved holding companies, where MOFTEC approved holding company applications which permitted services to investee companies so long as there was an

---

28. Explanation, Article 6.

29. Id.

30. Holding Company Tentative Provisions, Article 5(2).

authorizing board resolution from the investee company. The previous practice usually enabled a majority foreign investor to pass an appropriate board resolution. MOFTEC is very firm on this condition. The services which can be provided to investee companies are outlined below.

Purchase agent[31]

A holding company may assist or represent its investee companies in purchasing domestic and imported raw materials, machinery, equipment, parts and components and office supplies for use by the investee companies. It is intended that the holding company may be able to take advantage of purchasing in larger quantities and in a coordinated fashion.

Sales agent[32]

A holding company may assist or represent its investee companies in selling products manufactured by them in domestic and overseas markets. For example, a holding company could appoint wholesalers, retailers and distributors domestically in China.

Until August, 1999, MOFTEC would not permit a holding company to buy and sell inputs and outputs in its own name; all purchasing and selling was to be done as an agent on behalf of the investee company. The 1999 Supplement now permits a holding company, with approval from MOFTEC to change the previously approved Scope of Business, to buy from its investee companies – in its own name – in the China market, and sell – in its own name – in the China market and outside China. In addition, a holding company can buy – in its own name – from any source in the domestic market, for export (provided such goods are not subject to PRC export quotas on export licences.) However, MOFTEC still will not approve in a holding company's Scope of Business the import and sale of foreign products to third parties, even if manufactured by the foreign parent or its overseas subsidiary. One narrow exception is for imports to be used by an investee company, but even in this case, the holding company cannot import in its own name.

The 1999 Supplement also allows a holding company to provide transportation, warehousing and other such services to its investee companies.

MOFTEC views these changes as a substantial liberalization of its previous position. Clearly, China's objective is to encourage exports, while strictly controlling imports. Foreign investors welcome these changes, but remain frustrated by the inability of their holding companies to import goods manufactured by the relevant parent company or one of its overseas subsidiaries.

31. Id. Article 5(2)(i).

32. Id.

After-sales service and support[33]

A holding company may provide after-sales service and support for the products of its investee companies. This includes after-sales maintenance and repair functions. Further, MOFTEC has advised that a holding company may also provide after-sales service and support for the imported products of its foreign parent.

Centralized administration and accounting services

While not explicitly stated in the Holding Company Tentative Provisions, MOFTEC has indicated that a holding company may provide centralized administrative and accounting services to its investee companies. However, a holding company and its investee companies are treated as separate and distinct entities for accounting and tax purposes. Presently, consolidation for accounting or tax purposes is not permitted.

Centralized research and development ("R&D")

While not explicitly stated in the Holding Company Tentative Provisions, MOFTEC has indicated that a holding company may provide centralized research and development activities to its investee companies. Under this authority, a holding company could, for example, introduce uniformity in information technology and information reporting. The 1999 Supplement clearly encourages holding companies to establish scientific research and development centers.[34]

Centralized recruitment and training[35]

A holding company is permitted to assist its investee enterprises in the recruitment and training of personnel. In theory, a holding company should permit a more efficient allocation within China of human resources. In practice, however, it may be difficult to move Chinese personnel from one investee company to another so long as there are domestic restrictions on people moving city to city and province to province.

Centralized market development and consultations[36]

A holding company is permitted to provide its investee companies with assistance in developing the domestic and oversees markets for its products. This would include advertising and public relations. More generally, a holding company may assist with 'consultations' and 'advice'. This provision is intended to be broad and flexible, to accommodate a wide range of advisory services.

---

33. Id.

34. 1999 Supplement, Article 2.

35. Holding Company Tentative Provisions, Article 5(2)(iii)

36. Id.

In discussions with MOFTEC, it is interesting to note that MOFTEC encourages the training and consultation services to extend beyond the investee companies to the domestic customer base of the investee companies as well.

Coordinate foreign exchange and local currency balancing[37]

This is one of the principal powers of interest to a foreign investor in considering whether to establish a holding company and merits a detailed analysis.
A holding company may arrange and coordinate currency (foreign and local) exchanges among its investee companies. Presently, it is not possible for a holding company to freely move surplus foreign exchange or surplus Renminbi intra-group. MOFTEC explains that a holding company can arrange currency exchanges in two ways:

- directly between investee companies; and
- between an investee company and the holding company.

In each case, these exchanges must take place "with the consent and under the supervision of the Foreign Exchange authorities".[38] This means the State Administration of Foreign Exchange (SAFE) under the People's Bank of China (PBOC) will be involved in the process, and presently either a swap centre or an authorized bank. Presently, a holding company may not directly exchange foreign exchange for Renminbi, or vice versa, without going through a swap centre or authorized bank. In a typical transaction, the local SAFE unit where the swap centre or bank is located will be the approving and supervising body.

Some of the confusion in this area may have arisen because, at this important intersection of national level authorities – MOFTEC and the PBOC both directly report to the State Council – there is perhaps a tendency for the lines of authority to blur a little bit. For example, consider the following dialogue:

Foreign investor: "Once a holding company is approved by MOFTEC, is that approval sufficient for foreign exchange swapping, or does one also need local SAFE approval?"

MOFTEC: "When a holding company is approved by MOFTEC, the special Holding Company Tentative Provisions permit the holding company to transfer foreign exchange among its investee companies. The local SAFE will permit it."

Foreign investor: "Automatically, due to MOFTEC approval?"

MOFTEC: "The holding company will have to register itself with the local SAFE, then inform the local SAFE about the foreign exchange transfers."

---

37. Id. Article 5(2)(ii)

38. Id.

The reality is that the appearance of the Holding Company Tentative Provisions in 1995 has not (as of 2000) empowered MOFTEC to grant authority to do something which is under the authority of the PBOC and one of its departments, the SAFE. For more than 15 years, the difficult issue of balancing a foreign exchange surplus in one FIE against a foreign exchange deficit in another FIE has been clearly under the SAFE's authority:

"Where one foreign joint venturer establishes two or more joint ventures in China (including where these are in different locations and in different sectors) and where the legitimate foreign exchange income of one is in surplus and another is in deficit, that joint venturer may, with the approval of the foreign exchange control department, solve the problem through adjustment between the various enterprises in which the joint venturer is involved."[39]

In short, the Holding Company Tentative Provisions permit a holding company to effect currency balancing between itself and an investee company, or between investee companies, provided all parties to the investee company agree, and provided the local SAFE unit at the location where the exchange will take place approves the transaction. The "national standing" of a holding company will give the holding company access to the national SAFE if its assistance is needed.

By what other means, without involving the SAFE, might a holding company coordinate a currency exchange? Consider the three approaches discussed below.

holding company lends currency

Since a foreign exchange (or Renminbi) surplus FIE can get the foreign exchange (or Renminbi) upstream to a holding company via a foreign exchange (or Renminbi) dividend payment, if the holding company has authority to lend foreign exchange downstream, a currency balancing could be achieved. Many foreign investors have been pressing MOFTEC very hard for this authority. It should be noted that the "provide financial support" power of a holding company is listed in a separate Article (Article 7) from the other services. One of the reasons for this may be that it is clearly not a power which can be given by MOFTEC. Article 7 explicitly states: "With the approval of the People's Bank of China...". The official view of the PBOC is that a holding company is not a bank or a financial institution and thus should not be authorized to lend money.

Since currency balancing is such a priority issue for foreign investors, it is likely there will be continuous pressure to find solutions of one kind or another. If the authority of a holding company to lend continues to remain wholly with the PBOC, then one probable regulatory development will be guidelines to establish a financial vehicle, either as a WFOE or an EJV

39. *State Council, Question of the Balancing of Foreign Exchange Income and Expenditure of Sino-foreign Equity Joint Ventures Provisions*, Article 9.

under a holding company which has limited powers to make loans to, and receive deposits from, its investee companies. The PBOC will no doubt insist it should be the supervising authority for any such "financial holding company", rather than MOFTEC, and the PBOC will want to write its own regulations with its own capital requirements. As of end 1999, it appears one such "non-bank financial institution" had been authorized by PBOC in 1998 and began operations in that year.

holding company charges and is charged for services

A holding company may charge for services rendered to its investee companies, provided the investee company's board unanimously agrees, and taking into account MOFTEC general policy that such services should ideally be provided at cost. So, a holding company could charge a foreign exchange-rich investee company in foreign exchange, and a Renminbi-rich investee company in Renminbi. This will permit the holding company to collect the "surplus" funds. This still leaves the problem of downstreaming the surplus funds. One can envision various methods of downstreaming (for example, the holding company's paying for something of value rendered by the investee companies), but most seem artificial.

Downstreaming via changes to the equity capital structure of the investee company (which are permitted) may pose difficulties for the Chinese investor (for example, potential dilution if the Chinese investor cannot fund pro-rata its equity stake) and may make unanimous consent a problem.

"countertrade"

One complicated approach for the holding company to generate foreign exchange for an investee company is to act as an agent on behalf of the investee company for the purchase of products in China for export in foreign currency. The investee company is entitled to the foreign exchange if the holding company is only an agent. If the goods purchased are not produced by the investee company, the investee company can pay Renminbi to the holding company so the holding company can pay for the goods. The result would be a flow of Renminbi to the holding company and a flow of foreign exchange to the investee company. The holding company's authority, on behalf of the investee company, to purchase goods in Renminbi not produced by an investee company, is not explicitly provided for in the Holding Company Tentative Provisions but has been orally confirmed with MOFTEC and is implicit in the 1999 Supplement. This would be an activity one may want to include in the Scope of Business to be submitted to MOFTEC for approval. Approval will be facilitated if the investee company's Scope of Business permits domestic purchases in Renminbi for foreign sale in foreign exchange.

As can be seen from the above, a holding company is limited in its authority to efficiently and effectively balance currency intra-group. Swap centres and authorized banks, supervised by the SAFE, will be involved for the foreseeable future.

Swap centres offer a means of exchanging foreign exchange and Renminbi. The seller, the buyer and the transaction must be approved by the SAFE. Originally, swap centres were established throughout China and operated independently. There are presently more than 100. Initially, there were different rates for different markets. By 1994, the rate was unified so the foreign investor was faced with the same rate, but different markets (for example, an FIE in Fuzhou would not be approved to use the swap centre in Shanghai). The PBOC's ultimate objective is to have a unified rate and a unified market.

Since Shanghai has historically had the biggest swap market, as long as the markets are not unified, there may be reason for a foreign investor to consider registering its holding company in Shanghai. For example, where the foreign investor outside China wants a foreign exchange dividend but the FIE has a Renminbi surplus and its local swap market is small, one pattern would be:

- foreign investor establishes a holding company registered in Shanghai;
- FIE declares and pays a Renminbi dividend to the holding company (this assumes the FIE is unable to do the Renminbi/foreign exchange swap locally);
- holding company swaps Renminbi for foreign exchange in larger Shanghai swap centre or larger branch of authorized bank; and
- holding company pays foreign exchange dividend to offshore foreign investor.

When the swap markets are unified, of course, there should be equal access to foreign exchange in Shanghai and in the 100 other swap markets in China. Full unification of the markets will take time, although there is already at present a computer network linking many cities for daily spot foreign exchange/Renminbi trading. As long as investee companies have to compete with domestic enterprises for access to foreign exchange in the local swap markets, it will continue to make sense to consider registering a holding company in one of the larger swap market locations where SAFE approval of the transaction, while not "automatic", should be easier for the holding company. It should be noted MOFTEC's position is, for this purpose, the location of holding company registration should make no difference. Another approach is to establish a "branch" of a holding company. Branches are not mentioned in the Holding Company Tentative Provisions but are permitted by MOFTEC. Several of the approved holding companies have one, or more than one, branch, and several have one, or more than one, representative offices as well.

Arrange loans and guarantees[40]

A holding company may assist its investee companies seeking loans and guarantees. This power may prove to be very useful, particularly in conjunction with the powers to coordinate currency balancing and to provide financial support. Such assistance by the holding company does not require separate approval by the PBOC.

provide financial support[41]

A holding company is permitted to provide financial support to its investee companies. It is encouraging that MOFTEC has seen fit to include this provision. This is stated in a separate Article of the Holding Company Tentative Provisions, perhaps at the request of the PBOC. Depending on the nature of the financial support, approval of the PBOC may be needed. Examining five common means of financial support, is a holding company authorized to make foreign currency available to an investee company by means of:

- an increase in registered capital? – yes;
- a reinvestment of holding company earnings? – yes;
- a direct loan? – yes, but subject to the approval of the PBOC, which presently is quite restrictive on authorizing lending activities for non-financial companies (it will be useful nonetheless to include the authority to lend and place deposits, subject to prevailing restrictions, in the Scope of Business of the holding company);
- borrowing on behalf of the investee company? –

  qualified yes. The holding company has authority to borrow in its own name (subject to a newly imposed limit specified in the 1999 Supplement of four times its registered, paid-up capital).[42] Whether it could borrow "on behalf of" of "for the benefit of" its investee company without needing PBOC approval to make a loan is questionable;
- issuing a holding company guarantee on behalf of the borrowing investee company? – qualified yes. MOFTEC gives an unqualified yes, but practical concerns include:
  - the lender will want to be satisfied that the holding company has such authority (it will be helpful to include the authority to issue guarantees in the Scope of Business of the holding company); and
  - the lender may want to try to register the holding company guarantee with the SAFE, for which the SAFE is not presently prepared.

    Theoretically, the authority to lend directly and the authority to guarantee a loan (which if called would result in the guarantor's effectively becoming a lender) should be treated in the same way. However, historically in China the authority to guarantee has, in other

---

40. Holding Company Tentative Provisions, Article 5(2)(iv).

41. Id. Article 7.

42. 1999 Supplement, Article 1.

contexts, been less tightly controlled than the authority to lend. Thus, an investee company's authority to borrow, coupled with a holding company's authority to guarantee, may prove to be valuable tools to achieve intra-group currency balancing; and

- currency exchange? (for example, a holding company receives Renminbi and pays foreign exchange) – yes, but not directly. The present method is through a swap centre, provided the relevant authorities in charge of the swap centre approve (see "coordinate foreign exchange and local currency balancing" above).

Consulting services[43]

A holding company is permitted to provide consultancy services to its foreign parent and to other investors in the holding company (if a joint venture) and to the investors in the investee companies. This explicit provision in the Holding Company Tentative Provisions serves to affirm that a holding company can perform the functions usually handled by a representative office. Further, it is intended to encourage the foreign investor to provide services such as research, training, market development and consulting services to the PRC investors in the holding company and in the investee companies, not just to the personnel employed in the holding company and in the investee companies.

Other activities

While not explicitly stated in the Holding Company Tentative Provisions, activities beyond those listed can be approved by MOFTEC. It was slightly curious that the Holding Company Tentative Provisions did not make explicit provision for the holding company to engage in "productive" activities (for example, manufacturing) of its own. Some pre-1995 approved holding companies do engage in production activities and at the same time hold equity interests in investee companies. The subsequent Explanation clarified that a holding company is prohibited from performing production activities.

A holding company was initially explicitly not allowed to act as a trade intermediary.[44] But since August, 1999, a holding company can do one of the two"legs" of trading, namely buy in China in its own name and sell inside or outside China in its own name.

Table 5 below summarizes the Scope of Business that holding companies are permitted to engage in under the Holding Company Tentative Provisions.

43. Holding Company Tentative Provisions, Article 5(3).

44. Id. Article 6, paragraph 3.

Points of interest

pricing

The Holding Company Tentative Provisions do not mention any pricing guidelines for holding company services. MOFTEC officials indicate agency and other services should be provided at cost to the investee companies, and that any commissions charged (for example, for arranging an export sale) should not contain a profit margin for the holding company. Actual practice may differ from this position.

currency

MOFTEC indicates holding companies as PRC legal entities may only charge in Renminbi for their services. Holding companies have in practice charged in foreign exchange as well as Renminbi for their services.

Table 5: Scope of Business

Permitted Activities	Activities not Permitted
• Investment • Provide services to its investee companies, with their consent – purchasing agent – sales agent – after-sales service and support – centralized administrative and accounting services – centralized research and development – centralized recruitment and training – centralized market development and consultations – coordinate foreign exchange and local currency balancing – arrange loans and guarantees – provide financial support • Provide services to investors in the holding company and in investee companies – consulting	• Trading as an intermediary for imports into China

centralized management control

It may be difficult to achieve the desired level of centralized management control over the investee companies if the PRC investors in such companies are different, and if their objectives are different from the objectives of the holding company.

holding company cost

A holding company imposes an additional level of record keeping and financial management. It may also prove more costly to run the sale of an investee company's products through the holding company (compared, for example, against a sale by an investee company in a bonded import/export zone). So cost should be a consideration in deciding whether and when to establish a holding company.

limited trading

Although the Holding Company Tentative Provisions explicitly do not allow a holding company to import for itself and sell domestically finished products made by the foreign parent (this would be "trading as an intermediary"), it may nonetheless be possible for MOFTEC to agree to permit the holding company to import a limited quantity of such finished products for its investee company, related in some way to that company's production, to be sold in conjunction with, or as a complement to, the investee company's finished products. In negotiating for MOFTEC's approval, the foreign investor's position will naturally be stronger if the investee company is prospective rather than existing and if the foreign investor's prospective contribution in terms of cash and technology is noteworthy.

amend scope of business

The scope of business applied for and approved by MOFTEC will define the authorized activities of the holding company. Indeed, the Business Licence issued to the holding company states the permitted business activities. In the event the holding company seeks to invest in new businesses or to expand its range of permitted activities, the MOFTEC approval and the Business Licence can be amended to incorporate those activities.

Other Holding Company Issues

Taxation

A holding company is an FIE and enjoys the tax treatment accorded to FIEs generally. The relevant tax law which is applicable to FIEs is the *PRC, Foreign Investment Enterprise and Foreign Enterprise Income Tax Law*[45] (the "FIET" Law) and the *PRC, Foreign Investment*

45. Passed by the National People's Congress on April 9, 1991 and effective from July 1, 1991.

Enterprise and Foreign Enterprise Law Implementing Rules[46] (the "FIET Law Implementing Rules"). However, under Chinese law, a joint venture between a holding company and a Chinese domestic enterprise constitutes a "jointly operated enterprise" and is technically not a foreign enterprise. The reason is that both the holding company and the Chinese entity are Chinese legal persons. Similarly, a company wholly-owned by a holding company is not an FIE because it is a subsidiary of a Chinese legal person rather than an FIE. In principle, a subsidiary of a holding company, as a purely domestic enterprise, should be taxed as a domestic enterprise rather than as an FIE. This principle would render the holding company structure unattractive to foreign investors, since FIEs often enjoy tax benefits that domestic enterprises do not. The Holding Company Tentative Provisions solve this problem. If a holding company's investee company is established with not less than 25% of its registered capital coming from the holding company or other foreign investors, the investee company will enjoy the benefits of an FIE. The State Administration of Taxation (the "State Tax") has confirmed its acceptance of MOFTEC's Holding Company Tentative Provisions and it appears that the investee companies of most holding companies have been approved by the local tax authorities to be treated for tax purposes as FIEs.[47]

taxation of a holding company

A holding company is exempt from income tax on the dividends it receives from its investee companies.[48]

A holding company generally will not enjoy income tax holidays or reductions otherwise available to FIEs because a holding company is engaged in services not production.

A holding company is entitled to a tax rebate for the reinvestment of the profits that the holding company receives from its investee companies.[49] The current rebate is usually 40% for profits reinvested, and 100% for reinvestment of profits from an advanced technology investee company. Since reinvestment rebates are not available to domestic enterprises, and previously were not available to holding companies, it is a good idea to confirm with the State Tax that reinvestment rebates (particularly 100% rebates) will be extended to the proposed holding company.

46. Promulgated by State Council Decree No. 85 on June 30, 1991.

47. *Ministry of Finance and State Administration of Taxation, Certain Taxation Issues concerning Foreign Investment Enterprises Engaging in Investment Business Notice*, Document No. 083, promulgated on January 13, 1995.

48. FIET Law Implementing Rules, Article 18.

49. FIET Law, Article 10.

taxation of an investee company

An investee company will enjoy all of the benefits available to FIEs. An investee company probably cannot deduct service fees paid to its holding company, following the tax principles for FIEs where "royalties paid to head office"[50] and "other expenditures not related to production or business operation"[51] are not deductible. However, the State Tax (or the relevant local tax unit) may be willing to make a distinction between a "passive" management fee and fees for services charged in "active" support of the investee company's business.

transfer of equity interests

There are a number of unclear points regarding the tax impact of a transfer of an equity interest from an (offshore) foreign investor to its (onshore) holding company. There is potentially a tax on any capital gain (actual or deemed) arising from the transfer.

It should be noted that the FIET Law states:

"Income tax shall be paid in accordance with the provisions of this Law by foreign enterprises on the income derived on production, business operations, and <u>other</u> <u>sources</u> [emphasis added] within the territory of the People's Republic of China."[52]

The FIET Law Implementing Rules state that income from other sources includes:

"Income from the alienation of property ... and other non-business income."[53]

A transfer at book value may be subject to scrutiny as between "associated companies"[54]

Although foreign investors who have actually gone through the transfer experience are reticent to comment, it would appear that transfers have been completed with the only potential tax event being a modest stamp duty, the amount of which can be subject to negotiation. MOFTEC supports the view that the transfer (particularly a simple transfer from a foreign investor to that same foreign investor's WFOE holding company) should not give rise to any taxable event.

For clarification of the tax result for a particular transaction, it may be desirable to seek a tax ruling. Depending on the issue, it should be obtained from the State Tax national office or from the local Tax Bureau where the existing FIE is located.

---

50. FIET Law Implementing Rules, Article 19(4).

51. Id. Article 19(10).

52. FIET Law, Article 1, paragraph 2.

53. FIET Law Implementing Rules, Article 2, paragraph 2.

54. Id. Articles 54 and 57.

Contracts and dispute resolution

Holding companies are considered Chinese legal persons under Chinese law. As noted above (see "Taxation"), general Chinese policy is that a joint venture between a holding company and another domestic Chinese entity is not considered an FIE. MOFTEC's Holding Company Tentative Provisions clarify that if the investee company meets the requirements of the Holding Company Tentative Provisions (minimum 25% foreign invested) and the Explanation (minimum 10% holding company invested), that investee company will be deemed an FIE and enjoy FIE status for many purposes. Nonetheless, the contractual relationship between a holding company and its investee company will generally not be governed by Sino-foreign joint venture legislation unless the investee company has a separate foreign investor. This can be a third party, or the foreign investor in the holding company can hold a direct offshore equity interest in the investee company.

With respect to arbitration, until May 1998, it was doubtful that arbitration could be referred to the China International Economic and Trade Arbitration Commission ("CIETAC"), China's international arbitration organization, for disputes arising between a holding company and another Chinese domestic enterprise, including PRC joint venture partners in the holding company or the investee companies, because both sides to the dispute, in such cases, are Chinese legal persons. Accordingly, such disputes were likely to be settled pursuant to Chinese domestic arbitral regimes. However, the 1998 revisions[55] to the CIETAC rules specifically provide for CIETAC to handle such disputes, which is a welcome development as CIETAC specializes in disputes involving foreign investors and has a track record in such matters.

These issues are important ones for a holding company and need definitive clarification.

Conclusion

Foreign investors have been seeking to establish some form of Western-style, non-manufacturing "holding company" for many years in China. The three basic reasons for this are:

- to bring together and to aggregate in one vehicle all of a foreign investor's strengths in China, whether for purchasing, marketing or government relations;
- to facilitate intra-group financial needs, a basic function of a Western-style holding company; and
- to consolidate for tax and accounting purposes.

55. *China international Economic and Trade Arbitration Commission, Arbitration Rules*, Second Revision, effective as of May 10, 1998.

China has recognized the foreign investors' desire for holding companies but has been reluctant to grant the foreign investor the desired level of operating authority and other objectives sought. At the same time, China has developed its own set of objectives for holding companies.

The result is the Holding Company Tentative Provisions and MOFTEC policy permitting the establishment of holding companies in China, with Chinese characteristics. The approval process is difficult. This is intentional, since the Chinese are unsure that holding companies are a good idea for China, although they feel holding companies can be useful to meet China's objectives of increased foreign investment and the transfer of advanced technology, particularly for priority industries. For the foreign investor, the present limited scope of authorized activities (see "Scope of Business" above) does not meet two of the three basic reasons for establishing a holding company. Nonetheless, more than 170 holding companies have been established by year-end 1999 and there is a backlog of applications. It will be very interesting to see how holding companies evolve, as their presence and importance in China grows.

Summary Checklist

1. Holding companies are a relatively new form of foreign investment permitted by China. The current guidelines consist of the Holding Company Tentative Provisions (1995), the Explanation (1996), the Opinion (1996) and the Supplement (1999), and MOFTEC policy. This provisional status offers opportunity as well as uncertainty. At yearend 1999, MOFTEC does not anticipate publication in the foreseeable future of any Final Provisions for holding companies.
2. A holding company may invest its "registered capital" in subsidiary and affiliated enterprises. Hence, the assets comprising US$30 million of the holding company's registered capital may also constitute the registered capital of its investee enterprises.
3. The principal advantages of a holding company are:
   - centralized coordination of investee companies, including sourcing and sales;
   - handling of representative office functions and more;
   - increased influence with authorities, suppliers, customers; and
   - future benefits if restrictions are loosened:
     - trading;
     - foreign exchange balancing; and
     - group consolidation for accounting and tax purposes.
4. Only MOFTEC in Beijing has the authority to grant final approval to the establishment of a holding company. Local municipal and provincial authorities lack this authority.
5. In evaluating holding company applications, MOFTEC will give priority to well-known multinational corporations which have something to offer China (such as valuable technology), those with export-oriented manufacturing plans, and those intending to make substantial additional investments in China in high-priority industries.
6. A favourable approval decision can be encouraged by demonstrating the necessity or desirability of the holding company, explaining how existing and future activities will contribute to the economic development of China and emphasising substantial future investment plans.
7. The permitted Scope of Business activities include:
   - investment;
   - purchase and sales agency and after-sales service support;
   - centralized administration, R&D, recruitment and training;
   - coordinating currency balancing;
   - arranging loans and guarantees; and
   - providing financial support.

A holding company may not trade imports as an intermediary in its own name; it may now source domestically and sell domestically or export in its own name.

8. Depending on the type of financial support provided, separate approval from the PBOC may be required.
9. A holding company is permitted to arrange and coordinate currency exchanges between itself and its investee companies and between investee companies, but there are presently severe limitations (typically due to third-party approvals) on the ability of a holding company to efficiently balance intra-group currency needs.
10. The Holding Company Tentative Provisions do not make provisions for a holding company to engage in "productive" activities. The Explanation clarifies that a holding company is prohibited from performing production activities.

CHAPTER 4

SPECIAL CASES: RETAIL AND FOREIGN TRADE OPERATIONS

Professor Liu Chu, Senior China Counsel
Shearman & Sterling, Hong Kong and Los Angeles

China's imminent entry into the WTO will have a dramatic impact on the retail and foreign trade sectors as many if not most of the current restrictions described below are expected to be lifted with the opening of China's domestic markets.

Ever since the establishment of the People's Republic of China (PRC) in 1949, the Chinese government has exerted strict and severe control over foreign trade business. There are several reasons for this centralized control: the control and planning of foreign exchange, the protection of the domestic industry from foreign goods and, in general, a fear of foreign forces affecting, or even controlling, the Chinese economy. For a long period before China started opening up and reforming in 1979, its foreign trade was monopolized by about a dozen national import and export companies directly under the then Ministry of Foreign Trade and its local branches. No other Chinese companies were permitted to engage in foreign trade. After 1979, more Chinese companies were granted the "foreign-trade-right" but still, foreign investments were not permitted in China's retail and foreign trade businesses. In the 1990s, China began allowing Sino-foreign joint ventures to be established in these two sectors on an "experimental basis". The *Foreign Investment Industrial Guidance Catalogue*,[1] (see **Legislation Appendices**) formally put these two industries into the category of "Projects Restricted for Foreign Investments, (Part II N, 1, 2).

Retail Operations

Legal framework

On June 25, 1999, the State Economic and Trade Commission (SETC) and the Ministry of Foreign Trade and Economic Cooperation (MOFTEC) promulgated the detailed "Pilot Projects for Commercial Enterprises with Foreign Investment Procedures" (the "Procedures").

The Procedures have seemingly been more readily applied to cases where enterprising foreign retailers, under various contract management arrangements, frequently team up with existing domestic Chinese companies already possessing the desired retail licenses. Such operations appear to continue to thrive despite a rectification campaign intended to clean them up.

The Procedures apply to commercial enterprises in the form of Sino-foreign equity or cooperative joint ventures established in China by foreign companies (or enterprises) with Chinese companies (or enterprises) ("Commercial Joint Ventures"). For the time being, the establishment of wholly foreign-owned commercial enterprises is not permitted.[2]

According to the Procedures, the State Council decides in which areas Commercial Joint Ventures may be established. For the time being, those areas are limited to provincial capitals,

1. Revised and promulgated by the State Council on December 31, 1997 with effect on January 1, 1998.
2. Procedures, Article 2.

the capitals of autonomous regions, municipalities directly under the central government, municipalities with independent development plans and special economic zones (the "Pilot Areas").[3]

The Procedures stipulate that Investors in Commercial Joint Ventures shall satisfy the following conditions:

1. The foreign party, or the major party of foreign parties, (the "Foreign Party") shall be an enterprise which is economically relatively strong, which has advanced experience in commercial operations and management, which has mastered advanced marketing techniques, and which has an extensive international sales network, a sound reputation and good business results. In addition, it shall be able to promote the export of Chinese products through the proposed Commercial Joint Venture.

   A Foreign Party which applies for establishment of a Commercial Joint Venture to engage in retail business shall have had an average annual merchandise sales volume of at least US$2 billion during the three years preceding the application and assets worth at least US$200 million during the year preceding the application.

   A Foreign Party which applies for the establishment of a Commercial Joint Venture to engage in wholesale business shall have had an average annual merchandise wholesale volume of at least US$2.5 billion during the three years preceding the application and assets worth at least US$300 million during the year preceding the application.

2. The Chinese party, or the major party of Chinese parties, (the "Chinese Party") shall be an enterprise which is engaged in the circulation of merchandise, which is economically relatively strong, which has relatively strong business capabilities and which has had assets worth at least Rmb50 million (Rmb300 million if located in central or western China) during the year preceding the application. If such a Chinese Party is a commercial enterprise, its average annual sales volume during the three years preceding the application shall have been at least Rmb30 million (Rmb200 million if located in central or western China). If the said Chinese Party is a foreign trade enterprise, the average annual volume of imports and exports for its own account during the three years preceding the application shall have been at least US$50 million (of which exports shall account for at least US$30 million).[4]

3. Procedures, Article 4.

4. Procedures, Article 5.

A Commercial Joint Venture shall meet the following conditions:

1. it shall comply with relevant Chinese laws, regulations and rules;

2. it shall comply with the commercial development plans of the city in which it is located;

3. if the Commercial Joint venture is engaged in retail business, it shall have registered capital of at least Rmb50 million or, in central or western China, at least Rmb30 million; if it is engaged in wholesale business, it shall have registered capital of at least Rmb80 million or at least Rmb60 million in central or western China;

4. if the Commercial Joint Venture carries on business through more than three chain stores (excluding convenience stores, specialist stores and exclusive stores), the ratio of the Chinese Party's capital contribution shall account for at least 51% subject to State Council approval; the Foreign Party to such a chain store Commercial Joint Venture may be permitted to have a controlling interest therein if the Commercial Joint Venture's own business situation is relatively good, the Foreign Party has already purchased large amounts of goods from China and the Commercial Joint Venture is able to use the Foreign Party's international marketing network to further expand the export of Chinese products; the ratio of the capital contribution of the Chinese Party to either a Commercial Joint Venture which establishes not more than three branch stores, or to convenience stores, specialist stores or exclusive stores operated as a chain shall account for at least 35%; and the ratio of the capital contribution of the Chinese Party to a Commercial Joint Venture which is engaged in wholesale business (including a retail enterprise which is engaged in wholesale business as a sideline) shall not be less than 51%;

5. the type of branch stores to be established by the Commercial Joint Venture shall be limited to directly operated chain stores, i.e. chain stores which are directly invested in and directly operated by the Chinese Party and the Foreign Party; for the time being, Commercial Joint Ventures shall not be permitted to develop other types of chain stores such as voluntary chain stores and franchised chain stores, etc; and

6. the term of operation shall not exceed 30 years or, in central or western China, 40 years.[5]

If the Foreign Party and the Commercial Joint Venture enter into a trademark or trade name license contract and/or a technology transfer contract, the total amount of the relevant fee collected by the Foreign Party may not be more than 0.3% of the Commercial Joint Venture's sales (net of value added tax) during the year concerned, and the period over which such fee is collected may not be longer than 10 years.[6]

---

5. Procedures, Article 6.

6. Procedures, Article 7.

Establishing a commercial joint venture

The Procedure for establishment of a Commercial Joint Venture is as follows:

The Chinese Party shall submit a feasibility study (instead of a project proposal) and relevant documents to the economic and trade commission (or the economic commission or the planning and economic commission) of the Pilot Area in which it is located. The commission of the Pilot Area, together with the competent authority for internal trade, shall submit the same to SETC according to the prescribed procedure. After SETC has solicited the opinion of MOFTEC, it shall examine the submitted documents and decide whether or not to approve them.

After the feasibility study (submitted instead of a project proposal) has been approved, the foreign trade and economic cooperation authority of the Pilot Area shall submit the contract and articles of association to MOFTEC according to the prescribed procedure. MOFTEC shall examine the contract and articles of association and decide whether or not to approve them.

Within one month of the date on which a Commercial Joint Venture receives the Approval Certificate issued by MOFTEC for a Foreign Investment Enterprise, it shall register with the State's administrative authority for industry and commerce on the strength of such certificate.[7]

The following documents shall be submitted when applying to establish a Commercial Joint Venture:

1. Documents to be included in the submission of the feasibility study:
   i. a feasibility study (instead of a project proposal) prepared jointly by all the parties to the joint venture;
   ii. a banker's certificate of creditworthiness, (a photocopy of) the registration certificate and (a photocopy of) the legal representative certificate of each party to the joint venture;
   iii. annual balance sheets and profit and loss statements for the most recent three years of each party to the joint venture, audited by an accounting firm;
   iv. (if the Chinese Party invests State-owned assets) the document in which an administration for State-owned assets confirms the appraisal report for the State-owned assets which the Chinese Party intends to invest;
   v. the types of merchandise to be dealt in by the proposed Commercial Joint Venture; and
   vi. other relevant documents.

2. Documents to be included in the submission of the contract and articles of association:
   i. the documents included in the submission of the feasibility study and the approval document in respect thereof;

7. Procedures, Article 8.

ii. the contract for, and articles of association of, the proposed Commercial Joint Venture executed by the authorized representative of each party to the joint venture;
iii. a list of import and export merchandise;
iv. a name list of the members of the board of directors of the proposed Commercial Joint Venture and the instruments of appointment of the directors appointed by each party to the joint venture;
v. the notice of advance approval of the enterprise name, issued by the State Administration for Industry and Commerce; and
vi. other relevant documents.[8]

Wholesale operations

The Procedures also stipulate that, if an established Commercial Joint Venture applies for engagement in wholesale business as a sideline, the establishment of a branch store or the replacement of a joint venture party, MOFTEC shall examine the application, and decide whether or not to approve it, after obtaining the consent of SETC. Other changes in respect of an established Commercial Joint Venture shall be submitted for examination and approval by the original examination and approval authority in accordance with the existing regulations for foreign investment enterprises. When applying for approval, the Commercial Joint Venture shall submit the following documents:

1. an application;
2. a report on the enterprise's business situation;
3. the enterprise's capital contribution verification report;
4. a report on the enterprise's exports and documents in support thereof;
5. the relevant resolution of the board of directors;
6. the agreement to amend the contract and/or articles of association; and
7. other relevant documents.

The enterprise shall carry out the procedures for change of registration etc. with the State's administrative authority for industry and commerce within one month of the date of approval of the amended contract and/or articles of association.[9]

Scope of business

The scope of business of Commercial Joint Venture is stipulated by the Procedures as follows:

1. Scope of business of a Commercial Joint Venture engaged in retail business:
   i. to engage in the business of commercial retailing (including sales on an agency basis and sales on a commission basis).

8. Procedures, Article 9.

9. Procedures, Article 11.

ii. the business of organizing the export of domestic products;
iii. import and export business for merchandise dealt in by itself; and
iv. engagement in the provision of relevant ancillary services.

2. Scope of business of a Commercial Joint Venture engaged in wholesale business:

   domestic wholesale of domestic merchandise and merchandise imported for its own account, and organization of the export of domestic products.[10]

Subject to approval, Commercial Joint Ventures engaged in retail business may engage in wholesale business as a sideline.[11]

Commercial Joint Ventures may not engage in the business of merchandise import and export agency.[12]

Commercial Joint Ventures that wish to deal in merchandise governed by special State regulations or in import or export merchandise subject to quotas and licensing shall carry out examination and approval procedures in accordance with relevant State regulations.[13]

Foreign Trade Operations

Legal framework

On September 30, 1996, MOFTEC promulgated the *Establishment of Pilot Sino-foreign Foreign Trading Equity Joint Ventures Tentative Procedures* (the "Procedures"). As with the restrictions on foreign participation in the retail sector, restrictions on trading have been circumvented by various means including the inappropriate use of Sino-foreign joint ventures' import and distribution powers and bonded warehouse zone privileges.

Foreign trading joint ventures

According to the Procedures, foreign trading joint ventures shall be limited liability companies. The proportion of the registered capital of a foreign trading joint venture contributed by the Chinese companies must be at least 51 per cent, and the proportion contributed by the foreign companies shall be at least 25%. The legal representative shall be appointed by the Chinese companies.[14]

10. Procedures, Article 12.

11. Procedures, Article 13.

12. Procedures, Article 14.

13. Procedures, Article 15.

14. Procedures, Article 3.

Establishment

The Procedures stipulate that, the establishment of a foreign trading joint venture shall comply with the following conditions:

1. The foreign companies shall fulfil the following conditions:
   i. turnover in the year prior to application must be over US$5 billion;
   ii. average annual trade volume with China over the previous three years must be over US$30 million;
   iii. must have established a representative office in China for at least three years prior to application, or have invested over US$30 million in China.

2. The Chinese companies shall fulfil the following conditions:
   i. have the right to engage in foreign trade;
   ii. average annual import and export volume over the previous three years must be over US$200 million, of which the export volume must be at least US$100 million;
   iii. must have already established at least three branches, subsidiaries or joint ventures outside China, and have an average annual turnover of those enterprises outside China of more than US$10 million over the previous three years prior to application.

3. The foreign trading joint venture shall fulfil the following conditions:
   i. must have a registered capital of at least Rmb100 million;
   ii. must have its own name and organizational structure; and
   iii. must have a business location, specialized personnel and other necessary material conditions appropriate to its foreign trade business.[15]

A Chinese company applying to establish a foreign trading joint venture must provide the following documents to the local departments in charge of foreign trade and economic cooperation to be reported to the State departments in charge of foreign trade and economic cooperation for examination:

1. a project proposal, and a feasibility study report, joint venture contract and articles of association signed by the Chinese and foreign companies;

2. copies of the supporting documents in respect of the registration, creditworthiness and the legal representatives of the Chinese and foreign companies;

3. copies of the approval certificates and business licences of enterprises in China in which the foreign companies has already invested, copies of the approval documents and business licenses of resident representative offices already established by the foreign companies in China, and copies of the capital verification reports issued by registered Chinese accountants.

15. Procedures, Article 4.

4. copies of the registration documents of branches, subsidiaries or joint ventures established outside China by the Chinese companies.

5. assets liabilities sheets and confirmation certification issued by an auditing organization, for the past three years of the Chinese and foreign companies.

6. scope of the business and products to be handled by the foreign trading joint venture to be established, and

7. other documents required by the State departments in charge of foreign trade and economic cooperation.

After a foreign trading joint venture has undergone examination by the State departments in charge of foreign trade and economic cooperation and reported to the State Council for approval, the State departments in charge of foreign trade and economic cooperation shall issue an approval certificate.[16]

After an application for the establishment of a foreign trading joint venture obtains State approval, the Chinese company shall, within one month of the date of approval, take the approval certificate to the administrative departments in charge of industry and commerce to handle registration procedures, and within one month of registration, handle financial registration with the financial authority in charge of registration.[17]

The foreign company shall use freely convertible currency as its capital contribution to the registered capital of the foreign trading joint venture, and the Chinese company may use Renminbi, material goods, intangible assets or other property rights as its capital contribution.

Each joint venture party to a foreign trading joint venture shall pay up the capital contribution to which it has subscribed within one month of the date on which the business license is signed and issued.[18]

Scope of business

A foreign trading joint venture shall engage in the import and export of goods and technology on its own behalf or as an agent within the scope of the business and products for which it has been approved, and shall not engage in any other business.[19]

---

16. Procedures, Article 5.

17. Procedures, Article 6.

18. Procedures, Article 7.

19. Procedures, Article 8.

Products for import and export which are subject to State-imposed quotas and license control, may only be imported or exported after the approvals of the relevant State departments-in-charge are applied for and obtained, in accordance with relevant provisions of the State. To import or export products which are subject to State-imposed quota tender invitation for import and export, a foreign trading joint venture must participate in tender bidding in accordance with the provisions regarding tender bidding and tender invitation for the import and export of goods of the departments-in-charge.[20]

A foreign trading joint venture shall handle settlement, sale and payment of foreign exchange in accordance with relevant provisions of the State regarding State-owned foreign trade companies. A foreign trading joint venture must maintain a balance of foreign exchange. Specific administration procedures shall be formulated by the People's Bank of China in consultation with State departments in charge of foreign trade and economic cooperation.[21]

Coordination

The Procedures specifically stipulate that, a foreign trading joint venture shall apply to join an import and export chamber of commerce or foreign commercial investment enterprise association, and must comply with the co-ordination of such chamber of commerce or association.[22]

Pilot areas

The Procedures also make it clear that, the pilot regions and number of pilot companies shall be determined by the State Council. At present, the only pilot regions are the Shanghai Pudong New Area and the Shenzhen Special Economic Zone.[23]

On September 1, 1997, the Development Department of MOFTEC issued a *Policy on Pilot Sino-foreign Foreign Trading Equity Joint Ventures Provisions* (the "Provisions") which, while mainly re-stating several stipulations of the Procedures, make further clarifications on the following issues.

1. scope of business

The scope of the import and export business of foreign trading equity joint ventures must conform to the provisions of the Foreign Trade Law with respect to the licensing system for

20. Procedures, Article 9.

21. Procedures, Article 10.

22. Procedures, Article 13.

23. Procedures, Article 16.

foreign trade business and to State laws, regulations and administrative measures with respect to the administration of import and export. Foreign trading equity joint ventures may not deal in goods whose import or export is prohibited by the State. Foreign trading equity joint ventures shall require approval before they dealing in export goods that the State organizes to be dealt in centrally or jointly and import goods that are to be dealt in by approved companies.[24]

2. policy towards foreign trading equity joint ventures

The general policy towards foreign trading equity joint ventures shall be equal treatment and fair competition with State-owned foreign trade companies. In terms of scope of business, foreign trading equity joint ventures shall be subject to the provisions of the Foreign Trade Law concerning the licensing system for foreign trade business in the same way as are State-owned foreign trade companies. In terms of policies concerning tax rebates for exports tax collection, foreign trading equity joint ventures shall be treated equally with State-owned foreign trade companies. Other matters shall be handled in accordance with the relevant State regulations concerning foreign investment enterprises.[25]

3. governing law for the establishment of foreign Trading equity joint ventures

The establishment of foreign trading equity joint ventures shall mainly be governed by the *PRC, Foreign Trade Law*, the *PRC, Sino-foreign Equity Joint Venture Law* and the *Establishment of Pilot Sino-foreign Foreign Trading Equity Joint Ventures Tentative Procedures.*[26]

In reality, the cumbersome regulatory regimes for foreign participation in both the retail and trading sections described above have not succeeded in keeping foreign participation at bay or under control. A post - WTO regime permitting open participation by foreign retailers and traders subject to reasonable restrictions is to be welcomed.

24. Provisions, Article 3.

25. Provisions, Article 5.

26. Provisions, Article 6.

Summary Checklist

1. The retail and foreign trade areas are "restricted areas" for establishing Sino-foreign joint ventures. In these joint ventures, the Chinese party has to command the majority stake. WFOEs are not permitted in these areas.
2. For the time being, foreign investment in the retail business is permitted only in provincial capitals, the capitals of autonomous regions, municipalities directly under the central government, municipalities with independent development plans and Special Economic Zones.
3. All foreign investment retail projects must be approved by the central government.
4. The Scope of Business of retail joint ventures is restricted, in general, to the commercial retailing of general merchandise and related imports and exports. Subject to specific approval, retail joint ventures may engage in wholesale business as a sideline. Retail joint ventures may not engage in the business of merchandise import and export agency.
5. Foreign parties must be those that are "relatively strong economically" and have advanced management experience and international prestige; the Chinese party must also be "relatively strong economically".
6. Retail joint ventures engaged in retail business shall have a registered capital of not less than RMB50 million or, in central or western China, not less than RMB30 million; if it is engaged in wholesale business, it shall have registered capital of not less than RMB80 million or, in central or western China, not less than RMB60 million.
7. The duration of retail joint ventures shall not exceed 30 years or , in central or western China, 40 years.

Foreign trade operations

8. At present, foreign trade joint ventures are permitted only in Shanghai Pudong New Area and the Shenzhen Special Economic Zone.
9. Foreign trade joint ventures must have a registered capital of no less than RMB 100 million.
10. Bonded Areas are economic areas under the control of the Chinese Customs authorities which receive preferential tariff treatment within the Bonded Areas, foreign businesses are allowed to undertake transit trade, export trade and import-export trade, and act as an agent in the export business for enterprises located in the Bonded Areas.

CHAPTER 5

APPROVALS FOR ESTABLISHING BANKING OPERATIONS

Ariel Lu Ye, Todd Benson, Celina Chew & Wei-Min Zhang
Updated by Ariel Lu Ye & Wei-Min Zhang
Clifford Chance, Hong Kong

In 1979, three decades after the establishment of the People's Republic of China ("PRC"), only four foreign banks in Shanghai with special status were allowed to carry on symbolic banking operations. Since that time, as a result of the comprehensive economic reforms introduced with the open-door policy in 1979, a tremendous number of foreign investors have established foreign investment enterprises ("FIEs") in the PRC. For example, by the end of August 1999 and according to official statistics, 335,507[1] FIEs had been established in China. In order to keep pace with China's economic growth, and particularly to serve the growing number of FIEs in China, China's domestic banking system is gradually being reformed by the adoption of modern banking technology, banking management techniques and competition-based market mechanisms. A crucial aspect of meeting demand is an open-door policy allowing foreign banks and foreign financial institutions ("FFIs") to set up operations in China.

The process of permitting foreign financial institutions to gain access to the China market has proceeded slowly and cautiously. In 1980, on a trial basis, China began permitting representative offices of a small number of foreign banks to be opened in China. Originally restricted to Beijing and four Special Economic Zones ("SEZs"), Shenzhen, Zhuhai, Shantou and Xiamen, the geographical limitations of such representative offices were later extended to include other designated cities in China. In the mid-1980s, facing increasing domestic demand for foreign capital, Chinese authorities began granting permission for the establishment of foreign bank branches and Sino-foreign joint venture banks to open in China to engage in foreign currency banking services. Since early 1997, particularly since the onset of the Asian financial crisis in the summer of 1997, Chinese authorities have been alerted to the various problems existing in the domestic banking system and have shown a determination to further open up the banking sector to FFI banks.

For instance, in December 1996, China's central bank, the People's Bank of China ("PBOC") announced landmark measures allowing foreign banks to engage for the first time in Renminbi business. Initially, only eight foreign banks and one Sino-French joint venture bank were issued licenses to engage in Renminbi business. Since August 1998, an additional 10 foreign banks obtained such licenses. By August 1999, a total of 25 foreign banks and Sino-foreign joint venture banks in Shenzhen and in the Pudong New Area in Shanghai had been allowed to conduct limited Renminbi business. Since August 1999, foreign banks approved to conduct Renminbi business have been allowed to expand their business scope to include such areas as participating in syndicated loans. In addition, China has further relaxed its geographical restriction by allowing FFIs operating in Shanghai and Shenzhen to expand to neighbouring provinces.

1. Reported by Xin Hua News Agency in *International Commercial Daily*, a Beijing based newspaper, on September 29, 1999.

By the end of September 1999, FFIs (including banks, insurance companies and other financial service institutions) from 20 countries and regions had established 544 representative offices and 173 branch offices in 23 cities in China. 155 of these are branches of foreign banks and 248 are representative offices of foreign banks. According to PBOC, assets of foreign banks in China totalled US$31.4 billion, with outstanding loans totalling US$22.65 billion and liabilities amounting to US$28.7 billion[2].

If China, following its agreement with the US on November 15, 1999, enters the World Trade Organization ("WTO"), it may allow foreign banks to have full market access within five years. Following China's accession, foreign banks will be able to conduct local currency business with Chinese enterprises within 2 years and they will be able to conduct local currency business with Chinese individuals within 5 years. All customer restrictions and geographic restrictions will be removed within 5 years. Foreign banks will also enjoy the same rights as Chinese banks, i. e. they will receive national treatment.

But before this becomes reality, China will have to carry out substantial modifications in its egal regime vis-à-vis FFIs in order to satisfy various requirements of the WTO.

The current legal framework to regulate the activities of FFIs in China has largely been developed over the past decade. However, as with the establishment of any other type of foreign invested enterprise in China, obtaining approval from the Chinese authorities remains the first and key step for entry into the PRC market. PBOC, as China's central bank, is the governmental authority in charge of approval and macro supervision over the activities of foreign-funded banks and financial institutions within China. PBOC used to have regional branches situated in every provincial capital. Since the 1998 restructuring, PBOC now has nine regional branches and is headquartered in Beijing[3].

This chapter will address procedural issues and strategic concerns related to obtaining approval for the establishment of the following four permitted types of banking operations in the PRC:

- a representative office;
- foreign bank branch;
- a Sino-foreign joint venture bank (joint venture bank); and
- a foreign-funded bank with headquarters in the PRC (fully foreign-funded bank).

In addition, this chapter will discuss the approval requirements for foreign banks to conduct Renminbi business in the PRC.

2. Reported by *China Securities Daily*, a Beijing based newspaper, on November 17, 1999.

3. The nine branches are situated in Shanghai, Guangzhou, Chengdu, Shenyang, Wuhan, Jinan, Tianjin, Xi'an and Nanjing.

Features of the Banking Operations

Setting up a representative office is a prerequisite for foreign banks aiming to develop business opportunities in the Chinese market. Regulations governing the establishment of foreign bank branches, fully foreign funded banks and joint venture banks, require the prior establishment of a representative office.

As a business planning matter, setting up a representative office may be viewed as part of the natural sequence of business development in the PRC as a representative office is generally the most suitable vehicle for establishing an initial presence in the PRC market. A representative office is relatively easy to set up as there is no requirement of paying in a large amount of capital except to fund the representative office's operating expenses. A representative office is limited to engaging only in market research, information collection and liaison services. In the course of engaging in such permitted activities, representative offices are able to develop valuable connections for facilitating future business development.

Setting up a bank branch is significantly more cumbersome as the operation of a branch involves engaging in financial services. In addition to setting up operations, it is first necessary to obtain approval to engage in such services from the relevant authorities. A foreign bank branch is permitted to engage in foreign currency deposits, foreign currency loans, trade finance and limited business or services involving Chinese currency (although there are indications that this may change in some areas).

Establishing a joint venture bank offers different advantages and drawbacks in comparison with foreign bank branches. Some FFIs have favoured establishing joint venture banks because of their ease of access to the domestic market and the broader scopes of business granted. Some foreign banks are wary, however, about cooperation with Chinese partners to a joint venture. In fact, according to statistics published in China, only five joint venture banks had been established by the end of 1995. The number of joint venture banks increased from five to seven by the end of September 1999[4].

Fully foreign-funded banks are also a minority among foreign banking operations as only six have been set up for operation[5]. Although setting up this kind of banking operation may be viewed as avoiding the potential difficulties of cooperation with Chinese partners, this perceived advantage may be outweighed in some cases by the perceived drawbacks of negotiating the Chinese market without such partners.

4. Reported by *Economic Daily*, a Beijing based newspaper, on November 18, 1999.

5. Reported by *Economic Daily*, on November 18, 1999.

Foreign investors must decide which investment vehicle to establish in light of on their business objectives and plans for the future.

Approval Process for Establishing a Representative Office

Legal framework

The establishment of foreign bank representative offices is governed by the *PBOC, Administration of the Establishment of Resident Representative Offices in China by Foreign Invested Financial Institutions Procedures*[6] (the "FFI Representative Office Regulations") (see **Legislation Appendices**). In addition, the legislation governing resident representative offices of foreign enterprises also apply to the representative offices of banks, such as those relating obtaining visas for foreign employees of the representative office, taxation and employment of local staff.

Approval jurisdiction

The PBOC is responsible for the examination, approval and administration of the representative offices of foreign banks. If a foreign bank wishes to establish a representative office in Beijing, it must apply to the Foreign Financial Institutions Administration Department within the head office of the PBOC. Foreign banks wishing to establish representative offices in cities other than Beijing should apply to the corresponding department of the local branch of the PBOC. After examining the application, the local branch of the PBOC must submit the application to the head office of the PBOC.

Approval procedures

The procedure for establishing a representative office in China consists of two stages: approval and registration.

approval

The FFI Representative Office Regulations sets out the documents which a foreign bank must submit to the PBOC or its local branch when applying to establish a representative office[7]. The foreign bank should submit a letter of application, signed by its chairman or the general manager of its head office addressed to the president of the PBOC, containing a brief description of the foreign bank and the reasons for applying to establish a representative office in the PRC, and accompanied by the following documents:

- certified true copy of the foreign bank's certificate of incorporation and business registration certificate or its equivalent;

---

6. Promulgated by the PBOC on June15, 1991.

7. FFI Representative Office Regulations, Article 5.

- the annual reports of the foreign bank for the preceding three years;
- a letter of authorization to the Chinese sponsor;
- a letter of credit standing issued by a financial institution which has dealings with the foreign bank;
- a power of attorney for the chief representative appointed to the office, together with brief biographical notes, copies of his or her passport and a photograph (similarly for other representatives appointed);
- the latest annual balance sheet and profit and loss account of the foreign bank's head office;
- the memorandum and Articles of Association (or equivalent) of the foreign bank's head office;
- a list of the members of the board of directors of the foreign bank's head office;
- a tenancy agreement for office premises (or other evidence of having rented accommodation) (which should not be effective until the approval has been granted); and
- copies of documents evidencing business relations with China.

It will be beneficial to the application for all documents to have Chinese translations attached (where practical) to facilitate their review by the Chinese authorities responsible for approval.

Even though the FFI Representative Office Regulations do not expressly require a Chinese sponsor to act on behalf of the applicant of a representative office, a foreign bank must appoint a sponsor to submit the application in compliance with the provisions of the *Administration of Permanent Representative Organizations of Foreign Enterprises Interim Provisions*[8] (the Interim Provisions) and the *Administration of Permanent Representative Organizations of Foreign Enterprises Interim Provisions Implementing Rules*[9]. An experienced sponsor with good business standing and good connections with the approval authority may substantially facilitate the speed of approval (see "Approval Strategies" below).

The PBOC or its local branch must accept or reject the application within three months of receipt. If accepted, an official application form will be issued. If there is no receipt of the official application form within three months of the date of filing of the preliminary application, it means that the application has been rejected. The approval process takes three months at most, but is usually completed within one or two months.

The applicant must complete the application form and submit it to the head office of PBOC or its local branch together with a document of authorization for the chief representative

8. Promulgated by the State Council on October 30, 1980.

9. Issued by MOFTEC on February 13, 1995.

signed by the chairman or the general manager of the head office. This must be done within two months of the date of its receipt and an Approval Certificate will be issued by the PBOC or its relevant local branch upon approval.

Technically speaking, the approval of a representative office is similar to a process of notification as it involves essentially a routine checking of documentation. The PBOC usually tends to grant approval for representative offices of foreign banks unless there are technical deficiencies in the documentation.

registration

Within 30 days of the date of issue of the Approval Certificate, the foreign bank must register with the local State Administration of Industry and Commerce ("SAIC") to obtain a business licence.

In support of this registration, the foreign bank must submit:

- the Approval Certificate;
- an application for registration (this form can be obtained from the relevant SAIC branch);
- all documents submitted when applying for approval (see "approval" above); and
- the registration fee.

Post-approval formalities

Upon the issue of a Registration Certificate, the representative office and its personnel must go through the following formalities:

- opening of bank accounts – accounts must be opened by the representative office and its personnel with the Bank of China or another bank designated by it;
- residence registration – representative offices must maintain a Residence Registration Booklet with the local public security bureau;
- tax bureau registration – both the representative office and its personnel must register with the local tax bureau;
- acquiring a seal – the seal of the representative office will often need to be affixed to documents in China. Applications for seals to be made should be submitted to the public security bureau; and
- registration of personnel – the representative office's foreign personnel should be registered with the SAIC which will then issue the requisite work permits. Work permits should then be taken to the foreign affairs department of the local Public Security Bureau together with the relevant passports where a foreigner's residence permit will be issued.

Approval Process for Establishing a Foreign Bank Branch, a Joint Venture Bank and a Fully Foreign-funded Bank

It is worth noting that the law and regulations applicable to the establishment of branches, Sino-foreign joint venture companies or WFOEs in general, do not apply to the establishment of foreign bank branches, joint venture banks or fully foreign-funded banks (collectively referred to as "foreign-funded banks").

In the belief that the financial and banking sector is a special and influential segment in China's economy, the State Council has issued regulations to address various issues relating to the administration of FFIs including foreign-funded banks. At present, all FFIs are governed by the *PRC, Administration of Foreign Investment Financial Institutions Regulations*[10] (the "FFI Regulations") (see **Legislation Appendices**) and the *PRC, Administration of Foreign Investment Financial Institutions Regulations Implementing Rules*[11]. The FFI Regulations are the first national regulations for the establishment and governance of financial institutions with foreign ownership and supersede two previous regulations: *PRC, Administration of SEZ Wholly Foreign-owned Banks and Equity Joint Venture Banks Regulations*[12]; and *Shanghai Municipality, Administration of Foreign-owned Financial Institutions and Sino-foreign Equity Joint Venture Financial Institutions Procedures*[13]. The new national regulations provide a nationwide standard and should therefore bring more consistency to the overall administration of foreign banking operations.

Preliminary requirements

There are various preliminary requirements which must be met before a prospective applicant may apply to establish foreign-funded banks. Different requirements apply depending on the type of institution to be established.

According to the FFI Regulations, the preliminary requirements for establishing a foreign bank branch are:

- the applicant must have a representative office in the PRC of over two years standing;
- the foreign bank should have total assets of US$20 billion at the end of the year prior to the application for establishment; and
- the home country or region of the foreign bank should have a sound financial supervisory and regulatory system[14].

10. Issued on February 25, 1994 and effective on April 1, 1994.

11. Issued on March 29, 1994.

12. Promulgated by the State Council on April 2, 1985.

13. Adopted by the State Council on September 7, 1990 and adopted by the PBOC on September 8, 1990.

14. FFI Regulations, Article 7.

Most applicants from developed countries and advanced developing countries or regions will have little difficulty meeting these preliminary requirements. However, applicants should be aware that, in addition to the preliminary requirements, there are other requirements that will apply once a foreign bank branch is established. For example, working funds of the branch appropriated gratis from its head office must be in freely convertible currencies up to a value of not less than Rmb100 million.

The preliminary requirements for establishing a joint venture bank are:

- each party to the joint venture must be a financial institution;
- the foreign party must have a representative office in the PRC of over two years' standing;
- the foreign party should have total assets of US$10 billion at the end of the year prior to the application for establishment; and
- the home country or region where the foreign party is located should have a sound financial supervisory and regulatory system.

The preliminary requirements for applying to establish a fully foreign-funded bank are the same as those for a joint venture bank in so far as foreign investors are concerned.

Approval jurisdiction

The PBOC is the authority in charge of the approval and supervision of foreign-funded banks. Foreign-funded Banks should first submit their application to the relevant local branch of the PBOC. Following examination of the application by the local branch, the application documents together with an opinion on the application must be submitted to the Foreign Financial Institutions Administration Department within the head office of the PBOC for approval.

Present economic policies suggest that applicants applying to establish foreign-funded banks should be able to obtain a bank licence provided that the prescribed technical requirements are satisfied. However, there are additional factors that may influence whether an application is approved or not. For example, the political and economic relationship between the PRC and the home country of the foreign bank is one significant factor that may be taken into consideration by the Chinese authorities in the approval process (see "Approval Strategies" below).

Preliminary application

The PBOC reviews the application and submitted documents and, if it decides to grant approval, it will issue a formal application form to the applicant.

foreign bank branch

The following documents must be submitted to the president of the PBOC during preliminary application in order to establish a foreign bank branch:

- an application signed by the applicant's chairman (or its managing director, chief executive or president) including the intended name of the foreign bank branch and the amount of working funds to be appropriated gratis from the head office;
- the type of business for which application is being made;
- a copy of the applicant's certificate of incorporation and business registration certificate (or its equivalent) notarized in the country in which the documents are produced or subject to authentication by the Chinese diplomatic mission in that country;
- the applicant's annual reports for the preceding three years;
- information on the condition of the financial system in the applicant's country, its financial regulations and other relevant economic regulations (if required by the PBOC);
- the recommendation of the financial supervision and administration authority in the country or region of origin concerning the institution to be established (if required by the PBOC); and
- the applicant's business development plans in the PRC (if required by the PBOC)[15].

It appears that the authorities will favour those applicants with strong financial capabilities and representative offices which have been active performers in the PRC market.

joint venture bank

Both parties to the joint venture bank must jointly submit the following documents to the PBOC:

- an application signed by both parties to the joint venture bank including its intended name, the name of each party to the joint venture bank, the amount of registered capital and paid-up capital, the proportions each party will contribute to the joint venture bank, and the type of business for which application is being made;
- a Feasibility Study Report;
- the Joint Venture Contract and draft Articles of Association of the joint venture bank to be established;
- a notarized copy of each party's business licence, certificate of incorporation and business registration certificate (or its equivalent); and
- the documents mentioned in the last four points of "foreign bank branch" above[16].

---

15. Id. Article 10.
16. Id. Article 11.

wholly foreign-funded bank

The head office of the foreign bank must submit the following documents to the president of the PBOC:

- an application signed by the applicant's chairman (or its managing director, chief executive or president) including the intended name of the foreign bank, the amount of registered capital and paid-up capital and the type of business for which application to conduct is being made;
- a Feasibility Study Report;
- draft Articles of Association of the foreign bank to be established;
- a copy of the applicant's certificate of incorporation and business registration certificate (or its equivalent) notarized in the country in which the documents are produced or subject to authentication by the Chinese diplomatic mission in that country; and
- the documents mentioned in the last point of "joint venture bank" above[17].

A Chinese translation should be attached to all documents to facilitate their review by the relevant Chinese officials. It appears that no preliminary project listing (*lixiang*) is required in respect of the establishment of a joint venture bank or a fully foreign-funded bank.

Formal application

If the applicant does not receive a formal application form within 90 days of submitting its preliminary application, it should assume that its application has been rejected[18]. The applicant must complete the formal application form within 60 days of receipt and deliver it to the PBOC for approval together with the following documents:

- the name list and curricula vitae of the principal responsible officers (that is, the managing director of the foreign bank branch, or the chairperson of the board of directors and the general manager of the joint venture bank or the fully foreign-funded bank);
- the letters of authorization of the principal responsible officers;
- in the case of a foreign bank branch, a letter of guarantee from the branch's head office agreeing to bear liability for taxation and debts which should be notarized by certified notary public offices in the country in which such documentation is produced or subject to authentication by the Chinese diplomatic mission in that country; and
- any other documents required by the PBOC[19].

17. Id. Article 9.

18. Id. Article 13.

19. Id. Article 14.

Post-approval formalities

Foreign-funded banks must raise in full their paid-in capital or working capital and must transfer the paid-in capital or working capital to China within 30 days of the PBOC head office issuing the document of approval[20]. The minimum amount of registered capital of a foreign bank in freely convertible currencies must be Rmb300 million and its paid-up capital must not be less than half of its registered capital.

After the paid-up capital or working capital has been verified by a certified public accountant registered in China, the institution must also complete registration procedures with the SAIC for a business licence and, within 30 days of commencement of business must register with the relevant tax authorities[21].

Within 30 days of the date on which the PBOC issues the document of approval, the institution must apply to the State Administration of Foreign Exchange ("SAFE") for a Foreign Exchange Operation Permit[22]. As SAFE is the major governmental department in charge of the administration of foreign exchange, it functions to develop national policy in connection with foreign exchange and to draft relevant laws and regulations to monitor China's total foreign debt exposure. Further, it administers screening procedures for the issuance of foreign exchange licences to certain Chinese domestic entities and foreign banking operations in China (Foreign-funded banks are therefore subject to supervision and administration by both the SAIC and SAFE). Therefore, in addition to the necessary business licence issued by the SAIC for business organizations, all financial institutions which desire to engage in banking services in foreign currencies must obtain a Foreign Exchange Business Operation Permit.

Approved foreign-funded banks must commence their business operations within 12 months from the date on which the document of approval is issued by the PBOC. The commencement of business operations must be reported to the relevant local branch of the PBOC in advance and the date of commencement must be published in local newspapers.

Approval strategies

Geographical areas for opening foreign bank branches have been extended from the SEZs and Shanghai to include 13 other coastal cities and 11 additional cities including:

- Beijing;
- Shijiazhuang;

20. Id. Article 15.

21. Id.

22. Id. Article 16.

- Wuhan;
- Xi'an;
- Chengdu;
- Chongqing;
- Hangzhou;
- Hefei;
- Shengyang;
- Kunming; and
- Suzhou.

Factors that may affect the process and speed of approval include:

- the applicant's commitment to the Chinese market. Factors here include the business relationship between the applicant bank and China, the applicant's relationship with Taiwan, business activities such as offshore lending to Chinese entities, the total amount of lending or amounts involved in other business activities, the applicant's speed of expanding China related business, and the applicant's business plans in connection with China;
- the reputation and financial capacity of the applicant in its home country and other countries;
- the bank's history of doing business with China (the authorities may favour those who began the relationship earlier);
- the encouragement of foreign bank operations in remote and less-developed regions other than the coastal areas. There are a number of new cities open to foreign banking operations (see above) where foreign banking operations are welcomed and would be expected to be greeted with more enthusiasm;
- existing competition among foreign banking operations and the PBOC's supervision capacity in certain locations. Each year the PBOC and its local branches, in accordance with a plan determined at State Council level, allocate short-term loan quotas of a term of 365 days or less to all financial institutions, including foreign-funded banks, for the purpose of controlling the increase of foreign debt at the national level within certain limitations set forth by the Chinese authorities. Thus, in an area where a number of foreign-funded banks have been established, the PBOC may consider the extent of local competition and particularly, the administrative capacity of the PBOC to supervise the activities of additional banking establishments; and
- the effect of foreign competition on PRC banks. As China gradually eases its restrictions on foreign banks engaging in local currency business, the regulatory authorities will closely monitor the effects of foreign competition on PRC banks.

A number of additional issues relating to the approval process should also be considered:

Engaging a sponsor or joint venture partner

Where an applicant is intending to establish a representative office, it is necessary to engage a Chinese sponsor. For the establishment of a foreign bank branch or a fully foreign-funded bank, it may also be highly useful to engage a Chinese sponsor who can assist in liaising with the approval authorities. In this regard it is important that the sponsor possess the requisite industry and political connections (*guanxi*) necessary for smoothing the process of approval and operation in China. These considerations apply even more strongly to the selection of a Chinese partner by a foreign investor who is intending to establish a joint venture bank in the PRC.

In addition to possessing relevant industry and political knowledge, it is essential that a Chinese partner to a joint venture bank also possesses the relevant formal business and legal qualifications. The foreign financial institution must determine at an early stage that the entity that will sign the Joint Venture Contract is authorized to enter into contracts with foreigners of the type being contemplated. To make such a determination, it is advisable to make independent inquiries and also to request directly from the potential Chinese partner a copy of its business licence and Articles of Association. In carrying out such a due diligence exercise, the FFI should note that the *PBOC, Administration of Financial Institutions Provisions*[23], which applies to all financial institutions established in China, contains a provision prohibiting financial institution legal person licences and financial institution business licences issued to financial institutions from being photocopied without the approval of the PBOC[24]. This may complicate the due diligence process undertaken by foreign financiers with potential PRC counterparts. Further, the *PBOC, Administration of Financial Institutions Provisions* provides that branch organizations of financial institutions are not permitted to have legal person status[25]. This differs from previous regulations on the establishment of financial institutions which did not contain such a prohibition on branch entities, and many financial institutions have established branches as separate legal entities on the basis of previous legislation.

Foreign financial institutions which are considering relying on a Chinese entity as a joint venture partner should therefore, in addition to viewing the entity's constitutive documents, clarify from the outset whether the Chinese entity is a branch, head office or subsidiary of the institution.

23. Issued August 9,1994.

24. PBOC, Administration of Financial Institutions Provisions, Article 27.

25. Id. Article 33.

Scope of business

foreign exchange business

It is important that foreign-funded banks ensure that their approved Scope of Business includes all the types of activities they intend to carry out. PRC business entities, including banking and financial institutions, are subject to strict capacity limitations as to the types of business in which they may engage as all such activities must be authorized in the entity's approved Scope of Business by the relevant approval authorities. Under the administration of the SAIC, and in accordance with the *Supreme People's Court, Issuing Explanation of Several Questions Concerning the Application of the Foreign Economic Contract Law Circular and Explanation*[21] any contract entered into between parties involving activities beyond either of their approved scopes of business is invalid at its inception.

The types of foreign exchange business in which foreign-funded banks may engage include:

- foreign exchange deposits;
- foreign exchange lending;
- foreign exchange note discounts;
- approved foreign exchange investment;
- foreign exchange remittances;
- foreign exchange guarantees;
- import and export clearing;
- trading in foreign exchange on their own account and for clients;
- acting as agents for foreign currency credit card payment;
- custody and safety deposit box services;
- credit investigation and advice;
- approved domestic currency business; and
- other approved foreign currency business.

Renminbi business

Articles 17(13) and 18(9) of the FFI Regulations contemplate that FFIs may also engage in approved Renminbi business.

Many foreign banking operations have become involved in Renminbi transactions in indirect ways. For example, Citibank in conjunction with the Industrial and Commercial Bank of China ("ICBC") established a 24-hour ATM service centre in Shanghai for Citibank credit card holders to withdraw Renminbi cash directly by a mechanism through which Citibank acts as an agent for ICBC.

26. Issued by the Supreme People's Court on October 19, 1987.

In early 1996, the PBOC began permitting designated foreign banking operations in Shanghai, Dalian, Shenzhen and Eastern Jiangsu to engage in limited Renminbi business for FIEs on a trial basis.

In March 1997, Shanghai became the first city in which FFIs are allowed to engaged in direct, albeit limited, Renminbi business. This was followed in August 1998 by Shenzhen which became the second city in which FFIs are allowed to conducted limited Renminbi business.

To regulate the Renminbi business of FFIs, the PBOC has issued the *Provisional Administrative Measures of Shanghai Pudong on Foreign-funded Financial Institutions Conducting Trial Renminbi Business Operations* ("Shanghai Renminbi Rules") dated December 2, 1996 and the *Pilot Operation of Renminbi Business by Foreign-funded Financial Institutions in Shenzhen Principal Guidance* ("Shenzhen Renminbi Rules") dated August 13, 1998.

(a) permitted business area

An approved FFI may engage in the following Renminbi business:

- Deposit
- Loans
- Settlement
- Guarantees
- Investment in public debt and financial bonds
- Other approved Renminbi business.

However, an approved FFI may only take deposit from foreign investment enterprises and foreigners, and transferred deposits of Renminbi loans made by such FFI to non-foreign investment enterprises. In addition, it may only provide loans or guarantees to foreign investment enterprises, and non-foreign investment enterprises to which such FFI has granted foreign loans or guarantees. Furthermore, all FFIs are required to comply with the Renminbi deposit interest rate promulgated by PBOC.

(b) pre-conditions

The Shanghai RMB Rules and the Shenzhen RMB Rules contain similar pre-conditions which must be satisfied before a FFI may apply to conduct the specified RMB business:

- FFI must have been operating in China for at least 3 years, have committed no violations of the law and have a sound record. In addition, it must have recorded a profit in the two consecutive year preceding the application;
- In the year preceding the application, its monthly average balance of foreign exchange loan must be more than US$150 million if it is a branch of a foreign bank or more than

US$100 million if it is a joint venture bank, independent bank or independent finance company. Its monthly average balance of foreign exchange loan shall also be more than 50% of the monthly average balance of its total foreign exchange assets; and

- Other pre-conditions that PBOC may require.

(c) formal application

The applicant must complete the formal application form signed by its Chairman or the branch's head officer and submit the same to the Shanghai branch or Shenzhen branch of PBOC (depending on where the applicant would like to conduct RMB business). It should be noted that there are two regions in which FFIs may apply to conduct RMB business. The first region is administered by the Shanghai branch of PBOC and covers Shanghai, Jiangsu province and Zhejiang province. The second region is administered by the Shenzhen branch of PBOC and covers Guangdong province, Jiangxi province and Hunan province.

After the application is approved, FFI should apply to re-new its Financial Institution Operation Permit.

(d) post approval formalities

FFIs approved to conduct RMB business shall inject fresh capital equal to not less than RMB30 million as working capital for RMB business within 30 days of the approval of PBOC. A certified public accountant should then be appointed to verify the capital injection and produce a capital verification report.

In Shenzhen, before a FFI commences its RMB business, it must make another application to the Shenzhen branch of PBOC who will inspect, among other things, the place of business, computer system, accounting system and training of personnel, etc. of FFI. A FFI will only be allowed to commence its RMB business after it has passed the inspections.

Conclusion

Although establishing banking operations in the PRC has never been an easy proposition, the opportunities afforded to those institutions willing to make the effort appear increasingly attractive. Those institutions entering the PRC market will be well advised to understand both the legal requirements and practical strategies designed to ensure the most satisfactory achievement of long-term business objectives. A knowledgeable sponsor with the proper qualifications should be viewed as a necessary prerequisite for entry into the PRC banking market. In the process of establishing and operating representative offices, foreign banking and financial institutions can gain essential know-how, a deeper understanding of the PRC market and can cultivate important connections for facilitating later applications to establish PRC banking operations.

Summary Checklist

1. Foreign banks are permitted to establish representative offices, foreign bank branches, joint venture banks or fully foreign-funded banks in China.
2. Each of the four types of banking operations have different advantages and drawbacks. A foreign investor must decide which one best suits their business objectives and needs.

representative office

3. Representative office establishment is governed by the legislation regulating the establishment of representative offices in general, as well as specific PBOC regulations governing their establishment by financial institutions with foreign investment.
4. The PBOC is responsible for the approval of foreign bank representative offices. Application begins with the Foreign Financial Institutions Administration Department in Beijing or at the local branch of the PBOC and then proceeds to the head office of the PBOC.
5. Applications must be in writing, addressed to the president of the PBOC and a Chinese sponsor must be appointed to submit the application.
6. After preliminary approval is granted, a formal application form will be issued and must be submitted to the PBOC within two months of its receipt.
7. Once approval has been granted, the representative office must register with the local SAIC to obtain its business licence and must then undertake various post-approval formalities such as opening bank accounts and registering with the tax bureau.
8. Attaching Chinese translations to submitted documents and selecting a well-connected Chinese sponsor with good business standing may facilitate the approval process.

foreign-funded Banks

9. In general, the regulations and legislation governing the establishment of branches, joint ventures and WFOEs do not apply to the establishment of foreign-funded banks. These are governed by the FFI Regulations.
10. Preliminary applications must be submitted to the local branch of the PBOC and, once approved, the formal application form must be submitted with additional documentation to the Foreign Financial Institutions Administration Department of the head office of the PBOC, within 60 days of its receipt.

11. For a joint venture bank, both parties to the joint venture must jointly submit the documents to the PBOC.
12. Once approval is granted, foreign-funded banks can apply for business registration. The paid-up capital must be verified, and a Foreign Exchange Business Operation Permit obtained.
13. An applicant's commitment to the China market, their reputation and financial capacity in their home country and abroad, their history of doing business in the PRC, and the selection of a well connected sponsor or joint venture partner with good business standing are some of the factors which may facilitate the approval process.
14. Foreign-funded banks are strictly limited in the types of activities they can conduct. They should ensure that their approved Scope of Business covers all the activities in which they wish to engage.

CHAPTER 6

APPROVALS FOR ESTABLISHING AN INSURANCE COMPANY

Xiaowei Ye, attorney
Shearman & Sterling, Beijing and
Mark J. Harty, Asian Counsel,
Shearman & Sterling, Hong Kong

China is gradually opening up its insurance market to foreign companies and this process will only gather speed once China has entered the WTO. China's market of 1.2 billion potential customers has attracted the interest of many foreign companies. In all, some 113 foreign insurance companies from 17 countries have set up 202 representative offices in the country in the hope of eventually upgrading them and obtaining operating licences to penetrate this vast market.[1] However, obtaining licences to engage in the insurance business in China has proven to be difficult for foreign insurance companies. At present, the government has only allowed foreign insurance companies to operate in Shanghai and Guangzhou. In the near future, it is expected that Shenzhen, Haikou, Chongqing and Dalian will also open up for foreign insurance business. Currently, foreign insurers are only allowed to open branch offices or set up joint ventures with domestic insurance companies or other domestic financial entities approved by China Insurance Regulatory Commission ("CIRC").

Following China's accession into the WTO, however, a number of liberalizations are expected. First, foreign property and casualty firms may be permitted to insure large-scale risks nationwide. Current geographic limitations may gradually be eliminated. The scope of activities for foreign insurance companies is expected to be broadened to include group, health and pension lines of insurance. The issuance of licences may no longer be subject to numerical quotas or limits. 50% foreign ownership of joint ventures may be allowed and internal branching restrictions are expected to be relaxed or eliminated.

As of October, 1999 there are five foreign insurance companies with nine branch offices in China. They are:

- American International Assurance Co. Ltd. ("AIA") of the United States (two separate offices in Shanghai and Guangzhou),
- American International Underwriter ("AIU") of the United States (two separate offices in Shanghai and Guangzhou),
- Tokio Marine & Fire Insurance Co., Ltd. ("Tokio Marine") of Japan (Shanghai),
- Winterthur Insurance Co. Ltd. ("Winterthur") of Switzerland (Shanghai),
- Royal Sun Alliance Insurance Group ("Royal Sun") of the United Kingdom (Shanghai) and
- Min An Insurance Co. (HK), Ltd. ("Min An") of Hong Kong (two offices in Haikou and Shenzhen)

Four additional foreign insurance companies that have set up joint venture insurance companies with domestic institutions are:

- Manufacturers Life Insurance ("Manulife") of Canada (Shanghai),
- Aetna Life Insurance Company ("Aetna") of the United States (Shanghai),

1. *China Economic News*, No. 8, Vol. XX, March 1, 1999.

- AXA-UAP ("AXA") of France (Shanghai) and
- Allianz ("Allianz") of Germany (Shanghai)

It has been reported that seven additional foreign insurance companies have received the approvals from CIRC in preparation of establishing joint ventures or branches in the near future.

AIA, Tokio Marine and Manulife were the first three foreign insurance companies that obtained licenses in China. AIA received its first licence covering both life and property and casualty insurance in Shanghai in 1992 and obtained separate licences for both life insurance and property and casualty insurance in Guangzhou in 1995. AIU, the sister company of AIA, in 1996, took over the property insurance from AIA in both Shanghai and Guangzhou. Tokio Marine obtained its licence for property and casualty insurance in Shanghai in 1994. Manulife in 1995 received approval to set up a joint venture life insurance company in Shanghai. AXA and Allianz received life insurance licences to set up joint ventures in Shanghai. Winterthur and Royal Sun obtained approval to establish property insurance branch offices in Shanghai. Min An, as a special case, was permitted to operate a joint venture property insurance company in Shenzhen and Haikou as early as 1987 before the enactment of the *PRC, Insurance Law.*

This chapter will provide a step-by-step analysis of the approval process for establishing an insurance company in China and examine strategies for the successful completion of this process.

Legal Framework

In June 1995, the National People's Congress passed the *PRC, Insurance Law.*[2] Before the enactment of the *PRC, Insurance Law* in 1995, Shanghai was the only city in China with specific regulations concerning foreign insurance companies, having adopted the *Shanghai Municipality Administration of Concerning Foreign-funded Insurance Institutions Provisional Measures*[3] of (the "Shanghai Provisional Measures"). Pursuant to Article 148 of the *PRC, Insurance Law* as interpreted by CIRC, the Shanghai Provisional Measures will continue to be applicable to foreign insurance companies in Shanghai and Guangzhou until a new set of national regulations are issued by the CIRC. For example, the Shanghai Provisional Measures were applied with respect to AIA's application to set up a branch in Guangzhou. However, it should be noted that, although the CIRC applies the Shanghai Provisional Measures in the absence of national regulations, it appears that in practice the CIRC follows the procedural aspects of the Shanghai Provisional Measures more closely than some of its substance although the CIRC reserves the right to deny approval if an application substantively contradicts the

2. Adopted June 30, 1995 and effective October 1, 1995.

3. Adopted September 11, 1992.

PRC, Insurance Law. When a domestic company applies to establish an insurance company, it has to satisfy the requirements set forth under the *PRC, Insurance Law*, not the Shanghai Provisional Measures.

A new set of national regulations has been expected from the CIRC for some time. The new regulations should clarify various issues and may result in significant and substantive changes. For example, it is possible that the new regulations may increase the capital requirements for foreign insurance companies. The existing insurance regulations will reportedly be amended in the near future.

Legal Requirements

The Shanghai Provisional Measures require foreign applicants to satisfy the following conditions before submitting applications:

- have had more than 30 years experience in the insurance business;
- total assets of over US$5 billion in the year preceding the application; and
- have had a representative office in China for more than two years at the time of application.

In addition, the applicant needs to demonstrate that it meets the following conditions stipulated by the *PRC, Insurance Law*:

- to have Articles of Association that comply with the *PRC, Insurance Law* and the *PRC, Company Law*;
- to satisfy the minimum registered capital requirement under the *PRC, Insurance Law* (see "minimum registered capital requirement" below);
- to have senior management personnel with professional knowledge of their positions and with working experience in the business;
- to have a complete organizational structure and management system; and
- to have a business site that meets the requirements and other business related facilities.[4]

Furthermore, pursuant to Article 11 of the *Management Qualifications of Senior Management Personnel of Insurance Companies Provisional Regulations* issued by the CIRC in January, 1999, foreign senior management must satisfy the following conditions: (1) chairman, vice chairman, executive director and general manager must have working experience in the insurance business for more than 10 years or in the relevant businesses for more than 15 years of which over five years in junior management ; and (2) the deputy general manager or the assistance general manager must have worked in the insurance business for more than

4. *PRC, Insurance Law*, Article 71.

five years' of which at least three years in junior management . The term "relevant businesses" refers to any financial and banking institutions.

Minimum Registered Capital Requirement

The *PRC, Insurance Law* requires a domestic applicant to have a minimum registered capital of Rmb200 million. However, the Shanghai Provisional Measures stipulate different minimum capital requirements for foreign applicants:

- a minimum of US$20 million for a company engaged in the life insurance business;
- a minimum of US$20 million for a company engaged in the non-life insurance business; and
- a minimum of US$40 million for a company engaged in both the life insurance and the non-life insurance business.[5]

The above capital requirements are likely to be increased by the forthcoming national regulations.

Approval Jurisdiction

The government agency in charge of the approval process is the CIRC. At the CIRC, the key department involved in the decision making process is the Department of International Cooperation ("DIC"). DIC will review and comment on an application submitted by a foreign insurance company. DIC will then examine the applications and make suggestions before forwarding them to the office of the chairman and vice chairmen for final approval.

CIRC has five other departments including the Department of Policy and Regulation, the Department of Finance and Accounting, the Department of Property Insurance, the Department of Life Insurance and the Department of Insurance Medium. Currently, Ma Yongwei is the Chairman of CIRC.

Approval Process

Choice of legal form

Before a foreign insurance company submits an application, it has to choose the legal form under which it will operate its business in China. It may choose between a branch office or a joint venture insurance company with a domestic insurance company or another domestic financial entity approved by the CIRC. Each form of operation has its advantages and disadvantages.

5. It is no longer possible to obtain a licence to engage in both of these types of business (See "Choice of business scope" below).

On the one hand, it appears easier for a foreign insurance company to receive approval to set up a joint venture than a branch. As a general policy, the Chinese government encourages joint ventures because it sees certain benefits being brought by the foreign insurance company, such as the introduction of advanced management and innovative types of policies and marketing techniques. A joint venture may also be attractive to a foreign insurance company because the domestic partner may have an existing marketing network and personnel that the joint venture company can utilize.

On the other hand, foreign insurance companies may find it hard to establish a joint venture because of the difficulty in finding a suitable Chinese partner, different management styles, cultural differences and issues relating to control of the joint venture, among other things, and therefore such companies may prefer to establish a branch. Ultimately, the choice of form is a business decision to be made by each foreign insurance company depending on its particular circumstances.

Choice of business scope

Following the enactment of the *PRC, Insurance Law*, insurance companies, whether foreign or domestic, are required by the *PRC, Insurance Law* to choose between property and personal insurance even though the Shanghai Provisional Measures permit the business scope of one licence to cover both personal and property insurance. The *PRC, Insurance Law* states:

"The scope of business of an insurance company:

- property insurance business which includes property loss insurance, liability insurance, credit insurance and other insurance business; or
- personal insurance business which covers life insurance, health insurance, accident insurance, etc.

An insurer may not at the same time engage in both the property and personal insurance business."[6]

The Shanghai Provisional Measures, on the other hand, provide that:

"Depending on the application, the People's Bank of China[7] shall approve foreign insurance institutions to engage in part or all of the following businesses except legally required insurance:

- All types of insurance insured by overseas enterprises, and property insurance and liability insurance of foreign-invested enterprises in China;

6. *PRC, Insurance Law*, Article 91.

7. The People's Bank of China ("PBOC") was formerly the agency in charge of the approval process for insurance companies before the establishment of CIRC in 1998.

- Life insurance of foreign and domestic individuals;
- The reinsurance of the above two types; and
- Other businesses."[8]

Because it received its licence pursuant to the Shanghai Provisional Measures, prior to the enactment of the *PRC, Insurance Law*, AIA received a licence in Shanghai that includes both life and property insurance. AIA subsequently separated the licences into two by transferring the property insurance business to AIU, its sister company.

The *PRC, Insurance Law* provides that insurance companies, whether foreign or domestic, may engage in reinsurance[9] business and requires that insurance companies reinsure 20% of each insurance that they accept, except for life insurance.[10]

Preliminary application

branch office documents

Pursuant to the Shanghai Provisional Measures, the application for establishing a branch office requires the submission of the following documents:

- an application letter specifying the name of the company, letter of guarantee prepared by the parent company and the type of insurance;
- Articles of Association (recommended even though not specifically required under the Shanghai Provisional Measures; the CIRC may require them at a later stage);
- Feasibility Study (recommended even though not specifically required under the Shanghai Provisional Measures; the CIRC may require it at a later stage);
- annual reports or financial statements of the parent company for the past three years;
- the business licence of the parent company from its home country (an officially certified copy); and
- other relevant documents as required by the CIRC (the CIRC may ask for additional credit information from those insurance companies that it is unfamiliar with or for any other information to explain the above required items).[11]

---

8. Shanghai Provisional Measures, Article 17.
9. *PRC, Insurance Law*, Article 92
10. Id. Article 101.
11. Shanghai Provisional Measures, Article 6.

joint venture documents

For a joint venture insurance company, the Shanghai Provisional Measures require the Chinese and foreign parties to jointly apply to the CIRC and to submit the following documents:

- an application letter signed by both parties containing the name of the company, the name of each party, registered capital and paid-in capital, ratio of each party's capital contribution, and business scope;
- Articles of Association (recommended even though not specifically required under the Shanghai Provisional Measures; the CIRC may require them at a later stage);
- Feasibility Study prepared by both parties, including the type of insurance, the basic terms of the contract and the method of calculating premium rates;
- Joint Venture Contract signed by an authorized representative of each party and Articles of Association of the company to be established;
- annual reports or financial statements of each party for the past three years and other relevant documents of proof;
- the business licence of each party issued by the competent authorities of the home country or region (an officially certified copy); and
- other relevant documents as required by the CIRC (the CIRC may ask for additional credit information from those insurance companies that it is unfamiliar with or any additional information to further explain the above required items).[12]

registered capital

Under the Shanghai Provisional Measures, a branch does not need to specify the amount of registered capital. Instead, the foreign parent company must provide a letter of guarantee of all tax and debt obligations incurred by the branch office to CIRC payable to an account maintained at a local PBOC office designated by CIRC. At the same time, the foreign parent company has to make a cash deposit acting as another guarantee of obligations to CIRC which should also be deposited with the local PBOC office designated by CIRC. For either life or personal insurance, the parent company has to make a guarantee deposit of US$4 million.[13]

On the other hand, the joint-venture insurance company must have a minimum of US$20 million as registered capital for either life or property insurance.[14] Of the US$20 million, the actual paid-in capital must be at least 50% of the total amount. Exactly 20% of the paid-in capital will be submitted to CIRC as the joint venture company's guarantee deposit.

---

12. Id. Article 7.

13. Id. Article 16.

14. Id. Article 14.

Chart 1: The Application Process

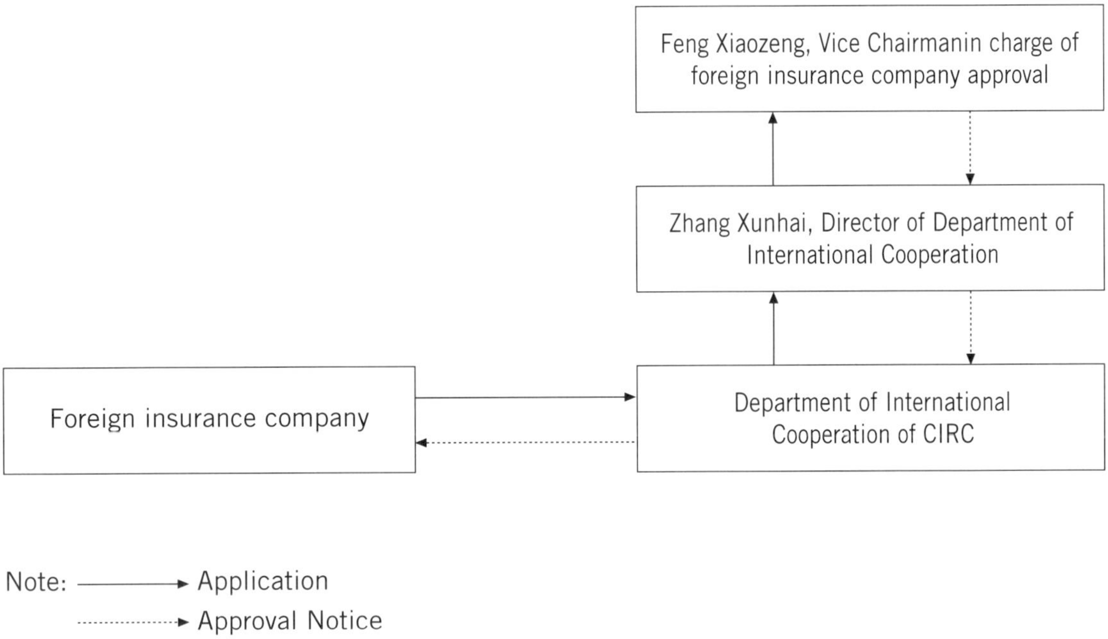

Applications must be filed with the DIC of CIRC in Beijing. Before the establishment of CIRC in 1998, applications were filed with the local offices of PBOC. Since CIRC has no local offices in either Shanghai or Guangzhou, the applications are filed with CIRC in Beijing.

Official application

An official application form must be accompanied by the following additional documents:

- the resumés and credential certifications of senior management;
- letter of authorization of the senior management (usually, it is a letter of appointment of a certain person signed by the general manager or CEO of the parent company or the general manager or CEO of the regional company);
- for a branch office, the parent company has to submit a guarantee letter in its own name for all tax and debt obligations of its wholly foreign-owned subsidiary; and
- other relevant documents as required by the CIRC.[15]

15. Id. Article 10.

Other relevant documents that may be required for a joint venture insurance company under the *PRC, Insurance Law* are:

- name list of the shareholders, as well as their portions of shares or amounts of investment; and
- credit certificates of the shareholders holding more than 10% of shares.[16]

The CIRC reserves the right to request additional information whenever it deems it necessary.

After the CIRC is satisfied with the documentation, it will either approve or reject the application within three months. If an application is rejected, the applicant may amend the application and apply again after a few months.

Company Registration

After receiving approval, the applicant will have its capital contribution to the company verified by a certified public accountant. After receiving the verification report, the applicant must register with the State Administration for Industry and Commerce to obtain a business licence. If the applicant fails to start business within 12 months, the approval document issued by the CIRC will automatically become void.

Post-approval Formalities

When an applicant has all three documents (the approval certificate, the business licence and the capital contribution verification report) it will need to apply for a Foreign Exchange Business Operation Permit at the State Administration of Foreign Exchange in order to open bank accounts in local or foreign currencies. In the process of applying for the approval documents, the applicant should prepare at least ten certified copies of each document that it receives. These should be used for filing to different government agencies in order to receive approvals for opening bank accounts in foreign exchange and local currency, and approvals for making a corporate seal. The process may take a long time depending on the completeness of documentation. Before the applicant can start business, a building inspection must also be passed.

Approval Strategies

Those companies that have received approval to date first approached the CIRC or PBOC, the former agency in charge of the approval process and obtained positive indications that approval would be accepted before filing the preliminary applications with CIRC. Now applicants usually have to approach both the working level officials and the chairman or vice chairmen of the CIRC as well as central government officials, namely, the premier or vice premiers of

---

16. *PRC, Insurance Law*, Article 10.

the country. This is very much public relations intensive work that involves strategic planning and careful presentation. The approval decision is ultimately political and arbitrary.

Those companies that have successfully received approvals used some of the following approaches:

- kept in regular and close contact with the CIRC;
- worked with their governments in approaching the Chinese central leadership and receiving their support;
- made contributions to the Chinese insurance industry by introducing training programmes, conferences and workshops;
- invested in China to show commitment to the market and the country; and
- demonstrated the need for their company's entry into the market by showing substantial bilateral trade and investment.

It has been reported that in 1993 a major international insurance company donated 10 antique bronze windows to China at a cost of US$515,000. These were windows that had been stolen from the Summer Palace in Beijing over 100 years ago.

Applications from several additional foreign insurers will reportedly be approved. It is likely that the foreign insurers who receive approvals will mostly come from different countries than those foreign insurance companies that have already received approval. Because the Chinese insurance industry is considered to be an infant industry, the government policy for the foreseeable future will likely be to encourage more domestic insurance companies to become established, and only gradually open the market to more foreign insurance companies.

At present there are twelve domestic insurance companies, some of which have a strong political background. Xinhua Life has the State Development and Planning Commission behind it and Taikang Life was organized by the China Travel Service Holding Corp. Huatai was formed by the State Economic and Trade Commission. Other domestic organizations, such as the Women's Federation, China Everbright Trust and Investment Corp., and China International Trust and Investment Corp., have reportedly applied to set up insurance companies.

The existing domestic insurance companies at the national level are:

- the People's Insurance Company of China (established in 1949)
- Xinhua Life Insurance Co. Ltd. (established in 1996)
- Taikang Life Insurance Co. Ltd. (established in 1996)
- Huatai Property Insurance Co. Ltd. (established in 1996)

- China Pacific Insurance Co. (established in 1991)
- China Ping An Insurance Co. (established in 1988)

The existing domestic insurance companies at the regional level are:

- Xinjiang Army Corp. Insurance Co. (established in 1986 in Xinjiang Autonomous Region)
- Tian An Insurance Co. (established in 1994 in Shanghai)
- Dazhong Insurance Co., Ltd. (established in 1995 in Jiangsu and Zhejiang provinces)
- Hua An Property Insurance Co., Ltd. (established in 1996 in Guangxi Autonomous Region and Guangdong, Hunan and Fujian provinces)
- Yong An Insurance Co., Ltd. (established in 1996 in Xi'an)

Summary Checklist

1. Foreign insurance companies experience difficulty in obtaining operating licences to engage in the insurance business in China. They are only allowed to operate in Guangzhou and Shanghai and, to date, nine have been granted approval.
2. The establishment of foreign insurance companies is governed by the Shanghai Provisional Measures, until a new set of national regulations are issued. Investors should also adhere to the *PRC, Insurance Law*. If an application substantively contradicts the *PRC, Insurance Law*, the CIRC reserves the right to deny approval.
3. Before beginning the approval process, the foreign insurance company must decide on the legal form it will take, that is, either a branch office or a joint venture. The Chinese Government encourages joint ventures as it sees certain benefits being brought to China by the foreign insurance company.
4. The foreign insurance company must also decide on the scope of business it is to follow, that is, either property or personal insurance.
5. The approval process begins with preliminary application to the Department of International Cooperation of CIRC. Different documents and procedures are required for establishing a joint venture rather than for a branch office.
6. Additional documents must accompany the official application and approval (or rejection) is granted within three months of receipt of these.
7. After company registration, the foreign insurance company must apply for the Permit to Engage in Foreign Exchange Business and pass a building inspection before business can commence.
8. Keeping in close contact with the CIRC, approaching Chinese central leadership to gain their support, demonstrating the company's commitment to the market and to China, and demonstrating the need for the company's entry into the market are all methods which can be used to facilitate a favourable approval decision.
9. Chinese Government policy for the foreseeable future is to encourage more domestic insurance companies, while only gradually allowing more foreign insurance companies (mostly from different countries than those already granted approval) to become established.
10. It is expected that China's entry into the WTO will result in further liberalization with respect to access to the Chinese market for foreign insurance companies.

CHAPTER 7

APPROVALS FOR ESTABLISHING REAL ESTATE DEVELOPMENT AND PROPERTY MANAGEMENT OPERATIONS

Ada P.Y. Lee (first edition)

Updated by Patty Chan of **Vivien Chan & Co., Hong Kong**

At the early stages of China's open door economic policy, foreign investors were primarily allowed to engage in tourist-orientated hotel projects and production joint ventures while approval for foreign investment in real estate development, such as residential or commercial complexes, was restricted. In the wake of the economy's rapid and continuous growth, both the Chinese central and local governments have drawn up urban redevelopment plans for the old districts in inner cities. The Chinese authorities concede that without foreign funds, technology and management they cannot accomplish their goals. During the past decade, foreign investors have shown a greater interest in the development and management of real property in China. Despite the emphasis on the open door policy, Chinese authorities are anxious that real estate development and management operations be carried out smoothly and steadily. Hence various complex regulations and policies have been promulgated with a view to exerting control, especially where previous legislation has not been adequate.

This chapter will examine the legal framework and strategies for foreign investment enterprises (FIEs) in China wishing to obtain approvals, permits and licences for establishing real estate development companies and engaging in property management operations.

The legislation discussed in this chapter represents an outline of the types of approvals and permits required for real estate development and property management operations. Such legislation should not be treated as comprehensive. In practice, the requisite approvals and application procedures do not strictly follow a systematic timetable and the procedural order of seeking various approvals may vary depending on the particular circumstances of the FIE developing the real estate in question. Furthermore, local regulations may differ. It is therefore essential for the FIE to exercise due diligence, and consult its legal advisers in any real estate transactions in the People's Republic of China (PRC).

Approval Process for Establishing Real Estate Development Operations

For the purposes of this chapter, real estate development refers to the activity in which developers acquire land and construct buildings (either residential or commercial) to be sold or leased.

Legal framework

The legal basis on which foreign investors may invest in the PRC property market is found in the following national regulations:

- *PRC, Granting and Assigning Leaseholds in State-owned Urban Land Tentative Regulations*[1] ("the Leaseholds Regulations");

1. Promulgated by the State Council on May 24, 1990.

- *PRC, Administration of Foreign Business Entities Investing in Large Tracts of Land Tentative Procedures*[2] ("the Tentative Procedures");
- *PRC, Administration of Urban Real Property Law*[3] ("the Real Property Law");
- *PRC, Administration of Urban Real Property Development Tentative Procedures*[4] ("the Real Property Development Tentative Procedures") (see **Legislation Appendices**); and
- *PRC, Administration of Urban Real Property Development and Business Regulations*[5] ("the Real Property Business Regulations").

Obtaining land use rights

Since the PRC upholds the socialist system of public ownership of land, a foreign developer can not purchase any plot of land in the PRC for property development. For urban State-owned land, the State has a system for the granting and assigning of leaseholds. A foreign property developer, like any other local property developer, can only obtain the right to use land. Therefore, as a first step, a foreign developer has to obtain land use rights of the plot of land intended for property development. According to the Leaseholds Regulations, both foreign and local individuals and entities may obtain land use rights in the PRC, and may develop and utilize the land and engage in commercial activity relating to such land[6]. This means that any foreign developer from a country that has diplomatic relations with the PRC can obtain the right to use land in accordance with the law.

Obtaining the right to use land can be achieved through either the grant or the transfer of land use rights. Either way, the recipient of the land use rights is entitled to use the subject land for a certain period of time depending on the purpose for which the land is to be used. For example, where the land is used for residential purposes, the maximum term for which leaseholds may be granted by the State is 70 years[7]. The procedure for the two methods is as follows:

by grant:

- land use rights are granted through agreement, invitation of tenders or auction;
- a grant contract shall be entered into by the land user and the land administration department of the municipal or county people's government;

2. Promulgated by the State Council on May 19, 1990.
3. Promulgated July 5, 1994 and effective January 1, 1995.
4. Promulgated by the Ministry of Construction on January 23, 1995 and effective March 1, 1995.
5. Promulgated July 20, 1998.
6. Leaseholds Regulations, Article 3.
7. Leaseholds Regulations, Article 12.

- the land user shall pay in full the fee for the grant of the right to use the land within 60 days after execution of the contract for the grant of the right; and
- the land user shall carry out registration procedures and obtain a land use certificate and thus acquire the right to use land.

by transfer:

- land use rights are transferred through sale, exchange or gift;
- an assignment contract shall be entered into between the transferor and transferee; and
- formalities shall be carried out to register the assignment contract.

Unless the Chinese party holds the right to use the land and contributes it to the joint venture of the real estate development company (see "Establishment of the FIE" below), obtaining the right to use land is a necessary step after the establishment of the real estate development company.

National legal requirements

The *Real Property Development Tentative Procedures* and the *Real Property Business Regulations* are both formulated in accordance with the Real Property Law and aim to regulate real estate development. Foreign investors wishing to set up real estate development companies will need to ensure that a proposed real estate development company complies not only with the legislation for establishing an FIE in general, but with additional conditions under both the *Real Property Development Tentative Procedures* and the *Real Property Business Regulations*, which include:

- the proposed real estate development company must have a name and an organizational structure which may be registered as a legal person;
- the proposed real estate development company must have a permanent place of business;
- both the registered capital and working capital of the proposed real estate development company, may not be less than Rmb1 million;
- the proposed real estate development company must have at least four employees who hold professional qualifications in real estate and construction engineering and at least two accountants holding professional qualifications; and
- conditions imposed by other laws and regulations[8].

The last condition is a classic example of PRC legislative style with its all-embracing reference. Although not identifying the specific requisite conditions, the last condition in practice intends

8. *Real Property Development Tentative Procedures*, Article 28.

to cover items such as the Articles of Association of the company, its management structure and financial controls.

Local legal requirements

The *Real Property Development Tentative Procedures* and the *Real Property Business Regulations* further provide that the administrative authorities in charge of construction of the People's Government at the level of province, autonomous region or municipality may set a higher requirement for the minimum amount of registered capital or working capital and number of professionals. In Shanghai, the minimum registered capital for an FIE real estate development company is US$10 million pursuant to the Specialized Company Standard[9] handed down by the Shanghai Foreign Investment Administrative Committee. On the other hand, the *Beijing Municipality, Administration of Real Property Development Business Provisions*[10] (the "Beijing Provisions"), promulgated to regulate real estate development in Beijing, specify that real estate development companies must satisfy the following conditions:

- it must have a permanent place of business;
- the minimum registered capital must be Rmb10 million if the development is adjacent to Beijing City, and only Rmb5 million if the project is situated outside Beijing City;
- the land acquired for development complies with the planning needs of Beijing City; and
- it has the requisite number of professional staff.

Establishing a real estate development company

Potential foreign investors should consider their business aims and needs before deciding which type of real estate development company best suits their objectives, resources and capital available for property investment (see "specialized company" and "project company" below).

The Real Property Development Tentative Procedures provide that a real property development enterprise (which includes a real estate-orientated FIE) can be one of two types:

- a specialized real estate development company (specialized company); or
- a project real estate development company (project company)[11].

9. Handed down in spring 1994.
10. Promulgated by the Beijing Municipal Government on May 21, 1994.
11. Real Property Development Tentative Procedures, Article 26.

specialized company

A specialized company is defined as a company which can develop and manage real property or contract to construct buildings on behalf of others, or undertake building construction work jointly with other companies by raising the funds required.

When a specialized company is approved and established, it can invest and engage in any kind of real estate project. Furthermore there are no regional limitations on the scope of its business and it can enjoy a longer term of business than the project company (see "project company" below) since, unlike a project company, it does not need to be wound up upon completion of a particular project. So far, specialized companies are not common in China as tight requirements have been imposed on their establishment and obtaining approval is therefore difficult. If a specialized company does not actually carry out any property development project or investment within one year from the time it obtains the right to real estate development and management, its business licence and its right to engage in property development and management could be withdrawn.

project company

A project company is limited to investing and developing real estate on a specific plot of land, and is wound up upon completion of the project.

The proposed project company must, therefore, obtain a specific project or the right to develop a particular plot of land. Accordingly, a condition precedent of setting up a project company is that the proposed FIE has to obtain the land-use rights in accordance with the Real Property Law (see "Obtaining land use rights" above) and other relevant local regulations for the grant and assignment of land-use rights.

To date, most FIE real estate development companies in China are in the form of project companies since in practice, it is quite difficult for an FIE to obtain approval for establishing a specialized real estate company. Although a project company will normally be terminated upon completion of the development (even if this may occur prior to its original approved term of business) an FIE may apply to alter its nature from a project company into a specialized company.

From looking at the different limitations of specialized and project companies, it is clear that the legal procedure and requirements for their establishment will differ. For example, in the case of a specialized company, the first step is usually to form the company before seeking any property project for development. On the contrary, an FIE will need to ensure its proposed project is feasible before taking any steps to form a project company. It would be meaningless to establish a project company if the proposed project was subsequently discovered to be unfeasible.

Construction qualification certificate approval

Besides the minimum capital requirements, a proposed FIE real estate development company must have its Construction Qualification Certificate examined and approved by the Construction Administration authorities at or above county level[12]. Construction Qualification Certificates are divided into several grades. Real estate development companies require a particular grade of Construction Qualification Certificate to undertake a certain type of building project throughout China.

A Grade One certificate will enable a company to undertake projects for developing residential, commercial and industrial areas with a gross floor area of anything more than 200,000 square metres. A company with a Grade Two certificate can only undertake projects for developing residential, commercial and industrial areas with a gross floor area of less than 200,000 square metres, and cannot undertake technically complicated construction projects. A Grade Three certificate will permit a company to undertake projects for developing residential, commercial and industrial areas with a gross floor area of less than 120,000 square metres as long as the intended building is less than 12 storeys high and within the height restriction of 24 metres. Companies with Grade Four or Five certificates are not permitted to undertake any construction projects in the main cities in China.

The government department in charge of the issuance of Construction Qualification Certificates is the Ministry of Construction and the local construction commissions at or above county level. What grade of certificate the real estate development company can receive depends on the following criteria:

- the amount of its registered capital and of its working fund;
- the number of professionals employed and their professional posts; and
- total gross floor area which has been developed and constructed.

When applying for the Construction Qualification Certificate, an FIE must submit the following documents:

- application for the desired grade of Construction Qualification Certificate;
- documents for the appointment of its general manager;
- documentary proof of the respective amounts of registered and working capital
- its Articles of Association; and
- other relevant documents as required.

12. Promulgated by the State Planning Commission on December 31, 1997 (**see Legislation Applendices**).

The *Administration of Real Property Development Enterprises Qualification Provisions* have not specified the period within which the construction administration authorities must complete the approval process. In practice, the FIE will normally be granted the certificate within two months of its application. It is very rare for the construction administration authorities to reject an FIE application unless it cannot even meet the criteria for a Grade Five construction qualification certificate. If, however, the authorities consider that an FIE cannot fulfil the criteria for the grades for which it applied, it will be granted a lower grade certificate.

Establishment of the FIE

While the Construction Qualification Certificate is being applied for, the foreign applicant can apply for setting up an FIE real estate development company. The procedures for the establishment of an FIE real estate development company will be similar to those applicable to the setting up of FIEs engaging in other types of business (see Chapter 1: **Approvals for Establishing a Joint Venture**). The relevant regulations are laid down in:

- *PRC, Sino-foreign Equity Joint Venture Law*[13] ; and
- *PRC, Sino-foreign Cooperative Joint Venture Law*[14]

The Tentative Procedures allow foreign investors to choose one of the following investment vehicles to carry out real property project development in China:

- Sino-foreign equity joint venture (EJV);
- Sino-foreign cooperative joint venture (CJV); and
- wholly foreign-owned enterprise (WFOE).

There used to be no special provision prohibiting WFOEs from engaging in real estate development activities, although applications by WFOEs have never been encouraged or easily approved. Between 1993 and 1994, it is known that only 10 WFOEs were approved to engage in real estate development in China. However, as from mid- 1995, the PRC Government began imposing stricter control and approval procedures on foreign investors in luxury real estate development. According to the *State Council Issues a Circular Calling for Strict Control of Luxury Real Property Development Projects*[15], project proposals for certain types of luxurious development such as holiday resorts, luxurious office and residential development and four- and five star hotels and guesthouses will not be approved for that calendar year nor may any construction work commence in that year. The *Foreign Investment Industrial Guidance*

13. Promulgated July 1, 1979.

14. Promulgated by the National People's Congress on, and effective from April 13, 1998.

15. Announced by the State Council on June 14, 1995.

Catalogue[16] (see **Legislation Appendices**) further stipulated that a WFOE is prohibited from engaging in luxury real estate development which includes, inter alia, villas, high grade office buildings, high grade hotels and development of large tracts of land. In the latest revised Catalogue, the same prohibition still applies. Therefore, FIE real estate development companies are now to be set up mostly as EJVs or CJVs.

The CJV is more flexible than the EJV in that the parties involved may structure the CJV according to their mutual agreement, including the division of profits of the venture in any manner they choose. Furthermore, the profit sharing ratio need not reflect the ratio of the parties' respective contributions as in the case of the EJV.

Insight into the preference for joint ventures may be gleaned from a review of the Beijing Provisions which apply to real estate development enterprises in Beijing, including EJVs and CJVs. Foreign enterprises and individuals are encouraged to establish joint ventures with Beijing enterprises which are already qualified to engage in real estate development.

Apart from fulfilling the usual requirements for establishing joint ventures (see Chapter 1: **Approvals for Establishing a Joint Venture**), property development joint ventures need to satisfy an additional requirement: the Chinese party must have a business licence empowering it to carry out real property development.

Generally speaking, property development joint ventures are set up with the Chinese party contributing the land, and the foreign party providing the necessary funding for the property development on the land.

The structure of a joint venture property development company can be divided into two categories:

- the Chinese party holds the right to use the land which is allocated by the government. The Chinese party normally does not have sufficient capital to pay for the land premium, therefore the foreign party is willing to cooperate with the Chinese partner by paying the fee for the land grant and the required capital for the construction of the building on the land. Under this arrangement, the land will be granted to the joint venture company; or
- the Chinese party holds the right to use the land which has already been granted or assigned. The Chinese party has already paid the fee for the grant of the land and obtained the State-owned land use certificate. It will contribute the land to the proposed joint venture while the foreign party will raise funds for the construction of the building on the land. The common issue is how to evaluate the value of the land.

16. Promulgated by the State Planing Commission, the State Economic and Trade Commission and MOFTEC on June 27, 1995.

Land valuation is a pre-condition to signing the agreement for the grant of leasehold land (see "Obtaining Land Use Rights" above). The land user should apply to a capable land valuation organization approved by the local land administrative departments for land valuation purposes. A survey on the site will have to be carried out. After payment of the land valuation fee, the land user will get a land valuation report. The price set by the land valuation report will be the guideline for the land user and the competent land administration department to negotiate the price for the grant.

In the second situation described above, when the Chinese party has obtained the State owned land use certificate (that is, the Chinese party has already carried out the land valuation once when the land is granted by the government), there will be another land valuation required when the Chinese party contributes land to the joint venture. Due to the rapid economic growth in China, the price of land is rising. Therefore, the second land valuation price may be higher or at least at the same premium as when the Chinese party originally acquired the land.

Approval Process for Engaging in Real Estate Development Activities

Apart from the statutory regulations on the formation of a real estate development company (see "national legal requirements" and "local legal requirements" above), the Chinese authorities have adopted a national policy to govern and monitor construction work undertaken by developers. The *PRC, Urban Planning Law*[17] was promulgated for:

"regularizing urban construction and development and standardizing and systematizing urban construction and management."

The *PRC, Urban Planning Law* provides that the use of the land and all construction within urban planning districts must conform with urban planning and must be subject to planning administration. Construction work cannot begin until various written approvals and permits are obtained.

After obtaining its business licence (see Chapter 1: **Approvals for Establishing a Joint Venture**) and prior to the start of any construction work, a real estate development FIE must obtain the following permits from the administrative department in charge of urban planning:

- Planning Permit for Land to be Built Upon (see "Planning Permit for Land to be Built Upon" below); and
- Construction Project Planning Permit (see "Construction Project Planning Permit" below).

17. Promulgated by the Standing Committee of the National People's Congress on December 26, 1989.

Legal requirements

The rules governing the application of these permits are found in:

- *the PRC, Urban Planning Law*; and
- *Planning Administration for the Grant or Assignment of Urban State-owned Leaseholds Procedures*[18] (the Planning Administration Procedures) and various local urban planning regulations such as:
- *Beijing Municipality, Urban Planning Regulations*[19]; and
- *Tianjin Municipality, Urban Planning Regulations*[20]

Planning permit for land to be built upon

Under the *PRC, Urban Planning Law* and its relevant regulations such as the *Planning Administration Procedures, and the Drawing up Urban Plan Procedures*[21], a real estate development FIE, after entering into an agreement for the grant of leasehold land, will not be issued with a State-owned Land Use Certificate until it has obtained the Planning Permit for Land to be Built Upon.

documents

The following documents must be submitted when applying for the Planning Permit for Land to be Built Upon:

- a written application stating the nature of the proposed construction project, the scope of the construction, construction project and approval documents;
- copies of the agreement for the grant of leasehold land; and
- planning and design proposals.

planning and design proposals

A real estate development company must follow the conditions laid down in the Land Use Grant Contract when it devises planning and design proposals for the proposed construction project. When there is a need to formulate detailed planning, the developer must entrust a qualified planning and design work unit to formulate such plans, and submit them for approval to the administration department in charge of urban planning, outlining planning and design

18. Promulgated by the Ministry of Construction on December 4, 1992 and effective from January 1993.
19. Adopted by the 35th Session of the Standing Committee of the ninth Beijing Municipal People's Congress on July 24, 1992.
20. Adopted by the 31st Session of the Standing Committee of the 11th Tianjin Municipal People's Congress on December 21, 1991 and amended on May 25, 1994 by the 8th Session of the Standing Committee of the 12th Tianjin Municipal People's Congress.
21. Promulgated by the Ministry of Construction on September 3, 1991 and implemented from October 1, 1991.

details in respect of the proposed construction project. If a foreign enterprise is appointed to design a construction project, the developer is required to hire a Chinese work unit or Chinese cooperative design work unit as a consultant[22]. The planning and design proposals should include the following documents:

- two pieces of the general plane figure (*zong pingmian sheji tu*) (with a scale of 1:500 or 1:1000) and environmental design drawings of the land granted, including the location of the construction, its entries and exits, parking lot, transportation plan, fire prevention and garden areas;
- plane, elevation and sectional drawings (*ping li gemiantu*);
- structural design proposals, including the classification of the foundations, structural systems, analyzing the effect on the neighbouring structures caused by the carrying out of piling work and detailing the appropriate protective measures;
- design proposals for utility equipment, including water, heating, electricity, gas and communications; and
- colour prospective drawing of the planning and design proposal and its general model.

review and examination

Upon receipt of the application for the Planning Permit for Land to Be Built Upon, the administrative department in charge of urban planning shall review the application and make a decision within the time specified. Different local regulations have different specifications for the time required for review and examination.

In Shanghai, the administrative department is required to complete its examination process within 45 days upon receipt of the application. However, in Beijing, no specified time limits have been laid down for the administrative department to carry out the review and complete its examination.

sanctions

Should land be occupied without a Planning Permit for Land to Be Built Upon, notwithstanding the fact that the approval documents for land usage for the purpose of construction (the Approval Certificate for Land Usage for the Purpose of Urban Construction or the Approval Certificate for Land Usage for the Purpose of State Construction) have been secured, the approval documents are deemed to be void. The current sanction is that the land must be returned to the State and the buildings or construction on that land must be demolished within a specified time.

22. *Works and Projects Design Jointly Carried Out by Chinese and Foreign Parties Interim Provisions*, promulgated by the State Development and Planning Commission and MOFTEC on May 26, 1986.

Construction Project Planning Permit

When the development company applies for the Construction Project Planning Permit, it should submit the following drawings, documents and materials:

- land-use right certificate;
- industrial and commercial registration certificate and the tax registration certificate;
- waste discharge permit;
- two sets of the general plane figures (with a scale of 1:500);
- two sets of the construction working drawings (plane figure, elevation drawings and sectional drawings with a scale of 1:100); and
- one set of working drawings of the structure and equipment.

review and examination

After the developer submits the construction project design plan, the administrative department in charge of urban planning should solicit and coordinate opinions from the relevant departments on the initial construction project design plan, upon receipt of which, the design plan should be examined and rectified. The construction project design drawings submitted by the applicant should conform with the examined and rectified design plan. If, upon examination, the drawings are found to be satisfactory, they will be approved by the urban planning administrative department, upon which a Construction Project Planning Permit will be verified and issued. In Beijing, the usual practice for completing the process is 22 days.

sanctions

Where construction is carried out without a Construction Project Planning Permit, or in violation of the provisions of the permit, and seriously affects urban planning or affects urban planning in such a way that rectification measures cannot be taken, the administrative department in charge of urban planning shall order the construction to be suspended, and buildings, structures or other facilities in violation of the law must be demolished within a specified time frame.

Upon securing the Construction Project Planning Permit, the development company must appoint a survey work unit, approved by the administrative department in charge of urban planning to survey the construction site before carrying out construction work with the Construction Work Commencement Permit (see box below).

The Construction Work Commencement Permit is issued by the Construction Commission. The aim of the permit is to check whether the development company has complied with all legal requirements before commencing with construction work.

To apply for the permit, the following documents must be submitted:

- approval given by the planning commission and the construction commission when the proposed construction work has been incorporated into their annual plans for formal work commencement;
- building demolition licence issued by the housing and land administration department;
- agreements for the supply for water, gas, electricity and provision of sewage disposal;
- registration document for the supervision of construction quality; and
- construction contracts for the project.

If the FIE does not commence construction work within one year of the granting of a Construction Project Planning Permit, then an application for postponement must be made to the urban planning departments responsible for its issuance. However, the period of extension must not exceed six months. If a postponement application is not made, or where construction work does not actually commence within the permitted period of extension, the Construction Project Planning Permit will automatically become invalid.

Foreign pre-sale of "commodity building" permit (foreign pre-sale permit)

Foreign investors often raise funds to finance the construction of their property project by selling uncompleted "commodity" buildings. This activity is commonly known as "pre-sale". "Commodity building" is a term used in China to denote a building capable of being transferred as a commodity on the property market. An FIE needs to pay special attention when securing the necessary approvals for a pre-sale. The Real Property Law, the Real Property Business Regulations and the *Administration of the Pre-Sale of Urban Commodity Buildings Procedures*[23] ("the Pre-sale Procedures") all serve to regulate the pre-sale activities regarding commodity buildings. These provisions (see "legal requirements" below) set out:

- the minimum investment that should be contributed by the developer prior to pre-sale;
- approval procedures;
- advertisement guidelines; and
- penalties for violation.

23. Promulgated by the Ministry of Construction on November 15, 1994 and effective on January 1, 1995.

legal requirements

Under the Real Property Law, the Real Property Business Regulations and the Pre-Sale Procedures, the prescribed requirements for overseas pre-sales are:

- the land premium has been paid in full and the State-owned Land Use Certificate has been obtained;
- the Construction Work Planning Permit has been obtained;
- more than 25% of the total construction investment for the commodity building (excluding land premium) has been injected in respect of a commodity building; and
- the time schedule for completion of the construction, the date of delivery of the buildings and the scheme for pre-sale of the commodity premises have been determined[24].

review and examination

After meeting the requirements, the developer should file its pre-sale application with the real property administration bureau of the People's Government at county level or above. The real property administration department will grant pre-sale approval by issuing a Foreign Pre-sale Permit within 10 days of the site inspection and after verifying that the requirements have been met. If the application is rejected, the real property administration department will explain the grounds for such rejection. The development company can not proceed with any pre-sale activity until it has re-applied and duly fulfilled the legal criteria.

documents

In applying for the Foreign Pre-sale Permit, the following documents prescribed by local regulations such as the *Beijing Municipality, Administration of Commodity Buildings for Foreign Sale Provisions*[25] are required for submission:

- business licence of the enterprise;
- Construction Project Planning Permit issued by the administrative department in charge of urban planning (see "Construction Project Planning Permit" above);
- Construction Work Commencement Permit (see box above);
- construction contract;
- proof of the injection of at least 25% of the total construction investment;
- settlement account number opened at a bank for holding proceeds from the pre-sale of buildings and the agreement signed with the bank on supervision of the proceeds;

24. Real Property Law. Article 44, The Real Property Business Regulations, Article 24 and The Pre-Sale Procedures, Article 7.

25. Promulgated on and effective from February 26, 1994.

- prospectus and the agreement for the use, maintenance and management of the building; and
- power of attorney for or agreement on the management of the building.

A foreign developer is required to show the Foreign Pre-sale Permit to purchasers in the pre-sale of commodity buildings[26].

In Shanghai, when a developer has secured the Foreign Pre-sale Permit, the real property administrative department will issue a public announcement, listing the commodity buildings which have been approved for foreign pre-sale. Advertisements in respect of the foreign pre-sale of commodity buildings must contain the approval number[27].

Although a foreign developer may very well meet all the pre-sale prerequisites and successfully obtain a Foreign Pre-sale Permit, there is still a lack of practical control in terms of ensuring that the proceeds of the sale received during the pre-sale are properly and promptly remitted by the developer into the designated bank account. However, under the Pre-sale Procedures, it is provided that proceeds of the pre-sale of commodity buildings obtained by a developer must be used in the relevant construction projects[28]. In theory, if the developer fails to remit the money into the designated bank account, it will be punished under the Pre-sale Procedures. This may lead to the cessation of the pre-sale or even a revocation of the pre-sale permit[29]. Certain provinces in the PRC now have their own local legislation governing the use of pre-sale proceeds. For example, under the *Guangdong Province, Administration of Pre-Sale of Commodity Premises Regulations*[30], proceeds received from purchasers for pre-sale of commodity premises have to be deposited in a stakeholder bank account by the developer and can only be used for the purchase of building materials and equipment for construction of project and for payment of project construction schedule fees and statutory taxes and fees.

26. The Real Property Business Regulations, Article 27 and the Pre-Sale Procedures Article 9.

27. *Shanghai Municipality, Strengthening of the Administration of Foreign Pre-sale of Commodity Building in Shanghai Notice*, promulgated by Shanghai Municipal Real Property Administration Bureau in December 1992.

28. The Pre-Sale Procedures Article 11.

29. The Pre-Sale Procedures Article 13.

30. Promulgated on August 22, 1998 and effective as of October 1, 1998.

Approval Process for Engaging in Property Management Operations

In order to keep pace with the large amount of property construction within China, the Chinese authorities have also formulated rules on regulating enterprises engaged in property management operations.

Legal framework

In 1994, the *Administration of Newly Constructed Residential Districts in Cities Procedures*[31] was promulgated (the Administration of Residential Districts), which defines the term "property management" to include a range of activities from maintaining, repairing and renovating buildings, public facilities, greening and gardening, sanitation, transportation, to security. It provides that residential areas should be managed by property management companies performing specialized management tasks in a unified fashion. It further provides that a prospective property management company should not commence its business until it has secured its business licence. However, the Administration of Residential Districts has not laid down any special requirements on how to establish a property management company. Therefore, foreign investors who intend to set up property management operations should follow the procedures for establishing FIEs under the national legislation (see Chapter 1: **Approvals for Establishing a Joint Venture**, and Chapter 2: **Approvals for Establishing a Wholly Foreign-Owned Enterprise**).

The Shanghai experience

In 1996, the *Shanghai Municipality, Administration of Qualifications and Quality Standards of Real property Management Enterprises Tentative Procedures*[32] ("the Shanghai Administration Procedures") came into effect. The Shanghai Administration Procedures apply to enterprises that carry out real property management business in the Shanghai Municipality.

Under the Shanghai Administration Procedures, real property management enterprises are classified into two types: a 'specialized' real property management enterprise and a 'secondary operated' real property management enterprise[33]. As the name implies, a 'specialized' real property management enterprise refers to those enterprises whose main business is in property management work. They must be capable of independent management and operations and must possess all the qualities of a legal person. A 'secondary operated' real property management enterprise on the other hand, refers to those enterprises whose main business is

31. Promulgated by the Ministry of Construction on March 23, 1994 and effective April 1, 1994.

32. Effective on September 1, 1996.

33. Article 3 of the Shanghai Administration Procedures.

not in property management work, for example, a real property developer engaging primarily in real property development work engages also in property management work. According to the Shanghai Administration Procedures, a company's branch office which does not possess the qualities of a legal person and which therefore cannot sue or be sued independently can also be set up as a 'secondary operated' real property management enterprise.

The Shanghai Administration Procedures expressly permits a foreign investor to establish a property management company by means of an EJV, CJV or WFOE. However, the ranking of qualifications and quality of such management companies are subject to the examination and approval of the Shanghai Land and Property Bureau which is the authority responsible for the overall administration of property management companies in Shanghai.

legal requirements

Under the Shanghai Administration Procedures, real property management enterprises are classified into three ranks according to their qualifications and quality. In addition to the three ranks, there is a "no rank" classification which can be given to those management enterprises whose qualifications and quality will for the time being not be classified by the Shanghai Municipal Real Property Bureau such as smaller scale management enterprises which cannot satisfy even the prescribed requirements of the third rank. Thus, in setting up a property management company in Shanghai, a FIE can first make a self assessment as to its qualifications of the different ranks before making the requisite application.

The prescribed requirements for the setting up of different ranks of real property management enterprises are set out as follows:

1. Scale of property management in terms of the area of the property

   First Rank: more than 500,000 square metres or more than 200,000 square metres for "property for foreign use";

   Second Rank: 200,000 to 500,000 square metres or 50,000 to 200,000 square metres for "property for foreign use";

   Third Rank: 30,000 to 200,000 square metres or 10,000 to 50,000 square metres for "property for foreign use"

   "property for foreign use" refers to those type of real property which can be sold or leased to foreign enterprises or foreign individuals together with ancillary facilities and related space.

2. Number of different types of properties managed: multi-storey, high rise residential premises, mansions, villas, commercial and residential buildings, office buildings, plazas, factories and other special types of buildings.

First Rank: more than three types or at least two types for "property for foreign use";

Second Rank: at least two types or managing "property for foreign use";

Third Rank: no requirement

3. Types of properties managed:

   First Rank: more than two types of properties managed must be outstanding small districts or buildings and the management of such districts must reach at least 50% of the standard requirements for management as laid down for such districts in Shanghai;

   Second Rank: more than one type of properties managed must be outstanding small districts or buildings and the management of such districts must reach at least 30% of the standard requirements for management as laid down for such districts in Shanghai;

   Third Rank: no requirement

4. Personnel:

   First Rank: the enterprise's manager or the deputy manager in charge of general affairs must possess at least three years experience specializing in property management and the number of competent middle rank economical and engineering management personnel must not be less than ten;

   Second Rank: the number of competent middle rank economical and engineering management personnel must not be less than six;

   Third Rank: the number of middle rank competent personnel possessing professional skills must not be less than three.

5. Registered capital

   First Rank: minimum Rmb1,000,000.00;

   Second Rank: minimum Rmb500,000.00;

   Third Rank: Rmb100,000.00.

6. Duration of operation of the property management enterprise

   First Rank: at least three years;

   Second Rank: at least two years;

   Third Rank: no requirement.

Apart from the duly completed application form, other prescribed documents for the application of the certificate of the qualifications and ranking of property management companies in Shanghai include:

- Articles of Association of the enterprise;

- management contract;
- the enterprise's management licence issued by the administrative authorities for Industry and Commerce;
- proof of qualifications for senior staff of the real property management enterprise such as the diplomas or certificates of staff holding professional or technical posts;
- other documents as required under different individual rankings as referred to above such as the proof of the registered capital of the property management enterprise

After receiving a complete set of the required documents, the Shanghai Land and Property Bureau will examine and process the application. A Certificate of Qualification and Ranking of Real Property Management Enterprise in the Shanghai Municipality in respect of the relevant ranking of the enterprise will be issued if the application is successful. The qualifications and ranking of management enterprises will be valid for two years after which the said qualifications and ranking will be subject to review again. After receiving the Certificate of Qualification, the applicant must apply to the Shanghai Foreign Investment Commission for approval and can then proceed with business registration in the same way as other companies do in China (see Chapter 1: **Approvals for Establishing a Joint Venture**).

It should be noted that the carrying out of the relevant application procedures and the obtaining of the certificate of the relevant ranking is a prerequisite for the operation of any real property management enterprise in Shanghai under the Shanghai Administration Procedures since the Shanghai Land and Property Bureau can either order any real property management enterprise to carry out the said application procedures or – in case the real property management enterprise without good reason fails to carry out the procedures – propose to the administrative authorities for Industry and Commerce to cancel the enterprise's qualifications for management operations. Further, the Shanghai Land and Property Bureau has the authority to alter the validity period of the Certificate of Qualifications and Ranking of the real property management enterprise, to downgrade the ranking of such enterprise or even cancel the enterprise's qualifications for management operations under certain circumstances, such as the non-observance or non-performance of the property management contract, poor management, frequent complaints from the owners and occupiers of the managed property, not attending to complaints from the owners and occupiers of the managed property and so on.

The *Shanghai Municipality, Management of Residential Property Regulations*[34] provide that work units selling newly constructed commodity dwellings should, before sale, draw up a users' covenant and sign an initial period management service contract with a real property management enterprise. The dwellings are to be managed by the appointed real property management enterprise in the initial period until an owners committee is formed.

34. Promulgated May 28, 1997.

The Beijing experience

The *Beijing Municipality, Examination and Approval of the Business Qualifications of Property Management Work Units Provisions*[35] (the Beijing Management Provisions) were issued in 1995, to regulate property management companies setting up in Beijing. Under the Beijing Management Regulations, all companies in the property management business within the Beijing Municipal administrative region are now directly administered by the Beijing Municipal Real Estate and Land Administration Bureau, whose responsibility it is to examine and approve the qualifications of property management companies set up with a foreign investor.

legal requirements

Under the Beijing Management Regulations, a property management company need to comply with the following requirements:

- has a company name and a regular place of business;
- has different types of managerial and technical personnel suitable for the proposed management operation;
- has the requisite registered capital; and
- has designed relevant rules and regulations concerning maintenance, service and management.

All property management companies must now have their management qualifications examined before being issued with a Certificate of Quality for Property Management Qualification (Certificate of Quality). Property management companies set up by foreign investors in Beijing must gain the Certificate of Quality before applying for other approvals applicable in setting up an FIE (see Chapter 1: **Approvals for Establishing a Joint Venture** and Chapter 2: **Approvals for Establishing a Wholly Foreign-Owned Enterprise**).

approval procedure

The foreign investor should file a written application directly to the Beijing Municipal Real Estate and Land Administration Bureau, together with documents showing proof of the:

- establishment of the organization;
- numbers of professional personnel;
- numbers of staff;
- place of business;
- management rules; and
- registered capital.

35. Promulgated by the Beijing Municipal Government and effective on November 13, 1995.

The Bureau will examine the materials and decide whether the applicant has approval within 10 days of receiving the application. If approval is granted the Certificate of Quality will be issued. Once the applicant has received this, they can then apply for the business licence in the same way as business registration for all companies in China.

Conclusion

China's central government has clearly recognized the importance of the property market in the development of its "socialist market economy". Over the years, a complex legal structure has been developed to assert administrative control over real estate development and property management. The regulations highlighted in this chapter are intended to safeguard and regulate the real estate market. However, a comprehensive system of administrative scrutiny to regulate non-compliance has not been fully developed. One needs to wait to see how and when enforcement will be improved.

Summary Checklist

Real estate development

1. Foreign entities and individuals are legally permitted, under the Leasehold Regulations, to obtain land use rights in the PRC for the purpose of real estate development.
2. Foreign investors should consider the different methods of obtaining land use rights and choose the most appropriate one according to the circumstances of the FIE.
3. Foreign investors must decide whether to form a specialized real estate development company or a project real estate development company (a project company is more common in China).
4. Foreign investors must fulfil the legal criteria for setting up a real estate development company under the national regulations and pay attention to any higher requirements under local regulations.
5. A real estate development company needs to have its Construction Qualification Certificate duly approved.
6. Foreign investors must choose a suitable investment vehicle to carry out the project development and follow the procedure for setting up FIEs under the national regulations.
7. The FIE real estate development company can then follow the usual legal procedure for obtaining a business licence for the company.
8. An FIE real estate development company needs to consider its use of land and construction work to fit in with urban planning issues and must proceed with the following:
   - obtain the Planning Permit for Land to be Built Upon;
   - submit planning and design proposals concerning the project to the administrative department in charge of urban planning;
   - apply for the Construction Project Planning Permit; and
   - appoint a survey work unit to survey the construction work before carrying out the construction work.
9. Construction work can then be commenced with the Construction Work Commencement Permit.
10. FIEs may pre-sell the incomplete buildings by obtaining a Foreign Pre-Sale of Commodity Building Permit. The legal requirements under the Real Property Law as well as local requirements must be met.

Property management operations

11. Foreign investors intending to set up property management operations should follow the procedure for establishing FIEs (that is, EJVs, CJVs and WFOEs) under the national regulations.
12. Legal requirements under local regulations must also be complied with.
13. A Qualification Certificate will be issued if the FIE is approved.
14. The FIE can then apply for a business licence.
15. In Beijing, the Certificate of Quality must be obtained before applying for the establishment of the FIE.

SECTION II:

ESTABLISHING INFRASTRUCTURE PROJECTS

CHAPTER 8

POWER PROJECT APPROVALS

Edward L. Turner III[1]
Shearman & Sterling, Hong Kong

1. The revisions to this chapter would not have been possible without the diligent research and insightful analysis of our associates, Alan D. Seem and Don H. Bennett.

Any form of direct investment in China is intrinsically risky by nature, but power projects arguably present the greatest hazards and offer the highest potential rewards of all types of Chinese investment. The long-term nature of the investment, large amounts of capital involved, uncertainty regarding future energy prices, foreign currency convertibility concerns, and close dependence on the transient state of the economy and political environment are just some of the factors to consider when investing in Chinese power projects. Therefore, the degree of transparency and predictability of the government approval process takes on greater significance for power projects than for other forms of investment in China. However, the lack of publicly-available published guidelines concerning the official requirements for approval makes developing a successful power plant in China all the more challenging.

Fortunately, past experiences in obtaining these approvals have yielded a fairly reliable road map which can help to make the approval process less intimidating. This chapter presents this road map in an easily digestible format, informs readers of the common pitfalls and new legal developments surrounding the approval of foreign-invested power projects[2], and provides remarks and suggestions to help investors navigate through the elaborate approval process.

Background

The Chinese economy grew at an average annual rate of 10.7% from 1993 through 1997. The Asian financial crisis began in July 1997, yet in 1998 the Chinese economy grew by 7.8%. Although this rate fell short of the officially declared target of 8% in 1998, it still ranked China foremost in the world.[3]

China has a population of 1.2 billion people that is increasing at a rate of 14 million people per year. Despite China's economic growth, only about 80% of the population is now connected to the electrical grid.[4] The installed power capacity per capita was a mere 0.21 kilowatts in

2. Most foreign-invested power projects take the form of a joint venture between a Chinese party (usually a corporate investment subsidiary of a local power bureau) and a foreign party or parties. Nevertheless, barring those aspects relating to agreement between the parties, the approval process is virtually identical for wholly foreign-owned projects.

3. It should be noted that many Western and Chinese observers doubt the accuracy of the PRC government's economic statistics. For example, even Premier Zhu Rongji expressed concern that economic data submitted by local governments are subject to some exaggeration. See *China Energy Watch*, January 1999, Volume 2, No. 1, Page 2. Economist Angus Maddison estimates that China's GDP annual growth from 1978 – 1994 was 7.4% against the official rate of 9.8%. On the other hand, economist Ren Ruo'en conservatively estimates that China's GDP annual growth from 1986 – 1994 was 6% against the official rate of 9.8%. See Asia Law & Practice, *Power In Asia*, March 8, 1999, Issue 272, Page 4.

   The PRC government has projected that the economy will grow by 7% in 1999, but initial reports have shown a 7.6% growth rate for the first half of the year. See *China Economic News*: April 19, 1999, Supplement No. 5, Page 3; August 16, 1999, Weekly No. 31, Page 1

4. *Power In Asia*, March 8, 1999, Issue 272, Page 5, citing *World Energy Outlook*, 1998 Edition, International Energy Agency Publications.

1997, placing China 85th in the world. Per capita power consumption in 1999 averages 900 kilowatt-hours, or only 40% of the world average.[5]

Owing to the tremendous scale of its recent power infrastructure investment, China is already second only to the United States in the production of electricity. Before 1997, this build-up in electrical capacity was not able to keep pace with the increasing demand arising from China's fast-growing economy. However, during the economic turbulence of 1997 and 1998, China saw supply outpace demand in almost half of its provinces.[6] This over-supply of power has prompted the State Power Corporation to ban (with several exceptions) the construction of new large-scale greenfield thermal power plants for the next three years.[7] In addition, the PRC government has undertaken an ambitious plan to phase out up to 10.86 Gigawatts worth of small-scale thermal power plants by the end of 2000 in order to reduce the current over-supply and to improve efficiency in the power sector. There is no official megawattage threshold to determine which plants will be phased out. Instead, the targeted plants will be those which are "small", expensive, inefficient and environmentally damaging.[8]

The recent over-supply in power and the three year ban on certain new plants does not mean that China is not planning for its anticipated power needs. However, the new power policy will focus on (i) building only large plants that use cutting-edge technology and are highly efficient and (ii) building power networks.[9] The PRC government intends to add more than 10,000 megawatts (MW) a year[10] and expects to meet its objective set forth in the Ninth Five Year Plan of achieving 290,000 MW of total annual production capacity by the year 2000. It is estimated that the power industry will require an aggregate of 17 billion US dollars in foreign investment during the current 1996-2000 period, representing 20% of the total investment in the power industry worldwide during this period. To put the magnitude of this

5. *China Economic News*, June 14, 1999, Weekly No. 22, Page 8.

6. Some reasons for the increase in supply over demand include: the Asia financial crisis, recent industrial restructuring and the poor electricity transmission structure. See *China Energy Watch*: March 1999, Volume 2, No. 3, Page 3; June 14, 1999, Weekly No. 22, Page 7.

7. The ban on new power projects does not include the following projects: "big-for-small"; hydro-thermal adjustment; peaking; "Western power sent to East"; necessary projects in developing Western and Central areas; improvements to power and water supplies in major cities, and those utilizing foreign capital that are in a mature stage of development. See *China Energy Watch*, March 1999, Volume 2, No. 3, Pages 2-3; *Project Finance International*, February 10, 1999, Issue 162, Page 7.

8. Most plants that are 25 MW or smaller will be phased out by the end of 1999, thereafter, several 50 MW plants are to be phased-out. See *Ji Jichu* (Planning, Infrastructure) [1999] No. 538, issued by the SDPC cited in *China Energy Watch*, July 1999, Volume 2, No. 7, Page 3.

9. *China Energy Watch*, January 1999, Volume 2, No. 1, Page 9.

10. The 10,000 MW per annum increase in installed electricity capacity is expected to continue for the entirety of the first decade of the coming century. See *China Economic News*, June 14, 1999, Weekly No. 22, Page 8. The projected increase in China's energy consumption between 1995 to 2020 is expected to account for almost 25% of the increase in world demand. See *Power In Asia*, March 8, 1999, Issue 272, page 3. However, compare note 3 above, where applying economist Angus Maddison's methodology, the increase in commercial energy need in China is dampened significantly from what China officially claims, putting the per annum electricity need growth rate figure at 3.4% compared to the PRC government's official 5.6% growth rate figure.

endeavour in context, China's annual demand for new power stations is equivalent to the production capacity a country such as Switzerland builds in a century.[11]

When considering the breadth of this undertaking, the large capital costs involved and the fact that Chinese manufacturers are only capable of producing two-thirds of the required hardware, it becomes clear that the PRC government must look abroad for a large part of the funding, technology and hardware for these projects.

Recent Restructuring in the Chinese Power Industry

The PRC government made a significant stride towards revitalizing its governmental structure at the Ninth National People's Congress in March 1998. At that meeting, it was announced that 15 ministries would be dissolved in order to begin the process of streamlining a unwieldy bureaucracy that has often hindered its developing market economy. Two of the main goals of this restructuring were delineating more clearly the spheres of control of these high-level organs of government and reducing the complexity and uncertainty of the governmental approval procedures.

The Ministry of Electric Power (MOEP), which formerly served both as the regulatory agency and the government's corporate arm in the Chinese power industry, was one of the ministries that was dissolved and it has since been replaced with the State Power Corporation.[12] This is however only the first step in the process of clearly separating the business functions and the regulatory authority in the power industry. It is expected that the operation and management functions will remain with the State Power Corporation, while macro-policy formulation and regulatory authority over power plants and the various grids will eventually be assumed by the Electric Power Division of the Economic Operation Department of the State Economic and Trade Commission (SETC). Most of the other dissolved industrial ministries have also had their former duties assumed by sub-administrations created under the umbrella of the SETC, which has now become a "super-ministry."

As part of this restructuring, 80% of the current staff in the dissolved industrial ministries are slated to be reassigned to government-run enterprises. In order to allow sufficient time for these workers to be absorbed into the economy, a similar restructuring on the provincial level and below will be delayed for three years.

While, as stated above, it is expected that the ultimate result of this restructuring will be a more streamlined and transparent bureaucracy and approval system, the short to medium term prospects continue to be unclear. As a result, there could be additional delays in the

11. Vladimir Baum, "Supply Industry to Undergo Radical Shift in Next Century: Global Electricity Generation", *Petroleum Economist*, February 1995.

12. *China Energy Watch*, May 1998, Volume 1, No. 7, Page 11.

approval process for a power project until the government clearly delineates the lines and scope of authority that result from this restructuring.[13]

Approval Thresholds

A common complaint often heard from foreigners in China is that the hardest part of doing business there is not getting the approvals you need, but determining which ones are necessary. One might say this is especially true for power projects, since a wide variety and large number of governmental ministries, bureaus and commissions, as well as government-related agencies, become involved at one stage or another.

Power generation projects differ from other types of investment schemes not only in their character and magnitude, but also in terms of the approval process. The State Power Corporation, as successor to the Ministry of Electric power (MOEP), currently has jurisdiction over all foreign investment in Chinese power projects.[14] This means that foreign-invested power project companies not only must obtain the Ministry of Foreign Trade and Economic Cooperation (MOFTEC) and, if large enough, State Council approvals that are necessary for all foreign investment enterprises (including both Sino-foreign joint ventures and wholly foreign-owned enterprises), such projects must also undergo a separate and more rigorous series of State Power Corporation and State Development and Planning Commission (SDPC)[15] inspections and approvals. In fact, as will be discussed in more detail later in this chapter, it is the SDPC that is the key approval agency with respect to power projects in China. All of the different approvals and permits from the other agencies and bureaus hinge upon the approval document issued by the SDPC.

In an arrangement similar to the hierarchy and vertical chain of authority under MOFTEC, there are local, municipal, provincial and even regional power bureaus that directly or indirectly report to the State Power Corporation (for ease of reference, the various power bureaus will hereinafter be referred to as "provincial or regional power bureaus"). Depending on the magnitude of the project in question, these subordinate provincial or regional power bureaus may be granted jurisdiction by the State Power Corporation to carry out the industry side of the approval process.

It is universally recognized that central MOFTEC approval is required for any project utilizing 30 million US dollars or more in total investment. Until recently, it was unclear how and where divisions in approval authority were made with respect to the State Power Corporation and its subordinate bureaus. Recent regulations have made clear that any power project in

13. Due to the PRC government restructuring, it will be several months before new approval patterns become fully established and clearly delineated to foreign investors. See Crosby, *China Mail*, April 1998, Page 2.

14. See Articles 15 and 35 of the *Ministry of Power Industry, Foreign Investment in Power Projects Several Provisions*, promulgated on and effective as of March 20, 1997 (hereinafter the "Foreign Investment Provisions").

15. As part of the recent restructuring, this agency's name was changed from the "State Planning Commission."

excess of 25 MW requires the approval of the State Power Corporation and the SDPC (or the SETC if the project involves the improvement of existing assets).[16] Therefore, the industry side of approvals for power projects has shifted away from an examination of the total amount of investment in the project and now focuses instead on the size of the project in terms of the amount of electricity produced. Since the types and magnitude of the projects that we are concerned with in this chapter clearly exceed this 25 MW threshold, our analysis will assume that both State Power Corporation and SDPC approvals are required. Furthermore, it should be noted that the PRC government has clearly shifted its support towards large projects that utilize domestically produced 300 MW or, more recently 600 MW, turbines. In fact, under such policy, it is unlikely that any project under 25 MW would receive the necessary approvals for synchronization to the relevant grid.[17] An additional requirement is that any joint venture or wholly foreign-owned enterprise with total investment of over 100 million US dollars must receive approval from the central State Council itself, the highest level of approval authority in China.

Table 1 below summarizes the relevant approval thresholds for power plants and the main government organs involved.[18]

Table 1: Approval Thresholds

Total Value or Megawattage	Approval Authority
US$100 million or above	State Council approval required (may delegate authority to the State Development and Planning Commission)
US$30 million or above[19]	Central Ministry of Foreign Trade and Economic Cooperation approval required
25 MW or above	State Power Corporation and State Development and Planning Commission approval required

16. See note 8 and accompanying text above.

17. In fact, Article 10 of the Foreign Investment Provisions explicitly states that "The State asks that newly built coal-fired power plants generally use units with single unit installed capacity of more than 300 MW, high parameters and high efficiency. The State strictly restricts 25 MW and smaller coal-fired condensing units and conventional fuel oil units and other projects that consume high levels of energy and produce high levels of pollution." Furthermore, according to a "departmental rule" issued by the State Economic and Trade Commission, which does not carry the force of an "administrative rule or regulation", conventional coal-fuel generating units within the coverage of large power grids that have a unit capacity of 100 MW and less (excluding generating units involving comprehensive utilization of resources), will be banned starting September 1, 1999. See the *Commercial and Industrial Investment Sector Catalogue to Halt Redundant Construction*, August 13, 1999

18. Exceptions: Municipalities which are subject to the Provisions of Provincial governments may only approve a project whose total investment does not exceed the thresholds established by the provincial government (usually less than US$30 million). Beijing, Shanghai, Tianjin and Chongqing, which are directly administered municipalities, may approve projects of up to US$30 million.

19. Some PRC government sources state that this threshold will be raised to US$50 million in the near future. See Crosby, *China Mail*, April 1998, Page 2.

The Approval Process

No project can commence in China without the informal (but fundamental) support of the local and provincial authorities. As a matter of public relations, the project sponsors should first determine whether the project is wanted and needed by the local people before further steps are taken. While this type of informal consent is not a substitute for the formal approvals that will be outlined here, it is crucial for ensuring that the project starts out on the right track.

Preliminary approval of the project proposal (lixiang)

The first official step in the approval process is to apply for a preliminary approval (*lixiang*) from the necessary industry-related approval authorities (municipal and provincial power bureaus, State Power Corporation and SDPC). In order to do so, the following initial documentation is required.

preliminary feasibility study report

Often, even before a foreign investor has been identified, the Chinese party (in the case of a joint venture) will have prepared what is known as a preliminary feasibility study report (*chubu kexingxing yanjiu baogao*).[20] The report will generally be written in Chinese only and is prepared strictly for the purpose of submission to the relevant government authorities. It consists of a general outline of the proposed project and usually includes a rough description of its most fundamental parameters and goals. Subjects that should be addressed include the size of the proposed project, both in projected power output and capital demands, sites under consideration, preliminary construction plans, possible sources of raw materials and potential purchasers of the electricity produced.

Once approved (as described below), the preliminary feasibility study report is often used as a promotional document for the project and is presented to potential foreign investors as evidence of a basic level of acceptance by the authorities. However, the preliminary feasibility study report should not be relied upon as anything more than a general introduction to the proposed project, and the government's approval of the report as well as the information contained in the report could become stale if the project encounters delays prior to identifying a potential foreign partner.

letter of intent of memorandum of understanding

In the case of a joint venture project, once the Chinese party (which, in many cases, is an investment arm of a provincial, municipal or local power bureau) has identified a potential

---

20. *Administration of Project Financing Conducted Outside China Tentative Procedures*, April 16, 1997 (the "1997 Procedures"), Articles 8 – 9; Foreign Investment Provisions, Article 17.

foreign investor to serve as project partner and the initial meetings between the parties have been productive, a letter of intent (*yixiang shu*) or memorandum of understanding (*liangjie beiwanglu*) will be executed between the parties. It is the first document to set out the primary terms of the understanding reached by the parties during their introductory meetings. The letter of intent or memorandum of understanding is similar to the Western legal concept of an agreement-in-principle and has no binding legal power. Nevertheless, since it will remain one of the basic components of the documentary package utilized throughout the approval process, its contents should be carefully considered and understood by both parties.

The letter of intent, or memorandum of understanding, tends to be at most a few pages long and should, in general terms, address such issues as:

- the proposed name of the project;
- its scope of operations;
- ratio of ownership;
- capital contributions of each party;
- preliminary schedule of such contributions;
- debt to equity ratio;
- project term;
- period of depreciation;
- method of profit allocation between the parties;
- factors for determining calculation of electricity tariffs;
- predicted annual output and method of sale;
- foreign exchange considerations; and
- confidentiality and exclusivity provisions covering the period of negotiation between the parties.

When deciding on the degree of specificity to employ at this stage of the negotiations, the foreign investor should weigh the benefits of flexibility and the fostering of good will against the importance of the specific deal points it wishes to secure. For example, while it may not matter if the specific monetary size of the project is approximated at this stage, it might be of crucial importance to the foreign party to insist on precise language regarding the determination of the tariff rate.

For a wholly foreign-owned project, the equivalent to the letter of intent might be a term sheet or project summary prepared by the foreign party or parties as an outline for the type of project that is being proposed.

project proposal

A document which is very similar to (or may incorporate) the letter of intent is the project proposal (*xiangmu jianyi shu*).[21] It may generally be thought of (although not always) as a more detailed and comprehensive version of the letter of intent. Both the letter of intent (or term sheet for wholly foreign-owned projects) and the project proposal are required for power projects.

When preparing the project proposal, particular emphasis should be given to:

- whether foreign or domestic equipment will be used;[22]
- the details of the construction and technical standards of the plant;[23]
- methods of financing; and
- projections regarding the future output and revenue generation of the plant during its lifetime and corresponding tariff rate setting mechanism or formula to be used.[24]

These crucial issues should be closely analyzed and discussed among the foreign investors and, if applicable, the relevant corporate arm of the Chinese power bureau that typically serves as joint venture partner in the project. Thoroughness at this stage can save the time and delay of having to redraft and renegotiate the finalized feasibility study report (see below) at a later time. It could also serve as evidence of a well-considered project and therefore leave a favourable impression with the approval authorities. Ultimately, however, the time and expense of this initial attention to detail must, of course, be weighed against the project's potential for success. And, as always, the foreign investor should be careful not to concede too much at such an early stage in the negotiations.

application report

Another document that may be necessary in order to obtain preliminary approval of a joint venture project proposal is the application report (*shenqing baogao*). It must be prepared when the Chinese partner intends to use State-owned assets as part of its contribution to the project. The report must address the scope and purpose of the joint venture project, the ratio of capital contributions of the parties, as well as details concerning the assets themselves.

---

21. 1997 Procedures, Article 8; Foreign Investment Provisions, Article 17.

22. The type of equipment used for the project (i.e., Chinese vs. imported) has become one of the main factors in determining whether a project will be favored for approval. The PRC government has made it very clear in recent years that plants utilizing Chinese equipment will receive priority treatment. Article 18 of the Foreign Investment Provisions states that, "The State will encourage the use of domestic equipment."

23. Particular attention should be paid to the *Measures of the Ministry of Electric Power, the Administration of Standardization Procedures*, promulgated March 16, 1994.

24. For obvious reasons, the tariff rate mechanism or formula is often the most highly negotiated issue for power projects in China and elsewhere.

If these assets are to be sold to the joint venture instead of contributed as part of the registered capital, then both the letter of intent and a certificate of creditworthiness of the foreign party must be included in the report. If the assets are currently owned directly by a central government organ, the application report must be submitted to the State Power Corporation; otherwise, for assets owned by a lower-level government entity, submission to the relevant subordinate power bureau will be sufficient.

After reviewing the application report, the relevant authority will issue a response in the form of an application report approval. Both the application report and the application report approval will then constitute part of the set of documents required for preliminary approval. For obvious reasons, a greenfield project will usually not require the preparation of an application report.

At this stage, the document package should include:
- the preliminary feasibility study report;
- the letter of intent (or term sheet);
- the project proposal; and
- the application report (if applicable).

provincial or regional power bureau approval

Once finalized by the project parties, all the project proposal preliminary approval documentation will be delivered by the Chinese party or, in the case of a wholly foreign-owned project, the foreign investor itself, to the relevant intermediate provincial or regional power bureau for approval.[25]

Once the proper provincial or regional power bureau with jurisdiction has been identified, it is the planning department (*guihua chu*) of that power bureau that coordinates the review of the preliminary approval documentation by the other departments of that power bureau. The planning department also submits the preliminary feasibility study report to other relevant non-power-related government organs, such as those related to:

- environmental protection;
- procurement of building materials;
- fuel supply;
- land use;
- construction;
- transportation;

25. In some cases, this intermediate approval authority may be one of the five regional power bureaus which concurrently oversee energy projects in several neighbouring provinces (divided geographically into north, northeast, east, central and northwest regions based on historical political and administrative divisions).

- utilities; and
- most importantly, the provincial development and planning commission.

After the provincial or regional power bureau planning department has collected and assimilated all of these intra- and extra-bureau recommendations, that power bureau will issue an examination opinion (*shencha yijian*) which either approves or rejects the project. If rejection hinges upon a correctable problem concerning the preliminary feasibility study report, then that power bureau will also inform the project applicants how the preliminary feasibility study report should be amended in order to gain approval. After being amended, the preliminary feasibility study report may then be resubmitted for review. When the preliminary feasibility study report is approved, the project will be assigned a document number which will be used throughout the rest of the approval process to refer to that project.

Assuming that the Chinese joint venture party or the sole foreign investor has obtained from the provincial or regional power bureau a favourable examination opinion concerning the preliminary feasibility study report, the planning department of that power bureau will then circulate the other preliminary documentation among the departments in that power bureau for review. At this stage, the document package should include:

- the preliminary feasibility study report;
- the examination opinion;
- the letter of intent (or term sheet);
- the project proposal;
- the application report and its approval certificate (if applicable); and
- a certificate of creditworthiness of the foreign partner (if applicable).

Once all departments within the provincial or regional power bureau have signed off on the preliminary project approval documentation, its general planning department (*zonghe guihua si*) will pass the documentation to the central State Power Corporation for review.

approval by the State Power Corporation

Within the State Power Corporation, the preliminary project approval documentation undergoes further detailed inspection. As at the lower level, the general planning department serves as coordinator of the project within the State Power Corporation. It distributes necessary documentation to internal departments such as the design department, the policy and legislation department and the international cooperation department. After each department has completed its review, the general planning department then has the task of synthesizing the various other departmental opinions into one unified recommendation of approval or denial for submission to the relevant official in the State Power Corporation who will make the final decision.

State Development and Planning Commission approval

Assuming the State Power Corporation approves the project, it will then submit a preliminary approval report (*lixiang baogao*) to the SDPC. A copy of the report will also be submitted to the provincial or regional power bureau(s) concerned with the project, who will forward a copy to the project applicants.

The role of the SDPC is to formulate the industrial plan for the whole country. The SDPC structures China's industry in the context of five-year plans, and China is currently in its ninth five-year plan, extending from 1996 to 2000. The SDPC is in charge of distributing Rmb50 billion of government resources to the projects it selects every year. Power projects account for a large portion of these allocated funds. For example, there were 23 power projects included on the SDPC list of 102 Key National Infrastructure Projects of 1999.[26]

Key departments within the SDPC include the foreign investment department (*waizi si*) and the long-term planning department (*changqi jihua si*). Once these and other departments conduct their reviews and give their recommendations, the findings are presented to the relevant SDPC official in charge of power projects, who, based upon these recommendations, either approves or rejects the project.[27] Evidence of SDPC approval takes the form of a report outlining the details of the project and suggesting what should be addressed in the final draft of the feasibility study report. In addition to providing the SDPC approval report to the power bureau and the project applicants, the SDPC will also send copies to various other government organs and ministries that will become more directly involved with the project at a later stage. This action effectively completes the process of preliminary approval (*lixiang*).

It must be noted that, for joint venture projects, submission and inspection of the preliminary feasibility study report may be undertaken at any time by the Chinese party, whether or not a foreign partner has been identified. Therefore, the preliminary approval is often a starting point for foreign investment. While entering into a project that has already obtained such preliminary approval may seem like a blessing to a foreign investor, this is not always the case. The foreign investor is often not entirely satisfied with the terms of the project as approved, therefore requiring time-consuming and costly re-approvals and amendments to the *lixiang* documentation before further steps are taken.

---

26. *China Energy Watch*, June 1999, Volume 2, No. 6, Page 6.

27. If a project originally gains approval from the SDPC as a wholly domestically funded project, but later has to seek foreign funding due to lack of local capital, the project will have to reapply for approval from the SDPC. Other changes such as in debt/equity ratio, equipment procurement and increased size, might also necessitate such re-approval if they are great enough to have a material impact upon the fundamental characteristics of the project.

Final industry approval

finalized feasibility study report

After preliminary approval (*lixiang*) is obtained from the SDPC, the project documentation must undergo substantially the same round of review in order to obtain final approval. However, for this round, the feasibility study report is submitted in its finalized form and an initialed joint venture contract (or articles of association of the wholly foreign-owned enterprise), instead of a mere letter of intent (or term sheet), must be provided as evidence of the terms of the project and/or the parties' agreement to cooperate.

The following is a list of standard items to include in a finalized feasibility study report:

- general survey of the project and description of objectives;
- financing proposal and schedule;
- total cost estimate and break-down;
- electricity tariff;
- project schedule and milestone dates;
- procurement and equipment;
- description of the proposed project company and operation;
- maintenance and transferral proposal; and
- environmental impact report.

It is at this stage that the heavy negotiation begins between the project sponsors, lenders and the relevant approval authorities and related parties; they know that the project is theoretically viable and the task at hand is to hammer out the gritty details. The most important (and probably most contentious) issues include:

- the formula for calculating the electricity tariff;
- allocation of exchange rate fluctuations;
- inflation and price fluctuation risk;
- division of management responsibilities; and
- the detailed technical specifications for all the equipment to be utilized for the project.

ancillary documentation

Once again, the more documentation that can be assembled at an early stage, the better. In addition, it is important to obtain as early as possible the declarations and statements of support from all the bureaus, agencies and organizations that are crucial to the success of the project, such as:

- State Environmental Protection Administratiion;
- Ministry of Railways;

- Ministry of Transportation;
- Ministry of Construction;
- MOFTEC;
- People's Bank of China;
- Ministry of Finance;
- State Price Bureau;
- Ministry of Labour and Social Security;
- Local Land Bureau; and
- State Administration of Foreign Exchange.

These "ancillary" approvals will differ from those obtained at the *lixiang* stage both in the degree of specificity and the level of authority consulted. For example, if coal is going to be procured domestically, firm commitments to supply specific quantities should be obtained, not just statements that adequate amounts are available, and a document evidencing such commitment may have to be requested in this instance from the Ministry of Land Resources (which will assume or has assumed the responsibilities of the Ministry of Coal) instead of from one of its subordinate bureaus or the local mine. Similarly, the Ministry of Railways would now review and approve the transportation arrangements that were negotiated locally at the *lixiang* stage. Therefore, the ultimate package submitted for final approval should consist of the finalized feasibility study report itself and multiple annexes consisting of such departmental statements and declarations.

Because a significant amount of crucial new information is included in the finalized feasibility study report, this is the time when issues previously ignored or avoided may suddenly come to the fore. In addition, there may be points of disagreement between the approval authorities and the project applicants from the first round that remain unresolved in the finalized feasibility study report. Such a disagreement might, for instance, relate to the procurement of fuel or the proposed tariff formula. If either situation arises, the process could become greatly delayed while these points are being resolved.

One way around this type of obstacle is to employ a PRC consulting company that may have close ties with the relevant bureaus involved in the dispute. In many cases, the government bureau or agency involved in the dispute may itself have a corporate consulting arm that can be hired by the project company to "facilitate" the dispute. Upon payment of the fee to this consulting company, the foreign investor may see the issues in dispute become resolved in a very short time! Therefore, it may be worthwhile to ask the opposing party in the dispute whether such "consulting" services are available for hire.

State Council approval

It should be reiterated that any projects over the $100 million threshold for total investment must go through one more layer of approval – the State Council (see "Table 1: Approval Thresholds" above). However, it is the usual practice of the State Council to designate the SDPC to act on its behalf in reviewing the project. The SDPC will prepare a short summary of the project along with its recommendation and submit this to the State Council. Assuming all has gone relatively smoothly up to this point, notification of final State Council approval should be received shortly thereafter.

MOFTEC approval

Once the SDPC official in charge of power projects gives the final approval, the provincial power bureau is notified that it may authorize the formal execution of the joint venture contract (or the articles of association in the case of a wholly foreign-owned project). It is only at this stage that the MOFTEC approval process commences. This means that the proposed project must undergo a review for conformance with the more general rules of foreign investment and the formation of foreign investment enterprises. Generally, while MOFTEC approval is not simply a rubber stamp, any project that has already been blessed by the SDPC (or the State Council) should have little trouble in eventually securing approval from MOFTEC. Because MOFTEC's review focuses specifically on compliance with the relevant foreign investment laws, the fact that the subject of the review is a project company for a power project should not be an insignificant factor (regardless of whether it takes the form of a joint venture or a wholly foreign-owned enterprise).

Documents that should be prepared for submission to MOFTEC include:

- executed joint venture contract (if applicable);
- executed articles of association (roughly similar to the Western legal concept of articles or certificate of incorporation);
- draft of the power purchase (off-take) contract[28] between the proposed project company and the provincial or regional power bureau (as well as any other contractual buyers of the project's output);
- draft of the dispatch contract;
- draft of the connection (grid access) contract;
- draft of the fuel supply contract;
- drafts of all credit agreements with the financiers of the project;

28. Many of the required terms of this document are stipulated in the Foreign Investment Provisions, the State Council Administration of the Operation of Power Grid Regulations, issued June 29, 1993 and effective November 1, 1993, and the Ministry of *Power Industry, Standardizing the Administration of Power Purchase Contracts Tentative Procedures*, promulgated and effective on September 29, 1996.

- drafts of any necessary equipment leases or purchase contracts;
- construction plans and preliminary draft of the EPC contract, assuming a lead construction company has been identified;
- draft of the operation and maintenance contract, assuming the joint venture company will not operate the facility itself;
- land use certificate for the proposed project site;
- environmental compliance certificate;
- confirmation of foreign exchange availability issued by the relevant branch of the State Administration of Foreign Exchange (the issue of foreign exchange is discussed in more detail below);
- MOFTEC certificates of approval and business licenses of all Chinese joint venture partners (if applicable);
- evidence that the foreign party or parties have been duly established in their home countries; and
- appraisal certificates for any assets to be contributed by the parties to the project as part of their registered capital (for the Chinese party, the State Administration for State-owned Assets and/or the relevant land administration bureau must be consulted).

When MOFTEC approval is received in the form of an official certificate of approval (*pizhun zhengshu*) the joint venture or wholly foreign-owned enterprise must register with the State Administration of Industry and Commerce (SAIC) within 30 days to obtain its business license. At this point, the power project has completed the entire approval process and the interested parties may begin to focus on bringing the first phase of the project on-line. The project company shall commence operation by holding its first board meeting within the period specified in its articles of association and, at that time, may formally execute the ancillary contracts referred to above (power purchase contract, etc.).

State Administration of Foreign Exchange

During this final round of review, many additional bureaus and ministries will become involved in the approval process as peripheral, but still very important, players. One of these is the State Administration of Foreign Exchange (SAFE, whose English name prior to October 1, 1996 was the State Administration of Exchange Control, or SAEC). SAFE is the powerful national governmental body which is responsible for allocating foreign exchange to projects and allowing Renminbi-denominated profits to be converted into foreign exchange for remittance to foreign investors. Without the consent of this vital organ, a project that might otherwise be perfectly viable would face serious problems, since foreign investors would be stymied in their ability to realize exportable proceeds from their investments. For this reason, most project developers will seek acquiescence from the national SAFE or one of its provincial branches as soon as the preliminary feasibility study report is approved. Such foresight helps to insure against unpleasant surprises after much time, effort and expense has been sunk into the project.[29]

Improper approval

If a project receives insufficient approvals or an investor attempts to portray a project as being smaller than it actually is (by purposely under-reporting its size or attempting to split it into several phases), there is a risk that it could be decommissioned by the relevant authorities and have sanctions imposed upon the parties thereto. While a belief that time is of the essence has spurred some investors to take such a risk, many have found that any time saved by avoiding the process of seeking central approval is not worth the time and effort required for investors and financiers to "get comfortable" with the project's lack of standard national-level approvals. In fact, a project will most likely fail to obtain financing from foreign banks without being able to show that it has been properly approved and fully sanctioned by all interested government authorities.

Strategies for re-approval

As mentioned earlier, the most important milestone for the establishment of a power project is to obtain approval from the SDPC. The SDPC approval certificate underpins all other project approvals and is the clearest evidence of central government support. However, as projects often take many years to complete, some of the approvals obtained along the way, including the SDPC approval, may become stale as the project begins to diverge in scope or scale from its approved parameters. What often occurs is that, as the project becomes delayed, costs escalate until they eventually exceed the pre-approved limit. At that point, the issue becomes whether the project should proceed with an inaccurate SDPC approval certificate, or whether the project sponsors should reapply to the SDPC for an amendment to its original approval.

One factor to bear in mind when making this decision is what is known as the "10% Rule." This informal rule-of-thumb states that so long as a project does not exceed (or fall short of) its originally approved investment amount (or such other relevant financial target), by a margin of 10% there is no need to apply for an amendment to the approval certificate in hand. The 10% Rule is generally accepted by both the foreign investment community in China, and (unofficially) the governmental bureaucracy, and it generally applies to approvals from any governmental agency with respect to numerical objectives. Therefore, under current practice, there is some flexibility with respect to approval targets.

29. Several provisions relating to SAFE and project financing can be found in the 1997 Procedures, Articles 11 – 16.

Assuming that the project has already exceeded the 10% Rule limit, a difficult dilemma faces the investors. If they apply for re-approval too early, it will cause delay for the project and drain its "forward momentum" (which can be a very important factor with respect to the morale of the project development team, both on the foreign and Chinese side). If a request for re-approval is delayed for too long, there is a risk that approval may be denied, and by that time, much additional time and expense would have been invested in the development of the project. Furthermore, all of the "ancillary" approvals (from MOFTEC, SAFE, etc.) that cited the terms of the original SDPC approval would also have to be amended so as to be faithful to the ultimate terms of the project. Seeking re-approval may also preclude the project's ability to apply for re-approval at the end of the project after financing has been arranged, which can be instrumental in providing additional comfort to the project's financiers that their financing package has been accepted (the SDPC will review the same project only so many times).

While the best strategy would obviously be to obtain SDPC approval for the correct terms and parameters in the first instance, this is not always possible in the context of a large and complicated power project that may involve project financing (see below). Therefore, once SDPC approval has been obtained, the project sponsors should cautiously monitor the status of the proposed project in relation to the approved terms and parameters. If it starts to deviate from the terms and parameters (especially if it exceeds the 10% Rule), the project sponsors need to consider carefully how to proceed to ensure that, in the end, the project that is financed and built is the same project described in the final approval certificates.

Duration and Strategies of the Approval Process

There are several factors that make it extremely difficult to estimate the amount of time required for each stage of the approval process, and, consequently, for completion of the entire procedure as detailed above. Such factors include:

- the size and complexity of the project;
- the sophistication and experience of the individual governmental officials involved;
- the work load of the approval organizations at the time of review;
- the political importance of the specific project or the political atmosphere surrounding power projects in general at that time;
- the region involved and the relative need for power in that region; and
- the speed of progression of the negotiations conducted between the parties.

This list, however, is by no means exhaustive. Therefore, it should come as no surprise that the most important virtue to possess when attempting to establish a power project (or any other project in China, for that matter) is patience. Closing deals could take anything from 18 months to five years. Individual projects are bound to differ due to the unique nature of power projects in general, the specific details of each individual project and the customary unpredictability involved in gaining approvals in China.

By far the most important factor influencing the speed of the approval process is the time it takes to assemble a complete package of letters of support and other approval documentation from the myriad of non-power industry bodies that must be consulted. Once the parties have been able to make arrangements for the fuel supply, obtain environment clearance for the constructions plans and cover all of the other details of the project, it is possible for State Power Corporation approval to be obtained within a matter of weeks or days. However, if it turns out that crucial parts of the documentary package are missing, the project sponsors will be required to obtain the necessary certificates or other documents before the old support letters obtained at the *lixiang* stage become outdated. Therefore, a high degree of organization, preparation and cooperation at the early phases of both preliminary and final approval can be invaluable towards facilitating the approval process.

Regional and national politics undoubtedly play a significant role in the approval process as interested local officials lobby the relevant agencies for favors with respect to their particular pet projects. This largely obscure process leads to slower and less predictable approvals as the pending projects vie for position behind closed doors in Beijing. Obviously, the political connections of the local project sponsors as well as the economic and technical soundness of the project itself are key factors in achieving necessary approvals and neither factor should be overlooked by the foreign sponsor. Whether this process will become more transparent and predictable in light of the recent reforms and the government crackdown on corruption is still unclear.

Approval-related Issues

Project financing

As China's need for electricity grows and the sizes of plants being built continues to increase (both due to governmental regulations and in order to capitalize on economies of scale), projects are increasingly being financed on a project finance basis, whereby only the anticipated proceeds from the project and project assets are liable to be used for repayment of the debt to foreign financiers. In fact, foreign investment of this kind has enjoyed a top seat on the mantle of state policy in recent years.[30] In order to more closely regulate this phenomenon, the PRC government has promulgated two regulations: the *Administration of Project Financing Conducted Outside China Tentative Procedures*, effective as of April 16, 1997 (the "1997 Procedures") and the *Administration of Taking Out of International Commercial Loans by Organizations in China Procedures*, promulgated by SAFE on September 24, 1997 effective as of January 1, 1998 (the "1998 Procedures").

30. *China Energy Watch*, March 1999, Volume 2, No. 3, Page 15.

1997 Procedures

The 1997 Procedures, jointly issued by the SDPC and SAFE, constitute the comprehensive set of rules that are expressly applicable to projects financed on a project finance basis and call for additional approvals to be obtained for project financed projects that are not required for other types of financing methods. Both the 1997 Procedures and the 1998 Procedures define project finance as a method of financing whereby foreign exchange funds are raised outside China in the name of a construction project itself and in which only anticipated revenues from the project and project assets are liable to be used for repayment of the foreign debt. The 1997 Procedures set forth detailed guidelines not only on procedural requirements for approvals, but also substantive requirements and restrictions. The 1997 Procedures also provide that the terms and conditions of all project financing must be reviewed and approved by SAFE in order to confirm that they are "competitive." As neither the 1997 Procedures nor the 1998 Procedures clarify what is meant by "competitive," SAFE is effectively vested with the power to review the substantive terms of the project financing. This authority to coordinate and review project financing may be viewed as analogous to MOFTEC's authority over foreign investment.

The 1997 Procedures call for approval by the central government of all project financing, regardless of the amount involved. After preliminary examination by the local department-in-charge of the electric power industry, the project proposal and finalized feasibility study report must be submitted to the central SDPC (via the local planning commission) for final examination and approval. One important point about this step is that the 1997 Procedures stipulate that letters of intent from the relevant foreign lending institutions must be included in the submitted finalized feasibility study report. As most financiers would be very reluctant to provide such a commitment at such an early stage in the development of the project and may require additional incentives to do so, it seems clear that this requirement (if it continues to be enforced) will raise controversy and cause the developmental costs of any project financed project to be increased.

According to the 1997 Procedures, determination of the electricity tariffs must be approved by the relevant price control authorities, and domestic revenues earned by the project may not be denominated in foreign currency. However, tariff formulas are allowed to contain provisions to take into account exchange rate fluctuations and the prices of inputs, so long as they comply with price control provisions, enable the project to generate a stable stream of anticipated revenues and take into account local sustainability.

The 1997 Procedures also reiterate the standing policy that no domestic financial institutions are permitted to issue guarantees in connection with project finance nor are non-financial domestic institutions permitted to make any form of financial guarantee. Under these restrictions, performance guarantees by domestic entities seem to be allowed (provided all other necessary approvals are obtained from the various departments-in-charge), but guarantees relating to the availability of foreign exchange (which, in the past, have usually been issued by the government itself) are more suspect under this new wording.

One problem presented by the 1997 Procedures is that, owing to the ban on financial guarantees by financial and non-financial institutions in China, it is more challenging to structure the financing as a limited recourse loan. This restriction on domestic guarantees may be overcome by structuring the investment as a loan to the principal foreign investor in the project company, who subsequently loans the funds to the project as a shareholder loan and guarantees repayment to the lenders through a pledge of its interests in the project.

1998 Procedures

The 1998 Procedures relate to the borrowing of international commercial loans and, unlike previous similar regulations, apply also to foreign-invested enterprises. Under these Procedures, any international commercial loans borrowed for the purposes of project finance must be approved by SAFE (on behalf of the People's Bank of China). Without SAFE approval, borrowers are banned from depositing funds onshore, paying funds offshore or converting foreign loans into Renminbi for local use.

Build-operate-transfer project financing and its approval process

China began to experiment with the build-operate-transfer (BOT)[31] method for power projects beginning in 1995. In that year, MOFTEC released the *Notice Regarding Issues Relating to Using BOT Methods to Attract Foreign Investment*, which provided that the PRC government was and will continue to be actively investigating ways of adopting BOT financing to attract foreign investment.[32] A few months later, the State Power Corporation, the former Ministry of Power Industry (MPI), and the Ministry of Communications jointly issued a Circular which states that China has begun experimentation with BOT and other concessionary arrangements; and that the scope of this "pilot" program should include 2 x 300 MW or above thermal generation plants and 250 MW and under hydro-electric projects of medium- to long-term duration.[33]

Foreign developers of independent power production projects initially had high expectations for utilizing the BOT method in China, because in theory, the BOT method offers several

31. Or build-own-operate-transfer (BOOT). This increasingly popular form of international project financing involves a plant being build by a private entity with non-recourse loans (usually funded by a combination of foreign and/or domestic investors), owned and operated by that entity for a specified period of time to allow investors to recoup their investment plus a premium, and then turned over to the Government free-of-charge or, perhaps, for nominal consideration.

32. Issued January 16, 1995.

33. *Several Issues Concerning the Examination, Approval and Administration of Experimental Foreign-invested Concession Projects Circular* (the "Circular"), issued August 21, 1995.

major advantages to both foreign investors and the PRC government, including: (i) the competitive bidding process will give an indication of (A) the true market value of a power project and (B) what constitutes a satisfactory return on equity for foreign bidders, (ii) the practice of provincial authorities agreeing to projects without central government approval will be curbed, (iii) the regulatory delays resulting from "pre-packaged" project approvals prior to bidding will be reduced, (iv) the potential for enhancing operating efficiencies due to 100% foreign ownership and control over projects will increase and (v) the rate of return on investment can potentially be above those customarily allowed in joint venture model projects assuming that the outcome of the competitive bidding process is in one's favor and assuming that the project sponsors can achieve operational efficiencies.[34]

Despite the early optimism for BOT projects, only two power projects and one water treatment facility have been established pursuant to the procedures outlined in the BOT Circular.[35] Nevertheless, the Circular seems like a step in the right direction from the standpoint of foreign investors. A new BOT law and related regulations were expected to be issued by the end of 1997, however, promulgation has been delayed due in part to the major governmental restructuring that took place in 1998 and to the related intergovernmental confusion it has created. Therefore, despite the lack of clarity and certainty in the BOT Circular, it will remain the principal law governing BOT projects until the BOT law is promulgated.[36]

As noted above, the BOT method is attractive to foreign independent power producers because it is viewed as a potential way to avoid the extremely long, uncertain and arduous approval process that is a fact of life for traditional joint venture or wholly foreign-owned power projects in China.[37]

The BOT approval and tendering process is covered in Articles five through eight of the BOT Circular. The BOT approval process begins with the preparation of a preliminary feasibility study report[38] by the planning department of the provincial (district or municipal) government where the project is located and the relevant industry department in charge in accordance

34. *Power In China*, 1998, see note 3, Page 57.

35. The three government approved "pilot" BOT projects include the Guangxi Zhuang Autonomous Region Laibin B Power Plant BOT Project, the Hunan Changsha Power Plant BOT Project and the Chengdu Water Plant BOT Project. It is important to note that other recent power projects in China have been described as "BOT" projects because they contained concession elements, however, none of the projects were carried out pursuant to the BOT Circular procedures. These quasi-BOT projects include the Meizhou Wan, Puqi and Shandong Zhonghua power projects. For example, the main difference between the BOT pilot projects and the Puqi project is that bidders for the Puqi project were selected by invitation rather than by public tender. See *Power in China*, Page 52, 61 – 62.

36. The new BOT laws and regulations will most likely follow the basic principles of the BOT Circular. See *Power in China*, Page 57.

37. *Power In China*, Page 54.

38. Article 5 of the BOT Circular requires that the feasibility study report must fall within the medium- and long-term plans of the PRC government.

with the current administrative planning system (usually the provincial or regional power bureau). The preliminary feasibility study report will be examined for approval by the State Power Corporation, the SDPC and, if the project involves investment over US$100 million, the State Council.[39]

Once the preliminary approval is received, (i) the provincial (district or municipal) government must draft the project agreements, the documents relating to sponsor pre-qualification and the bid tender invitations, and (ii) the SDPC must organize a bid evaluation committee.[40] The bid evaluation committee will issue an open invitation to sponsors for pre-qualification and will compile a short list of qualified bidders based on the responses received. Thereafter, the qualified sponsors are given the opportunity to ask questions and seek clarification from the bid evaluation committee on any issue. The evaluation committee will issue supplementary answers to all qualified bidders answering such questions.

The qualified bidders then submit bids to the evaluation committee for evaluation. The bid submission package includes the following information:

- feasibility study;
- tariff structure;
- financing proposal;
- timetable; and
- comments on the project documents (including assumptions and required modifications).[41]

After the winning bidder is selected,[42] the Concession Agreement will be (i) initialed by the winning bidder and the relevant provincial (district or municipal) government, (ii) submitted for approval to the SDPC and (iii) if the project involves investment over US$100 million, submitted for approval to the State Council.[43]

---

39. BOT Circular, Article 5.

40. BOT Circular, Article 6. The bid evaluation committee is composed of representatives from the provincial or regional power bureau, the relevant provincial (district or municipal) government departments and technical advisors.

41. Lenders' comments will be incorporated into the documents at this stage because it is difficult to amend the Concession Agreement once it has been approved. See *Power in China*, Page 58.

42. The winning bidder is selected largely based on two factors: the lowest tariff and the technical merits of the project proposal. See *Power in China*, Page 58.

43. Whereas Article 18 of the 1997 Procedures provides that laws that govern particular types of project financing shall take precedence over the 1997 Procedures, it may be the case that the financing documents under a BOT project need not be submitted to SDPC and SAFE for approval as is required by the 1997 Procedures. However, it is probably wise to submit the financing documents to SDPC and SAFE for approval regardless of this provision in the 1997 Procedures.

Once the Concession Agreement is approved, it will be signed by the relevant parties. Thereafter, the sponsor party must go through the regular process of seeking approval from MOFTEC for the articles of association of the project company (in the case of a WFOE) and of registering the project company with the relevant administration of industry and commerce.[44]

To date, the BOT pilot projects in China have all enjoyed a relatively efficient approval process. This efficiency is mainly the result of: (i) the priority and support given to the projects by the central government, (ii) the guidance and advice given to the provincial governments from foreign legal and financial advisors and (iii) the reliance on precedents set in the successive BOT projects which has lead to more standardized documentation. One can only hope that past practice and the promulgation of the new BOT law and regulations will further improve the efficiency of the BOT approval process.[45]

Capped Returns vs. Tariff Controls

One major problem in recent years for investors in Chinese power projects has been de facto caps imposed by the PRC government on investment returns. While projects in other Asian countries have had projected rates of return of around 18 to 20% or even more, investors in Chinese power projects in recent years have complained that they have been limited to returns of 12 to 15%. These caps are easy to enforce by the government, since it often both supplies the raw building materials and fuel to the plant, and regulates the sale price of the output electricity. When such relatively low returns are viewed in conjunction with the risks that accompany any investment in China (not to mention large, capital-intensive power projects), it is no surprise to find that many foreign investors have taken their power project business elsewhere.

There is evidence, however, that the PRC government has been attempting to ease this "bamboo ceiling" in order to re-attract foreign investors, whose capital is an absolute necessity if China is to meet its electricity needs in the coming decades. Under new policies of the Chinese Government, there has been a shift away from the former emphasis on the level of returns enjoyed by the investor and the focus is now instead on the tariff level and the operational efficiency of the project. In other words, if the investors are able to manage the plant well and keep costs down, their returns will be high. If the plant is run inefficiently, the tariff will not be increased to allow for compensation and returns will correspondingly be lower. Furthermore, under the Electricity Law (see below), the tariff level is to be reviewed annually by the SDPC, State Power Corporation and Provincial Price Control Bureau.

Limitations on Foreign Ownership

Due to the crucial economic and social importance of power plants, the PRC government has historically been reluctant to allow foreigners to own a majority stake in power projects.

---

44. See BOT Circular, Articles 7 – 8; *Power In China*, Page 59.

45. *Power In China*, Page 65.

However, not only has the government loosened the restrictions on foreign ownership of power plants, it has also increased the investment channels for such projects (see BOT projects above). Currently, foreign investors are allowed to invest in both new and expansion coal-fired, hydro-electric, nuclear and new technology power plants. Under the Foreign Investment Provisions[46] such investment may be made by way of establishing an equity joint venture enterprise, cooperative joint venture enterprise[47] or wholly foreign-owned enterprise, purchasing shares in a project company that are either issued internationally or within China in the form of B shares, purchasing inventory assets of an existing plant or investing in a BOT project by sponsoring a project company. The only restrictions remaining on foreign ownership of power plants are that wholly foreign-owned enterprises may not independently operate nuclear power plants or 250 MW and larger hydro-electric plants; in such types of projects, PRC entities must have a major holding or leadership position. Therefore, foreign investors now have a wide range of possibilities with respect to both the type and size of power project in which to invest and the manner of making such investment.

Foreign Exchange Convertibility

The PRC government has made it clear that neither it nor any other PRC entity shall be permitted to grant guarantees for an investor's ability to exchange Renminbi profits for foreign exchange. As a result, unless a project is fortunate enough to find a purchaser that will pay for the power in foreign exchange (which would be unlikely), investors are left without firm assurance that they will have the ability to exchange Renminbi profits for foreign exchange and to remit such profits out of China in hard currency.[48]

While attempts have been made to allay these currency convertibility fears through other means, the central government has made it clear that it does not approve of domestic foreign exchange guarantees and deems them to be unenforceable. It views such local dealings as attempts to circumvent central government control over the power industry and has even threatened to take punitive action against the parties involved. Therefore, relying upon local or provincial guarantees, whether from government or bank sources, could result in both financial losses and tarnished reputations for foreign investors.

---

46. Foreign Investment Provisions, Article 9.

47. The main difference between an equity joint venture and a cooperative joint venture is in the permitted division of control and profit distribution. While profits of equity joint ventures must be distributed according to the ratio of contributions to registered capital by each investor, the parties to a cooperative joint venture may agree upon profit distribution and control provisions in the joint venture contract that differ from the ratio of ownership.

48. While the PRC government has expressed a desire to make the Renminbi fully convertible in the near future, in light of the recent financial crisis in Asia, such a step is unlikely to be taken soon. In the meantime, the government will continue to rely on foreign exchange adjustment centers (swap centers) (first established in 1986) as a stop-gap measure before full convertibility is achieved. However, there are limits on the amount of foreign exchange available for conversion from Renminbi at government-controlled swap centers. In fact, only 10% of China's foreign exchange volume changes hands in the swap centers; the other 90% is traded on the China Foreign Exchange Trading Center or interbank market. Thus, even having a swap center access permit in hand does not guarantee that adequate foreign exchange will be available to the foreign investor, especially if there is a national or regional shortage of such reserves in effect.

Finally, while no explicit sovereign currency convertibility guarantees are available, some investors view approval of the SDPC and the State Council essentially as tacit guarantees. In other words, in the event of a currency shortage, projects which have received such high-level central government approvals will likely be given priority access to reserves, even though such a provision is nowhere stated explicitly. The reasoning is that although there may be a shortage, the foreign-invested enterprises that will bear the brunt of the shortage will be the smaller projects that are viewed as less significant by the government or projects that have failed to gain the proper approvals. Larger and more politically and socially significant power projects will most likely be protected from such a fate. Therefore, while foreign currency remains a great concern to investors and financiers alike, some comfort may be taken once a project has been sanctioned by the highest levels of government.

Term Limitations

Article 12 of the Foreign Investment Provisions stipulates that the term (not including the construction period) of Sino-foreign joint venture power projects (as well as wholly foreign-owned projects) shall be limited to 20 years for coal-fired projects, 30 years for hydro-electric projects and 25 years for nuclear power plants. At the end of this period, the plant must be turned over in BOT fashion to the Chinese party, and there is no mention of any opportunity to extend these terms. Therefore, when negotiating power project agreements, and tariff arrangements in particular, investors must keep these term limitations in mind.

Four-Stage Reform of the Power Industry

A very significant development in recent years affecting power projects in China was the decision by the PRC government to implement a major four-stage reform of the power industry. The first stage took place from 1997 to 1998 and involved the abolition of the Ministry of Power Industry (MPI) and the establishment of the State Power Corporation. The second stage runs from 1998 to 2000 and requires the corporatization of all existing provincial and regional power bureaus and the separation of distribution and production functions (*changwang fenkai*).[49] The third stage will run from 2001 to 2010 and will involve the establishment of a competitive electricity market (*jianli fadian shichang*) (see "Merchant Power" below). The fourth stage will take place from 2010 onwards, and will involve the complete separation of production, distribution, sales and delivery functions and assets, resulting in a power production and supply network that is handled on a competitive market basis.[50]

49. *State Economic and Trade Commission, Relevant Questions Concerning Intensifying the Reform of the Power Industry System Opinion*, issued by the SETC and circulated by the Office of the State Council on December 24, 1998.

50. See *China Law & Practice*, August 1999, Volume 18, No. 6, Page 66; *China Energy Watch*, February 1999, Volume 2, No. 2, Pages 4 – 9.

Merchant Power

The PRC government's new policy that prohibits guaranteed tariffs or minimum off-take obligations is aimed at the implementation of a pool market system nation-wide by 2001. The move is designed to increase competition among generators thus resulting in lower on-grid tariffs. The government has already begun implementing experimental pool power markets in Shanghai municipality and Shandong, Fujian, Zhejiang, Liaoning, Heilongjiang and Jilin provinces. Foreign developers and their bankers with existing long-term off-take agreements already in place have scrambled to meet with government officials to discuss the impact the pool system will have on their off-take agreements, and were initially assured that the new policy does not affect projects with signed power purchase agreements that have received final approval from the SDPC. However, some officials in the State Power Corporation have stated that the new policy will be applied retroactively to projects in the experimental locations but only prospectively with regard to projects in other locations. Therefore, it is highly likely that the pool market will have an impact on the foreign invested projects in experimental areas because the off-take agreements may have to be renegotiated, possibly as early as 2001, and because they will eventually have to compete with other projects to sell into the pool market.[51]

Electricity Law

The national Electricity Law, which became effective on April 1, 1996, serves as the basis for a relatively new system of administration of the electric power industry. While the Electricity Law does not directly relate to the approval process, there are many provisions which may be relevant for foreign investors. For example, while the State Council is responsible for the nation-wide supervision and management of the electric power industry,[52] any necessary approvals for projects or network interaction below the autonomous region, municipality or provincial level may be undertaken by local approval authorities.[53] The ones which prospectively may have the most impact on foreigners are outlined below.

While the State Council is responsible for the nation-wide supervision and management of the electric power industry,[54] any necessary approvals for projects or network interaction below the autonomous region, municipality or provincial level may be undertaken by local-level approval authorities.[55] Investors in electric power production should be given priority access to the electricity produced by their projects.[56] Power projects must abide by the

51. See *Project Finance International*, Issue 159, Pages 14-15; *China Law & Practice* February 1999, Volume 13, No. 1, Pages 81-82.

52. *PRC, Electricity Law*, Article 6.

53. Id. Articles 38, 39 and 40.

54. Id. Article 6.

55. Id. Articles 38, 39 and 40.

56. Id. Article 13.

national policies regarding electric power development, and equipment and techniques officially declared obsolete by the government may not be used in power projects.[57]

Electric power supply units shall supply electricity to consumers within certain approved 'operational zones' and there shall be only one electric power supply unit within each 'operational zone.' Each electric power supply unit must also obtain an 'electric power supply permit' before beginning operations.[58] Electricity rates should include such important items as costs, reasonable profits and tax allowances according to law.[59] Electricity tariffs shall vary according to the category and time period of consumption and, within the same power network, identical rates should apply to similar consumers.[60] The government should encourage power development in rural areas,[61] but the electricity rate for agricultural consumption should be determined based on a low rate of return for investors.[62]

The last sixteen substantive articles of the Electricity Law are devoted to the subject of legal liabilities, and provide for fairly precise penalties for violation of any of the foregoing provisions. For instance, if obsolete equipment is utilized in violation of Article 14, the obsolete equipment shall be confiscated and a fine of not more than Rmb50,000 shall be imposed.[63]

Conclusion

As can be seen from the information presented in this chapter, obtaining approvals for power projects in China is a formidable task. Not only must the conventional MOFTEC approvals be received, but separate State Power Corporation and SDPC power industry approvals must be obtained as well. While such an arduous and time-consuming process may seem wasteful and inefficient to some investors, it is nonetheless entirely consistent with the Chinese practice of governance and regulation by mutual consent. Only after all governmental authorities with any degree of interest in and authority over the project have given their consent may a project proceed as planned. This is meant to ensure that the project has received all necessary approvals prior to the start of construction and will not encounter any regulatory road blocks in the future. For projects in which so much capital is put at risk, this assurance, for what it its worth, is critical. Therefore, it could be said that the approval process in its present form serves to reassure foreign investors as much as it allows the Chinese authorities to protect China's national sovereignty.

57. Id. Article 14.

58. Id. Article 25.

59. Id. Article 36.

60. Id. Article 41.

61. Id. Article 47.

62. Id. Article 50.

63. *PRC, Electricity Law,* Article 62.

While it may not seem ideal to those who have to endure it, the present Chinese approval system has been greatly improved in recent years. Less than two decades ago, China suffered from an underdeveloped economy and an almost complete lack of regulations governing foreign investment, and government-promoted prejudice against foreign investment was widespread. This situation has changed rapidly, to the benefit of Chinese and foreigners alike. The recent national reforms at the ministry level are a testament to China's commitment to improving this system, no matter how daunting such task may be. Ultimately, it seems that foreign investors can be sure of one thing: China's need for foreign capital to upgrade its power industry over the coming decades makes it practically inevitable that the approval process will continue to evolve, becoming more transparent, efficient, economical and manageable for foreign investors.[64]

64. One of the SDPC's proposals for enhancing economic performance in China in 1999 is to reform the investment examination and approval system by turning it into a simple filing system for certain industrial sectors where no state investment is involved. The intention would be to facilitate non-governmental investment activities. See *China Energy Watch*, January 1999, Volume 2, No. 1, Page 6.

Summary Checklist

1. Approval of foreign investment power projects in China is a complex exercise requiring Provincial or Regional Power Bureau and foreign investment (MOFTEC) review and approval.
2. The approval process for power projects starts with preliminary approval (*lixiang*) by the local, lower-level power bureau. Documents to be submitted include the preliminary Feasibility Study report and, if a potential foreign investor has been identified, a Letter of Intent and Project Proposal.
3. Provincial or Regional Power Bureaus approve the power project based on the lower-level power bureau's recommendation and by reviewing the preliminary Feasibility Study report, the Project Proposal and other relevant issues (for example, environmental protection, fuel supply and certificate of creditworthiness of the foreign investor).
4. For large projects, the Provincial or Regional Power Bureau performs a detailed review based on the submitted documents and makes a recommendation to the State Development and Planning Commission ("SDPC").
5. Relevant departments of the SDPC, based on the foregoing recommendation, will conduct a general review and make recommendations to the department-in-charge within the SDPC; the SDPC vice-minister decides whether to approve the project based upon the recommendation made by the department-in-charge.
6. After the project proposal is preliminary approved (*lixiang*) by the SDPC, the project documentation including the Finalized Feasibility Study Report must undergo in essence the same round of review in order to obtain final approval. In this next round, a Joint Venture Contract replaces the Letter of Intent. Ancillary documents which will facilitate the final approval include various support letters from related departments (for example, local land bureau, environmental protection bureau and Ministry of Railway).
7. MOFTEC approval commences once the SDPC vice-minister gives final approval to the project. MOFTEC will review the project to see whether it conforms with the general rules of foreign investment and formation of a Sino-foreign joint venture or a wholly foreign-owned enterprise. A decision will be made within 90 days.
8. There are now no hard caps on investment returns allowed for power projects, although 15% is generally seen as the "soft" ceiling.
9. China's BOT pilot projects as well as the promulgation of the 1997 project financing procedures and the 1998 international commercial law procedures indicate that China's power industry is moving to accommodate the requirements of internationally sponsored and financed power development.

CHAPTER 9

TELECOMMUNICATIONS PROJECT APPROVALS

David Fu, Associate[1]
Shearman & Sterling, Beijing

1. This chapter would not have been possible without the diligent research and insightful analysis of Andrew Zhang, associate, Shearman & Sterling, Beijing.

With the transformation of the Chinese economy from a planned economy to a more market-oriented economy, the telecommunications industry in China has experienced rapid growth. China has become the world's fastest growing telecommunications market today, and in absolute terms it has recently become the third largest mobile telephone market and the second largest for fixed-line telephone services. According to State statistics, the business of China's telecommunications sector grew 35.7% in 1998, far exceeding the national GDP growth of 7.8%. While the number of subscribers of fixed-line telephone services, mobile communications services and paging in China has grown substantially in the last five years, the penetration rates[2] remain relatively low compared to other Asian and international markets, indicating significant potential for continued rapid growth.

Telecommunications Services Development

As of end 1998, there were 110,920,000 telephone subscribers in the whole country, 27,380,000 more than the previous year; the total number of mobile subscribers reached 23,570,000, including 17,320,000 for the digital mobile telephone, 10,470,000 more than the previous year; there were 2,670,000 public telephone sets installed, 732,000 of which were added in 1998 alone; there were 37,830,000 radio pagers in operation, 8,140,000 more than the previous year; data communications subscribers totaled 1,510,000, including 74 national group subscribers.[3]

Telecommunications Capacity

As of end 1998, the total switching capacity of central office exchanges reached 134,900,000 lines 22,210,000 lines more than to the previous year. During 1998, 460,000 circuit terminals were added to the line-distance automatic switching network, driving the total up to 4,830,000; of the present total of 1,630,000 long-distance telephone circuits, 490,000 were added in 1998. As of end 1998, 99.6% of the long-distance transmission circuits nationwide were digitized and 99.8% of the central office exchanges were composed of stored program control systems; telephone sets in operation totaled 131,430,000, the national teledensity was 10.53% while the urban teledensity was 27.70%. Mobile switching capacity topped 41.62 million subscribers. The GSM networks currently cover 330 cities and more than 2000 counties with capacity of automatic roaming covering 38 countries and regions. The construction of the planned public data and multimedia communications network in 1998 was basically completed. As of end 1998, the data communications network had the capacity to serve 750,000 terminal ports, 610,000 of which basic network ports and the other 140,000 public multimedia communications and CHINANET network ports. The

2. As of end 1998, the national fixed-line teledensity was 10.53% and the mobile teledensity was 1.9%. See *China Telecom 1998 Annual Report*.

3. See *China Telecom 1998 Annual Report*.

CHINAPAC and CHINADDN had covered all the cities at and above the prefecture level and over 2,000 counties and some townships; the CHINANET and the multimedia communications network had covered all 31 provinces; the CHINAFRN had covered 23 provincial capital cities and the wireless data network had been under construction[4].

Recent Development

In the first eight months of 1999, the number of fixed-line subscribers increased by 14.06 million while the number of mobile telephone subscribers increased by 10.91 million, according to the MII.[5]

Despite this impressive growth, China's telecommunications market still remains under-developed compared to the much higher telecommunications penetration rates in advanced economies. The numbers mentioned above have spelled out the potential for massive growth in China's telecommunications services, and have also sparked a keen interest on the part of nearly all of the world's major telecommunications equipment manufactures and service providers, many of which have made gaining a strategic foothold in this "market of the next century" a top priority.

Government Policies on Foreign Investment

Pursuant to the *Guide Catalogue of Industries for Foreign Investment*, as revised and approved by the State Council on December 29, 1997, effective as of January 1, 1998, China encourages foreign investment in the following telecommunications sectors:

(i) Manufacturing of equipment for DCS/CDMA;

(ii) Manufacturing of digital serialized transmission equipment of photo timing and micro-wave synchronization of 2.5 GB/s and above;

(iii) Manufacturing of measuring meters of 2.5 GB/s for photo communication, wireless communication and data communication;

(iv) Manufacturing of ATM exchange equipment;

(v) Manufacturing of equipment for multimedia data communications systems;

(vi) Production of monomode optic fibers;

(vii) Manufacturing of equipment for access network communications systems;

(viii) Manufacturing of new technical equipment for supporting communications systems; and

(ix) Manufacturing of wide-band ISDN equipment.

4. See *China Telecom 1998 Annual Report*.

5. See Wang Chuandong, "Telecom Investment Slows but Usage Soars," *China Daily*, September 17, 1999.

Foreign investment is restricted in the following industries:

(i) Analog type mobile communications systems (cellular, grouping, paging and wireless telephones);

(ii) Satellite navigation receiving equipment and key parts (wholly foreign-owned operations not allowed);

(iii) Manufacturing of equipment for VSAT systems; and

(iv) Manufacturing of digital serialized transmission equipment of photo-timing synchronization below 2.5 GB/s, and manufacturing of microwave communications equipment of 144 MB/s and below.

Foreign investment is prohibited in:

(i) Operation and management of telecommunications services.

Foreign investment in the telecommunications sectors which are not specified above is permitted under the *Guide Catalogue of Industries for Foreign Investment.* (See **Legislation Appendices**)

Overview of the Telecommunications Industry in China

Regulatory structure

The telecommunications industry in China is subject to a high degree of regulation by the government. Regulations issued or implemented by the State Council, the Ministry of Information Industry (the "MII") and other relevant government authorities, including the State Development and Planning Commission (the "SDPC") and the Ministry of Foreign Trade and Economic Cooperation (the "MOFTEC"), encompass virtually every aspect of operating a telecommunications network, including entry into the telecommunications industry, scope of permissible business, interconnection and transmission line arrangements, technology and equipment standards, tariff policy, capital investment priorities, foreign investment and spectrum allocation.

In March 1998, the National People's Congress approved a government restructuring plan that created the MII to assume, among other things, the regulatory, administrative and other responsibilities of, and rights previously exercised or enjoyed by, the former Ministry of Posts and Telecommunications (the "MPT"). The MII, under the leadership of the State Council, is responsible for, among other things:

- formulating overall industry policy and regulations;
- coordinating telecommunications projects and networks at the national level;
- enforcing industry standards and regulations;
- granting of licenses to provide telecommunications services;

- formulating interconnection and settlement standards for implementation between telecommunications networks;
- formulating tariff and service charge policies for telecommunications services;
- supervising the operations of telecommunications service providers;
- maintaining a fair and orderly market competition among operators;
- allocating and administering public communications resources, such as national radio frequencies and code numbers and domain names and addresses of communications networks;
- examining and approving the establishment of radio stations; and
- managing the day-to-day administration of the national telecommunications sector.

In order to provide a uniform regulatory framework to encourage the orderly development of the telecommunications industry, the government is currently preparing a draft telecommunications law. If and when the telecommunications law is adopted by the National People's Congress, it is expected to become the basic telecommunications statute and the legal source of telecommunications regulations in China. In addition, the MII is preparing a draft of the telecommunications administration regulations, which will be subject to approval by the State Council. The regulations are expected to provide and clarify the regulatory rules and guidelines for the telecommunications industry in the interim period prior to the adoption of the telecommunications law. The telecommunications law and the regulations would have a positive effect on the overall development of the telecommunications industry in China.

History of China Telecom system

Prior to 1993, the China Telecom system, under the control of the MPT, was the sole provider of all public telecommunications services in China. The China Telecom system comprises the Directorate General of Telecommunications (the "DGT", or "China Telecom"), a State-owned enterprise, and the provincial Posts and Telecommunications Administration (the "PTA") and city and county Posts and Telecommunications Bureau (the "PTB"). Prior to the industry restructuring described below, the China Telecom system provided a range of telecommunications services, including domestic and international telephone, telegraph, data, facsimile, Internet access and electronic mail services, as well as mobile and satellite communications. The DGT was responsible for determining operational goals and policies for the China Telecom system at the national level. The PTAs and PTBs are local entities established with the approval and under the administrative authority of the MPT. Prior to the industry restructuring, they exercised day-to-day operational responsibilities over the China Telecom system's networks. The PTAs also exercised regulatory responsibilities over posts and telecommunications operations and services at the provincial level as well as administrative responsibilities over posts and telecommunications services provided by the PTBs within their respective jurisdictions.

Introduction of Competition

In 1993, the State Council issued regulations permitting the MPT to license domestic companies other than China Telecom to provide non-basic telecommunications services, such as radio paging, VSAT, computer information services, electronic data interchange (EDI), e-mail and other domestic communications services. In December 1993, the State Council approved the establishment of China United Telecommunications Corporation ("China Unicom") to introduce competition to the telecommunications sector. China Unicom provides cellular, fixed line, paging and other telecommunications services. Currently, China Unicom is the second largest cellular telecommunications service provider and the leading provider of paging services in China.

In January 1994, Ji Tong Communications Company ("*Ji Tong*") was established to construct and operate the China Golden Bridge Network, a national public data communications network. Ji Tong provides Internet Protocol (IP) telephone services, Internet international direct access and services, data communications services and other value-added telecommunications services.

In August 1995, Great Wall Telecommunications Corporation ("Great Wall") was established between the MPT and China Electronics Systems Engineering Corporation to explore the feasibility of deploying 800 MHz CDMA technology in public cellular networks in China. The trial operations of services, developed and operated by the Great Wall, has been completed in Beijing, Shanghai, Guangzhou and Xi'an. After initial service rollout, the CDMA mobile service is available in these four cities with a total network capacity of 140,000. However, the MII has not officially sanctioned the commercial operation of Great Wall yet. It remains unclear when the MII will issue a license for CDMA rollout in China.

In October 1999, China Network Communications Corporation ("China Netcom") was established to construct and operate one of the world's fastest IP-based optical fibre commercial networks. China Netcom is licensed to offer IP backbone services and international integrated data communications services.

Industry restructuring

In February 1999, the State Council approved a restructuring plan for the telecommunication industry in China. According to the plan, the telecommunications operations of China Telecom are to be separated along four business lines: fixed line communications, mobile communications, paging and satellite communications services. China Mobile Communications Group Corporation was established in July 1999 as a State-owned company to hold the mobile communications assets resulting from this separation and operate the mobile communications network nationwide. A separate company will be responsible for satellite networks following the restructuring, while the paging operations have been merged into

China Unicom. As a result of the restructuring, China Telecom now operates only fixed-line networks and provides only fixed line telephone and data communications services. China Telecom is expected to become the holding company of the China Telecom system.

As part of the Chinese government's industry restructuring initiatives, the regulatory functions of the MII and the PTAs will be separated from the operational functions of the State-owned companies under their control. Following this separation, it is expected that the MII will act exclusively as the industry regulator and will not longer manage the day-to-day operations of telecommunications service providers in China. The separation of the regulatory and operational functions of the MII and the PTAs has not been completed. As a result, the MII continues to exercise administrative control over the operational goals and policies and the personnel of telecommunications service providers formerly under the control of China Telecom. In addition, the provincial PTAs continue to operate the fixed line telephone networks in their respective provinces. According to the restructuring plan, separation of regulatory and operational functions of the MII and the provincial PTAs is expected to be completed by the end of 1999.

Though the MII restructuring plan gives no definite timetable for the introduction of cross-sector competition and opening to foreign investors, the plan institutionalizes existing divisions within China Telecom system. The restructuring would speed passage of the long-awaited telecommunications law, rationalize interconnection policy and legitimize a multi-vendor market. These structural adjustments could restore confidence in the market, and the potential for foreign investors may be great.

Agenda for Opening Telecommunications Services Sector to Foreign Investors

The restructuring move is designed to develop a market-oriented mechanism for competition and to strengthen the domestic telecommunications operators in preparation for China's entry into the World Trade Organization ("WTO"). Given that opening up the country's telecommunications service market is on the top of the government's agenda, the move would prepare the ground for a limited opening of the market to overseas players.

There is profound reason for China to step up its efforts to open the domestic telecommunications market. Previously, inside the government, China took the year 2004 as a critical milestone, because it is the time when the majority of Asian countries (including Malaysia, Thailand, The Philippines, Indonesia and India) have promised to deregulate their domestic telecommunications market as a pre-condition for joining the WTO. This will put China under tremendous pressure in doing business with its neighbors in the region; in fact, it may hurt China's long term relations with the region, both economically and politically. However, the recent signing of the market access agreement between the U.S. and China (the "WTO Agreement") has advanced China's agenda for opening the telecommunications services sector.[6] Pursuant to the WTO Agreement, China will allow 49% foreign investment and ownership in all telecommunications services in the first year of accession and 50% foreign ownership in value-added services in two years and paging services in three years.

To open the telecommunications market gradually, domestic companies are used in an experiment to weigh different options and compare results. The recent restructuring move and the emergence of China Netcom have demonstrated that the government has decided to push the timetable for entry by domestic companies to 1999, so that China will have enough time to strengthen its competitive position before permitting foreign companies to participate.

The prospect of opening the telecommunications service market should create opportunities for overseas firms, many of which believe they should be able to get a share of the huge market as it continues to grow. But it should be cautioned that conditions of market opening are still uncertain. The WTO Agreement will not become effective until China's accession to the WTO. Moreover, the WTO Agreement and the laws and regulations to be adopted to implement the WTO Agreement may contain restrictions on ownership structure or permissible activities or stringent approval requirements. It remains to be seen how these possible restrictions or requirements affect the abilities of foreign telecommunications firms to become directly involved in one of the mainland's most lucrative sectors. Until the WTO Agreement becomes effective, no foreign involvement is allowed in the management and operation of telecommunication services. The recent outlawing of Chinese-Chinese-Foreign ventures affirms such prohibition.

Chinese-Chinese-Foreign ("CCF") Ventures – the Involvement of Foreign Companies

The CCF investment structure was invented by China Unicom in late 1994, a few months following its official establishment in July 1994, when it wanted to get investments from foreign companies. A CCF venture is created when a foreign company forms a telecom engineering service or technological consulting service joint venture ("JVCO") with a Chinese company (usually, a subsidiary of China Unicom or a shareholder of China Unicom or its subsidiary, as local partner). The JVCO provides financing, technical support and operation consultation to China Unicom for construction, development and operations of one of its telecommunications projects (GSM, fixed line telephone or wireless paging network) pursuant to a complex web of project cooperation contract, consultation agreement and equipment sale or leasing agreement, in return for sharing revenues generated from the project, in which the JVCO participates. To avoid the prohibition of foreign operation and management of telecommunications services, the project cooperation contract provides that during the term

6. See, "Summary of U.S. - China Bilateral WTO Agreement", released from the White House of the U.S. on November 15, 1999.

of the project cooperation contract (typically, 12-15 years), the JVCO shall not participate in the management and operation of the project. Under the CCF structure, the foreign partner injects capital into the JVCO, which in turn injects the funds in China Unicom's project for a share of the latter's revenues. On paper the final venture/cooperation is between two mainland firms (China Unicom and JVCO), however, it is backed by the foreign partner of the JVCO financially and technically.

The CCF structure has provided a route for investors to circumvent China's longstanding prohibition of foreign ownership in, operation and management of telecommunications service companies. With the help of the CCF, China Unicom was able to build up its nationwide GSM network in less than three years. It signed its first CCF contract with Shanghai Science & Technology Investment Corporation ("SSTIC")[7] in April 1995 for construction and development of China Unicom's GSM project in Shanghai. By the end of 1997, China Unicom had signed 23 GSM project contracts with 46 foreign companies and raised about US$1.4 billion or 72% of the total investment in China Unicom's GSM projects. Foreign firms participating in the CCF ventures include France Telecom[8], Deutsche Telecom, Sprint[9], Bell Canada, NTT International, Sumitomo, Itochu, AmTec[10], LTC Telecommunications[11], Korea Telecom and Hong Kong firms First Pacific, New World and Star Telecom International.

In early September 1998, the State Council ordered all foreign involvement in China Unicom to be stopped immediately because of violations against existing regulations. The ban effectively closes off almost all opportunities for foreign telecommunications service providers to participate in the market. The ban on CCF ventures reportedly was prompted by the government's concerns that capital-rich foreign telecommunications companies might eventually control China's strategic telecommunications market, repatriating handsome profits out of the country. Another concern was that the telecommunications market was becoming more liberal than the government was promising to make it in connection with China's accession to the WTO.

7. As a shareholder of China Unicom, SSTIC is an investment company engaged in investment in telecommunications and other infrastructure projects. In connection with its CCF contract with China Unicom, SSTIC established a Sino-foreign joint venture with McCaw International Ltd. in October 1995 to implement the CCF contract.

8. France Telecom's GSM projects in two cities in the booming southern province of Guangdong demonstrate that foreign companies stand to lose more in future prospects than in current revenues. The company has spent only US$60 million of a planned US$350 million investment that was designed to reap its greatest returns toward the end of the projects' life.

9. A SSTIC contact confirmed that the mechanism by which Sprint had invested US$30 million in setting up a fixed line network with China Unicom in Tianjin was no longer applicable for China Unicom's Shanghai fixed line network. The contracts between Sprint and SSTIC are pending for signature due to the ban on CCF ventures.

10. AmTec is developing 10 regional cellular networks in Hebei Province in partnership with China Unicom, NTT International, Itochu, and Hebei Provincial Government. AmTec is also participating in a cable TV programming network in Hunan Province.

11. LTC Telecommunications, a wholly-owned subsidiary of Lion Tech Chiang Ltd., a Singapore-listed company with main businesses in property, steel and telecom, participated in China Unicom's GSM projects in Henan, Shanxi, Hubei and Guizhou.

Following a close investigation by the government, the following "irregularities" were found in the CCF venture :

- *JVCO's Participation in the Operation and Management of Telecommunications Services*: Under the CCF structure, a joint committee comprising of members appointed by China Unicom and JVCO is created by China Unicom and JVCO pursuant to a project cooperation contract. The joint committee is responsible for examining and deciding major matters relating to business development, network operations, pricing and marketing of the project in which JVCO is involved. Although China Unicom appoints the majority of, and controls the joint committee, JVCO's participation in the business decision of China Unicom's project is deemed to participate indirectly in the operation and management of the telecommunications services, which is prohibited by current Chinese law.
- *JVCO's Ownership of China Unicom's Network Assets*: Under the CCF, the foreign investor, through the JVCO, maintains ownership of the network assets until its investment is recouped through sharing revenues generated from the project. By controlling the ownership of the network assets, the foreign investor could leverage the operational rights of the operator. Such retention by JVCO of network assets is deemed as JVCO's indirect ownership in the telecommunications company, which is prohibited by current Chinese law.
- *JVCO's Activities of Financing*: Under the CCF structure, the JVCO provides financing for the network assets, owns such network assets and allows the operator to use such network assets. Such financing activities of JVCO should be deemed as leasing activities, which shall require the approval of the MOFTEC. However, none of the JVCOs engaged in CCF projects has obtained such approval. Accordingly, JVCO's provision of financing to China Unicom is illegal unless the business license of JVCO permits it to engage in such financing.
- *JVCO's Sharing of Installation Fee*: Under the CCF structure, the "distributable cash flow" split by China Unicom and JVCO equals to the aggregate amount of (i) installation fee, (ii) depreciation of the network assets and (iii) after-tax profit of the project. However, the regulations of the MPT and the Ministry of Finance provide that installation fee shall be used only for infrastructure construction, especially in the more marginal areas of the country. Accordingly, JVCO's sharing revenue from the installation fee violates the provisions of such regulations.
- *WTO Concerns*: Under the CCF structure, a significant percentage of the revenue is distributed to the foreign investors. The benefits that the foreign investor obtained under the CCF structure may have exceeded what he will receive if the Chinese government liberalises the telecommunications market and permits foreign minority equity interest in telecommunications companies – as it has pledged in its attempts to gain WTO membership.

By banning the CCF ventures, the Chinese government set out plans for China Unicom to finance its projects through domestic bank loans, issuing bonds and shares domestically and overseas. There is a growing sense in official circles that the fast-growing telecommunications industry does not require as much foreign direct investment as previously thought. The successful listing of China Telecom (Hong Kong) Limited in Hong Kong and New York in

October 1997 demonstrated that China can raise capital without ceding operational and management control. The MII would like to see this success repeated for the regional China Unicom joint ventures. China Unicom has been recently approved to issue shares overseas and list such shares in Hong Kong and New York. But foreign investors own the local companies' network assets, and a mechanism for converting joint venture equity into shares is a prerequisite to public listing. How the existing assets will be valued has not yet been worked out. China Unicom is currently involved in serious negotiations with foreign telecommunications companies which had been involved in the CCF ventures and are now seeking compensation. If disputes are not promptly and properly settled, China Unicom's listing plan would be prevented. It remains to be seen how the CCF ventures will be restructured.

Currently the ban on the CCF ventures looks like a setback for foreign investments. However, it could be a prelude to official recognition by the Chinese government and may be the first step in a rationalization which will eventually lead to foreigners being granted permission for direct, but minority, equity participation in telecommunications services, as part of China's WTO entry obligations. The MII may wish to standardize the telecommunications industry in anticipation of further liberalization. In connection with the ban on CCF ventures, China is reviewing foreign equity participation in the telecommunications market in preparation for its negotiations over the country's membership of the WTO. The WTO requires all members to open their telecommunications services market to foreign participation. As China is likely to gain membership of the WTO in the near future, foreigners will eventually be granted permission for direct equity ownership and operation of telecommunications services in China.

Pursuant to the "grandfather" clause under the WTO Agreement, China will grandfather all existing current market access and activities in all services sector. Therefore, the existing foreign investment in the CCF ventures would be likely to be legalized subject to a restructuring following which the foreign investment and ownership in these ventures will not exceed the 49% limit in the first year of China's accession to the WTO.

Regulatory Approval for Computer Information Services and Multimedia Communications Services

The Ministry of Posts and Telecommunications, Administration of Examination and Approval for Engaging in Deregulated Telecommunications Industry Tentative Procedures, promulgated by the MPT on September 11, 1993, and effective as of November 1, 1993 (the "Deregulation Procedures") have classified computer information services, electronic mail (e-mail) and electronic data interchange (EDI) as liberalized telecommunications services. Such services are off-limits to foreign investment, ownership, operation and management. Computer information services, Internet services and multimedia communications services are still considered telecommunications businesses, and therefore are regulated by the MII in the same manner that it regulates telecommunications services.

The computer information and Internet services have grown rapidly over the past few years. Chinese Internet subscribers reached 4 million in the first half of 1999, up from 2 million in 1998. The amount of time subscribers spend online has increased from 1-5 hours to 10 hours a month per account, according to a survey conducted by China National Information Center. Internet Content Providers (ICPs) and Internet Service Providers (ISPs) are also growing rapidly in China. However, strict content regulations and the prohibition against foreign companies providing Internet service in China continue to block the entry of foreign ISPs and ICPs.

The Information Highway Hierarchy and Regulatory Approval

The *Administration of International Linkups of Computer Information Networks Tentative Provisions*, promulgated by the State Council on May 20, 1997 (the "CIN Tentative Provisions") lay out the basic organizational and administrative structure of China's computer information services networks. The *Implementing Procedures of the Tentative Provisions for the Administration of Computer Information Networks and the Internet*, promulgated by the State Council on March 6, 1998 (the "CIN Implementing Procedures") reiterate the network connection relations set out in the CIN Tentative Provisions. The CIN Tentative Provisions and the CIN Implementing Procedures specify three tiers of computer information networks in China.

The first tier is international computer information networks (*jisuanji xinxi wangluo guoji lianwang*), or Internet, which are computer information networks within PRC territory that link directly to foreign computer networks for international information exchange.

There is only one way to access the World Wide Web (WWW) from PRC and that is through the international gateway controlled by the MII, and operated by China Telecom[12]. Any new connection from China to the WWW requires the approval of the State Council. The State Council has not approved any entity other than the MII to connect to the global Internet.

The second tier is interlinked networks (*hulian wangluo*), which are computer information networks that link to the international computer networks, or Internet. The work units that provide interlinked network services are the so-called Internet Service Providers ("ISPs").

Only five interlinked networks have actually been authorized and established in China. These five networks are ChinaNet of the MII, GBNet of Jitong, the Chinese Science and Technology Network ("CSTNET") of the Chinese Academy of Sciences, the China Education and Research

12. See *Administration Procedures for Gateway Access Channels of International Linkups of Computer Information Networks*, promulgated by the MPT on April 9, 1996.

Network (CERNET) of the State Education Commission and UniNet of China Unicom.[13] Of these five interlinked networks, only ChinaNet, GBNet and UniNet are licensed to provide commercial services to the public. The MII regulates the existing three commercial ISP operators. The MII is responsible for the examination and approval of all applications for new interlinked networks before submitting them to the State Council for final approval.

The third tier is interfacing networks (*jieru wangluo*), which are computer information networks that link to the ISP's interlinked networks in order to provide access to the Internet. "Interfacing units" (*jieru danwei*) refers to those organizations responsible for the operation of interfacing networks. Interfacing networks must carry out international linkup through an ISP.

The CIN Tentative Provisions and the CIN Implementing Procedures establish a licensing system for commercial interfacing units that provide Internet access through an ISP. No interfacing unit may engage in international linkups services without having obtained an international linkups service license.

Pursuant to Article 9 of the CIN Tentative Provisions, an interfacing unit that engages in international linkup services must:

- Be a legally established enterprise legal person;
- Have a corresponding computer network and equipment and corresponding technical and management personnel;
- Have a sound system for security control and confidentiality protection, and sound technical protection measures;
- Have the ability to provide long-term services to subscribers; and
- Satisfy other conditions provided for in laws and State Council regulations.

Pursuant to Article 10 of the CIN Implementing Procedures, an interfacing unit that satisfies the conditions as specified above, shall submit (i) an application and (ii) a feasibility study report for the interfacing networks to the relevant department of the ISP or the MII, which shall, within 20 days, examine such application and report and notify such interfacing network organization the results of examination.

- Interfacing units that intend to provide services across provincial borders must apply to the MII for an international linkup service license. Interfacing units that intend to provide services within a province shall apply to the local PTA for an international linkups service license.
- An interfacing unit operator shall, on the strength of its international linkup service license, handle registration procedures with the local administration of industry and commerce, and lease telecommunications lines from telecommunications operators, which shall, within 30 days, provide leased lines and related services.

13. "China Telecom Face Competitions", *Economics Daily*, August 17, 1999.

The *Certain Issues Concerning the Implementation of the Operating Licence System for the Computer Information Networks and the Internet Services Circular*, issued by the MII on September 18, 1998 sets forth further details with respect to the license system for interfacing networks and reiterates the two level administration system for the approval of the license for interfacing network:

- The MII is responsible for examination and approval of, and licensing the interfacing units that offer inter-province Internet services;
- The PTA is responsible for examination and approval of, and licensing the interfacing units that offer intra-province Internet services.

Multimedia Network Services and Regulatory Approval

Multimedia networks are being developed separately from the Internet networks in China although the public multimedia communications network is based on Internet technology. Pursuant to the *Administration of China's Public Multimedia Communications Procedures* issued by the MPT on September 10, 1997 and effective as of December 1, 1997 (the "Multimedia Administration Measures"), the MPT, now the MII, is responsible for the overall administration of China's public multimedia communications services, formulating the policies and regulations relating to development, operations, tariff and technical standards of the multimedia communications services. The relevant PTA administers the public multimedia communications services within its respective jurisdiction.

Pursuant to Article 8 of the Multimedia Administration Measures, provision of communications and information services through China's public multimedia communications network shall be regulated as deregulated telecommunications services according to applicable regulations. The Multimedia Administration Measures defines the operator of multimedia communications services as operator of China's multimedia communications network, operator of multimedia information access service and operator of multimedia information content service. The key player in the development and operation of China's multimedia communications is China Telecom. Pursuant to Article 4 of the Multimedia Administration Measures, China Telecom is responsible for the construction and operation of China's public multimedia communications network. Article 8 of the Multimedia Administration Measures establishes a license system for the provision of multimedia information access service and an approval system for the provision of multimedia information content. Without obtaining a license or an approval from the MII or the relevant PTA (depending on the scope of territory in which the service is to be offered), no entity or individual shall be permitted to engage in the provision of multimedia information access service or provision of multimedia information content service.

The *Examination and Approval of the Operation of Multimedia Communications Services Circular*, issued by the Telecommunications Administration Department of the MPT on November 26, 1997 (the "Multimedia Circular") established the approval procedures for the provision of multimedia information access service and the provision of multimedia information content service. To provide public multimedia communications services, an applicant must:

- Be a State-owned enterprise, institution or collectively-owned enterprise, legally established in China;
- Have relevant technical and managerial personnel, and financial resources to provide subscribers with long-term services;
- Have the necessary location and equipment to meet the technical requirements prescribed by the MPT, now the MII.

An application for a license for the provision of multimedia communications services must be submitted to the MII or the relevant PTA. Providers of multimedia information content must also apply to the appropriate level MII authorities to establish information databases for the multimedia information network and file the approval with the MII.

Prospects for Foreign Investment in Internet and Internet-related Services

In recent years, China's enormous growth in computer information services and Internet services has prompted many foreign media, network and venture capital firms to seek a toehold in China's Internet and Internet-related service market. Foreign companies that have been involved in the leading Internet access providers and ICPs in China include Intel Corp., Dow Jones & Co., Time Warner, International Data Group and Goldman Sachs (Asia).[14] However, recently the MII has reiterated China's prohibition on foreign participation in the ownership, operation and management of telecommunications services, including the Internet and Internet-related services. According to the MII, included in the ban, as prescribed in the Deregulation Procedures, were public and non-public, wire and wireless networks and services.

However, the MII shall follow through with any concessions in terms of access to the Chinese market if China makes certain commitments in its bid to gain WTO membership. Pursuant to the WTO Agreement, China will liberalize all aspects of Internet services at the same rate as other key telecommunications services. As with the CCF ventures, the existing foreign investments in Internet services are likely to be legalized subject to a restructuring following which the foreign investment and ownership in these services will not exceed the 49% limit in the first year of China's accession to the WTO.

At present, the only deal in place is a framework agreement between Shanghai PTA, Shanghai Information Investment Co., Ltd. and AT&T signed in March 1999 to set up a joint venture to

14. See, James Harding, Peter Montagnon & James Kynge, "Beijing Warns Foreigners off Online Sector", *Financial Times*, September 14, 1999.

operate value-added telecommunications services in Pudong New Area, Shanghai.[15] This agreement signals the first time a foreign party has taken part in providing telecommunications services (though not basic telecommunications services) in China. With China's efforts to open up its telecommunications services market in its bid to gain WTO membership, foreign companies will eventually be permitted to participate in this fastest growing industry in China.[16].

Regulatory Approval for Manufacturing and Importing Telecommunications Equipment

Several major regulations regarding the approval process for manufacturing and importing telecommunications equipment have been promulgated since the last article was published.[17] The new regulations apply not only to the "telecommunications terminal devices" but also to all the other telecommunications equipment defined hereinafter.

The MII requires all telecommunications equipment for network access to be licensed to enhance the management of telecommunications equipment and to ensure the security of telecommunications network. Pursuant to the *Administration of the Examination and Approval of Telecommunications Equipment for Network Access*, promulgated by the MII on December 31, 1998 and effective as of January 1, 1999 (the "Network Access Procedures Administration Procedures"), a Network Access Permit and a Network Access Symbol issued by the MII are required before any telecommunications equipment for network access can be used for the public and private telecommunications networks.

The term "telecommunications equipment" is defined in Article 2 of the *Network Access Administration Measures* as "any software and hardware systems which can be used for sending, receiving or transmitting voice, characters, data, pictures or any kind of information either through wires or wireless adopting electromagnetic or optical modes".

Any telecommunications equipment without a Network Access Permit and a Network Access Symbol is not allowed to be advertised, sold or used on telecommunications network in

15. See, Wang Chuandong, "Telecom Minister Stresses Policies for Foreign Funds", *China Daily, Business Weekly*, September 19-25, 1999.

16. The Provisional Opinions Concerning Foreign Investment in Computer Information Service Industry in Shanghai, jointly promulgated by Shanghai Municipal National Economy and Social Information Leading Group Office and Shanghai Municipal Foreign Investment Commission, on June 3, 1999, permit foreign investors, in the form of Sino-foreign equity joint venture or Sino-foreign cooperative joint venture, to engage in the following computer information services: (a) producing informaiton products (including developing on-line informaiton sources, producing, maintaining and upgrading network database); (b) designing, producing and posting web pages; (c) electronic ticketing, on-line shopping and network linking services; (d) consulting, surveying, economic forecasting and publishing on-line information using the networking information; (e) enterprise intranet and Internal technical training; and (f) design, installation, testing and maintenance of integrated computer information systems. Wholly foreign owned enterprises are also permitted to engage in the above computer information services, except for publishing on-line information.

17. Lee Edwards, "Telecommunications Project Approvals", *Obtaining PRC Approvals: Foreign Investment Enterprises and Infrastructure Projects*, Asia Law and Practice, 1996.

China. Article 4 of the Network Access Administration Measures provides that the MII shall exercise macro-control over telecommunications equipment to be applied for network access in line with industry policies and domestic market demands. Pursuant to Article 5 of the *Network Access Administration Measures, Telecommunications Administration Department* (the "TAD") of MII is responsible for the approval of an application for, and issuance of, the network access permits for telecommunications equipment. An application for a network access permit will be handled by a department authorized by TAD to accept and deal with such application (such department, being a "Network Access Handling Department"). The relevant PTAs are responsible for the supervision and management of the telecommunications equipment that will access to the telecommunications network under their jurisdiction.

Approval Procedure

Pursuant to Articles 6 of the *Network Access Administration Measures*, to obtain a Network Access Permit for its telecommunications equipment, a manufacturer must: (i) adhere to the State industry policies and related regulations, (ii) conform to the State standards and the industrial technical standards, and (iii) have a consummate system to guarantee quality.

Pursuant to Article 7 of the *Network Access Administration Measures*, an applicant must submit the following documents to the Network Access Handling Department:

- Application forms of network access permit for telecommunications equipment;
- Copies of the applicant's business license (overseas enterprises may submit valid licenses of their office or agent in China);
- Government-issued documents approving sales of such equipment in the domestic market (only required for Sino-foreign joint ventures and wholly foreign-owned enterprises in China);
- Introduction of the enterprise of the applicant (including enterprise profiles, production facilities, equipped instruments, quality guarantee system and measures for after-sale service);
- Certificates of authorization (only required when overseas enterprises entrust their agent in China with application for network access permits);
- A Letter of Guarantee signed by the legal representative of the applicant;
- Equipment introduction (including function, specification, system design and schematic diagram);
- Pictures of equipment with external and internal composition;
- User's manual;
- Overseas inspection reports of, and status of commercial use of, such equipment (only required for overseas enterprises).

Apart from the credentials, all documents stated above must be prepared in Chinese. Overseas enterprises may entrust their branches or agents in China with the application procedures.

Article 8 and 9 of the *Network Access Administration Measures* provide two different procedures to apply for a network access permit, depending on whether the manufacturer's products are "important telecommunications equipment or new products", or, "general telecommunications equipment". However, the *Network Access Administration Measures* do not define the "important telecommunications equipment or new products" or "general telecommunications equipment".

Enterprises applying for network access permits for "important telecommunications equipment or new products" shall follow the following procedures:

- Enterprises should first submit application documents for network access to the Network Access Handling Departments;
- The Network Access Handling Department shall, within five days, conduct a preliminary examination of the application documents, and report to the TAD the equipment that conforms with the TAD's requirements;
- The TAD will, within 30 days, organize experts to evaluate the overall technical scheme of the applicant and issue an evaluation report thereof;
- The TAD will notify Network Access Handling Department of the equipment which has been endorsed by experts. The Network Access Handling Departments should, within five days, notify the corresponding institutions that will be responsible for the sample test and examination of the quality guarantee system;
- The examination of the quality guarantee system shall be done in accordance with the relevant regulations and completed within 15 days after receiving the notice. The examination results should be submitted to the Network Access Handling Departments. After receiving the notice, the sampling inspection institutions should select samples for testing within 15 days. Upon receiving the samples for testing, the inspection institutions should, in accordance with the relevant standards, complete the inspections within 30 days and submit the results to the Network Access Handling Department;
- After passing the above examination and inspection, the network access tests will be performed on a designated experimental system for continuous testing not less than 3 months. Upon the completion of the experiment, the test reports should be submitted to the Network Access Handling Departments by the test institutions;
- After completion of all the work stated above, the Network Access Handling Departments will submit all the documents including application documents, inspection reports, examination reports on quality guarantee system and test reports, to the TAD. The TAD will, within 30 days, organize the experts for a comprehensive verification of the equipment and will issue a network access permit to the applicant if its equipment passes such verification.

Enterprises applying for network access permits for the "general telecommunications equipment" should follow the following procedures:

- Enterprises should submit application documents to the Network Access Handling Departments;
- The Network Access Accepting Departments should conduct a preliminary examination of the application documents within five days, and notify the inspection institution to conduct sampling test and examine quality guarantee system for the equipment which conforms with the TAD's requirements;
- After receiving the notice, the relevant inspection institution should complete the examination of the quality guarantee system in accordance with the relevant regulations within 15 days, and submit its findings to the Network Access Handling Departments.

  Upon receiving the notice, the sampling inspection institution will select the samples within 15 days. Upon receiving the samples for tests, the inspection institutions should, in accordance with the relevant standards, complete the inspections within 15 days and submit the results to the Network Access Handling Department;
- After completion of all the work stated above, the Network Access Handling Departments will submit all the documents including application documents, inspection reports and examination reports on quality guarantee system to the TAD. The DAT will make comprehensive verification of the equipment, and will issue within 15 days network access permits to the equipment which passes such verification.

Pursuant to Article 15 of the *Network Access Administration Measures*, Network Access Permits are valid for a duration of three years and may be renewed three months before their expiration.

Certificate for Radio Transmission Equipment

On April 26, 1999, the MII promulgated the *Strengthening Administration of Radio Transmission Equipment Circular* (the "Radio Circular"). The Radio Circular reiterates that both the "*Regulation on the Administration of Imported Radio Transmission Equipment*"[18] and the "*Regulation on Manufacturing of Radio Transmission Equipment*"[19] shall be strictly observed.

The MII requires manufacturers and importers of all equipment that emits radio waves to be certified. Pursuant to the Radio Circular, starting June 1, 1999 all manufacturers of radio transmission equipment in China shall obtain a "Technical Verification Certificate" issued by

18. Jointly issued by the former State Radio Regulatory Commission ("SRRC"), State Economic and Trade Commission, MOFTEC and Customs General Administration on July 24, 1995 and effective as of January 1, 1996.

19. Issued by the SRRC and State Bureau of Technology Supervision on October 7, 1997 and effective as of January 1, 1999.

Radio Administration Department under the MII for their radio transmission equipment. The "Technical Verification Certificate" issued by the former SRRC will still be valid until their expiration date.

The term "all equipment that emits radio waves" defined in Article 1 of the Radio Circular includes equipment for:

- radio communications
- navigation
- positioning
- direction measuring
- radar
- remote control
- remote measuring
- radio broadcasting
- television

The definition excludes equipment that emits electromagnetic waves which are used in industry, scientific research, medical care, electrical transportation and high-voltage power cables.

It is prohibited to manufacture (except for exports), sell, use or advertise any radio transmission equipment without a "Technical Verification Certificate" within China (excluding Hong Kong, Macao and Taiwan) and the radio administration authorities shall not approve for import of any equipment without such certificate, nor shall they allocate radio frequencies or issue a radio license for such equipment.

Conclusion

The Chinese telecommunications market offers a variety of opportunities for foreign investment. Pursuant to the WTO Agreement, the existing foreign investments in the CCF ventures and Internet services are likely to be grandfathered subject to a restructuring to comply with the 49% ownership limit. Under such a policy, foreign investors would relinquish their majority control over CCF ventures but would benefit from standing on firmer legal ground. The WTO Agreement will, upon its effectiveness, also permit 49% foreign investment and ownership in all telecommunications services.

However, the absence of a definitive telecommunications law in China makes it difficult for potential investors to participate in the fastest growing and lucrative industry in China or to turn these opportunities into profit. The telecommunications administration regulations that are reportedly drafted in a manner "beneficial for investment and development" are expected to be promulgated by the end of this year. Until a transparent regulatory frame is in place that permits foreign participation in China's telecommunications services, foreign investors seeking to profit from China's telecommunications and Internet boom must carefully structure any proposed venture and should be well advised to proceed with their investment.

Summary Checklist

1. There are many opportunities for foreign investment in China's rapidly developing telecommunications industry.
2. The recent industry restructuring broke up the monopoly of China Telecom, promoted the separation of regulatory and operational functions of the MII and created a pro-competition environment in the telecommunications industry.
3. Under existing PRC law, foreign companies, including foreign investment enterprises established in China, are prohibited from investing in, owning and operating a telecommunications network in China.
4. The recent outlawing of the CCF ventures could be the first step in a rationalization which may eventually lead to foreign investors being granted permission for direct, but minority, equity participation in telecommunications services, as part of China's WTO entry obligations.
5. The signing of the WTO Agreement between the U.S. and China heralds China's opening up of the telecommunications services sector to foreign investors.
6. Computer information and Internet services are regulated by the MII in the same manner that it regulates the deregulated telecommunications services, and are still off-limits to foreign investment, ownership and operation.
7. The PRC government continues to encourage the participation of foreign companies in the manufacturing in China, and importing into China, of telecommunication equipment and products that adopt advanced technologies.
8. Manufacturers of telecommunications equipment and products must obtain a Network Admission Permit from the MII for equipment and products that will be connected to telecommunications networks in China.

CHAPTER 10

TOLL ROAD APPROVALS: WHERE THE RUBBER MEETS THE ROAD

*Clark T. Randt, Jr. and Don H. Bennett**

Shearman & Sterling, Hong Kong

---

* Mr. Randt is a partner with Shearman & Sterling resident in Hong Kong, where Mr. Bennett is an associate specializing in infrastructure projects.

China is currently in the process of implementing its ambitious road[1] development programme to accommodate freight and passenger traffic volume growth of around 7% and 12% a year, respectively. These growth figures clearly reflect the increasing prosperity of the Chinese and the growing strength and geographical diversity of their industrial base. As a result, the road infrastructure market in China is in great need of foreign capital and is looking for foreign participation in construction and management.

Which level of government authority has responsibility over the planning, administration, and hence the approval, of the highway depends on (i) the location and size of investment in newly developed roads, bridges and tunnels within China's road network and (ii) whether they will be part of China's national highway grid. This chapter aims to sort out the various laws and administrative bodies that govern the approval, construction and operation of road infrastructure projects in China.

Background

Highway construction plans in the PRC

It is well known that China has a great need for road development and for funds to support such development.[2] The expansion of road infrastructure forms an integral part of the country's overall economic development, and road expansion continues to lag significantly behind the country's rapid growth in vehicular traffic. China is currently the world's largest infrastructural investment market with total demand for infrastructural investment for the five-year period from 1998 to 2002 estimated at US$280 billion, of which approximately US$19 billion per year will be required for road construction. Approximately US$30 billion, or 31%, of the five-year amount for road construction is targeted to come from overseas funds.[3] The average total investment in a given highway project in the PRC is around US$200 million.[4]

Under the Ninth Five-Year Plan the PRC government has set itself the target of constructing an additional 11,000 km of roads by 2000, including 6,000 km of Class I highways and expressways, in order to support China's continuous economic growth and to expedite the economic development of the inland provinces – a current PRC national priority. In addition, the Ministry of Communications ("MOC") has set itself the ambitious target of constructing the "National Trunk Highways System," comprising 12 trunk highways of 36,090 km in

1. The word "road" will be used herein as a generic term to mean "highway", "roadway", "tollway", etc.
2. In 1996, China had 855 km of highways per million people, compared to 25,300 km for the United States, 8,860 km for Japan and 2,103 km for India. In urban areas, Beijing had 570 km of highways per million people and Shanghai had 350 km, compared to 1,200 km in New York and 3,200 km in London. See *China Business Review*, March-April 1998, p. 8.
3. See *China Economic News*, August 18, 1997, No. 31; see also the Internet at http://irasia.com/listco/hk/roadking/annual/97/respress9712.htm.
4. See The *China Business Review*, p. 10, March-April 1998.

aggregate that will link all provincial capitals, most cities with populations over 500,000 and all cities with populations over one million by 2010. The goal is to link important local economic centres with a system of feeder highways and expressways, and thereby build an infrastructure foundation that will facilitate economic growth on a country-wide scale. The backbone of the National Trunk Highway System, referred to as the "two horizontals and three verticals," will be a system of roads of 16,390 km in aggregate that is currently under construction pursuant to the Ninth Five-Year Plan period (1996-2000).

In the face of the Asian Economic Crisis which started to be felt at the beginning of 1998, the PRC government improved road infrastructure investment prospects even further by pronouncing that it would speed up infrastructure development as a means of stimulating the domestic economy. Thus, road building has become a national priority, and foreign investment in the sector is strongly encouraged.[5]

Toll road investment opportunities

Investors in China's toll road projects typically fall into three groups of companies: (i) mainland provincial investment and development companies, (ii) Hong Kong investors and international finance institutions or funds and (iii) other Asian investors. First, mainland provincial investment and development companies technically are not private sector companies, however, they operate purely as commercial organizations. These provincial investment and development companies form the largest group soliciting foreign capital for China's road infrastructure development, often by raising funds in the Hong Kong and PRC securities markets. It is a common practice under existing PRC legislation for provincial investment and development companies to develop a roadway and then assign the operating rights to foreign road companies to raise capital and to establish a relationship with an experienced partner for future developments. Second, Hong Kong investors and international financial institutions or funds together make up the largest source of foreign investment in China with respect to road infrastructure. Hong Kong also provides much of the professional and financial services used to structure toll road investments. Third, companies based in other parts of Asia have shown interest in China's road infrastructure sector, but some have had disappointing results.[6] Furthermore, their enthusiasm for large-scale investments in foreign infrastructure projects may have been dampened by Asia's Economic Crisis.[7]

One of the most attractive features drawing investors to China's road infrastructure market is that the PRC government has provided for the development of service industry infrastructure along the roadways over which local investment and development companies and foreign

5. See PRC Highway Law, Article 4.

6. See text accompanying note 31 below.

7. See *The China Business Review*, pp. 9 - 10, March/April 1998.

investors can obtain operating rights. Such additional development rights have their origin in the *Foreign Investment Industrial Guidance Catalogue* (the "Catalogue"), together with the *Directing of Foreign Investment Tentative Provisions* (the "Provisions"), first issued in 1995, and are reflected in later laws relevant to roads in China.[8] The Catalogue is only meaningful when read together with the Provisions, which divide foreign investment into the categories of encouraged, permitted, restricted and prohibited.[9] Under the Catalogue and the *Administration of the Assignment of Highway Operating Rights for Compensation Procedures*, foreign investors in the highway construction sector may be permitted to operate retail businesses, such as restaurants and motels, alongside the roadway over which they have concession rights. Therefore, with an eye to obtaining a greater return on investment, foreign investors in highway construction are keen to secure the rights to develop such services infrastructure.[10]

Legal Regime

Despite targeting transportation infrastructure as one of the key investment areas to attract foreign investment over the next few years, the PRC government does not yet have a coherent or comprehensive legal regime in place to guide foreign investment in the sector. Foreign investors in highway infrastructure must rely on piecemeal, and sometimes inconsistent, rules and regulations and government practice. Under the PRC legal regime, the approach taken by the PRC government for dealing with the development and financing of infrastructure projects is to promulgate a separate rule for each different, officially sanctioned transaction structure. In comparison, the legal regime in most developed countries allows private parties to freely structure their deals according to neutral rules of general application. Because it is impossible to anticipate all possible transaction structures, the result is that there are gaps in the law that can either hurt an investor or be exploited by an investor, can result in unnecessary concessions being granted by authorities and can result in varying treatment of transactional issues. Arguably, the PRC government would be better able to achieve its infrastructural development goals if they had a unified programme rather than the current system that produces piecemeal legislation.[11]

Previously, the primary legislation relating to roads in China was the *PRC, Administration of Highways Regulations* promulgated by the State Council on October 13, 1987, which applies to national, provincial, county, village and special access roads. Other regulations, including notices, that regulate the use, management and ownership of roads in the PRC, include laws

8. See *Administration of the Assignment of Highway Operating Rights for Compensation Procedures*, 1996, Article 9.

9. It should be noted that anything not specifically listed in the Catalogue belongs to the permitted category, and that projects listed in the permitted category supposedly receive better treatment than those in the restricted category when it comes to the term of investment and approval procedures.

10. See *China Law & Practice*, January/February 1998, pp. 51 - 53.

11. See *China Law & Practice*, August 1998, p. 78.

and regulations enacted by provincial people's governments in accordance with the limits of their legislative authority, and rules and notices issued by the PRC Ministry of Communications (the "MOC").[12]

Two of the more recent laws governing highway construction and operation in the PRC are the *Administration of the Assignment for Compensation of Highway Operating Rights Procedures*, issued by the MOC on October 19, 1996 (the "Assignment Procedures"), which governs the transfer of operating rights of roads planned, constructed and managed by government transportation supervisory departments at various levels throughout the country; and the *PRC Highway Law*, issued by President's decree and effective as of January 1, 1998 (the "Highway Law"), which is aimed at strengthening the construction and maintenance of highways, facilitating the development of the highway industry and catering to the changing needs of the PRC's socialist modernization and its people.[13] The Assignment Procedures and the Highway Law, in conjunction, provide a legal basis for the granting and assignment of concession rights to foreign investors for the operation of highways and toll roads in the PRC. However, these two laws give only limited guidance on project structures and financing, and fail to address some of the major issues that concern lenders and sponsors. On the other hand, note should be taken that many highways were previously developed, approved and financed without the benefit of these two laws, so the field of play has only become greener in recent years.

Although China's build-operate-transfer ("BOT") law[14] specifically provides for experimental application of its provisions to 30 to 80 km highways of a high grade, free-standing bridges with a length of more than 1,000 metres, tunnels and urban water supply plants, to date no such projects have been developed using the BOT law , although the Beijing No. 10 water treatment project is currently being bid under a BOT structure. Chinese officials apparently are mindful of the regulatory gaps referred to above as there has been some discussion recently regarding the promulgation of new laws on granting concession rights under a BOT framework specifically with respect to transportation infrastructure, and regarding the promulgation of detailed rules on foreign investment in toll road projects.[15]

Finally, the new *PRC Invitation and Submission of Tenders Law* (the "Tendering Law" – See **Legislation Appendices**) will be applicable to new road infrastructure projects after January 1, 2000. The Tendering Law covers all contracts for major projects in which the government

---

12. See, *for example, <Administration of Highways Regulations> Implementing Rules, and the Urgent Notice for Strengthening the Regulation of Dealings in Ownership Rights of Road Assets*, issued by the Ministry of Communications.

13. See *PRC, Highway Law*, Articles 1 - 3.

14. See *Several Issues Concerning the Examination, Approval and Administration of Experimental Foreign-invested Concession Projects Circular*, 1995, Article 4. (See **Legislation Appendices**).

15. See *China Law & Practice*, December 1998/January 1999, p. 71.

has an interest (in particular, infrastructure projects). Under this law, projects will be awarded through a standardized system of public tender that is modeled on international standards.

How to fill perceived gaps in the laws

There are several useful resources to help fill the legislative lacunae, including : provincial level administrative measures, MOC and provincial level project approval notices, provincial level support letters and concession agreements. Perhaps stimulated by the lack of available domestic funds for local road development, local governments have become trailblazers when it comes to producing laws that assist the road development process in China.[16] These laws often provide additional details on subjects such as:

- term of the concession,
- transfer of land use rights,
- exemptions with respect to land use fees,
- description of other fees that may be levied,
- obligations of the concession grantee,
- preferential tax treatment,
- foreign exchange convertibility,
- toll collection and concession assignment rights,
- transfer of rights at the end of the concession period,
- events that may trigger early termination and disposal of project assets,
- remedies available to the concession grantor when the grantee breaches its duties.

Some provincial or other local governments have been willing to offer more detailed concession agreements only to those companies that are listed on various securities markets, presumably under pressure arising from the requirements of various securities regulatory authorities.[17]

Approval notices issued by MOC do not contain much substantive information relating to the road project being approved, although the date of commencement of the concession can be negotiated and included. Possible commencement dates may be:

- the date of listing (when funds are being raised through a public offering);
- the date of completion of the road (which may result in multiple commencement dates and concession terms in cases where the road is being completed in several sections); or
- simply the date of the notice itself.[18]

16. For example, see the following laws promulgated by Guangdong Province: *Guangdong Province, Administration of Highways Regulations,* 1992; *Further Clarification and Standardization of the Policies and Examination and Approval Process for Utilization of Foreign Investment in Highway Projects Circular,* 1999; *Administration of Expressways Regulations,* 1998; *Strictly Observing the Examination and Approval Procedures of Charged Items of Highways Circular,* 1998.

Support letters or comfort letters issued by the relevant PRC government authority can be used to fill perceived gaps in the regulatory framework and thereby render road projects more enticing to private and public lenders and foreign developers. Support letters should be sought from all government departments with separate functions that become involved in the project. Although such letters are likely not enforceable in PRC courts, the long-standing practice has been for government departments to stand behind them, to the extent possible, as if the law required such obligation.[17]

Foreign investors must, however, exercise caution in connection with supplemental commitments by overeager local governments as in the not uncommon case of purported "guaranteed" returns on the foreign investors' investment reflects. While such guarantees are unenforceable as contrary to Chinese law,[18] numerous local authorities gave their approval to such arrangements which, generally, worked in practice until the crackdown on foreign exchange abuses by the State Administration of Foreign Exchange ("SAFE") began in 1998.

Concession agreements can be used to cover a broad variety of issues relevant to road projects. Concession agreements can be relied upon to specify in greater detail issues relating to: toll collection terms and conditions, traffic volume guarantees, rights of first offer to operate other roads in the region, service facilities construction and management rights along roadways, limitations on vehicles exempt from tolls, non-competition covenants for roads above a certain grade that run parallel to the road in question, protection from government planning of new road projects unless certain traffic volumes are reached, toll rate adjustment guarantees, and options to extend the term of concession rights and toll collection.[19]

Right to collect tolls vs. right to tangible assets

Under the Assignment Procedures, "road operating rights" include the right to collect tolls and the right to operate service facilities (such as restaurants and rest areas) and to display advertising within the designated areas of the roads.[20] From this reading, such road operating rights appear to attach to the intangible operating rights as opposed to the tangible assets comprising the roads. A transfer or assignment of the operating rights does not transfer title to the fixed assets associated with the road, such as the land use rights. This distinction in the Assignment Procedures has caused confusion among developers regarding the extent of their rights under their respective concession arrangements. The apparent inability of a

---

17. See *China Law & Practice*, November 1998, pp. 66 – 67.

18. *Notice on Tightening Up of Control Over the Examination and Approval of the Establishment of Foreign-funded Enterprises and their Business Regulations*, paragraph 5, SAIC and MOFTEC, November 3, 1994. See **Legislation Appendices**.

19. See *China Law & Practice*, January/February 1998, pp. 82 - 83.

20. See Assignment Procedures, Article 5.

foreign investor to secure rights over the relevant tangible assets limits the investor's ability to secure financing by leveraging such assets and, in the case of CJV structures, to generate cash from the project by way of early recoupment of depreciation expenses, the latter being subject to Ministry of Finance approval.

Comparing the Assignment Procedures to the *PRC Land Administration Law (revised)* of 1999 (the "Land Law") creates additional confusion, because the Land Law specifically provides for the transfer of "land use rights" in road infrastructure projects. Thus, under the Assignment Procedures, it is possible to have operating rights over the intangible assets without having the right to use the underlying tangible assets, whereas under the Land Law, it is possible to obtain land use rights in respect of the underlying tangible real property. Unless such land use rights are "allocated" free of charge and the allocation is approved by the proper government authority pursuant to the Land Law, developers of transportation infrastructure projects could potentially be subject to land use fees. Therefore, developers should specifically enumerate all of the rights, intangible and tangible, which they will receive in the concession agreement and in all other applicable project documents. The distinction between intangible and tangible rights should provide leverage to foreign investors when negotiating the consideration to be paid for such rights.[21]

Approval Jurisdiction

In addition to dealing with the legal ambiguity and uncertainty described above, foreign investors must also deal with the difficulty of identifying exactly which government bodies have the authority to issue approvals in connection with their project. Furthermore, there is always the legal question as to whether a particular government authority has the legal capacity to enter into a concession agreement, which is essentially a contract with the government. Reliance upon the proper authority and its capacity is a critical issue because it is central to the ability of a project to repay the huge capital outlays provided by the foreign investors.[22] Without the proper formal PRC approvals, investors may not have the right to collect tolls and, in most cases, to convert these proceeds into foreign exchange for repatriation to the foreign investors and/or bondholders and banks.

Whether approval is required by the relevant authorities at the central level of government or entrusted to authorities at the local level depends on whether a road project involves a road that is part of the national highway grid and on the amount of total investment of a road project At the highest level, the State Council is responsible for national transportation laws and regulations and national road planning approvals. However, the State Council's approval authority has been vested in the State Development and Planning Commission (the "SDPC")

21. See *PRC, Land Administration Law* (revised), 1999, Article 54; see also *China Law & Practice*, December 1998/ January 1999, pp. 70 - 71. See **Legislation Appendices**.

22 See *China Law & Practice*, December 1997 p. 43.

(the SDPC, through its Communications Department, is responsible for the overall planning of all modes of transportation in China, including roads). In turn, the SDPC has delegated the authority to approve projects to provincial governments, provincial level bureaus of the central government and to certain municipalities, but the project approval authority of local governments is generally limited to approving projects worth no more than US$30 million, unless the project is one that has been approved under the "Encouraged Category" of the Foreign Investment Guidelines. If the project is one that is encouraged and is not "subject to the comprehensive balance of the State" (See the discussion in Chapter 1: **Approvals for Establishing a Joint Venture**), then, even though the total investment exceeds the US$30 million threshold, the province, autonomous region or directly administered municipality, through its COFTEC, may approve the transaction provided it files the principal documents with MOFTEC and that MOFTEC does not raise any objections within one month.[23]

MOC is the supervisory body for the planning, development, construction and management of all roads in the PRC and provides policy guidance in areas such as setting nationwide policies, regulations, standards and specifications in road design, construction and maintenance. MOC also participates directly in the development, construction and investment of certain key national highway projects. For example, for those major road projects under the National Trunk Highway System, MOC will initiate the planning, and then submit the proposals to the SDPC and the State Council for approval.

On the provincial level, the provincial communications bureau is the supervisory body for the planning, development, construction and management of all roads in the province, and it is responsible for reporting both to MOC as well as to the relevant provincial or municipal governments. The provincial communications bureaus propose detailed plans for road networks in accordance with the plans outlined by MOC, taking into account the particular conditions in the individual province. After the provincial government has approved such proposals for road development, the proposal will then be forwarded to the provincial communications department for implementation.

The Approval Process

Project approvals

Unfortunately, the laws pertaining to road infrastructure projects are not of much help in describing the relevant approval authorities or the steps for gaining approval for road projects. The Highway Law contains some procedures for obtaining concessions and some limited guidance on how new toll road projects should be planned, structured and financed, but it

23. *[MOFTEC, Relevant Issues Concerning the Approval of Foreign Investment Enterprises under the Encouraged Category in Localities by the Local Authorities and to be filed with MOFTEC Notice]*; MOFTEC, October 15, 1999 Waijing feizi fa No. 615. See **Legislation Appendices**.

does not contain a detailed or comprehensive set of rules regarding approvals, operation, toll adjustments or route monopoly protection. According to the Highway Law, construction of road infrastructure projects involving foreign investment must be examined and approved in accordance with "national regulations," which presumably includes all regulations applicable to foreign-invested enterprises.[24]

In fact, the approval process for toll roads is similar to that set forth in great detail in Chapter 9 on Power Project Approvals, because both power projects and transportation projects are large-scale public works projects which contain a government-approved and monitored tariff/toll element. The difference between the two approval processes lies in the identity of the industry-related government entities involved in the approval process. Whereas the State Power Corporation is the key PRC department-in-charge that is involved in the supervision and approval of power infrastructure projects, MOC is the key government entity that must be dealt with for the supervision and approval of transportation infrastructure projects. Exhibit 1 below provides a roadmap with respect to the government maze through which developers must manoeuvre in order to gain the necessary approvals to carry out transportation projects.

Assignment approvals

The Assignment Procedures contain additional approval-related information. For instance, the Assignment Procedures provide that MOC is responsible for the supervision and management of assignment of highway operating rights in the PRC and that the department of communications under the local government at the provincial, autonomous region and directly administered municipality level is responsible for the supervision and management of the work relating to the assignment of operating rights of roads within its jurisdiction.[25] The Assignment Procedures provide that the provincial communication authorities are required to obtain the approval of: (i) MOC for the assignment of operating rights for roads involving "central surcharges on vehicle purchases", roads completed with central financial investment and roads that are part of the national grid; and (ii) the provincial communications authority for the assignment of operating rights for roads in the provincial plan or for roads below the provincial level that are completed with local funds, local investments or funds raised by local entities.[26] Finally, the Assignment Procedures state that there can be no assignment of operating rights for roads constructed with financing from international financial institutions or foreign government loans except with the approval of the government department which approved the loan and the "window" department, the actual borrowing entity, with respect to such loans.[27] In addition, the Highway Law states that transfers of toll rights must be approved

24. See Highway Law, Article 60.

25. See Assignment Procedures, Article 4. (See **Legislation Appendices**)

26. See Assignment Procedures, Article 7. (See **Legislation Appendices**)

27. See Assignment Procedures, Article 10. (See **Legislation Appendices**)

by the government at the provincial, autonomous region or centrally-governed municipality level and reported to the State Council department-in-charge of communications.[28]

Foreign investment enterprise approvals

All foreign investment projects must be approved by MOFTEC or by one of its subordinate departments at the provincial or local government level (only if the total investment amount is below US$30 million or the project has been approved for inclusion into the Encouraged Category). Accordingly, foreign investment enterprises proposing to undertake projects must obtain approvals for the projects from the SDPC (or its provincial level designee), and approvals for the foreign investment from a similar level department of MOFTEC (or its provincial level designee), to establish the required Sino-foreign joint venture. (See generally Chapter 1: **Approvals for Establishing a Joint Venture**.)

Toll rate approvals and the length of the concession term

When a joint venture has been established or when an expressway has been completed, the joint venture may apply to the State Price Bureau at the appropriate level for approval of the toll amounts depending on the type of vehicle. Typically, provincial governments are responsible for toll rate approvals for roads within their administrative region. Decisions regarding toll rates are usually made collectively by the provincial Price Bureaus, provincial departments of communications and provincial finance departments. Upon obtaining the approval document from the provincial price bureau, the joint venture has the right to collect tolls. Although toll rates will be determined by the price bureau, together with the finance bureau (both at the provincial level), the actual approval document with respect to the toll rates will be issued by the price bureau at the provincial level.

The Highway Law does not specifically limit the maximum length of time allowed for concession rights to collect tolls on roads other than to say that the period of operation and toll collection may not exceed the number of years stipulated by the State Council (apparently 30 years).[29] On the other hand, the Assignment Procedures state that for the assignment of the right to collect tolls, the maximum period should be, in principle, based on the period required to recoup the initial capital invested plus a reasonable profit. The maximum toll collection period should not exceed 150% of the period required to recoup the initial capital invested, and the term of operating rights may not exceed 30 years.[30] These more recent laws correlate with past government practice, which has been to grant concession rights for a term of no more than 30 years.

28. See Highway Law, Article 61.

29. See Highway Law, Article 60.

30. See Assignment Procedures, Article 11. (See **Legislation Appendices**)

Exhibit 1 outlines the basic administrative framework for road development and approval in the PRC.

Exhibit 1

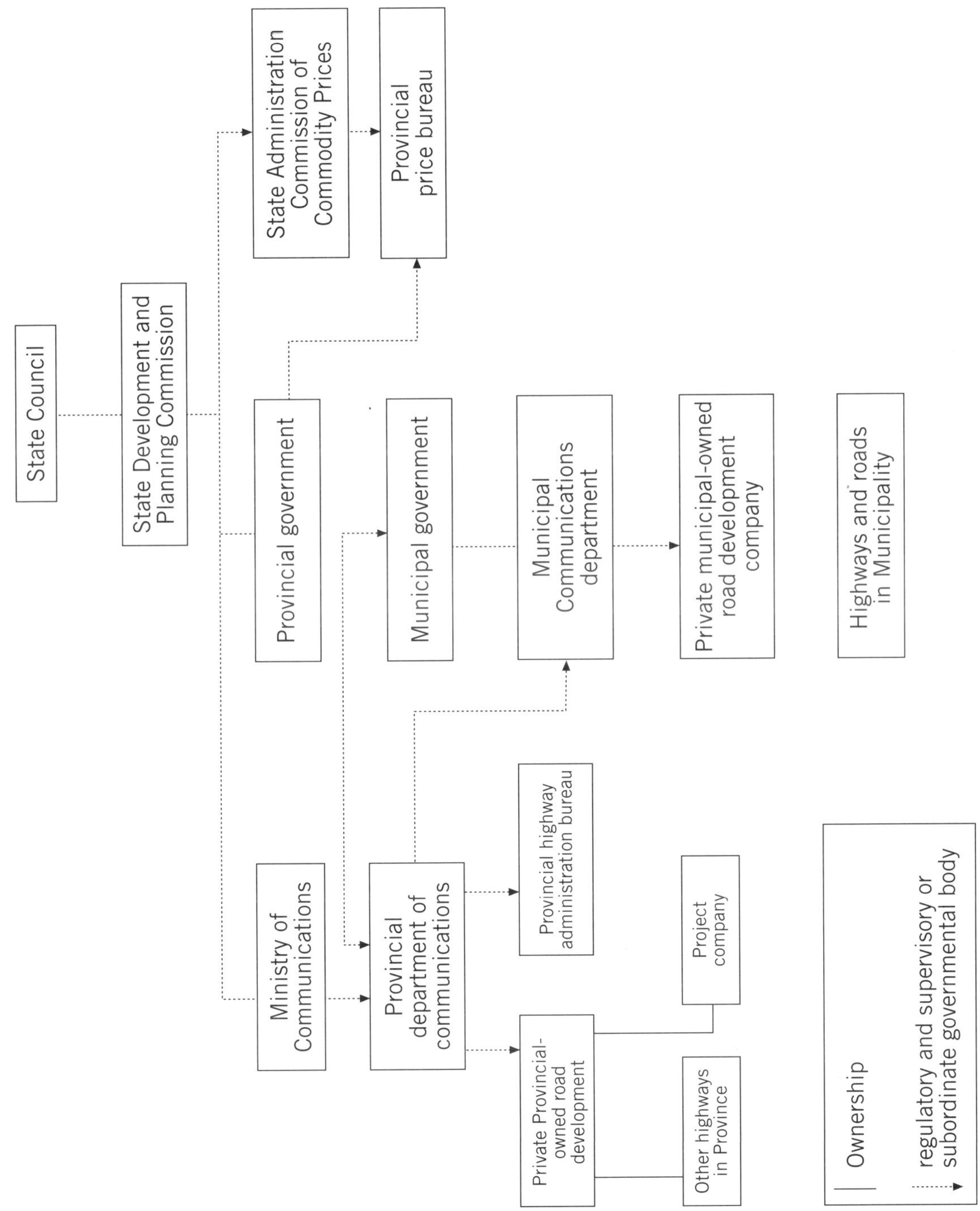

Effective Project Structures

Why projects fail

The way projects are structured and financed is critical to a project's success. It is usually the case that foreign investors team up with a local partner to form a joint venture to own the concession rights and to operate the toll road. Sometimes the relationship with the local partner turns sour. For example, recently, a Malaysian investor divested its controlling interest in a joint venture in China that owns concession rights to a toll road because of a disagreement with its local Chinese partner over issues relating to dividend distribution and other operational matters.[31] The most common issues that derail road projects include: relocation issues, delays in obtaining clearance for route plans (sometimes due to county level government lobbying), local taxation concerns, and land use and engineering disputes (most PRC parties insist that local engineers are sufficient for the job and will likely only agree to a Sino-foreign engineering partnership).[32] Ironically, many of these difficulties result from China's poor legal framework and regulatory structure. Control and supervision of the toll collection process has given rise to disputes in some cases. In addition, roadside service infrastructure may become overdeveloped, thereby reducing its profitability.[33]

Choosing a strategic local joint venture partner

One investment structure often used in Sino-foreign road ventures is to have the foreign partner hold only a majority interest in the project company. Even though management control of the project company is important to foreign investors, most foreign investors in road infrastructure projects in China have chosen to work with a PRC partner that is an entity established by the local government, precisely for the purpose of acquiring assistance with such governmental approval matters such as securing routing plans, land use rights and toll rate approvals.

The profitability of a toll road project depends to a large extent upon "toll strategies" and the ability to realize the property development potential along roadways. This is a situation where direct government involvement in one's project can produce beneficial results when time

---

31. See Internet at http://skali2.com/business/trp/199903/19/trp19990319_02.html.

32. In fact, the State Council and Ministry of Construction Regulations on Construction Project Supervision of 1995, require in practice that investors in construction projects using foreign investment must hire a PRC government-approved construction supervision unit to supervise the construction work. Foreign investors who undertake construction projects in the PRC usually prefer to employ a foreign construction management company with whom they have experience to supervise the construction process. Nevertheless, regardless of the reputation of the foreign contractor and the parties' relationship, the law requires the foreign investor to retain a PRC government approved construction supervision unit to perform these services, usually at a disproportionately high fee compared to the services performed, regardless of parallel work, in some instances, by a foreign construction management company. See *China Law & Practice*, March 1999, p. 50.

33. See The *China Business Review*, March-April 1998, pp. 10 - 11.

comes to have toll rate increases approved. Having a local government partner is not a guarantee, however, as some local pricing bureaus have opposed toll increases in spite of the fact that the government has a commercial stake in the venture. Such tariffs are, of course, often politically sensitive.

Financing alternatives

Some investment variables, such as the nature of one's relationship with a local Chinese partner, are less subject to control than other investment variables, such as how to structure the construction, operation and financing phases of a project. The requirement for large capital outlays from banks, international funds or public offerings of equity and debt usually dictates the overall structure of a project. Some of the structures used to finance toll roads (other than through international lending) will be outlined here.

A growing trend among Chinese-owned expressway companies is to list their shares on foreign or PRC stock exchanges. Despite several successful initial public offerings on the Hong Kong stock exchange, market volatility during the Asian financial crisis has caused share prices to fluctuate downward. Furthermore, the capital markets of the PRC are still relatively small and capable of handling only a modest number of issues each year. Equity-funded infrastructure projects tend to be more expensive, requiring net profits of around 18% to be viable.

On the other hand, several Sino-foreign owned expressway companies have undertaken large bond issues. Bond issues have become increasingly popular partly because of their less expensive annual interest cost (usually 10% to 11%). Bond issues are typically used to refinance projects that are complete or nearly complete, as revenue streams begin to become more closer to a reality. In addition, international rating agencies have graded PRC road bonds.

Unfortunately, an experimental and promising model of infrastructure financing based on industrial revenue bond structures employed in the successful Zhuhai Toll Road project financing was subsequently scrapped due to bureaucratic infighting in Beijing.

China's domestic commercial banking sector is limited in its ability to support investment on the scale needed for road infrastructure. Loans from domestic banks are unlikely to become a reliable source of financing road projects in the near future, but there is a trend towards domestic banks providing "bridge" financing in relatively small amounts (around US$25 million) in order to allow developers to finish projects.[34]

34. See *The China Business Review*, March-April 1998, Pp. 10 – 11.

Breaking projects into sections

One attractive feature of road projects versus other infrastructure projects in China is that roads can be broken into shorter or longer sections in accordance with the individual investor's particular funding limits, its requirement for certain levels of risk and return, or to avoid seeking central level MOFTEC approval for projects requiring a total investment in excess of US$30 million. Although this practice of separating a project into smaller parts is frowned upon and subject to risk, such structures have generally not been challenged by MOFTEC, in some cases at least, on the theory that such projects are not "production-type" projects utilizing foreign funds. One of the drawbacks to this approach is that the existence of numerous project companies may interfere with the overall construction planning process and the performance of the sectional investments. Furthermore, in some cases, investors are not willing to finance less attractive sections of the road, resulting in a scenario where the investor must sit and wait for the completion of the connecting sections before achieving the traffic levels and anticipated returns projected at the planning stage. The existence of a series of foreign-invested enterprises, each responsible for a section of the road, is awkward in the redundant administrative work it creates as well as the separate accounting statements and tax payments for each such entity. Nevertheless, this type of sectional financing approach has been successfully deployed and implemented.[35]

Road development vs. assignment of operating rights

As a risk reduction strategy, foreign investors might consider seeking out those provincial level investment and development companies which have already completed roads and which would be amenable to assigning their operating rights in the existing roads as an inducement to the foreign partner to pursue future greenfield development and operation opportunities within their jurisdiction.

Seeking concession terms up to 30 years

Developers may seek a concessionary operation period of up to 30 years. Formerly, concessionary terms were limited by PRC officials to 15-year periods. A recent trend for new projects is to grant concessionary rights for 25 to 30 years, and at least one provincial jurisdiction has required concessions for terms in excess of 30 years to be renegotiated.[36]

35. See *The China Business Review*, March-April 1998, p. 9.

36. See *Guangdong Province, Further Clarification and Standardization of the Policies and Examination and Approval Process for Utilization of Foreign Investment in Highway Projects Circular*, 1999; See also *The China Business Review*, March-April 1998, p. 10.

Approval Related Issues

Restrictions relating to road size

In China, highways are classified according to their technical grade and level of importance in the national road network. Road networks are classified into national highways, provincial highways, country roads and village roads. Roads may be further divided into two categories, namely vehicular roads and general roads, which are further distinguished by traffic volume, function (in terms of the design assumption for vehicle type) and scope of service (in terms of the points of linkage). Each category is divided into three grades. In terms of road quality, roads may be classified as either paved roads or non-paved roads whereas paved roads may be further divided into primary grade, secondary grade, medium grade and low grade roads. However, there are restrictions on the assignment of operating rights depending on the size of the roads in question. The Highway Law makes no mention of the particulars regarding the minimum size of roads subject to toll collection. On the other hand, the Assignment Procedures provide that the scope of assignment of operating rights is limited to (a) the right to collect tolls with respect to sections of roads with a minimum length of 44 km and having 4 lanes or more and, with respect to large-scale bridges and tunnels, those which are at least 500 meters wide, and (b) the right to operate service facilities such as restaurants, auto repair, shops and advertising along the designated areas of such roads. In addition, there are further restrictions that items (a) and (b) above may be assigned jointly, item (a) above may also be assigned separately independent of the service facilities, but item (b) above may not be assigned separately.[37]

Government guarantees

The average rate of return for an investment in China's toll roads is reported to be around 13 to 14%.[38] As noted earlier, guaranteed rates of returns are contrary to PRC regulations and, accordingly, not enforceable.

Risk factors

A number of factors involved in toll road projects give rise to risks with which developers and lenders must deal. Some of these risk factors are outlined briefly here.

interruption of operations

The use of the roads may be adversely interrupted or otherwise affected by a variety of events, such as natural disasters and serious traffic accidents. Typically, however, sponsors do not obtain property or business interruption insurance in respect of the roads they operate, leaving them vulnerable to such risks.

37. See Assignment Procedures, Article 9. (See **Legislation Appendices**)

38. See *China Economic News*, August 18, 1997, Weekly No. 31.

fluctuations in traffic volume

The volume of traffic on a toll road is influenced by factors such as the availability, quality, proximity and toll rate differentials of alternative routes, the existence of other means of transportation such as air or rail transportation, and other factors such as fuel prices, weather conditions, vehicle registration fees, taxation, environmental regulations and general economic conditions. Prospective foreign investors often hire professional traffic consultants to assess such risks for a specific project.

lack of control over toll rates

Normally, the right to receive subsequent adjustments to toll rates will require the prior approval of the provincial level price bureau, and may further require the approval of the provincial development and planning commission, finance department and communications department. These government authorities typically decline to agree in advance that future applications for increases of toll rates will be approved or covenant that they will not, in fact, require a toll reduction. Concessionary agreements usually provide for the periodic (one to two years) review and adjustment of toll rates according to the prevailing inflation rate (per the PRC Retail Price Index) so that the toll rates will be maintained at their present levels in constant price terms. In the end, a locality's pricing bureau has the final say over any increase in user fees. To protect against the risk of toll rate unpredictability, some projects include an assurance from a company owned by the provincial government's road infrastructure development and investment vehicle to compensate the project company for any shortfall in revenue sustained as a result of a failure to increase toll rates as set out in the concession agreement. As discussed above, such shortfall guarantees, while they may be implemented in practice, are contrary to the prohibition on guaranteed returns for foreign-invested companies and, accordingly, unenforceable.

Another risk relating to toll rates is the fact that many localities charge vehicle registration fees in addition to highway tolls as a source of funding. The higher the registration fees, the more expensive road use becomes. Efforts to implement a national fuel tax in place of local vehicle registration fees has been met with strong resistance at the provincial level and below.[39]

toll receipt efficiency

Toll collection can be affected by the integrity of the toll collection system and the number of vehicles exempted from the payment of tolls. Toll collectors should be closely monitored. Therefore, road operators must develop toll collection control systems to monitor the entire process of toll collection by each toll collector.

---

39. See *The China Business Review*, March-April 1998, p. 13.

construction problems

A considerable amount of capital expenditure is required for most road projects during the lengthy construction period. Significant delays and cost overruns in road construction will negatively affect the earnings and cashflow of a toll road operator. The way to mitigate construction risk is to enter into a fixed price/fixed term construction contract or turnkey contract. Such agreements should also provide for penalties to be payable by the contractors if they fail to adhere to the construction schedule.

financing problems

Many road projects are financed by a combination of equity and/or debt financing that is serviced by the cash flow generated by the project company. When new toll road projects are undertaken by developers, there can be no assurance that further equity and/or debt financing will be available or that it will be on attractive terms. Some developers have been successful in making their project bids "subject to financing".

seizure or termination of concession

It is possible, regardless of one's legal rights under the concession agreement, that the government authority that issued the concession may impose restrictions or onerous requirements or restrictions on the developer's rights under the concession agreement, which may adversely affect a company's operations.

neighbouring road competition

The existence of competing transportation and alternative road routes is a problem that could seriously effect revenues. Usually, the concession agreement will provide for a ban on building certain classes of highways in the designated area until specific traffic forecasts are realized, at which time the sponsor may have the right of first offer to construct the neighboring expansion highway.

issues affecting profitability

Competition from other roads, railways, etc., in China may affect the profitability of a toll road project. Additionally, the ability of local governments to set vehicle registration fees influences the overall number of vehicles that will be registered and in use. A way to solve these problems is to obtain assurances in the concession agreement from the relevant government authority that no new roads in the vicinity will be constructed until certain usage levels are exceeded on the toll road, and that the toll road company will be given the right to make the first proposal for the construction and operation of new roads on a preferential basis.

currency issues

Large-scale infrastructure projects such as toll roads require large amounts of domestic currency to be converted into foreign exchange for remittance abroad to pay interest and principal on any foreign loans or bonds. SAFE registration and approval is required with respect to such loans or bonds, as the case may be. Without such registration or approval, the project company will not be able to convert Renminbi into foreign currency for payment abroad. There is always an exchange rate risk involved when receiving revenue denominated in one currency to pay off debts denominated in another currency. Therefore, the profitability of road projects in China is vulnerable to exchange rate volatility and inflation.

legal system

Despite the progress made by China to improve its body of laws and their enforcement, the fact remains that these laws, regulations and legal requirements are relatively new, and their interpretation and enforcement are not always consistently applied.

completion delays

As indicated above, in some cases investors are not willing to finance the less attractive sections of the road which results in the project company having to wait for the completion of the connecting sections before they can begin operations. Such a scenario will impact the traffic levels and projected returns determined at the planning stage.

Conclusion

The development of China's road network is still in its infancy, providing ample opportunity for road development companies to add Chinese toll roads, bridges and tunnels to their portfolio. Nevertheless, the road along which investors must travel to become a profitable player in the Chinese transportation market still has some potholes. Regulatory considerations, such as the approval process and other procedural hoops relating to road projects in China, are no less daunting than the task of mitigating project risk through diligent legal and financial structuring. Fortunately, the Highway Law and the Assignment Procedures provide some guidance regarding the administration of toll roads in China, and past government practices in this regard provide assistance in filling in the gaps in China's regulatory framework.

As with any PRC infrastructure project, investors who are mindful of all the local and central governmental approvals required in respect of their particular project and actively and patiently seek to have any significant terms and conditions of their investment clearly reflected in the basic concession agreement and in the various required approval documents reduce the risk of unpleasant surprises leading to an unsuccessful project.

Summary Checklist

1. Determine appropriate level of government approval authority based upon
   - whether project is part of China's national highway grid;
   - total amount of investment required; and
   - location of project.
2. Consider related cash-generating opportunities in connection with establishing and operating roadside service facilities when seeking approval.
3. Check BOT and Tendering regulations, if applicable.
4. Use of Support Letters from relevant government authorities.
5. Concession Agreement Terms and Conditions including
   - legal capacity of PRC grantor
   - term
   - operating rights v. rights in respect of the tangible assets
   - toll collection details
   - vehicle registration fees
   - operation of roadside services
   - traffic volume guarantees
   - non-competition provisions and rights to develop and operate related roads
   - limits on toll-exempt vehicles
   - toll rate adjustment mechanism
   - right to extend term under certain conditions
6. In the case of CJV's, Ministry of Finance approval for early recoupment of capital by way of depreciation expenses.
7. Status of land
   - land use rights
   - leasehold interest
   - exclusive use
8. Financing structure
   - Debt
   - Foreign exchange and RMB loans
   - Foreign exchange bonds
   - Equity
   - private placements
   - public offerings, IPO's
9. Risk assessment and mitigation

APPENDICES

APPENDIX 1

CONTENTS REQUIREMENT FOR A JOINT VENTURE'S FEASIBILITY STUDY REPORT

1. General description:
   (1) Name of the joint venture enterprise, legal address, purpose, scope of business and its scale.
   (2) Name of respective partner, registered country, legal address. Name, position, and nationality of the legal representative. State the superior administration of Chinese partner.
   (3) Total investment of the joint venture, its registered capital, capital funds to be raised (self-owned fund, investment proportion, form of investment, term of payment of the investment funds).
   (4) Term of the joint venture, ratio of profit-sharing and loss-sharing of both parties.
   (5) Approval certificate of project proposal.
   (6) List of persons responsible for preparing the feasibility study report.
   (7) Summary and conclusion of the feasibility study report including problems, issues and suggestions.
2. Plans of production and their basis. Explain the demand of the market both at home and abroad and how the market survey is carried out. Also explain similar facilities already existing or being built at home and abroad, i.e. situations of both existing and potential competitors.
3. Sourcing of raw materials supply including power and transportation and their basis.
4. Selection of the location of the project and the reason thereof.
5. Selection of the equipment and the process of manufacturing, and their reason thereof. (Including classified list of domestic and imported equipment).
6. Organizational structure of the joint venture and its reason, including composition of management, departments, total number of employees, and their recruiting source.
7. Environment protection, security of labour, health care and their relevant measures.
8. Mode of construction, time schedule, and their reason.
9. Method of raising funds which include building and equipment as capital investment and their calculation.
10. Arrangement of foreign exchange balance, and its reason thereof.
11. Composite analysis (including economic, technical, financial and legal analysis) of benefit and foreign exchange revenue and expenditure using dynamic, risk, or sensitivity method.
12. Appendices:
    (1) Duplicate of business licences of both partners issued by their respective government or region;

(2) Certificates of legal representative of both partners;

(3) Annual financial reports including balance sheets and profit and loss statements of each partner;

(4) Market survey and prediction both at home and abroad. Expected international market share;

(5) Opinions of relevant superior administration on main supply of raw materials, auxiliary materials, subcontracting of components, localization of sourcing of components, as well as power and transportation;

(6) Opinions of relevant superior administration on the classified lists of domestic and imported equipment;

(7) Opinions of relevant superior administration on the import substitution of products;

(8) Opinions of relevant superior administration on the raising of capital funds;

(9) Opinions of relevant superior administration on the location of manufacturing site;

(10) Opinions of relevant superior administration on the environment protection, fire protection, security of labour, health care and earthquake;

(11) Opinions of relevant superior administration on the balance of foreign exchange;

(12) Opinions of relevant superior administration on the preview or evaluation of the project.

APPENDIX 2

SAMPLE CHECKLIST OF LICENCES, PERMITS AND APPROVALS REQUIRED PRIOR TO AND AFTER COMMENCEMENT OF A POWER PROJECT

Approval for the Establishment of the Company

After the Feasibility Study report is approved by the SPC (or the state council if necessary), the parties should put forward an application to COFTEC through the relevant local MOFTEC and must submit the following documents:

- Application Report for establishing a foreign investment enterprise in China, which includes the following:
  - names and registered address of the foreign investors and the Chinese investors and names, nationality and positions of their legal representatives;
  - name and address of the proposed company;
  - scope of operations, product type and production scale;
  - total amount of investment in the proposed company, amount of registered capital, each party's capital contribution in case of joint ventures, source of capital, method of investment and term of investment;
  - organizational format and structure of the proposed company and its legal representative; main types of production equipment to be used and respective age of equipment, production technology to be used, level of technology and source of supply;
  - product sales direction, regions, sales channels, methods and the product sales ratio on domestic and overseas markets;
  - foreign exchange income and expenditure arrangements;
  - personnel framework, including arrangements for employee recruitment, training, wages, welfare benefits, insurance and labour protection;
  - amount of environmental pollution likely to be caused and combative measures;
  - site selection and area of land to be used;
  - capital construction and capital, resources and raw materials required for production and operations and supply measures;
  - progress plans for project implementation; and
  - period of operation of the proposed company
- Feasibility Study Report
- Articles of Association of the company and Joint Venture Contract (if applicable);
- list of the legal representative (or name list of members of the Board of Directors) of the Company;
- certificates evidencing the legal status and the creditworthiness of investor(s);
- written response of the relevant local government to the investor's application for the establishment of the proposed company;

- the Feasibility Study Report approval document;
- list of items to be imported; and
- other documents required to be submitted (including an environmental evaluation report, supplied by the Environmental Protection Bureau and the MPI's opinion).

The Application Report, Feasibility Study, Articles of Association and the Joint Venture Contract must be in Chinese. The other documents can be prepared in a foreign language as agreed upon by both parties (in the case of joint ventures), but the Chinese version has to be attached.

Company Registration

Registration of company name

The company's name should be registered in advance. After receiving the Feasibility Study Report approval from the SPC, the Preparation Committee of the proposed company may apply to the State Administration for Industry and Commerce ("SAIC") for registration of the company's name and for obtaining the Certificate of Enterprise Name Registration by submitting the following documents:

- Application Form signed by the person in charge of the Preparation Committee of the proposed Company;
- Feasibility Study Report approval document from the SPC; and
- Incorporation Certificate of the investors in their home country.

Registration for operation

The Preparation Committee should apply to the SAIC for registration and for obtaining the business licence of the company as an enterprise legal person within 30 days after receiving the approval certificate from MOFTEC. The following documents must be submitted:

- Application Form signed by the person in charge of the Preparation Committee;
- Certificate of Enterprise Name Registration;
- MOFTEC's Approval Certificate;
- Articles of Association and Joint Venture Contract (if applicable) of the proposed Company;
- Certificates evidencing the creditworthiness of the investors;
- the list of names of the members of the Board of Directors and appointment documents of the members of the Board of Directors, the general manager and the deputy general manager and a copy of their identification certificates;
- evidence of use of an office; and
- other relevant documents and certificates.

Approvals Required after the Company is Formally Established

Foreign Investment Enterprise Foreign Exchange Registration Certificate

To open a foreign exchange bank account, the company should apply to the relevant local branch of the SAEC for the Foreign Investment Enterprise Foreign Exchange Registration Certificate ("FERC") by submitting the following documents:

- Application Form with the company's seal;
- the company's Articles of Association and Joint Venture Contract (if applicable);
- copy of the company's Business Licence;
- MOFTEC's Approval Certificate; and
- other documents required by the branch.

After obtaining the approval documents and the FERC from the SAEC local branch, the company should apply to a designated bank with foreign currency business for opening a foreign exchange account by submitting the above documents together with the FERC.

Tax registration

The company should register with the local tax authority 30 days after its establishment by submitting the following documents:

- Application Report and the Tax Registration Form;

- copy of the Business Licence issued by the SAIC;
- the company's Articles of Association and Joint Venture Contract (if applicable)
- copy of the basic bank savings account of the company;
- ID of the company's legal representative; and
- copy of the code given by the technology supervising authority.

Customs registration

The company should submit a written application to Customs for registration. Upon examination by Customs and the completion of the registration procedure, the company may apply to Customs for declaration of the import and export equipment and cargo. The company shall submit the following documents on registration:

- Application Form;
- copy or photocopy of the approval documents for establishment of the company;
- copies or photocopies of the business licence issued by the SAIC;
- economic guarantee issued by the bank (if Customs thinks it is necessary);
- Articles of Association and Joint Venture Contract (if applicable) and approval documents;
- capital verification report (photocopies); and
- approval documents for special purpose (if necessary).

Approvals Required Before Commencement of Construction Work

Qualification Certificate of Foreign Contractor Undertaking Contracted Projects

In accordance with the Administration for Qualification of Foreign Contractor Undertaking Contracted Projects in China Interim Measures, before undertaking contracted projects in China, a foreign contractor should go through the qualification examination and obtain a Qualification Certificate of Foreign Contractor Undertaking Contracted Projects (the "Qualification Certificate").

Foreign contractors undertaking contracted projects in a province or an autonomous region in China should apply to the construction administration authority of the provincial People's Government for the Qualification Certificate.

After receiving the Qualification Certificate, the foreign contractor shall register with the SAIC in accordance with Chinese laws before undertaking contracted projects in China. The foreign contractor shall submit the Qualification Certificate together with the following documents:

- the contract signed by the foreign contractor;
- the foreign contractor's certificate for business operation and capital credit;
- application for registration signed by the Chairman of the Board of the foreign contractor (the content of the application includes: business scope and the name list, positions and personal particulars of the main resident personnel in China); and
- the list of foreign subcontractors, items and content of subcontracted projects and the list of their main resident personnel in China.

After verification and approval of the registration of the foreign contractor by the SAIC, a PRC Business Licence should be issued.

Registration of foreign subcontractors shall be handled by the local SAIC. The following documents shall be submitted:

- the contract;
- the certificate given by the related company; and
- the application for registration signed by the Chairman of the Board of the foreign contractor (the content of the application includes: business scope and the name list, positions and personal particulars of the main resident personnel in China).

After the verification and approval of the registration of the foreign subcontractor, the

Registration Certificate for Foreign Enterprises Undertaking Subcontracted Projects in China shall be issued to the foreign subcontractor.

Investment Certificate and Certificate of Construction Permit

The Company applies to the relevant local planning commission for obtaining an Investment Certificate.

The Company applies to the relevant local construction commission and fills in the Construction Declaration Form to obtain the Certificate of Construction Permit.

Approval for Grid Synchronization

The company shall sign a grid access agreement with the Central Dispatching Station ("CDS") of the relevant power bureau no later than three months prior to the completion date on which the power plant (or part of the power plant) reaches commercial operation criteria ("Completion Date"). Upon satisfaction of the conditions for synchronization required by the agreement, the company should submit to the CDS of the relevant power bureau the design documents of the primary equipment of the power plant related to the synchronization. The CDS of the relevant power bureau should reply to the company within 30 days upon receipt of the above-mentioned technical material if the design of the power plant has satisfied the technical requirements of the grid system.

The company should submit a relevant power bureau application for synchronization with the grid system to the CDS no later than 20 days prior to the Completion Date. The contents of the application include:

- general situation of the power plant;
- target start-up date, target commissioning date and commissioning schedule; and
- person to contact during start-up and commissioning, and name list of primary staff conducting operations.

The following materials shall be submitted at the same time;

- specifications and parameters of main equipment;
- primary and secondary electric wiring diagram;
- floor plan for main equipment; and
- equipment operating rules.

The CDS of the relevant power bureau should reply in writing to the company within five days of receipt of the application and materials.

Approval Before Commencement of Commercial Operation

During the testing of the power plant, the company should apply promptly to the environment protection authority for as-built acceptance application of the environment protection equipment of the power plant, and the environmental protection authority should manage the as-built acceptance of the environment protection equipment.

After completion of the power plant, the company should apply to the relevant planning commission for as-built acceptance as stipulated by the SPC. The as-built report and drawing should be provided to the relevant provincial or municipal government.

APPENDIX 3

WHOLLY FOREIGN-OWNED ENTERPRISE APPLICATION FORM

Application No. : ____________________

Receiving Person : ____________________

Date : ____________________

Field of Operation : ____________________

APPLICATION FORM FOR THE ESTABLISHMENT OF A FOREIGN CAPITAL ENTERPRISE IN CHINA

I. INFORMATION CONCERNING THE COMPANY APPLYING FOR THE ESTABLISHMENT OF A FOREIGN CAPITAL ENTERPRISE (HEREIN AFTER THE "COMPANY")

1. Name of the Company: ____________________
2. Legal Address: ____________________
   Other Address (if any): ____________________
3. Country or Jurisdiction of Incorporation: ____________________
4. Date of Incorporation: ____________________
5. Name of the Legal Representative: ____________________
   Nationality: ____________________
6. Business Scope: ____________________
7. Scale of Production: ____________________
8. Total Asset: ____________________
9. Registered Capital: ____________________
10. Bank: ____________________
11. Countries Where Investment Has Been Made:
    ____
    ____
    ____
12. Attach Balance Sheets for the past 3 years. If the company has less than 3 years of operations, attach information for the parent company.
13. Name of the Contact Person for the company in China.

Address: ____________________

Telephone number: ____________________

II. THE FOREIGN CAPITAL ENTERPRISE TO BE ESTABLISHED IN CHINA

1. Name of the Foreign Capital Enterprise: ____________________
2. Address: ____________________
3. Total Amount of Investment: ____________________
4. Amount of Registered Capital: ____________________
5. Upon Establishment The Foreign Capital Enterprise Shall be a Limited Liability Company, Liability Shall be limited to ____________________ Amount of Registered Capital)
6. Form of Investment: ____________________
   a) Foreign Currency: ____________________
   b) Equipment: ____________________
   c) Technology: ____________________
   d) Other: ____________________
7. Land Surface Area and Building Surface Area Needed: ____________________
   a) Office: ____________________
   b) Manufacturing: ____________________
   c) Other Buildings: ____________________
8. Project Conditions:
   a) Scope: ____________________
   b) Production Scale: ____________________
   c) Raw Materials and Their Sources: ____________________
   d) Sources of Machine Fittings: ____________________
   e) Product Uses: ____________________
   f) Market for Sales: ____________________
   g) Export Ratio: ____________________
   h) Plan for the Balancing of Foreign Exchange Expenditures and Receipts (Please Attach)
9. Management of the Foreign Capital Enterprise
   a) Composition of the Board of Directors: ____________________
   ____
   b) Management Offices and Senior Staff: ____________________
   c) System of Financial Affairs and Accounting: ____________________
   d) Total Staff and Workers: ____________________
      Foreign Staff and Workers: ____________________
      Management Personnel: ____________________
      Technical Personnel: ____________________
      Workers: ____________________
10. Department in Charge: ____________________

III. CONSTRUCTION AND IMPLEMENTATION OF THE PROJECT

1. Technology to Be Used in Carrying out the Project:
2. Machinery and Equipment to Be Used for the Project:
3. The Volume of Water, Electricity, Gas, Fuel Etc. Which Will be Needed by the Project:
4. The Standard of the Treatment of "Three Wastes" and the Security Standard:
5. Schedule of Planned Construction:
   Year 1:______________________________
   Year 2:______________________________
6. Starting Date for Production:
7. Quantity of Products Planned in the First Three Years of Production:
   a) Year 1: ______________________________
   b) Year 2: ______________________________
   c) Year 3: ______________________________
8. Principal Raw Materials to be Purchased in China:
   a) Year 1: ______________________________
   b) Year 2: ______________________________
   c) Year 3: ______________________________
9. Raw Materials to Be Imported:
   a) Year 1: ______________________________
   b) Year 2: ______________________________
   c) Year 3: ______________________________
10. Plan for the Training of Chinese Staff and Workers: ____________________

IV. TERM OF OPERATION OF THE FOREIGN CAPITAL ENTERPRISE

____

V. THE COMPANY HEREBY AGREES TO THE FOLLOWING CONDITIONS FOR THE ESTABLISHMENT OF THE FOREIGN CAPITAL ENTERPRISE

1. All Activities of the Foreign Capital Enterprise Shall Comply With and be Protected by the Laws, Decrees and Relevant Regulations of the People's Republic of China.
2. The Foreign Capital Enterprise Shall pay the Relevant taxes in Accordance With the Laws, Decrees and Relevant Regulations of the People's Republic of China.

COMPANY:

____

SIGNATURE:

____

DATE:

____

LEGISLATION APPENDICES

DIRECTING OF FOREIGN INVESTMENT TENTATIVE PROVISIONS

(Reported by Xinhua News Agency on June 27, 1995, Beijing.)

Article 1: These Provisions are formulated in accordance with the provisions of laws concerning foreign investment and the requirements of industrial policies of the State, in order to direct foreign investment so as to bring in line with China's national economic and social development plans, and to protect the lawful rights and interests of investors.

Article 2: These Provisions apply to projects invested in and set up by Sino-foreign equity joint ventures, Sino-foreign cooperative joint ventures and wholly foreign-owned enterprises as well as foreign investment projects in other forms (hereafter, "Foreign Investment Projects") within the People's Republic of China.

Article 3: The State Planning Commission shall, in conjunction with the relevant departments of the State Council, draft on a regular basis, and amend when appropriate, a Foreign Investment Industrial Guidance Catalogue based on these Provisions and the development of the national economy and technology. Such Catalogue shall be promulgated after approval by the State Council.

The Foreign Investment Industrial Guidance Catalogue shall be the basis for guiding the examination and approval of Foreign Investment Projects.

Article 4: Foreign Investment Projects shall be divided into four categories: encouraged, permitted, restricted and prohibited projects.

Encouraged, restricted and prohibited Foreign Investment Projects shall be included in the Foreign Investment Industrial Guidance Catalogue. Foreign Investment Projects that do not fall into the encouraged, restricted or prohibited project categories shall be Foreign Investment Projects under the permitted project category. Foreign Investment Projects under the permitted project category shall not be included in the Foreign Investment Industrial Guidance Catalogue.

The Foreign Investment Industrial Guidance Catalogue may specify Foreign Investment Projects that may not be operated by wholly foreign-owned enterprises in which State-owned assets shall represent a controlling or leading position.

Article 5: Foreign Investment Projects of any of the following kinds shall be categorized as encouraged Foreign Investment Projects:

(1) those which involve new agricultural technology, overall agricultural development and energy, communications and major raw materials for industrial construction;

(2) those which involve high and new technology and advanced technology as well as new equipment and materials capable of improving product performance, saving

energy and raw materials, enhancing the technological and economic benefits and production of enterprises to meet market demand due to the lack of productivity in the domestic market;

(3) those which meet international market demand and are capable of upgrading products, opening up new markets, expanding the foreign sales of products and increasing exports;

(4) those which involve new technology or equipment for the comprehensive use of resources or recycled resources as well as for the prevention and control of environmental pollution;

(5) those which can bring into play the advantages of the manpower and resources in the central and western regions and which conform to the industrial policies of the State;

(6) other projects which are encouraged under laws or administrative regulations of the State.

Article 6: Foreign Investment Projects of any of the following kinds shall be categorized as restricted Foreign Investment Projects:

(1) those which have already been developed in China or for which technology has already been imported into China, and of which the productivity has already met domestic market demand;

(2) those which involve industries in which the State attracts foreign investment on a trial basis or exercises a monopoly;

(3) those which involve exploration or exploitation of rare or precious mineral resources;

(4) those which involve industries for which central planning is required by the State;

(5) other projects which are restricted under laws or administrative regulations of the State.

Restricted Foreign Investment Projects shall be placed under restricted project category (A) or restricted project category (B) respectively, according to the State's industrial policies and the requirements of macroeconomic controls.

Article 7: Foreign Investment Projects of any of the following kinds shall be categorized as prohibited Foreign Investment Projects:

(1) those which jeopardize national security or harm public interests;

(2) those which cause environmental pollution, destroy natural resources or damage people's health;

(3) those which occupy large tracts of cultivated land, are disadvantageous to the protection and development of land resources or jeopardize the security or efficiency of military installations;

(4) those in which techniques or technologies that are unique to China are applied to the manufacture of products;

(5) other projects which are prohibited under laws and administrative regulations of the State.

No companies, enterprises, other economic organizations or individuals may set up Foreign Investment Projects as specified in the preceding paragraph.

Article 8: In addition to the entitlement of preferential treatment under relevant laws or administrative regulations of the State, encouraged Foreign Investment Projects involved in the construction and operation of energy, communication or infrastructure facilities (coal, electricity, local railways, highways and ports) with a large amount of investment and a long payback period may be allowed to cover other related business upon approval.

Article 9: Restricted Foreign Investment Projects must conform to relevant laws or administrative regulations of the State and the provisions set forth below:

(1) the term of operation of an enterprise must be fixed for restricted Sino-foreign equity joint venture projects; and

(2) for Foreign Investment Projects under restricted project category (A), the fixed assets in the Chinese party's investment must consist

of the funds of the Chinese investor himself or assets owned by the Chinese investor.

Article 10: Encouraged and permitted Foreign Investment Projects shall be examined, approved and filed for the record in accordance with the stipulated procedures and measures currently in force.

Foreign Investment Projects under restricted project category (A) shall be examined, approved and filed for the record in accordance with the stipulated procedures and measures currently in force. Of these, Foreign Investment Projects under restricted project category (A) involving an amount below the limit for examination and approval set by the State Council shall be examined and approved respectively by the planning authorities or the authorities in charge of technical reform in enterprises, depending on the nature of the construction project, of provinces, autonomous regions, centrally-governed municipalities or municipalities with independent development plans. The power to examine and approve projects of this category may not be delegated.

Proposals on Foreign Investment Projects under restricted project category (B) involving an amount below the limit for examination and approval set by the State Council shall be examined and approved by the State Council authorities exclusively in charge of the industry; project feasibility studies shall be examined and approved respectively by the planning authorities or the authorities in charge of technical reform in enterprises, depending on the nature of the construction project, of the provinces, autonomous regions, centrally-governed municipalities or municipalities with independent development plans, and submitted to the State Planning Commission or the State Economic and Trade Commission for the record. The power to examine and approve projects of this category may not be delegated. Projects involving an amount above the limit for examination and approval set by the State Council shall be examined and approved in accordance with the stipulated procedures and measures currently in force.

With regard to Foreign Investment Projects involving quotas or licences, a prior applications for the quota or licence shall be made in advance to the authorities in charge of foreign trade and economic cooperation.

Where laws or administrative regulations contain separate provisions concerning the procedures and measures for the examination and approval of Foreign Investment Projects, such provisions shall be followed.

Article 11: Where Foreign Investment Projects under restricted project category (A) fall into the scope specified under item (1) of Article 6 hereof and their export product sales account for 70% or more of total product sales, they may be regarded as permitted Foreign Investment Projects subject to approval, and will not be subject to the restrictions specified under Article 9 hereof. Restrictions on the above-mentioned Foreign Investment Projects may also be relaxed to a certain extent if such projects can truly bring into play the advantages of the resources in the central and western regions and confrom to the industrial policies of the State.

Article 12: Foreign Investment Projects which have been examined and approved in violation of these Provisions shall be canceled by examination and approval authorities at a higher level within 30 days of receiving the projects' documents submitted for the record. The contracts and articles of association of such projects shall be void, enterprise registries shall deny registration or cancellation of registration, and the Customs shall not carry out import and export procedures.

Article 13: Where the parties to a Foreign Investment Project obtained approval of the project proposal by improper means such as fraud, legal liability shall be pursued in accordance with the law depending on the seriousness of the circumstances; the examination and approval authority shall revoke the approval of the project and the relevant authorities in charge shall appropriately deal with the matter in accordance with the law.

Article 14: In case of abuse of power, graft, dereliction of duty or ultra vires examination and approval by personnel of examination and approval authorities, administrative sanctions shall be imposed on such personnel and, if the circumstances are serious and a criminal offence is constituted, their criminal liability shall be pursued according to law.

Article 15: Reference shall be made to these Provisions for projects set up by overseas Chinese or from Hongkong, Macao or Taiwan.

Article 16: The implementation of these Provisions shall be organized by the State Planning Commission in conjunction with the State Economic and Trade Commission and the Ministry of Foreign Trade and Economic Cooperation.

Article 17: These Provisions shall be effective as of the date of promulgation.

LEGISLATION APPENDIX 2

INDUSTRIES, PRODUCTS AND TECHNOLOGIES CURRENTLY PARTICULARLY ENCOURAGED BY THE STATE FOR DEVELOPMENT CATALOGUE

Ref no: 2110/97.12.31(1)
(Promulgated by the State Planning Commission on December 31, 1997 and in trial implementation from January 1, 1998.)

1. **Agriculture**
   - Technology to improve good varieties of plants and animals and to prevent major plant diseases and insect pests
   - Poison-resistant seeds
   - Soil-less culturing of vegetables, flowers and plants
   - High-yield high-efficiency modular culturing
   - Development and popularization of advanced agricultural technology
   - Storage, preservation of freshness, processing and comprehensive utilization of agricultural products
   - Integrated administration of medium and low-yield fields
   - Development of wasteland, barren hills, desert and shorelines suitable for agriculture
   - Construction of bases for marketable agricultural products such as grain, cotton, oil, sugar
   - Dry agriculture, water-saving agriculture and eco-agriculture
   - Natural rubber
   - Construction of pasture and grassland
   - Culture of famous aquatic products
   - Dairy industry
   - Biological agricultural chemicals
   - High-efficiency low-toxicity non-environmentally polluting agricultural chemicals
   - New types of sheeting to be used in agriculture
   - New types of vaccines and medicines for use on animals
   - Embryo transfer for cattle and sheep
   - Technological renovation of fishing vessels
   - Feed additives and their integrated utilization

2. **Forestry**
   - Selective breeding and genetic improvement of good types of trees
   - Intensive raising and storage of trees of economic value and of good types of plants and flowers

- Prevention of natural disasters in forests
- Site afforestation of ecologically and environmentally fragile areas with special difficulties
- Fast-growing high-yield trees
- Forest protection projects
- Revival of forest resources projects
- Prevention of desertification
- Supplementary making of paper from wood pulp from the raw material tree base
- Advanced processing and serialized products of lumber, trees from plantations, small diameter lumber and leftovers from forest areas
- Bamboo engineering material and plant fibre engineering material
- Advanced processing of chemical products from trees
- Tree physiology reactive materials
- New materials for fixing sand, conserving water and improving soil

3. Water Conservancy

- Flood prevention and control projects on major rivers and lakes
- Interbasin water diversion projects
- Water resources projects in areas lacking water resources
- Drinking water for humans and livestock and water improvement projects in arid areas
- Safety construction in flood storage and detention basins
- Construction and protection of sea walls
- Desilting of rivers, lakes and reservoirs
- Making safe and reinforcement of dangerous reservoirs, dykes and dams
- Integrated use of key water control projects
- Water and soil conservancy technology and facilities construction
- Development and utilization of brackish water, poor water and sea water, and desalination of sea water
- Development and protection of hydro-energy resources
- Synthetic construction materials for water conservancy projects
- Technology, equipment and methods for high-efficiency water transmission and distribution and for economic irrigation
- High-efficiency wear-resistant and low-lift large-volume water pumps
- Automated regimen gauges and automated flood prevention management systems
- Computer aided design (CAD) software for water conservation projects
- Devices and equipment for collecting hydrologic data

4. Meteorology

- Automated weather station systems technology and equipment
- Special types of meteorological observation and analysis equipment
- Doppler radar technology and equipment

5. Coal

- Underground geological and geophysical prospecting
- Large and medium-sized high-efficiency open-cast mines
- Large and medium-sized high efficiency coal preparation plants
- Prevention of gas, coal dust, mine water and underground fires
- Industrial coal
- Water-coal slurry
- Coal gasification and liquefaction
- Coal-bed gas prospecting, development and utilization

- Development and utilization of low calorific value fuel and mine-associated resources
- Pipeline transport of coal

6. **Electric Power**
   - Hydroelectric power
   - Large-scale pit-head power stations
   - Joint production of heat and electricity
   - Electricity generation from solar energy, geothermal energy, ocean energy, rubbish and biomass energy, and large-scale electricity generation from wind power
   - Combined gas turbine cycle power generation
   - Clean coal power generation
   - Remote super-high pressure electricity transmission and transformation
   - Construction and upgrading of power grids

7. **Nuclear Energy**
   - 1 million kilowatt pressurized water reactor nuclear power stations
   - Low-temperature nuclear process heat reactors, fast breeder reactors and fusion reactors
   - Advanced uranium extraction
   - High-performance nuclear fuel elements
   - Handling of spent fuel
   - Nuclear analysis and detection instruments and meters
   - Use of isotopes and irradiation

8. **Oil and natural gas**
   - Oil and natural gas exploration
   - Oil and natural gas extraction
   - Pipeline transport of crude oil
   - Pipeline transport of natural gas
   - Liquefied natural gas
   - Oil storage
   - Integrated use of oil gas and associated resources

9. **Railways**
   - Railway trunk line networks
   - Speeding up of existing tracks
   - High-speed railway systems
   - 25-ton axle weight heavy freight transport
   - Railway carriage safety technology and protection systems
   - Heavy duty high-quality steel rails and new types of sleepers
   - Automation of marshalling stations, mechanization of loading and unloading, and equipment for goods yards
   - Railway passenger and freight transport equipment
   - Railway passenger and freight transport information systems
   - Railway container transport

10. **Roads**
    - National road trunk road networks
    - Intelligent road transport systems
    - High-speed passenger and freight road transport
    - New materials for road construction
    - Design and manufacture of new types of machinery and equipment for roads
    - Road container transport

11. **Water transport**
    - Key coastal ports
    - Inland river trunk shipping routes and wharves
    - Standardization, systemization and modernization of shipping transport
    - Automation of loading and unloading for large ports

- Oceangoing transport electronic data exchange systems
- Water traffic control systems
- Design and manufacture of new types of machinery and equipment for ports
- Water container transport
- Combined transport of different types of containers

12. Air Transport

- Civilian airports
- High-performance airport safety inspection equipment
- Air traffic control systems

13. Posts and Telecommunications

- Key technology and equipment for stratospheric communications systems
- More than 622 Mb/s digital synchronous series optical fibre communications systems and equipment
- More than 155 Mb/s digital synchronous series microwave communications systems and equipment
- Digital mobile communications systems and equipment (GSM, CDMA, DCS1800 etc.)
- Integrated service digital network (ISDN) systems and equipmen
- New technology and equipment to support communications systems
- Satellite communications systems and earth station equipment
- Broadcasting satellite and earth station equipment
- Mobile satellite communications systems and equipment
- Systems and equipment to connect cable and wireless users to the network
- Asynchronous transfer-type broadband photoelectric transmission systems and equipment
- Intelligent networks and corresponding equipment
- Digital centralized communications systems and equipment
- Automated handling systems for letters and parcels

14. Iron and steel

- High-efficiency ore dressing and integrated use of the resources produced by mines
- Direct reduction
- Small spherical and pellet sintering
- Blended coal coking and stamp coking
- Dry method extinction
- High-wind high-temperature long-burning wind furnaces
- High-heat oxygen-rich spray coal
- High-heat high-efficiency long-burning integration technology
- Super-high power electric furnaces and integrated energy-saving technology
- Converter spatter protection furnace technology
- High-efficiency continuous casting
- Continuous casting billet hot loading and hot feeding
- Melting reduction
- Near-finished continuous casting and continuous rolling of sheet bars and sheet strips
- Integrated automation of metallurgy
- Controlled rolling and controlled cooling
- Plate-type control
- Surface plating
- Low alloy steel and micro-alloy steel
- Converter steel smelting of 50 tons or more
- Stainless steel smelting
- Cold rolling of silicon steel plates
- Hot and cold rolling of stainless steel plates
- Steel pipes for oil

- Processing and handling of waste steel
- Development of high aluminium alumina and hard clay, and production of clinker
- Environmental protection when smelting and integrated use of waste materials from smelting

15. Nonferrous metals

- Mining of deep and difficult mineral deposits
- Compound nonferrous metal materials and new nonferrous metal alloys
- Production of aluminium oxides from boehmite-duralumin-diaspore ore
- Intensified smelting and temperature method smelting of nonferrous metals
- Thin non-crystal alloy sheets
- Supercritical extraction
- High-efficiency energy-saving ore dressing and electrochemically controlled floatation
- Large-scale pre-baked electrolytic aluminium
- Rapid casting and rolling of aluminium and aluminium alloys
- 8 inch or more single-crystal silicon sheets and polycrystal silicon
- High-efficiency ore dressing agents
- High-performance high-precision rigid alloys, tin compounds, antimony compounds and ceramic materials
- High-performance magnetic materials
- Superfine powder materials, electronic pastes, and products made from these
- New brake materials
- Integrated use of multimetal mineral intergrowths
- Mining and integrated use of rare-earth metals, rare metals and disperse metals
- Integrated use of salt lake resources
- Use of new baking skills, heat pressure pre-oxygenizing-cyaniding skills and bacteriological oxygenizing-cyaniding skills to mine and make use of metal ores that are difficult to process
- Integrated recovery of metal tailings in ores which are difficult to process

16. Chemical engineering

- Scientific fertilizer application (soil testing fertilizer application, new types of chemical fertilizers, and special-use fertilizers)
- Large-scale synthetic ammonia and urea
- Large and medium-scale high-density phospho-potash fertilizer and its compound fertilizers
- Compound fertilizers containing trace elements required by crops
- Pressure gasification of water-coal slurry
- New high-efficiency catalysts
- Annual production of 200,000 tons or more of potassium chloride and annual production of more than 100,000 tons of potassium sulphide
- Modified calcium magnesium phosphate compounds
- Manufacture of granular ammonium phosphate and triple compound fertilizers
- Coated urea
- Annual production of 30,000 tons or more of slurry method ammonium phosphate and of urea and sulfuric acid from phosphorus gypsum
- Sulphur-based triple fertilizer
- Rare earth compounds
- Very pure phosphorus pentasulfide
- Refinement of phosphoric acid by advanced wet methods
- Special anti-aging polyethylene
- Low-toxicity rogue alumen sodium
- 10,000 tons of sodium cyanide
- 5,000 tons per year of gas phase method white carbon projects

- Large and medium-sized chemical mines
- New chemical engineering products such as organic silicon monomers and organic fluorine
- New fine chemical engineering products
- Large-scale coal chemical engineering
- Ionic membranes using caustic soda
- Titanium dioxide by chlorination
- High performance meridian tyres
- High-performance for high performance meridian tyres
- Management and integrated use of the "three wastes" (solid wastes, waste water and waste gases)

17. Petroleum Engineering

- Oil refineries with a single line capacity of 5 million tons or more
- Intensive processing of crude oil on an economic scale
- more than 600,000 tons of ethylene and large-scale onward processing
- PVC resin
- Engineering plastics and new types of plastic alloys
- Complete sets of raw materials for synthetic materials: diphenol A, butadiene pyridine latex, pyridine, 4.4 diphenyl methane vulcabond, methylbenzene vulcabond
- Synthetic rubbers and their applications
- Single line capacity of 100,000 tons or more of acrylonitrile
- Single line capacity of 350,000 tons or more of PTA
- New products from nylon 6 and nylon 66
- New products from organic chemical engineering raw materials
- Integrated use of refinery gas and chemical engineering byproducts
- Management and integrated use of the "three wastes" (solid wastes, waste water and waste gases)

18. Construction Materials

- Daily production of 4000 tons or more of new types of aggregate dry method concrete
- New types of materials for walls, decorating, damp-proofing and heat retention
- 10,000 tons of glass fibre floss
- High quality plastic compound doors, windows, pipes and wall and floor lining materials
- Intensive processing of plate glass
- High-grade sanitary wares and hardware components
- Superfine modification processing and manufacture of products from non-metallic ores

19. Pharmaceuticals

- Medicines and reagents listed in the national catalogue of basic medicines
- Important superior products for export
- Biologically-engineered medicines and reagents
- Radioactive medicines and reagents
- New types of anti-tumour medicines (including anti-hepatitis medicines) and new types of cardio-cerebral vascular medicine
- Diagnostic preparations for AIDS and radio-immunity etc.
- New types of medicine for regional diseases
- New types of medicines to allay fever and kill pain
- New types of medicinal preparations and supplementary material, and medicinal preparations produced in accordance with GMP
- Special medicinal intermediates that are in short supply and new types of antibiotics

- New series of biochemical medicines and reagents (including biochemical diagnostic reagents)
- New types of pharmaceutical packaging material
- New types of medical apparatus and instruments
- New types of hygiene materials and dressings
- Family planning medicines and tools
- Screening technology and models for new types of medicines
- New amino acid growth mediums
- Fodder-grade biotins
- Vergimycin and tylosin
- Purification and increase in purity of penicillins
- Fermentation and automatic temperature control systems
- Large-scale synthesis and purification of polypeptides
- Large-scale synthesis and purification of nucleic acid for medical use
- High production of genetic engineering bacteria
- Naturally occurring medicines
- Research and development of new types of Chinese medicines

20. Machinery

- Precision technology and equipment
- Numerical control machines with more than three coupled axles, numerical control systems and servo mechanisms
- Development of mechanical products using advanced computer software technology and equipment
- Development of mechanical products using advanced testing and measuring technology and equipment
- High-speed super-hard precision cutters and automatic precision measuring devices
- New types of sensors
- Vehicle bearings, railway carriage bearings, precision bearings and high speed bearings
- Mixed flow and axial flow hydroelectric equipment with wheel diameter of 8.5 metres or more plus essential supplementary machinery
- Large-scale through-flow and pump storage hydroelectric machinery plus related essential supplementary machinery
- Supercritical fossil-fired power machinery
- Large-scale air-coolers of 600,000 kilowatts or more
- Circulation fluid bed boilers of 100,000 kilowatts or more
- Joint gas and steam fired circulation equipment of over 36,000 kilowatts
- Large-scale wind power electricity generating machinery
- Nuclear power machinery and related essential machinery
- Super-high pressure alternating current transformer equipment of 500,000 volts or more
- Equipment for testing heavy current cut-out capacity and sudden transformer short-circuits
- New types of insulation material
- Key manufacturing technology and equipment producing 450,000 tons or more per year of chemical fertilizer or ethylene
- Decentralized control systems for heavy technical equipment
- On-line automated measuring technology and systems
- New types of electrical and electronic technology and devices

- Precision and super-precision processing technology and equipment
- Laser processing technology and equipment
- Large precision instruments
- New types of water-pressure, sealed and pneumatic devices
- Electronic low pressure electrical items
- High-strength section fastenings
- Resin sand casting equipment producing more than 20 tons per hour
- Advanced die design and manufacturing technology and equipment
- Large-scale vacuum electronic beam welding technology and equipment
- Technology and equipment for controlling atmosphere and vacuum heat treatment
- New technology and equipment for, and manufacture of equipment for, production safety and environmental testing
- Urban rubbish treatment technology and equipment
- Large-scale waste water treatment equipment
- Smoke desulphurizing and nitrifying equipment
- Sea water desalination technology and equipment
- Industrial robots
- Trackless mining extraction, packing and moving equipment with a capacity of 5 million tons a year or more
- Sets of large-scale open cast mining equipment with a capacity of 20 million tons or more
- Tunneling machinery
- Underground railway blind tunneling equipment
- Large-scale cold and hot continuous rolling of more than 2 metres and process control technology and equipment
- Mechanical three-dimensional garage at more than 30,000 cubic metres per hour
- Natural gas collection and transport equipment
- Key flexible plate printing equipment
- Operating machinery and equipment suited to agriculture
- Equipment for advanced processing of agricultural and animal husbandry products and for integrated use of resources
- Equipment required for agricultural environmental protection and for ecological agriculture
- Agricultural harvesting machinery and parts (for cotton, rice, maize, beans and green fodder etc.)
- Vacuum precision smelting and casting technology and equipment
- New types of instrument components and materials
- Large-scale project construction machinery and equipment
- Advanced internal combustion engines and key parts

21. Electronic Information

- Large-scale integrated circuits of wire width of under 0.8 millimetres
- New types of electronic components (including chip components) and of electrical electronic components
- New types of surface attachment components
- Photoelectric devices, sensors and transducers
- Development of semiconductor and photoelectric materials
- Large and medium-sized electronic computers
- High-performance micro electronic computers
- Work stations and servers

- Software development
- Computer-aided design (three-dimensional CAD), computer-aided testing (CAT), computer-aided manufacturing (CAM) and computer-aided engineering (CAE) systems plus other computer application systems
- Electronic equipment, instruments and dies
- Digital cross-connection equipment
- Large capacity optical and magnetic disks and their components
- New types of displays (liquid crystal displays and panel displays)
- New types of printers (laser printers)
- Data and information multimedia systems equipment
- Single-mode optic fibres
- Network equipment such as routing devices
- Digital audio-visual frequency broadcasting systems and products
- High quality laser video disks (using MPEG-II standard, such as DVD)
- High definition televisions (HDTV)
- Digital video technology
- Digital colour televisions
- Wide-screen colour televisions
- VCD drivers, laser heads and special chips
- Ordinary paper fax machines
- New types of scramblers
- Multimedia terminals
- Wide-band digital programmed switchboards (asynchronous switching wide-band switchboards ATM)
- High-speed wire-less pagers
- Digital multifunction telephones

22. Vehicles

- Vehicle bodies and body parts
- New types of motors for vehicles and motor cycles
- Key vehicle components
- Precision forging and pressing, black casting, coloured casting and workblanks for main vehicle parts
- Vehicle dies
- Electronic products for vehicles
- New light-weight materials for vehicles
- Development systems for whole vehicles and motor cycles and for their engines and parts
- Vehicle exhaust emission control systems such as engine control systems and triplet catalytic transformation installations
- Inspection systems for State-level testing centres for automobiles and motor cycles

23. Shipping

- High-technology high-performance large vessels of over 60,000 tons
- Ship main engines
- Shipboard electrical stations
- Shipboard crankshafts, auxiliary engines and electronic instruments

24. Aeronautics and astronautics

- Civilian aircraft and parts
- Airborne engines
- Integrated airborne electronic systems
- Onboard equipment systems
- Helicopter bodies, rotor systems and transmission systems
- New aeronautical and astronautical materials and their applications
- Gas turbines
- Satellites and delivery rockets and their parts
- Applications of satellites
- Applications of space technology

25. Light industry and textiles

- Die design, processing and manufacture of non-metallic products
- Paper pulp, paper and cardboard in accord with economic scale and standards
- New types of high-speed corrugated paper with more than 9 layers
- End processing of hides
- Non-mercury alkaline secondary batteries, nickel hydrogen batteries, lithium batteries
- Special sorts of industrial sewing machines
- Enzyme preparations
- Compound perfumes and single perfumes
- Non-fluorine refrigeration technology and its applications
- Xanthic gum (edible grade)
- High quality paper packaging
- New types of packaging material
- Fully automatic high-speed multi-colour printing
- High quality textile printing and dyeing and high technology post-treatment processing
- Single line daily production of 400 tons or more of polyester
- High quality reproduction fine garment material
- Oil agents, auxiliaries and dyes for use on textiles
- Carbon fibres, aromatic synthetic fibres, and modified, unusual, super-fine and mixed chemical fibres
- Processing of special sorts of natural fibres
- Special sorts of textile products for industrial use
- High-technology light industrial and textile machinery
- More than 30,000 tons of directly spun and washed short synthetic fibre
- More than 10,000 tons of directly spun and washed long synthetic fibre

26. Construction

- Computer-aided design for construction projects
- Computer-aided design and manufacture of construction machinery
- Applications of computers in construction work
- Key technology for saving energy in construction work
- High-rise construction and mid-air structural equipment
- Key equipment for construction work
- High-performance external protection structural material and parts for housing

27. Urban infrastructure and real property

- Urban underground railways, light railways and public transport
- Urban roads
- Urban traffic control systems and equipment
- Urban flood prevention
- Urban water supplies, running water, waste water and sewage water disposal
- Disposal and integrated use of urban rubbish and other solid waste
- Urban gas supply stations
- Centralized urban heating
- Energy-saving low-pollution heaters
- Greening of urban parks
- Urban three-dimensional car park
- Upgrading of dangerous urban structures
- "Home ownership" building projects
- Economically appropriate commercial housing
- Management of housing estates

28. Integrated use of natural resources and environmental protection

- Ecological and environmental management
- Nature protection zones
- Integrated use of resources projects
- Integrated use of solid waste
- Integrated use of waste water (and liquids)
- Integrated use of waste gas
- Integrated use of waste obsolete objects
- Large-scale sewage handling
- Measuring of waste gas
- Marine development and marine environmental protection

29. Service industry

- Commercial facilities such as chain stores, supermarkets and storage-type markets
- Modern management methods such as distribution centres and agency systems
- Modern storage and transport facilities for major products such as grain, cotton, edible oil, chemical fertilizer and oil
- Large-scale wholesale markets for agricultural by-products
- Integrated trade/industry/agriculture and production/processing/sale management and circulation facilities for agricultural products
- Social service systems for agriculture
- Construction of tourist transport and infrastructure
- Major tourist resort projects and special tourism projects
- Projects for the integrated development of large-scale tourism resources
- Banks, financial companies, and trust and investment companies
- Insurance companies, insurance brokers and agent companies
- Securities companies, investment banks, commercial banks and fund management companies
- Foreign exchange brokers
- Financial, insurance and foreign exchange consultants
- Leasing services
- Cultural arts, radio broadcasting, television, film showing and sports facilities for the public
- Protection of cultural relics
- Facilities such as those for basic health, disease control, mother and baby healthcare, rehabilitation and welfare
- Key higher educational institutes, special sports academies and scientific research facilities
- State engineering research centres, State key laboratories, new high technology development centres, new product design and development centres and scientific research testing grounds
- Science and technology services such as those involving popularizing technology, exchanging science and technology, meteorology, environmental protection, surveying, earthquakes, the sea, patents and technology supervision
- Economic, science and technology, engineering, management, accounting and auditing, labour employment and legal consultancies
- Manufacture of new high technology advertisements, economic, scientific and technical exhibitions and popularization of science
- Maintenance and services for precision instruments and equipment

QUESTIONS CONCERNING FURTHER STRENGTHENING THE ADMINISTRATION OF THE EXAMINATION, APPROVAL AND REGISTRATION OF FOREIGN INVESTMENT ENTERPRISES CIRCULAR

(Promulgated by the State Administration for Industry and Commerce and the Ministry of Foreign Trade and Economic Cooperation of the People's Republic of China on November 3, 1994)

To: Administrations for Industry and Commerce and Commissions on and Departments for Foreign Trade and Economic Cooperation under the governments of the provinces, autonomous regions and municipalities directly under the central government.

Recent years always see a rapid growth in the inflow of foreign investment in China with an ever expanding area for the investment to a great alleviation of the shortage of funds used for economic construction in the country and thus a speedy development of the national economy. However, not a few problems have been given rise in the process with the more outstanding ones being:

In starting FEEs, certain localities would give an overstress in quality but to the neglect of quality, lavishly promise preferential terms to foreign businesses in contravention of State laws, regulations and policies, underestimate the value of State assets in the course of setting up joint equity ventures with foreign businesses, or selling the stocks to foreign businesses all to an erosion of State properties. There are also cases in which the Chinese or foreign partner in a joint equity venture fails to put in the corresponding fund in time according to the contract after business registration of the enterprise.

In order to properly guide the FFEs to a sound development, hereby a notice is given on the questions concerning the tightening up of control over the examination and approval of the establishment of FFEs and their business registration.

(1) The offices in charge of enterprise approval and registration (hereinafter referred to as approval and registration offices) should strengthen and perfect their work in regard to the examination of the establishment and actual capital input of FFEs and the handling of cases of their violations of the law and other rules. These offices should earnestly monitor how the enterprises are to observe the law, regulations and State policies in their business operations.

(2) For entering into joint equity or cooperative ventures with foreign businesses through the input of State assets or sales of part of the State assets in the form of stock transfer, in addition to present necessary document to the approval and registration offices as required by law, it should also submit the appraisal report on the value of the State assets involved and relevant documents confirming the appraisal as well as other papers officially required.

For sales of the entire State assets of an enterprise to foreign businesses, the whole transaction should be handled according to relevant regulations of the State including the presenting of the documents of approval.

(3) Whereas the foreign partner in a joint equity or cooperative venture uses equipment or other material objects as items of investment, the approval office should strictly examine the list of investment items. Whereas the approval and registration offices discover false presentation of prices of investment items during examining the report of verification of investment offered by the FFE, concurred, they have the right to ask the enterprise to present the documents confirming the price evaluation.

(4) The examination and approval and registration of Sino-foreign joint venture projects of a whole or trans-trade should be suspended. For those already set up, the original approval office should join the registration office and other departments concerned in doing a proper job of rectification.

(5) The articles of association and contracts presented by investors in Sino-foreign joint equity or cooperative ventures should strictly adhere to the principle of mutual sharing of benefits and risks by both sides. Whereas the Chinese side, in violation of regulations, offers guarantees for capital input by the foreign side or for the recovery rate of investment of the foreign investor in the form of loan or bond issues, the approval office should ask the partners in the joint venture to revise such stipulations in the documents according to law and regulations. Those ventures which refuse to make the revisions will be refused approval and registration by the offices concerned.

(6) The approval and registration offices should step up their supervision and check-up of the actual input of investment in the FFEs to see if the investors have strictly observed the regulations on "Some Provisions for Capital Disbursement by the Investors in Sino-foreign Joint Ventures" and paid up their shares of the registered capital. Clear time limits for capital disbursement should be included in the contract and articles of association of foreign-funded enterprises or cooperative ventures in accordance with the planned progress of the investment project. Those enterprises which fail to make the stipulations in the document will not be granted approval or business registration.

Unless otherwise stipulated by the State, hereby a timetable is given for the deadline for the actual payment of the investment by the investors in FFEs.

(I) For enterprises with a registered capital of US$500,000 or less, the time limit for the payment is one year after the issue of the business license.

(ii) For enterprises with a registered capital of more than US$500,000 to US$1million, the time limit for the payment is one and half years after.

iii. For enterprises with a registered capital of more than US$1million to US$3million, the time limit for the payment is two years after.

(iv) For enterprises with a registered capital of more than US$3million to US$10million, the time limit for the payment is three years after.

(v) For enterprises with a registered capital of more than US$10million, the time limit for the payment will be decided by the approval office with reference to actual conditions. Whereas a real need arises for extending time for the actual payment of the investment because of special circumstances after the approval of the enterprise contract, the enterprise concerned should report to the original approval office and obtain its permission for the postponement which should be reported to the registration office for record and perform the necessary procedures.

(7) The approval and registration offices will not handle the application of FFEs which fail to pay up the registered capital within the time limit for setting up of branches or an expansion of business scope.

(8) To normalize the actual payment of investment according to schedule, the registration office can issue to the FFEs business a temporary license with a specified time of validity in coincidence with time limit for their capital payment and after the payment of the capital a formal license in accordance with the contracted terms will be issued.

(9) Whereas one or both partners to a Sino-foreign joint equity venture violate the Article Four of "Some Provisions for Capital Disbursement by the Investors in Sino-Foreign Joint Equity Ventures" and the Article Six of this Notice, the document of approval for the establishment of the enterprises will automatically be invalidated and the registration office can decide on the penalty of revoking their business licenses and report the penalty decision to the State Administration for Industry and Commerce for record and send a copy of the decision to the original approval office.

(10) Whereas one or both partners to a Sino-foreign joint equity venture violate Articles Six and Seven of "Some Provisions for Capital Disbursement by the Investors in Sino-Foreign Joint Equity Ventures", or one of the partners violates the Article Six of this Notice, the approval and registration offices shall jointly or singly, after consultation with the other, send out a notice to ask for a full payment of the registered capital within a specified time limit. In case of failure to make the full payment as required, while the partner which has fulfilled its obligations may decide to dissolve the joint venture or seek a new partner for the venture, the approval office has the right to revoke the document of approval of the enterprise, and the registration office has the right to revoke its business license and report the case to the State Administration for Industry and Commerce for record and make a copy of the report to be sent to the original approval office.

(11) With justifiable reasons and on condition of not affecting its normal business operations and not encroaching on the interests of creditors, a FFE can, within its term of operations, apply to the original approval office for curtailing its production scale and readjusting the amount of its total capital input and registered capital. With approval by the original approval office and confirmation by the registration office, the FFE shall perform the procedures for the changes of registration, and report the changes to the State Administration for Industry and Commerce for record.

(12) When the approval and registration offices have found out that Chinese and foreign investors or a FFE have acted against the law and regulations, especially in a case of sham joint venturing, as soon as the acts are confirmed, the said offices should order the parties concerned to make corrections within a prescribed time limit. For those which fail to correct their misconduct within the set period, the original approval and registration offices have the right to revoke the approval document and business license to the enterprise and impose due penalties on the parties involved according to relevant laws and regulations. The decision on punishment will be reported to the Ministry of Foreign Trade and Economic Cooperation and the State Administration for Industry and Commerce for record.

Please carry out what has been told as soon as you receive this notice.

NOTICE REGARDING RELEVANT ISSUES IN REPORTING FOR THE RECORD TO MOFTEC FOREIGN INVESTMENT ENTERPRISES UNDER THE ENCOURAGED CATEGORY EXAMINED AND APPROVED BY LOCAL AUTHORITIES THEMSELVES

To the Foreign Economic Relations and Trade Commission (Departments and Bureaus) in the various provinces, autonomous regions, directly administered municipalities and municipalities with independent planning status:

Pursuant to the provisions of the "Opinion on the Current Further Encouragement of Foreign Investment" (ref: *Guofa* [1999] No. 73), the establishment (i.e. the approved equity joint venture contracts, articles of association and their appendices) of the foreign investment enterprises under the encouraged category and not requiring the comprehensive balance of the State, shall be filed with MOFTEC when such establishment is approved by the provinces themselves. In accordance with State laws and regulations for the attraction of foreign investment and the *Relevant Provisions for the Filing of Foreign Investment Enterprises* promulgated by MOFTEC in 1988, you are herewith given the following notice regarding relevant issues:

(1) The establishment of foreign investment enterprises under the encouraged category not requiring the comprehensive balance of the State shall be examined and approved by the departments in charge of the foreign economic relations and trade of the various provinces, autonomous regions, directly administered municipalities and municipalities with independent planning status (hereinafter referred to as the "Local Departments in Charge of Foreign Economic Relations and Trade"), and the examination and approval authority shall not be delegated to lower levels.

(2) The Local Departments in Charge of Foreign Economic Relations and Trade shall send the relevant materials for filing with MOFTEC on the date on which the contracts and articles of associations are approved.

(3) The materials required for filing:

(i) Approval Document for the feasibility study report;

(ii) Approval Document for the contract and articles of association. The Approval Document shall state the names of the investors, form of investment, total investment, registered capital, ratio of capital contributions of the parties, form of capital contributions, loans to be raised, business scope, production scale, percentage of export sales, operation term and other matters requiring special approval. If a technology import contract, as an appendix to the contract, is approved simultaneously, the name of the technology import contract shall be set out in the Approval Document;

(iii) Explanation by the Local Departments in Charge of the Foreign Economic Relations and Trade that a project does not require the comprehensive balance of the State.

(4) MOFTEC shall, within two working days from the date of receipt of the materials filed, give notice to the reporting unit to acknowledge receipt of the materials filed and to indicate whether the materials are complete. In case MOFTEC has a different opinion on the project filed, MOFTEC shall give a written reply within one month from the receipt of the complete materials filed, with copies to the State Administration for Industry and Commerce, the General Administration of Customs, Administration of Foreign Exchange and the State General Administration of Taxation.

(5) Only after MOFTEC raises no objection to the filed materials within one month from the receipt thereof, may the Local Departments in Charge of the Foreign Economic Relations and Trade issue a Certificate of Approval for Foreign Investment. No Certificate of Approval for Foreign Investment shall be issued for projects on which MOFTEC has a different opinion.

(6) Each month before the 5th, the Local Departments in Charge of Foreign Economic Relations and Trade shall transmit by facsimile to the Foreign Investment Administration of MOFTEC a list (a form of which is appended thereto) of the enterprises under the encouraged category that were approved in the preceding month and seek confirmation by telephone that such facsimile transmission has been received.

(7) The Foreign Investment Administration of MOFTEC shall verify the enterprises on the list and timely notify the reporting unit and the departments of industry and commerce, customs, foreign exchange and other relevant departments of those projects for which no filing materials have been received. Enterprises which have not been filed for the record with MOFTEC, or whose filings have not been approved, shall not be registered by, and shall not receive assistance in other matters from the departments of industry and commerce, customs, foreign exchange and other departments.

(8) On the strength of the Certificate of Approval for Foreign Investment and other documents which they require, the departments of industry and commerce, customs, foreign exchange and other relevant departments shall accept the enterprise registration and file the same for the record.

(9) Of existing enterprises under the encouraged category, not involved in the comprehensive balance of the State, of which the establishment was examined and approved by the Local Departments in Charge of Foreign Economic Relations and Trade, major amendments to their contract and articles of association, or increases in capital of their foreign investment shall be filed with MOFTEC in accordance with the relevant provisions mentioned above. Materials to be filed for approval of an increase in capital shall be submitted in accordance with the relevant provisions.

(10) In addition to filing with MOFTEC in written form by the Local Departments in Charge of the Foreign Economic Relations and Trade in accordance with the requirements set forth above, the relevant information and data of the enterprises filed for the record shall be transmitted to the Foreign Investment Administration of the MOFTEC in accordance with the *Notice Regarding Relevant Issues Concerning the Networking between the Local Departments in Charge of the Foreign Economic Relations and Trade and the Foreign Investment Administration of the MOFTEC* (ref: [1998] *Waijingmao zizonghanzi* No. 521). When the conditions mature, filing for the record through the networks will be implemented nationwide.

Appendix: as per the attached.

[Seal of the Ministry of Foreign Trade and Economic Cooperation of the People's Republic of China affixed]

October 15, 1999

CC: General Administration of Customs, State General Administration of Taxation, State Administration of Foreign Exchange and State Administration for Industry and Commerce.

MOFTEC: MOFTEC leaders (Shi and Ma), General Office, Foreign Investment Administration (9), Treaty and Law Department, Secretary, person on duty, and for filing.

Printed at 16:00 hours, 80 copies in total

Recorded by: Wang Hui

Checked by: Guo Shuqin and Han Huifen

Appendix

List of Enterprises under the Encouraged Category above the Local Approval Threshold for the Month of ____________.

____________ (Province, Autonomous Region, Directly Administered Municipality or City Separately Listed in the Plan)

Seal of the Reporting Unit:

No.	Project	Name	Industry	Approval Date	Date of Submission of Materials	New Establishment	Increase of Capital	Remarks

Date of Completion: Completed by: Contact Telephone:

(original translation: Shearman & Sterling)

ESTABLISHMENT OF COMPANIES WITH AN INVESTMENT NATURE BY FOREIGN INVESTORS TENTATIVE PROVISIONS

Ref: no: 2330/95.04.04

(Promulgated by the Ministry of Foreign Trade and Economic Cooperation on April 4, 1995. Effective as of the date of promulgation.)

In order to encourage foreign investors to invest in China and import foreign advanced technology and management expertise, foreign investors are permitted to establish companies of an investment nature (hereafter, "investment companies") in China in accordance with China's relevant laws and regulations on foreign investment and these Provisions.

Article 1: For the purposes of these Provisions, the term "an investment company" shall refer to a company established in China by a foreign investor either in the form of a wholly foreign-owned company or a joint venture in conjunction with a Chinese investor engaged in direct investments. The company shall take the form of a limited liability company.

Article 2: The application for the establishment of an investment company shall comply with the following requirements:

(1)

(i) the foreign investor shall have good credit standing, financial capability necessary for the establishment of an investment company, a total asset value of no less than US$400 million in the year prior to the submission of an application, also established foreign investment enterprise(s) in China with a capital contribution of more than US$10 million of the actual registered paid up capital and have had three investment project proposals or more approved; or,

(ii) the foreign investor shall have good credit standing, the financial strength required for the establishment of an investment company; have already established ten foreign investment enterprises or more engaged in production or infrastructure projects, with a capital contribution of more than US$30 million of the actual registered paid up capital;

(2) where an investment company is established in the form of a joint venture, the Chinese partner shall have good credit standing, the financial capability necessary for the establishment of an investment company and a total asset value of no less than Rmb100 million; and,

(3) the registered capital of an investment company shall not be less than US$30 million.

Article 3: When applying to establish an investment company, an investor shall submit the following documents to the Ministry of Foreign Trade and Economic Cooperation ("MOFTEC") for examination and approval after such documents have been examined and approved by the local economic trade and cooperation department of the relevant province, autonomous region, centrally-governed municipality or municipality with an independent development plan of the establishment location of such investment company:

(1) the project proposal for the establishment of an investment company in the form of a joint venture; the feasibility study report; contract and articles of association signed by all investment parties; the project proposal; application form for foreign investment enterprises; feasibility study report and articles of association signed by the foreign investor who establishes an investment company in the form of a wholly foreign-owned company;

(2) supporting documents on the credit standing of the investment parties as well as supporting documents (copies) of registration and legal person representatives;

(3) copies of the approval certificate(s), business licence(s) and the capital verification report(s) issued by a PRC registered accountant of the enterprise(s) invested by the foreign investor;

(4) balance sheets of the investment parties for the past three years; and,

(5) other documents required by MOFTEC.

The aforementioned documents shall be originals except where indicated as copies.

Where a document is not signed by a legal representative, a power of attorney from such legal representative shall be provided.

Where an agency established in accordance with the law is appointed to handle application procedures, a power of attorney signed by a legal representative of the investor shall be provided.

Article 4: A foreign investor shall contribute capital in a freely convertible currency to the registered capital of an investment company, and the Chinese investor may contribute capital in renminbi. The capital contribution shall be paid up within two years of the issue of a business licence.

Article 5: An investment company may operate in part or all of the following businesses upon approval:

(1) investment in sectors such as industry, agriculture, infrastructure and energy that are encouraged by the State and in which foreign investment is permitted;

(2) the investment company may be appointed in writing (subject to a unanimous resolution of the Board of Directors) by an enterprise invested by it to provide the following services to such enterprise:

   (i) assisting or acting as agent for an enterprise invested by it in the purchase of machinery, equipment and office equipment for the own use of such enterprise and in the purchase of raw materials, spare parts and components required for production from inside and outside China, and in the sale of products inside and outside China produced by such enterprise, as well as providing after-sale services;

   (ii) balancing foreign exchange among enterprises invested by it with the consent and under the supervision of the relevant department of exchange control;

   (iii) assisting in the employment of staff for enterprises invested by it and providing technical training, marketing and consulting;

   (iv) assisting enterprises invested by it in raising loans and providing guarantees; and/or,

(3) the investment company provides its investors with a consultancy service.

Article 6: For the purposes of these Provisions, the phrase "an enterprise invested by an investment company" referred to in Item 2 of Article 5 of these Provisions shall refer to:

(1) an enterprise invested by an investment company directly or in conjunction with other foreign and/or Chinese investors, with the capital contribution by such investment company, or in conjunction with other foreign investors, accounting for more than 25% of the registered capital of such enterprise; or,

(2) an established enterprise in China whose interests, owned by investors or associates of an investment company and other foreign investors, are partly or entirely acquired by such investment company so that the capital contributions by such investment company and other foreign investors account for more than 25% of the registered capital of such enterprise.

An investment company can only provide those services specified in Item 2 of Article 5 to the above-mentioned enterprises invested or established by it, unless with special permission from MOFTEC.

An investment company may not act on behalf of its investors to engage in intermediary services in China.

Article 7: Subject to the approval by the People's Bank of China, an investment company may provide financial support to enterprises invested and established by it.

Article 8: The term of an investment company shall be determined according to the relevant State regulations on the operating term of foreign investment enterprises and on the basis of the nature of the project to be invested by such investment company.

Article 9: The establishment of an enterprise by an investment company shall be submitted and approved individually in accordance with the limit of powers and procedures for the examination and approval of foreign investment enterprises.

Article 10: Where an investment company invests in the establishment of an enterprise in which the proportion of investment made in foreign exchange by such investment company or in conjunction with other foreign investors is not less than 25% of the registered capital of such enterprise, such enterprise shall enjoy preferential treatment as a foreign investment enterprise, and a foreign investment enterprise approval certificate and business licence shall be issued.

Article 11: A foreign investor who complies with the requirements of Item 1 (i) of Article 2 may invest in the establishment of an investment company in the name of its wholly-owned subsidiary.

Article 12: An investor applying to establish an investment company must provide the examination and approval authorities with a warranty on capital contribution and technology transfer by such investment company at the time it invests in China.

Where an investment company is established in the name of a wholly-owned subsidiary of a parent company, the parent company shall provide a warranty to the examination and approval authorities on the completion of capital contributions by such subsidiary to the registered capital of such investment company according to conditions stipulated by the examination and approval authorities, and on capital contribution to the registered capital and technology transfer by such investment company at the time it invests in China.

Article 13: The investment activities of an investment company shall not be restricted to the place where such investment company is registered.

Article 14: An investment company shall pay taxes in accordance with the relevant laws and regulations of China.

Article 15: An investment company shall zealously implement its project investment plans and shall report details of its investments in each year to MOFTEC for the record within the first three months prior to the following year.

Article 16: An investment company and the enterprise(s) established by such investment company are legal persons or entities independent of one another. The business contacts between such investment company and enterprise(s) shall be treated as business contacts between independent enterprises.

Article 17: An investment company and the enterprise(s) established by such investment company shall abide by the laws and regulations of China, and shall not employ any means to avoid administration and tax payments.

Article 18: These Provisions shall apply to investors from Taiwan, Hong Kong and Macao who invest in the establishment investment companies in China.

Article 19: The Ministry of Foreign Trade and Economic Cooperation shall be responsible for interpretation of these Provisions.

Article 20: These Provisions shall be effective as of the date of promulgation.

MOFTEC, ISSUES CONCERNING THE <ESTABLISHMENT OF COMPANIES WITH AN INVESTMENT NATURE BY FOREIGN INVESTORS TENTATIVE PROVISIONS> EXPLANATION

Ref no: 2330/96.02.16
(Promulgated by the Ministry of Foreign Trade and Economic Co-operation on February 16, 1996.)

The Establishment of Companies With an Investment Nature by Foreign Investors Tentative Provisions ("the Provisions") were promulgated on April 4 , 1995 with Ministry Order No. 4 of 1995 of the Ministry of Foreign Trade and Economic Co-operation, and have been implemented from the same date. In accordance with the provisions of Article 19 of the Provisions, we hereby provide the following explanation of issues regarding the Provisions.

(1) A foreign investor intending to establish an investment company shall be a foreign company, enterprise or economic organization. If there are two or more foreign investors, at least one of them shall be a foreign investor with a majority interest that holds a majority equity interest and conforms to the provisions of item (1) of Article 2 of the Provisions.

(2) If the registered capital of an investment company needs to be increased after establishment and the investment company possesses lawfully generated Renminbi profits, the investment company's investor may use such Renminbi profits as a capital contribution for such increase in the company's registered capital, provided that it submits evidence of the lawfulness of such Renminbi profits.

(3) At least US$30 million of the registered capital of investment companies shall be used as capital contributions to foreign investment enterprises invested in and newly established by them, or as contributions to the capital, or increases in capital, of foreign investment enterprises already invested in and established by their parent companies or affiliates (and for which procedures for the assignment of equity have been completed according to law), where such capital or increases in capital have not been fully paid up.

(4) Investment companies may not act as the promoters of joint stock limited companies or purchase or hold the shares of such companies.

(5) The scope of business of investment companies shall be restricted to the contents set forth in Article 5 of the Provisions. Investment companies may not directly engage in production and business operations. Sales inside and outside China by investment companies of products produced by the enterprises invested in by them in accordance with the provisions of item (2) of Article 5 of the Provisions may be carried out only by the method of acting as an agent upon entrustment.

(6) Where Article 10 of the Provisions specifies that "if, when an Investment Company invests in and establishes an enterprise, the foreign exchange investment of the Investment Company or of the Investment Company and (an)other foreign investor(s) accounts for not less than 25 per cent of the registered capital of the enterprise invested in and established

by it, the enterprises invested in and established by it shall be treated as a foreign investment enterprise," the Regulations mean that if foreign exchange investment made up solely of foreign exchange investment in the investment company attributable to its foreign investor, or made up jointly of said foreign exchange investment and that of (an)other foreign investor(s), accounts for not less than 25 per cent of the registered capital of the enterprise invested in and established by it (them), such enterprise invested in by it (them) shall be treated as a foreign investment enterprise. The interpretation of Article 6 of the Provisions shall be consistent with Article 10.

When an investment company invests in and establishes an enterprise, it shall conform to the above-mentioned provisions and, in addition, its amount of capital contribution may not be less that 10 per cent of the registered capital of the enterprise invested in and established by it.

(7) Article 11 of the Regulations means that if a foreign investor that intends to establish an investment company in China is the wholly-owned subsidiary of a foreign company, then only if such foreign company (the parent company) meets the conditions specified in item (1)(a) of Article 2 of the Provisions may the foreign investor that is the subsidiary apply to establish an investment company.

(8) The establishment of any branch by an investment company shall be submitted to the Ministry of Foreign Trade and Economic Co-operation for examination and approval. To apply for the establishment of a branch, an investment company must meet the following conditions:

(i) the registered capital of the investment company has been paid on schedule in accordance with the provisions of the contract or articles or association and the amount of capital contribution already paid is not less than US$30 million, or the investment company has already invested in and established or owns at least 10 foreign investment enterprises; and

(ii) the region in which the branch is to be established is a region in which the investment company has concentrated its investment or its product sales.

(9) Article 12 of the Provisions means that:

(i) if a foreign investor that intends to invest in and establish an investment company meets the conditions specified in item (1) of Article 2 of the Provisions, it shall submit a letter to the examination and approval authority in which it guarantees the contribution of registered capital, and the transfer of technology belonging to the said foreign investor or its affiliate(s), when the investment company established by it invests in and establishes enterprises; and

(ii) if a foreign investor that intends to invest in and establish an investment company is the wholly-owned subsidiary of a foreign company (the parent company), the parent company shall submit a letter to the examination and approval authority in which it guarantees payment of the registered capital of the investment company to be established by the above-mentioned foreign investor and, upon establishment of the investment company, payment of the registered capital of the enterprises invested in and established by such investment company and transfer of technology belonging to such parent company and its subsidiary (subsidiaries).

<ESTABLISHMENT OF COMPANIES WITH AN INVESTMENT NATURE BY FOREIGN INVESTORS TENTATIVE PROVISIONS> SUPPLEMENTARY PROVISIONS

Ref no: 2330/99.08.24

We hereby formulate the following Supplementary Provisions to the Establishment of Companies with an Investment Nature by Foreign Investors Tentative Provisions promulgated by the Ministry of Foreign Trade and Economic Cooperation on April 4, 1995, in order to promote investment in China by multinational companies, to introduce foreign advanced technology and management experience and to enhance the functions of investment companies.

1. The registered capital of an investment company may not be less than US$30 million. The amount of loans taken out by an investment company may not exceed four times the amount of its paid-up registered capital. If, due to business requirements, an investment company intends to have its amount of loans exceed four times the amount of its paid-up registered capital, it shall obtain the approval of the Ministry of Foreign Trade and Economic Cooperation.
2. Investment companies are encouraged to establish scientific research and development centers or departments in China for purposes of engaging in the research and development of new products, high technology and new technologies, and to transfer the resulting achievements and provide corresponding technical services.
3. Investment companies may act as sales agents or distributors on the domestic and foreign markets for the products produced by enterprises that they have invested in.
4. Investment companies may provide transportation, warehousing and other such comprehensive services to enterprises that they have invested in.
5. Investment companies may purchase in and subsequently export from China merchandise which is not subject to export quotas or export licensing.
6. To engage in any of the business activities set forth in Articles 3, 4 and 5 hereof, investment companies shall submit the amended investment company contract, articles of association and other such relevant application documents for examination and approval by the Ministry of Foreign Trade and Economic Cooperation in accordance with the submission procedure. In addition, they shall meet the following conditions:

   The registered capital of the investment company has been paid up on schedule in accordance with the contract and articles of association, and the amount of the registered capital actually paid up is not less than US$30 million. If the investment company+s application is for the engagement in any of the business activities set forth in Articles 3 and 4 hereof as a service for enterprises that it has invested in, then at least 10% of the registered capital of such enterprises must have been contributed by the investment company, and such enterprises must have entrusted the investment company in writing (and with the unanimous approval of their boards of directors) to provide such service.

7. In the event of any discrepancy between these Provisions and the Issues Concerning the <Establishment of Companies with an Investment Nature by Foreign Investors Tentative Provisions> Explanation promulgated by the Ministry of Foreign Trade and Economic Cooperation on February 16, 1996, these Provisions shall prevail.

8. These Provisions shall be implemented as of the date of promulgation.

PBOC, ADMINISTRATION OF THE ESTABLISHMENT OF RESIDENT REPRESENTATIVE OFFICES IN CHINA BY FOREIGN INVESTMENT FINANCIAL INSTITUTIONS PROCEDURES

(Announced by the People's Bank of China on June 15, 1991.)

Article 1: These Procedures are formulated according to the PRC State Council, Administration of the Resident Representative Offices of Foreign Enterprises Tentative Provisions in order to standardize the administration of resident representative offices of foreign investment financial institutions (hereafter, "resident representative offices") in China.

Article 2: For the purposes of these Procedures, the term "foreign investment financial institutions" shall refer to banks and securities, investment, insurance, finance, credit card and lease financing companies with foreign capital.

Article 3: A resident representative office shall be a detached office of its head office and shall be named as "xxx Representative Office". The main responsible person of such representative office shall be named as the principal representative and other personnel as representatives, consultants, assistants and secretaries.

Article 4: The People's Bank of China shall be the examination, approval and administration authority of resident representative offices. A foreign investment financial institution may apply to the People's Bank of China according to these Procedures for permission to establish a resident representative office in an open city in China.

Article 5: A foreign investment financial institution shall submit the following materials to the People's Bank of China for application of permission to establish a resident representative office in an open city in China:

(1) an application letter to the president of People's Bank of China signed by the chairman of the board of directors or the general manager of the head office of the work unit that submits the application;

(2) a lawful certificate for operations or a duplicate (or a copy) of the business licence issued by the relevant authorities of the country or region where such work unit is located;

(3) the articles of association and a list of the directors of the board or similar organization of such work unit's head office;

(4) the annual reports of such work unit in the last three years; and

(5) other information required by the People's Bank of China.

Except Item 4, the materials listed in the preceding paragraph that are in a foreign language shall be accompanied by a Chinese translation.

A foreign investment financial institution shall submit the materials to the head office of the People's Bank of China for the application of establishment of a resident representative office in Beijing. It shall submit the materials to the local branches of the People's Bank of China for the application of establishment of a resident representative office in cities other than Beijing and the materials shall be submitted to the head office of the People's Bank of China after being examined by such branches.

Article 6: The People's Bank of China shall decide, within three months of the receipt of the materials for application from a foreign investment financial institution, whether to accept the application. If such application is accepted, an "Application Form for the Establishment of a Resident Representative Office in China by a Foreign Investment Financial Institution" shall be issued. Where confirmation of the People's Bank of China has not been obtained in three months, such application shall be automatically void.

A foreign investment financial institution shall, within two months of the receipt of an "Application Form for the Establishment of a Resident Representative Office in China by a Foreign Investment Financial Institution" issued by the People's Bank of China, submit the duly completed form together with a letter of authorization for the principal representative of the resident representative office signed by the chairman of the board of directors or general manager as well as the resumes of the principal representative and other representatives, to the People's Bank of China for examination and approval.

The head office of the People's Bank of China shall issue an approval certificate after having approved a foreign investment financial institution to establish a resident representative office in China.

Article 7: A foreign investment financial institution that has been approved to establish a resident representative office in China shall, according to relevant Chinese regulations and on the strength of an approval certificate issued by the People's Bank of China, go to the industrial and commercial administration department and public security department of the place where such resident representative office is located to handle registration procedures and residence procedures for its personnel and the families of such personnel, and go to the local State's specialized bank to open an account and to the taxation department to handle taxation registration procedures.

Article 8: The scope of activities of a resident representative office shall include consulting, liaison, market research and other non-profit making activities. A resident representative office may not handle operational business in the course of its activities for its head office or branches (including branches established inside China).

Article 9: A resident representative office that wants to replace its principal representative shall submit an application letter signed by the chairman of the board of directors or general manager of its head office as well as a letter of authorization and resume of the newly-appointed principal representative to the head office of the People's Bank of China for approval.

A resident representative office established in Beijing that wants to replace or add a representative, an assistant, foreign nationals and persons from Hongkong or Macao shall submit an application letter signed by the responsible person of the department in charge of the head office and the resumes of the appointed persons to the head office of the People's Bank of China for approval.

A resident representative office established in cities other than Beijing that wants to replace or add a representative, an assistant, foreign nationals and persons from Hongkong or Macao shall submit an application letter signed by the responsible person of the department in charge of the head office and the resumes of the appointed persons to the local branches of the People's Bank of China for approval, and such branches shall submit the letter and resumes to the head office of the People's Bank of China for the record.

Article 10: A resident representative office that employs citizens inside China as consultants, secretaries, translators and personnel of general duties on the recommendation of a China foreign services work unit shall submit a list and resumes of the Chinese citizens to be employed to the head office or local branch of the People's Bank of China for the record. Persons who fail to complete procedures for filing the record may not engage in the work of a resident representative office.

Article 11: A resident representative office that wants to change its name shall submit an application letter signed by the chairman of the board of directors or general manager of its head office to the People's Bank of China and, following approval by the head office of the People's Bank of China, handle procedures for changing the registration at the local industrial and commercial administration department on the strength of the approval certificate.

Article 12: A resident representative office that wants to move its office shall submit an application letter signed by the person responsible for the office to the People's Bank of China and, following approval by the People's Bank of China, handle procedures for changing the registration at the local industrial and commercial administration department on the strength of the approval certificate. Office removal by a resident representative office in Beijing shall be reported to the head office of the People's Bank of China for approval. Office removal by a resident representative office in cities other than Beijing shall be reported to the local branch of the People's Bank of China for approval.

Article 13: The principal representative of a resident representative office shall reside in China in charge of day-to-day work. A principal representative who is away from China for one month or more, or who cannot reside in China in charge of day-to-day work due to other events shall assign a person in advance to assume his duties and shall mail or deliver an assignment document to the head office or local branch of the People's Bank of China for the record.

Article 14: A resident representative office shall submit the People's Bank of China a work report for the previous year by the end of February of each year. Such work report shall be written in Chinese in a table format specified by the People's Bank of China, and shall provide accurate details of the work of such office in China.

The report of a resident representative office in Beijing shall be delivered to the head office of the People's Bank of China. The report of a resident representative office in cities other than Beijing shall be delivered to the local branch of the People's Bank of China, which shall refer the report to the head office of the People's Bank of China.

Article 15: A foreign investment financial institution that wants to close its resident representative office shall submit an application letter issued by its head office in advance to the People's Bank of China and, following approval by the head office of the People's Bank of China, handle cancellation procedures at relevant departments. The head office of the resident representative office shall be responsible for any matter left unfinished by such office.

Article 16: The head office of the People's Bank of China shall be responsible for the supervision, inspection and administration of resident representative offices in Beijing and shall authorize the local branches of the People's Bank of China to supervise, inspect and administer resident representative offices in cities other than Beijing.

Article 17: Resident representative offices shall abide by the Chinese laws and regulations as well as these Procedures. The head office and local branches of the People's Bank of China shall have the right to deal with any resident representative office in violation of these Procedures.

Article 18: These Procedures shall apply to the administration of resident representative offices established by foreign investment financial institutions registered in Hongkong, Macao and Taiwan.

Article 19: These Procedures shall be effective as of date of promulgation. The People's Bank of China, Administration of the Establishment of Resident Representative Offices in China by Overseas Chinese and Foreign Investment Financial Institutions Procedures promulgated by the People's Bank of China in February 1983 shall be repealed at the same time.

LEGISLATION APPENDIX 5

PRC, ADMINISTRATION OF FOREIGN INVESTMENT FINANCIAL INSTITUTIONS REGULATIONS

(Adopted at the 14th Ordinary Meeting of the State Council on January 7, 1994, promulgated on February 25, 1994 and effective as of April 1, 1994.)

CHAPTER 1: GENERAL PROVISIONS

Article 1: These Regulations are formulated in order to meet the needs of opening up to the outside world and economic development, and to strengthen and improve the administration of foreign investment financial institutions.

Article 2: For the purposes of these Regulations, the term "foreign investment financial institutions" shall refer to the following financial institutions that are approved to be established and operated in the People's Republic of China in accordance with the relevant laws and regulations of the People's Republic of China:

(1) banks with foreign capital whose head offices are located within the People's Republic of China (hereafter, "foreign investment banks");

(2) branches of foreign banks in the People's Republic of China (hereafter, "branches of foreign banks");

(3) banks in the People's Republic of China that are equity joint ventures between foreign financial institutions and Chinese financial institutions (hereafter, "joint venture banks");

(4) finance companies with foreign capital whose head offices are located in the People's Republic of China (hereafter, "foreign investment finance companies"); and

(5) finance companies in the People's Republic of China that are equity joint ventures between foreign financial institutions and Chinese financial institutions (hereafter, "joint venture finance companies").

The State Council shall determine the regions where foreign investment financial institutions are to be established.

Article 3: Foreign investment financial institutions must abide by the laws and regulations of the People's Republic of China and may not harm the public interests of the People's Republic of China.

The normal business activities and lawful rights and interests of foreign investment financial institutions shall be protected by the laws of the People's Republic of China.

Article 4: The People's Bank of China shall be the authority in charge of the administration and supervision of foreign investment financial institutions. The branches of the People's Bank of China of the regions where foreign investment financial institutions are located shall exercise day-to-day administration and supervision of the foreign investment financial institutions in their regions.

CHAPTER 2: ESTABLISHMENT AND REGISTRATION

Article 5: The minimum amount of the registered capital of a foreign investment bank or a joint venture bank shall be freely convertible currencies equivalent to Rmb300 million in value; the minimum amount of the registered capital of a foreign investment finance company or a joint venture finance company shall be freely convertible currencies equivalent to Rmb200 million in value. Their paid-up capital shall be not less than 50% of their registered capital.

The branch of a foreign bank shall be allocated without consideration by its head office freely convertible currencies equivalent to Rmb100 million in value as its working capital.

Article 6: An applicant shall meet the following conditions for the establishment of a foreign investment bank or foreign investment finance company:

(1) the applicant is a financial institution;

(2) the applicant has maintained a representative office in the People's Republic of China for more than two years;

(3) the applicant possesses assets totalling not less than US$10 billion at the end of the year prior to the year of submitting the application; and

(4) the country or region where the applicant is located possesses a sound financial supervisory and administrative system.

Article 7: An applicant shall meet the following conditions for the establishment of a branch of a foreign bank:

(1) the applicant has maintained a representative office in the People's Republic of China for more than two years;

(2) the applicant possesses assets totalling not less than US$20 billion at the end of the year prior to the year or submitting the application; and

(3) the country or region where the applicant is located possesses a sound financial supervisory and administrative system.

Article 8: An applicant shall meet the following conditions for the establishment of a joint venture bank or joint venture finance company:

(1) each party in the joint venture is a financial institution;

(2) the foreign party in the joint venture has established a representative office in the People's Republic of China;

(3) the foreign party in the joint venture possesses assets totalling not less than US$10 billion at the end of the year prior to the year of submitting the application; and

(4) the country or region where the foreign party in the joint venture is located possesses a sound financial supervisory and administrative system.

Article 9: To establish a foreign investment bank or foreign investment finance company, an applicant shall apply in writing to the People's Bank of China and submit the following information:

(1) an application for the establishment of a foreign investment bank or foreign investment finance company. Such application shall include the name of the foreign investment bank or foreign investment finance company to be established, the amount of registered and paid-up capital, types of business operations applied for and so on;

(2) a feasibility study;

(3) the articles of association of the foreign investment bank or foreign investment finance company to be established;

(4) a copy of the business licence issued by the relevant authorities in charge in the country or region where the applicant is located;

(5) the annual reports of the applicant for the most recent three years; and

(6) other information required for submission by the People's Bank of China.

Article 10: To establish a branch of a foreign bank, the head office of such foreign bank shall apply in writing to the People's Bank of China and submit the following information:

(1) an application signed by legal representatives. Such application shall include the name of the branch of the foreign bank to be established, the amount of working capital allocated without consideration by its head office, types of business operations applied for and so on;

(2) a copy of the business licence issued by the relevant authorities in charge in the country or region where the applicant is located;

(3) the annual reports of the applicant for the most recent three years; and

(4) other information required for submission by the People's Bank of China.

Article 11: To establish a joint venture bank or joint venture finance company, parties in the joint venture shall jointly apply in writing to the People's Bank of China and submit the following information:

(1) an application for the establishment of a joint venture bank or joint venture finance company. Such application shall include the name of the joint venture bank or joint venture finance company to be established, the names of the parties in the joint venture, the amount of registered and paid-up capital, the ratio of capital contributions by the parties and the types of business operations applied for;

(2) a feasibility study;

(3) a joint venture contract and the articles of association of the joint venture bank or joint venture finance company to be established;

(4) a copy of the business licences of the parties in the joint venture issued by the authorities in charge in the countries or regions where the applicants are located;

(5) the annual reports of the parties in the joint venture for the most recent three years; and

(6) other information required for submission by the People's Bank of China.

Article 12: Except for annual reports, any of the information listed in Articles 9, 10 and 11 of these Regulations that is written in a foreign language shall be accompanied by a Chinese translation.

Article 13: After preliminarily examining and approving an application for establishing a foreign investment financial institution, the People's Bank of China shall issue an official application form to the applicant. Where such applicant fails to receive the official application form within 90 days of submitting the application, the application shall be considered not to be entertained.

Article 14: Within 60 days of receiving an official application from, an applicant shall submit to the People's Bank of China the duly completed application form together with the following documents for examination and approval:

(1) a list and resumes of the key persons in charge of the foreign investment financial institution to be established;

(2) the powers of attorney for the persons in charge that are to take up key positions at such foreign investment financial institution;

(3) where a branch of a foreign bank is to be established, a liability guarantee by its head office for the tax and debt liability of such branch; and

(4) other documents required for submission by the People's Bank of China.

Article 15: Within 30 days of receiving the approval documents issued by the People's Bank of China, a foreign investment financial institution must have raised the full amount of its paid-up capital or working capital and transferred such capital into the People's Republic of China. After verification by a Chinese registered accountant, the foreign investment financial institution shall register with the industrial and commercial administrative authorities in accordance with the law and shall, within 30 days of the commencement of business, handle tax registration with the taxation authorities in accordance with the law.

Article 16: Within 30 days of the examination and approval by the People's Bank of China, a foreign investment financial institution shall obtain a Foreign Exchange Business Operation Permit from the State Administration of Exchange Control.

CHAPTER 3: SCOPE OF BUSINESS

Article 17: A foreign investment bank, a branch of a foreign bank or a joint venture bank may operate part or all of the following types of business in line with the business scope approved by the People's Bank of China:

(1) foreign exchange deposits;

(2) foreign exchange lending;

(3) foreign exchange note discount;

(4) approved foreign exchange investment;

(5) foreign exchange remittances;

(6) foreign exchange guarantee;

(7) import and export clearing;

(8) trading in foreign exchange for its own account and for clients;

(9) acting as an agent for the exchange of foreign currencies and foreign exchange notes;

(10) acting as an agent for foreign currency credit card payments;

(11) custody and safe deposit box services;

(12) credit investigation and advice; and

(13) approved domestic currency business and other foreign currency business.

Article 18: A foreign investment finance company or joint venture finance company may operate part or all of the following types of business in line with the business scope approved by the People's Bank of China:

(1) foreign exchange deposits with each deposit being no less than US$100,000 and having a term of no less than three months;

(2) foreign exchange lending;

(3) foreign exchange note discount;

(4) approved foreign exchange investment;

(5) foreign exchange guarantee;

(6) trading in foreign exchange for its own account and for clients;

(7) credit investigation and advice;

(8) foreign exchange trust; and

(9) approved domestic currency business and other foreign currency business.

Article 19: For the purposes of this Chapter, the term "foreign exchange deposits" shall refer to the following deposits denominated in foreign currencies:

(1) interbank deposits inside and outside the People's Republic of China;

(2) non-interbank deposits outside the People's Republic of China;

(3) deposits of foreign nationals in the People's Republic of China;

(4) deposits of overseas Chinese and compatriots from Hong Kong, Macao and Taiwan;

(5) deposits of foreign investment enterprises;

(6) deposit with a foreign investment financial institution of a loan granted by such institution to a non-foreign investment enterprise; and

(7) other approved foreign exchange deposits.

Article 20: For the purposes of this Chapter, the term "foreign exchange remittances" shall refer to remittances remitted into the People's Republic of China and remittances remitted out of the People's Republic of China by foreign investment enterprises, foreign nationals, overseas Chinese and compatriots from Hong Kong, Macao and Taiwan inside the People's Republic of China.

Article 21: For the purposes of this Chapter, the term "import and export clearing" shall refer to import and export clearing for foreign investment enterprises, approved export clearing for non-foreign investment enterprises as well as approved clearing for imports under loans for non-foreign investment enterprises that are handled by foreign investment banks, branches of foreign banks and joint venture banks.

CHAPTER 4: SUPERVISION AND ADMINISTRATION

Article 22: The deposit and lending interest rates as well as handling charge rates of foreign investment financial institutions shall be determined by foreign investment financial institutions in accordance with the relevant regulations of the People's Bank of China.

Article 23: A foreign investment financial institution engaging in deposit business must place a deposit reserve with a branch of the People's Bank of China at the place where it is located. The ratio of such deposit reserve shall be determined and adjusted according to the needs by the People's Bank of China. Such deposit reserve shall not carry interest.

Article 24: Thirty per cent of the working capital of a branch of a foreign bank must exist in the form of interest-generating assets designated by the People's Bank of China. Such interest-generating assets shall include deposits at a bank designated by the People's Bank of China.

Article 25: The total assets of a foreign investment bank, joint venture bank, foreign investment finance company or joint venture finance company shall not exceed 20 times the sum of its paid-up capital and reserves.

Article 26: Loans to an enterprise and its affiliates by a foreign investment bank, joint venture bank, foreign investment finance company or joint venture finance company shall not exceed 30% of the sum of its paid-up capital and reserves, except for loans specially approved by the People's Bank of China.

Article 27: The total amount of investment of a foreign investment bank, joint venture bank, foreign investment finance company or joint venture finance company shall not exceed 30% of the sum of its paid-up capital and reserves, except for investment in financial institutions made with the approval by the People's Bank of China.

Article 28: The fixed assets of a foreign investment bank, joint venture bank, foreign investment finance company or joint venture finance company shall not exceed 40% of the sum of its paid-up capital and reserves.

Article 29: Foreign investment financial institutions shall ensure the liquidity of their assets. Specific procedures shall be separately formulated by the People's Bank of China.

Article 30: The total amount of deposits taken up in the People's Republic of China by a foreign investment financial institution shall not exceed 40% of its total assets.

Article 31: Foreign investment financial institutions must calculate and set reserves for idle (bad) debts in accordance with the regulations.

Article 32: A foreign investment bank, joint venture bank, foreign investment finance company or joint venture finance company whose paid-up capital is less than its registered capital must each year withdraw 25% of its after-tax profits to make up the deficiency until the sum of its paid-up capital and reserves equals its registered capital.

Article 33: A foreign investment financial institution shall employ at least one Chinese citizen as a senior manager.

Article 34: A foreign investment financial institution shall employ registered accountants in China that are also approved by a branch of the People's Bank of China at the place where it is located.

Article 35: A foreign investment financial institution must obtain approval of the People's Bank of China and handle relevant registration with the industrial and commercial administrative authorities in accordance with the law for any of the following activities:

(1) establishment of a branch;

(2) adjustment or assignment of registered capital and increase or decrease of working capital;

(3) change of the name or place of business of the institution; or

(4) change of senior management personnel.

Article 36: Foreign investment financial institutions must report and submit financial statements and relevant information to the People's Bank of China and its relevant branches in accordance with regulations.

Article 37: The People's Bank of China and its relevant branches shall have the right to examine or check the operation, management and financial situation of foreign investment financial institutions.

CHAPTER 5: DISSOLUTION AND LIQUIDATION

Article 38: A foreign investment financial institution that terminates its business activities of its own accord shall submit a written application to the People's Bank of China 30 days prior to the date of termination, and shall be dissolved and liquidated upon examination and approval by the People's Bank of China.

Article 39: Where a foreign investment financial institution is unable to repay its debts in full at maturity, the People's Bank of China may order it to suspend business and to clear up the debts within a specific period. Where repayment capability is restored during the period of clearing up the debts and business needs to be resumed, an application for business resumption must be submitted to the People's Bank of China. Where repayment capability is not yet restored within such period, liquidation must be conducted.

Article 40: Where a foreign investment financial institution terminates its business because of dissolution, being closed down or declared insolvent in accordance with the law, specific matters concerning its liquidation shall be handled by reference to the relevant laws and regulations of China.

Article 41: Upon completion of liquidation, a foreign investment financial institution must cancel its registration with the original registration authorities within the statutory period.

CHAPTER 6: PENALTIES

Article 42: Where a foreign investment financial institution is established without authorization in violation of Chapter 2 of these Regulations, the People's Bank of China shall forbid it and confiscate its illegal income, and may impose a fine in foreign exchange equivalent to Rmb50,000 to Rmb100,000 in value.

Article 43: Where a foreign investment financial institution engages in business beyond the approved scope of business in violation of Chapter 3 of these Regulations, the People's Bank of China or its relevant branch shall order it to stop the part of business activities that is beyond the scope of business and confiscate the illegal income from such part, and may impose a fine in foreign exchange equivalent to Rmb10,000 to Rmb50,000 in value.

Article 44: Where a foreign investment financial institution engages in business in violation of the relevant provisions of Chapter 4 of these Regulations, the People's Bank of China or its relevant branch shall have the right to order it to make rectification, to restructure its business or to make up the relevant deficient funds, and may impose a fine in foreign exchange equivalent to Rmb5,000 to Rmb30,000 in value.

Article 45: Where a foreign investment financial institution fails to report and submit financial statements and relevant information within a specific period in violation of the relevant provisions of Chapter 4, the People's Bank of China or its relevant branch shall issue a warning or a notice of criticism and order it to re-submit such financial statements and information within a specific period, and may impose a fine in foreign exchange equivalent to Rmb3,000 to Rmb20,000 in value.

Article 46: In addition to the penalties imposed in accordance with the relevant provisions of Articles 43, 44 and 45 of this Chapter on a foreign investment financial institution in violation of these Regulations, the People's Bank of China may order such institution to stop its business or even cancel its business permit where the situation is serious.

Article 47: A foreign investment financial institution that violates other laws and regulations of the People's Republic of China shall be handled by the relevant authorities in charge in accordance with the law.

CHAPTER 7: SUPPLEMENTARY

Article 48: These Regulations shall apply, by comparison, to financial institutions established and operated in the People's Republic of China by Hong Kong, Macao and Taiwan financial institutions.

Article 49: Administrative procedures for representative offices of foreign financial institutions in the People's Republic of China shall be formulated separately by the People's Bank of China.

Article 50: The People's Bank of China shall be responsible for interpreting these Regulations. The implementing rules shall be formulated by the People's Bank of China.

Article 51: These Regulations shall be effective as of April 1, 1994. At the same time, the PRC, Administration of Foreign Investment Banks and Sino-Foreign Joint Venture Banks in Special Economic Zones Regulations promulgated by the State Council on April 2, 1985 and the Administration of Foreign Investment Financial Institutions and Sino-Foreign Joint Venture Financial Institutions in Shanghai Procedures approved by the State Council on September 7, 1990 and promulgated by the People's Bank of China on September 8, 1990 shall be repealed.

PRC, LAND ADMINISTRATION LAW (REVISED)

Ref no: 4100/88.12.29

(Adopted at the 16th Session of the 6th National People's Congress Standing Committee on 25 June 1986, First Revision on 29 December 1988, Second Revision on August 29, 1998 and became effective as of January 1, 1999.)

PART ONE: GENERAL PROVISIONS

Article 1: This Law is formulated in accordance with the Constitution in order to strengthen the administration of land, to safeguard the system of socialist public ownership of land, to protect and develop land resources, to use land in a rational way, to effectively protect arable land and to promote sustainable social and economic development.

Article 2: The People's Republic of China implements the system of socialist public ownership of land, i.e. the system of ownership by the whole people and the system of collective ownership by the working people.

The State Council shall exercise the ownership by the whole people, i.e. the State ownership, of land, on behalf of the State.

No work unit or individual may seize, buy and sell, or illegally transfer land by other means. Leaseholds may be assigned according to law.

The State may implement requisition of collectively-owned land in the public interest according to law.

The State implements the system of use of State-owned land for compensation according to law except, however, where the State has allocated leaseholds within the scope prescribed by law.

Article 3: To cherish and rationally use land and to effectively protect arable land is the basic national policy of the State. Each level of the people's government shall take measures to carry out overall planning for and strictly administer, protect and develop land resources and prevent acts of illegal occupation of land.

Article 4: The State implements the system of land usage control.

The State shall prepare a master land use plan, which shall prescribe the usage of land and classify land as agricultural land, construction land and unutilized land. The State strictly limits the conversion of agricultural land into construction land, controls the total area of construction land and implements special protection for arable land.

In the preceding paragraph "agricultural land" means land that is directly used for agricultural production and includes arable land, forest, grassland, land used for cropland irrigation, bodies of water for breeding, etc. "Construction land" means land that is used for construction of buildings and structures and includes land used for urban and rural residences and public facilities, land used for industry and mining, land used for transportation and water project facilities, land used for tourism, land used for military facilities, etc. "Unutilized land" means land other than agricultural land and construction land.

Work units and individuals that use land must use the land strictly in accordance with the usage determined in the master land use plan.

Article 5: The State Council's administrative authority in charge of land shall assume overall responsibility for the administration and supervision of land nationwide.

The establishment and duties of the administrative authorities in charge of land of local people's governments at and above the county level shall be determined by the people's government of each province, autonomous region or municipality directly under the central government according to the relevant regulations of the State Council.

Article 6: All work units and individuals shall have the obligation to comply with the laws and regulations concerning the administration of land and the right to report and complain about any violation of laws and regulations concerning the administration of land.

Article 7: People's governments shall reward those work units and individuals with outstanding achievements in fields such as the protection and development of land resources, the rational use of land, the undertaking of relevant scientific research, etc.

PART TWO: LAND OWNERSHIP AND LEASEHOLDS

Article 8: Land in urban areas of cities shall be owned by the State.

Land in rural and suburban areas shall be owned by peasants' collectives, except for those portions which are owned by the State in accordance with the Law. Home lots, private plots of cropland and private lots of hilly land shall be owned by peasants' collectives.

Article 9: State-owned land and land owned by peasants' collectives may be lawfully designated to work units or individuals for use. Work units and individuals that use land shall have the obligation to protect, manage and rationally use the land.

Article 10: If land owned by a peasants' collective is lawfully owned by a village peasants' collective, it shall be operated and managed by the village collective economic organization or by the village committee. If the land owned by a peasants' collective is already separately owned by two or more village collective economic organizations within the village, it shall be operated and managed by each such village collective economic organization or villagers' group within the village. Land owned by township (town) peasants' collectives shall be operated and managed by township (town) village collective economic organizations.

Article 11: People's governments at the county level shall register, issue certificates for and confirm the ownership of land owned by peasants' collectives.

People's governments at the county level shall register, issue certificates for and confirm construction leaseholds in respect of land owned by peasants' collectives that is lawfully used for non-agricultural construction.

People's governments at or above the county level shall register, issue certificates for and confirm leaseholds in respect of State-owned land that is lawfully used by work units and individuals. Of this, the specific registration authority that issues certificates for the State-owned land used by central State authorities shall be determined by the State Council.

The confirmation of ownership or leaseholds in respect of forests, grasslands and the confirmation of breeding use rights in respect of bodies of water and tidal flats shall be handled in accordance with relevant provisions of, respectively, the PRC, Forestry Law, the PRC, Grassland Law and the PRC, Fishery Law.

Article 12: If the title or usage of land has been changed in accordance with law, the procedures for the registration of a change in the land use or title must be carried out.

Article 13: Land ownership and leaseholds that have been registered according to law shall be protected by law and may not be infringed by any work unit or individual.

Article 14: Land owned by peasants' collectives shall be contracted for operation by the members of the collective economic organization for plantation, forestry, animal husbandry and fishery production. The term of contract operation of land shall be 30 years. The owner and the contractor shall enter into an agreement for contract operation which shall stipulate the rights and obligations of both parties. Peasants who contract to operate land shall have the obligation to protect the land and use it rationally in accordance with the usage agreed in the agreement for contract operation. The peasants' rights of contract operation of land shall be protected by law.

If, during the term of an agreement for contract operation of land, appropriate adjustments are made to the land contracted by individual contract operators, the consent of not less than two-thirds of the members of the village council or not less than two-thirds of the village representatives must be obtained and the adjustments must be reported to the people's government at the township (town) level and the administrative authority in charge of agriculture of the people's government at the county level for approval.

Article 15: State-owned land may be contracted for operation by work units or individuals for plantation, forestry, animal husbandry and fishery production. Land owned by peasants' collectives may be contracted for operation by work units and individuals outside the relevant collective economic organization for plantation, forestry, animal husbandry and fishery production. The owner and the contractor shall enter into an agreement for contract operation of land which shall stipulate the rights and obligations of both parties. The term of contract operation of land shall be agreed in the agreement for contract operation. Work units and individuals that contract to operate land shall have the obligation to protect the land and rationally use it in accordance with the usage agreed in the agreement for contract operation.

If land owned by peasants' collectives is contracted for operation by work units or individuals outside the relevant collective economic organization, the consent of not less than two-thirds of the members of the village council or not less than two-thirds of the village representatives must be obtained and the matter reported to the people's government at the township (town) level for approval.

Article 16: In the event of a dispute over land ownership or leaseholds, the parties involved shall resolve the same through consultations. If consultations are unsuccessful, the matter shall be decided by the people's government.

Disputes between work units shall be decided by people's governments at or above the county level. Disputes between individuals or between individuals and work units shall be decided by people's governments at the township level or by people's governments at or above the county level.

If an involved party is dissatisfied with the decision of the relevant people's government, it may institute proceedings at the people's court within 30 days commencing from the date on which it received the notice concerning the decision.

Prior to settlement of a dispute over land ownership or leaseholds, no party involved may change the existing usage and condition of the land.

PART THREE: MASTER LAND USE PLAN

Article 17: Each level of the people's government shall organize the preparation of a master land use plan in accordance with the national economic and social development plan, and the requirements for rehabilitation of State land and protection of resources and the environment, the capacity to supply land and the demand for land for each construction project.

The State Council shall determine the planning period of master land use plans.

Article 18: The master land use plan at the lower level shall be formulated on the basis of the master land use plan at the next higher level.

The total area of construction land in the master land use plan formulated by the local people's government at each level may not exceed the control targets specified in the master land use plan at the next higher level. The reserved area of arable land may not be lower than the control targets specified in the master land use plan at the next higher level.

The master land use plan formulated by the people's government of each province, autonomous region and municipality directly under the central government shall ensure that the total area of arable land in their respective administrative regions is not reduced.

Article 19: Master land use plans shall be formulated according to the following principles:

(1) to strictly protect basic cropland and to control the occupation of agricultural land by non-agricultural construction

(2) to increase the land use efficiency ratio;

(3) to carry out overall planning and arrangements for the use of land under different categories and in different regions;

(4) to protect and improve the ecological environment and to safeguard the sustainable use of land;

(5) to balance the occupation of arable land with the development and restoration of arable land.

Article 20: Master land use plans at the county level shall delineate different land use zones and clearly specify their respective land usage.

Master land use plans at the township (town) level shall delineate different land use zones and confirm the usage of each parcel of land according to the land use conditions, and shall be publicly announced.

Article 21: Master land use plans shall be examined and approved at different levels.

The master land use plans of provinces, autonomous regions and municipalities directly under the central government shall be submitted to the State Council for approval.

The master land use plans of those municipalities where people's governments of the provinces and autonomous regions are located, those municipalities with a population of one million or more and those municipalities designated by the State Council shall, once examined and agreed upon by the people's government of the relevant province or autonomous region, be submitted to the State Council for approval.

Master land use plans other than those specified in the second and third paragraphs of this Article shall be submitted level by level to the people's government of the relevant province, autonomous region or municipality directly under the central government for approval. Of these, master land use plans at the township (town) level may be approved by the people's governments of municipalities established with sub-districts or autonomous prefectures that have been so authorized by the relevant people's governments at the provincial level.

Once a master land use plan has been approved, it must be strictly implemented.

Article 22: The scale of land used for urban construction shall comply with the standards prescribed by the State. Urban construction shall fully utilize existing construction land and shall not occupy, or shall minimize, the occupation of agricultural land.

The master plans for cities and the plans for villages and towns shall be linked to the master land use plans. The scale of construction land provided for in the master plans for cities and the plans for villages and towns may not exceed the scale of construction land for cities, villages and towns specified in the master land use plans.

Construction land that is located within urban planning zones or village or town planning zones shall comply with the urban planning and the village and town planning.

Article 23: Plans for the comprehensive rehabilitation, development and use of rivers and lakes shall be linked to the master land use plans. Use of land within areas for control and protection of rivers, lakes and reservoirs and areas for absorbing and retarding flood water shall conform to plans for the comprehensive rehabilitation, development and use of rivers and lakes as well as to the requirements for guiding and absorbing flood waters and conveying water in respect of rivers and lakes.

Article 24: Each level of the people's government shall strengthen its administration of land use plans and exercise control over the total amount of construction land.

Annual land use plans shall be prepared in accordance with plans for national economic and social development, State industrial policies, the master land use plan and the actual circumstances with respect to construction land and land use. The procedure for preparation, examination and approval of the annual land use plans shall be identical to the procedure for preparation, examination and approval of the master land use plans. Once approved and issued to the lower levels, annual land use plans must be strictly implemented.

Article 25: People's governments of provinces, autonomous regions and municipalities directly under the central government shall include the implementation status of their annual land use plans as part of the implementation status of the plan for national economic and social development and shall report the same to the people's congress at the same level.

Article 26: Amendments to an approved master land use plan must be approved by the original approval authority. The land usage determined in the master land use plan may not be changed without approval.

If the land requirements for the construction of large-scale power, communication, water or other infrastructure projects approved by the State Council necessitates a change in the master land use plan, the master land use plan shall be amended in accordance with the approval document of State Council.

If the land requirements for the construction of large-scale power, communication, water or other infrastructure projects approved by the people's government of a province, autonomous region or municipality under the central government necessitates a change in the master land use plan and the change is within the approval authority for master land use plan of the people's government at the provincial level, the master land use plan shall be changed in accordance with the approval document of the people's government at the provincial level.

Article 27: The State shall establish a land survey system.

The administrative authorities in charge of land of people's governments at or above the county level shall carry out land surveys in conjunction with the relevant authorities at the same level. Land owners or users shall cooperate with the surveys and shall supply the relevant information.

Article 28: The administrative authorities in charge of land of people's governments at or above the county level shall assess the grades of land in conjunction with the relevant authorities at the same level in accordance with the land survey results, the planned land usage and the unified standards formulated by the State.

Article 29: The State shall establish a system for land statistics.

The administrative authorities in charge of land of people's governments at or above the county level and the statistics authority at the same level shall jointly prepare plans for statistical surveys, carry out statistical surveys of land according to law and regularly publish statistical information concerning land. Land owners or users shall supply the relevant information and may not falsify the contents, conceal facts, or refuse to submit the information or delay the submission of information.

Statistical information concerning area of land jointly published by the administrative authority in charge of land and the statistics authority shall be the basis for the formulation of master land use plan by each level of the people's government.

Article 30: The State shall establish a national land administration information system to implement a dynamic monitor over the status of land use.

PART FOUR: PROTECTION OF ARABLE LAND

Article 31: The State protects arable land and strictly controls the conversion of arable land to non-arable land.

The State implements the system of occupation of arable land for compensation. If, upon approval, arable land is occupied by non-agricultural construction, the work unit that occupies the arable land shall be responsible for cultivating new arable land of the same quantity and quality as the arable land occupied according to the principle of "for each area of land occupied an equal area must be cultivated". If the conditions for cultivating new arable land do not exist or the newly cultivated arable land does not meet the requirements, fees for cultivating new arable land shall be paid in accordance with the regulations of the relevant province, autonomous region or municipality directly under the central government and shall be applied only to the cultivation of new arable land.

The people's government of each province, autonomous region and municipality directly under the central government shall formulate plans for the cultivation of new arable land, supervise the work units that occupy arable land in their cultivation of, or their arrangements for the cultivation of, new arable land according to the plans and shall carry out inspection and acceptance in respect of the newly cultivated arable land.

Article 32: Local people's governments at or above the county level may require work units that occupy arable land to use the top-soil of the arable land occupied by it for the improvement of the soil conditions of newly-cultivated arable land, inferior land or other arable land.

Article 33: The people's government of each province, autonomous region and municipality directly under the central government shall strictly implement the master use plan and the annual land use plan and adopt measures to ensure that the total area of arable land in their respective administrative regions is not reduced. If the area of arable land is reduced, the State Council shall order the cultivation of new arable land of an area and quality equal to those of the arable land lost within a specified time limit. Such arable land shall be inspected and accepted by the State Council's administrative authority in charge of land in conjunction with the administrative authority in charge of agriculture. If, due to a genuine lack of land reserve, the amount of newly-cultivated arable land in a particular province or municipality directly under the central government is insufficient to make up for the amount of arable land occupied as a result of an increase in construction land, it must be reported to the State Council for approval to reduce or exempt the area of arable land in that administrative region and to cultivate arable land in other places.

Article 34: The State implements the system of protection of basic cropland. The following types of arable land shall be included in basic cropland protection zones in accordance with the master land use plan and shall be subject to strict administration:

(1) arable land within the grain, cotton or oil production bases approved and determined by the relevant State Council authorities in charge or by local people's governments at or above the county level;

(2) arable land that has good water irrigation facilities and water and soil conservation facilities, and medium- and low-yield cropland that is currently subject to a transformation plan or that is transformable;

(3) vegetable production bases;

(4) experimental cropland for agricultural research and education;

(5) other arable land that should be included in basic cropland protection zones according to regulations of the State Council.

The basic cropland delineated by each province, autonomous region and municipality directly under the central government shall be not less than 80% of the arable land in its administrative region.

Basic cropland protection zones shall be zoned and delineated using townships (towns) as the unit. The administrative authority in charge of land of the people's government at the county level shall arrange for implementation of such zoning and delineation in conjunction with the administrative authority in charge of agriculture at the same level.

Article 35: Each level of the people's government shall adopt measures to safeguard drainage and irrigation facilities, improve soil conditions, enhance the fertility of the land and prevent desertification, salinization, soil erosion and pollution of the land.

Article 36: Land for non-agricultural construction must be used economically. If it is possible to use uncultivated land, arable land may not be occupied. If it is possible to use poor quality land, good quality land may not be occupied.

It is forbidden to occupy arable land for the construction of kilns or tombs or to carry out unauthorized construction of buildings, sand extraction, quarrying, mining or soil removal on arable land.

It is forbidden to occupy basic cropland for the development of forestry or fruit plantations or for digging of ponds for breeding fish.

Article 37: It is forbidden for any work unit or individual to leave arable land idle or allow it to become wasteland. If arable land for which the examination and approval procedures for occupation by non-agricultural construction have been carried out is not used within one year and it can still be farmed and produce a harvest, the collective or individual that originally farmed the said parcel of arable land shall resume farming the same or, alternatively, the work unit using the land may arrange for it to be farmed. If construction is not started for more than one year, an idle fee shall be paid in accordance with the regulations of the relevant province, autonomous region or municipality directly under the central government. If the land is not used for two consecutive years, upon the approval of the original approval authority, the relevant people's government at or above the county level shall recover the leaseholds of the work unit using the land without compensation. If the said parcel of land was originally owned by a peasants' collective, it shall be returned to the original village collective economic organization for resumption of farming.

Idle land within the scope of urban planning zones for which leaseholds are obtained by means of grant for real property development shall be handled in accordance with the relevant provisions of the PRC, Administration of Urban Real Property Law.

If a work unit or individual that has contracted to operate arable land leaves it uncultivated and idle for two consecutive years, the original owner shall terminate the agreement for contract operation and repossess the arable land contracted out.

Article 38: The State encourages work units and individuals to develop unutilized land according to master land use plans, provided that they shall protect and improve the ecological environment and prevent soil erosion and desertification. If unutilized land is suitable for developing into agricultural land, preference shall be given to developing it as agricultural land.

The State shall protect the lawful rights and interests of developers according to law.

Article 39: The cultivation of unutilized land must first undergo scientific evaluation and verification and must be carried out within the cultivatable areas delineated in the master land use plan and then only if approved according to law. It is forbidden to destroy forest and grassland for cultivation of arable land. It is forbidden to reclaim farmland from lakes or to encroach on river banks.

In accordance with the master land use plan, arable or reclaimed land that has damaged the ecological environment must be restored to forest, grassland or lake by ceasing cultivation in a planned and gradual manner.

Article 40: If State-owned barren hills, wasteland or barren shoals whose leaseholds have not been determined are developed for plantation, forestry, animal husbandry or fishery production, upon approval according to law by a people's government at or above the county level, the leaseholds may be granted to the developing work unit or individual for long-term use.

Article 41: The State encourages the rehabilitation of land. People's governments at the county and township (town) level shall organize village collective economic organizations to carry out comprehensive rehabilitation of cropland, water, roads, forests and villages in accordance with the master land use plans, enhance the quality of arable land, increase the effective area of arable land and improve the conditions of agricultural production and the ecological environment.

Each level of the local people's government shall adopt measures to transform medium and low-yield farmland, and rehabilitate idle and scattered plots of land and abandoned land.

Article 42: If land is damaged due to excavation, subsidence, pressure, etc. the work unit or individual using the land shall be responsible for restoring the land in accordance with the relevant State regulations. If it is not possible to restore the land or the restored land does not meet the requirements, a land restoration fee shall be paid, to be used solely for land restoration. Preference shall be given to using the restored land for agricultural purposes.

PART FIVE: CONSTRUCTION LAND

Article 43: Any work unit or individual that intends to carry out construction and needs to use land therefor must apply according to law to use State-owned land. However, the land owned by the farmers' collectives of collective economic organizations that has been approved according to law for use in the establishment of a township/town enterprise or for construction of residences by rural residents and land owned by farmers' collectives that has been approved according to law for use in the construction of township (town) village public facilities or public welfare undertakings is excepted.

For the purposes of the preceding paragraph, State-owned land the use of which is subject to application shall include both land belonging to the State and land originally owned by peasants' collectives that has been requisitioned by the State.

Article 44: If land to be occupied for construction involves the conversion of agricultural land into construction land, the procedures for examination and approval of the conversion of agricultural land shall be carried out.

If roads, pipelines or large-scale infrastructure construction projects approved by the people's government of a province, autonomous region or municipality directly under the central government or construction projects approved by the State Council involves the use and conversion of agricultural land into construction land, such use and conversion of land shall be approved by the State Council.

If, within the scale of construction land of cities, villages and towns determined in the master land use plan, agricultural land is to be converted into construction land in order to implement the plan, such conversion shall be approved by the approval authority that originally approved the master land use plan on a lot-by-lot basis in accordance with the annual land use plan. Within the approved scope of conversion of agricultural land, the details of land to be used for construction projects may be approved by people's governments at the municipal or county level.

If a construction project that is not covered by the second and third paragraphs of this Article involves the use and conversion of agricultural land into construction land, such use and conversion of land shall be approved by the people's government of the relevant province, autonomous region or municipality directly under the central government.

Article 45: Requisition of the following land shall be approved by the State Council:

(1) basic cropland;

(2) more than 35 hectares of arable land that is not basic cropland; and

(3) more than 70 hectares of other land.

The requisition of land that is not covered by the preceding paragraph shall be approved by the people's government of the relevant province, autonomous region or municipality directly under central government and reported to the State Council for the record.

If agricultural land is to be requisitioned, examination and approval of the conversion of agricultural land must first be carried out as prescribed in Article 44 hereof. Where the conversion of agricultural land is approved by the State Council, the examination and approval procedures for land requisition shall be handled simultaneously without need for examination and approval of land requisition to be handled separately. Where the conversion of agricultural land is approved by the people's government of a province, autonomous region or municipality directly under the central government within its land requisition authority, the examination and approval procedures for land requisition shall be carried out simultaneously without need for examination and approval of land requisition to be handled separately. If the land requisition authority is exceeded, examination and approval procedures for land requisition shall be handled in accordance with the provisions of the first paragraph of this Article.

Article 46: If land is to be requisitioned by the State, once the requisition is approved in accordance with the statutory procedures, the local people's government at or above the county level shall make a public announcement and organize the implementation thereof.

The owners and leaseholders of the requisitioned land shall, within the period specified in the announcement, carry out registration for land compensation with the administrative authority in charge of land of the local people's government on the strength of their land title certificates.

Article 47: When land is requisitioned, compensation shall be made according to the original usage of the land under requisition.

The compensation fee for requisitioned arable land shall include land compensation fee, resettlement allowance and compensation for attachments to the land and young crops. The land compensation fee for requisition of arable land shall be six to ten times the average annual yield value of the said arable land during the three years prior to requisition. The resettlement allowance for the requisition of arable land shall be calculated in accordance with the number of the rural residents to be resettled. The number of the rural residents to be resettled shall be calculated by dividing the area of the arable land under requisition by the average per capita area of occupation of arable land of the requisitioned work unit prior to the land requisition. The standard for the resettlement allowance for each member of the rural population to be resettled shall be four to six times the average annual yield value of the arable land during the three years prior to requisition. However, the maximum resettlement allowance per hectare of arable land under requisition may not exceed 15 times the average annual yield value of the land during the three years prior to requisition.

The standards for land compensation fees and resettlement allowances for the requisition of other types of land shall be prescribed by the provinces, autonomous regions and municipalities directly under the central government by reference to the standards for land compensation fees and resettlement allowances for the requisition of arable land.

The standards for compensation for attachments to and young crops on the land under requisition shall be prescribed by the provinces, autonomous regions and municipalities directly under the central government.

When suburban vegetable land is requisitioned, the work units that use the land shall make payments of new vegetable land development and construction funds pursuant to the relevant State regulations.

If the land compensation fee and the resettlement allowance paid pursuant to the second paragraph of this Article are still not sufficient to enable peasants who need to be resettled to maintain their original standard of living, the resettlement allowance may be increased upon the approval of the people's government of the relevant province, autonomous region or municipality directly under the central government. However, the aggregate amount of the land compensation fee and the resettlement allowance may not exceed 30 times the average annual yield value of the land under requisition during the three years prior to requisition.

In extraordinary circumstances, the State Council may raise the standards of land compensation fees and resettlement allowances for requisition of arable land in accordance with the level of social and economic development.

Article 48: After the compensation and resettlement scheme for land requisition has been determined, the relevant local people's government shall make a public announcement and listen to the opinions of the village collective economic organizations and peasants whose land is to be requisitioned.

Article 49: Village collective economic organizations whose land is requisitioned shall announce the details of receipts and payments of the compensation fees for land requisition to the members of the village collective economic organization, and shall accept their members' supervision.

It is forbidden to seize or misappropriate compensation fees for land requisition or other relevant fees belonging to a work unit whose land is requisitioned.

Article 50: Each level of local people's government shall support village collective economic organizations and peasants whose land is requisitioned to develop business and establish enterprises.

Article 51: The standards for compensation fees for land requisition and measures for the relocation and resettlement of inhabitants in connection with the construction of large- and medium-scale water projects and hydroelectric projects shall be separately specified by the State Council.

Article 52: During the evaluation of the feasibility study of construction projects, the administrative authority in charge of land may review matters relating to the land required for construction and give opinions in accordance with the master land use plan, the annual land use plan and the standards for construction land.

Article 53: Where State-owned construction land needs to be used for an approved construction project, the owner of the construction project shall, on the strength of the relevant documents specified in laws and administrative laws and regulations, submit an application for use of construction land to the administrative authority in charge of land of the people's government at or above the county level that has the right to approve the same. Once the application has been examined by the administrative authority in charge of land, it shall be submitted to the people's government at the same level for approval.

Article 54: When the owner of a construction project uses State-owned land, it shall obtain the land by way of grant or other modes of compensatory use of land. However, upon approval according to law by the people's government at or above the county level, the following types of construction land may be obtained by way of allocation:

(1) land used by State authorities and land for military purposes;

(2) land used for urban infrastructure facilities and land used for public welfare undertakings;

(3) land used for energy, transportation, water or other infrastructure projects that have key support from the State;

(4) land for other purposes prescribed by laws or administrative regulations.

Article 55: Owners of construction projects that have obtained State-owned leaseholds by way of grant or other compensatory modes of use may use the land only after paying the leasehold grant premium or other fees for compensatory use of land and other charges in accordance with the standards and measures specified by the State Council.

Commencing from the date of implementation of this Law, 30% of the fee for compensatory use of land in respect of all newly-created construction land shall be surrendered to the central fiscal authority and 70% shall be retained by the relevant local people's government. Both of these payments shall be used solely for the cultivation of new arable land.

Article 56: Owners of construction projects that use State-owned land shall use the land as agreed in contracts for compensatory use of land such as leasehold granting contracts, etc. or as stipulated in the document approving the allocation of the leaseholds. If it is truly necessary to change the construction usage of a parcel of land, upon the agreement of the administrative authority in charge of land of the relevant people's government, the matter shall be submitted for approval by the people's government that originally approved the use of the land. Where the usage of land within an urban planning zone is to be changed, the consent of the relevant administrative authority in charge of urban planning must be obtained before such change is submitted for approval.

Article 57: If a construction project needs to temporarily use State-owned land or land owned by peasants' collectives for construction works or geological surveys, the matter shall be approved by the administrative authority in charge of land of the relevant people's government at or above the county level. Where land in urban planning zones is to be temporarily used, the consent of the relevant administrative authority in charge of urban planning must be obtained before such temporary occupation is submitted for approval. The temporary land user shall enter into a temporary land use contract with the relevant administrative authority in charge of land, the village collective economic organization or the village committee, depending on the title to the land. The temporary land user shall also pay compensation for the temporary use of the land as agreed in the contract.

Users using land temporarily must use the land in accordance with the usage agreed in the temporary land use contract and may not construct permanent structures.

The term of temporary land use shall not normally exceed two years.

Article 58: In any of the following circumstances, the administrative authority in charge of land of the relevant people's government may recover the State-owned leaseholds upon the approval of the people's government that originally approved the use of the land or of the people's government that has approval authority:

(1) use of the land is required in the public interest;

(2) use of the land needs to be adjusted in order to carry out the reconstruction of old urban districts for implementation of urban planning;

(3) the term of use as agreed in contracts for compensatory use of land such as leasehold granting contracts, etc. has expired and the land user has not applied for an extension of the term or the application for an extension is not approved;

(4) State-owned land that was originally allocated to a work unit is no longer used due to the closure, relocation, etc. of the work unit;

(5) a highway, railway, airport, mine, etc. is to be retired after verification and approval.

When State-owned leaseholds are recovered pursuant to Item One or Two of the preceding paragraph, appropriate compensation shall be paid to the holder of the leaseholds.

Article 59: Township (town) and village construction such as township (town) enterprises, township (town) and village public facilities, public welfare undertakings, residences for rural villagers, etc. shall be rationally arranged, comprehensively developed and constructed as a whole in accordance with the village and town planning. The use of land for construction shall comply with the township (town) master land use plan and the annual land use plan. In addition, the examination and approval procedures shall be handled in accordance with the provisions of Articles 44, 60, 61 and 62 hereof.

Article 60: If village collective economic organizations intend to use construction land designated in the township (town) master land use plan to establish enterprises or to jointly establish enterprises with other work units or individuals by means of contributing leaseholds as capital or by joint operation, etc., they shall submit an application to the administrative authority in charge of land of the local people's government at or above the county level on the strength of the relevant approval documents. The application shall be approved by the local people's government at or above the county level in accordance with the approval authority prescribed by the relevant province, autonomous region or municipality directly under the central government. Where the occupation of agricultural land is involved, examination and approval procedures shall be handled in accordance with Article 44 hereof.

The construction land used for the establishment of enterprises specified in the preceding paragraph must be strictly controlled. Each province, autonomous region and municipality directly under the central government may prescribe different standards of land use for township enterprises of different business sectors and business scales.

Article 61: With respect to land required for the construction of township (town) and village public facilities and public welfare undertakings, after examination and verification by the relevant people's government at the township (town) level, an application shall be submitted to the administrative authority in charge of land of the local people's government at or above the county level. The application shall be approved by the local people's government at or above the county level in accordance with the approval authority prescribed by the relevant province, autonomous region or municipality directly under the central government. Where the occupation of agricultural land is involved, examination and approval procedures shall be handed in accordance with Article 44 hereof.

Article 62: Each village household may own only one home lot. The area of the home lot may not exceed the standard prescribed by the relevant province, autonomous region or municipality directly under the central government.

The residences constructed by rural residents shall comply with the township (town) master land use plan and shall use existing home lots and idle land in the village as far as possible.
Land to be used for residential purposes by rural residents shall, after examination and verification by the relevant people's government at the township (town) level, be approved by the relevant people's governments at the county level. Where the occupation of agricultural land is involved, examination and approval procedures shall be handled in accordance with Article 44 hereof.

If, after selling or leasing out their residences, a rural resident applies for another home lot, the application shall not be approved.

Article 63: The leaseholds with respect to land owned by peasants' collectives may not be granted, assigned or leased for non-agricultural construction, except, however, for the transfer according to law of the leaseholds by enterprises due to circumstances such as bankruptcy, merger, etc., provided that the construction land is in compliance with the master land use plan and was lawfully obtained.

Article 64: Buildings or structures constructed prior to the formulation of the master land use plan that fail to comply with the usage determined in the master land use plan may not be rebuilt or extended.

Article 65: In any of the following circumstances, village collective economic organizations may recover the leaseholds after reporting to and obtaining approval from the people's government that originally approved the use of the land:

(1) the land is required for the construction of township (town) village public facilities or public welfare undertakings;

(2) the land has not been used in accordance with the approved usage; or

(3) the land is no longer used due to reasons such as closure, relocation, etc.

If land owned by peasants' collectives is repossessed pursuant to Item One of the preceding paragraph, appropriate compensation shall be paid to the leaseholder.

PART SIX: SUPERVISION AND INVESTIGATION

Article 66: The administrative authorities in charge of land of the people's governments at or above the county level shall carry out supervision and investigation in respect of violations of laws and regulations concerning land administration.

Officials responsible for supervision and investigation of land administration shall familiarize themselves with laws and regulations concerning land administration, faithfully discharge their duties and enforce the law justly.

Article 67: When performing their supervision and investigation duties, the administrative authority in charge of land of the people's governments at or above the county level shall have the right to adopt the following measures:

(1) to require the work units or individuals under investigation to provide documents and information regarding land rights and to review and make copies of the same;

(2) to require the work units or individuals under investigation to give explanations concerning issues relating to land rights;

(3) to enter land that has been illegally occupied by the work units or individuals under investigation to carry out on-site surveys;

(4) to order work units or individuals that have illegally occupied land to cease their violation of the laws and regulations concerning land administration.

Article 68: When an official responsible for supervision and investigation of land administration needs to, in order to carry out their duties, enter a site to carry out surveys, or require the relevant work units or individuals to provide documents or information or to give explanations, he must produce his identity warrant for supervision and investigation of land administration.

Article 69: The relevant work units and individuals shall support, co-operate with, and facilitate the work of, the administrative authorities in charge of land of the people's governments at or above the county level in respect of the supervision and investigation of violations of law concerning land. Such work units and individuals may not obstruct or hinder the supervision and investigation officials for land administration in the performance of their duties according to law.

Article 70: If the administrative authority in charge of land of a people's government at or above the county level discovers violations of law by State officials during the course of its supervisory and investigative work and such violations are subject to administrative penalties according to law, the matter shall be handled according to law. If the administrative authority in charge of land does not have the authority to handle the matter, it shall submit a proposal for imposition of administrative penalties to the administrative supervisory authority of the people's government at the same level or at a higher level, and the relevant administrative supervisory authority shall handle the matter according to law.

Article 71: If the administrative authority in charge of land of a people's government at or above the county level discovers in the course of its supervisory and investigative work that a particular violation of land law amounts to a criminal offence, it shall transfer the case to the relevant authorities to pursue criminal liability according to law. If the violation does not amount to a criminal offence, administrative penalties shall be imposed according to law.

Article 72: If certain administrative penalties should be imposed pursuant to this Law, but the relevant administrative authority in charge of land fails to impose the administrative penalties, the administrative authority in charge of land of the people's government at a higher level shall have the authority to order the relevant administrative authority in charge of land to issue a decision to impose administrative penalties or to directly impose the administrative penalties, and, additionally, shall impose administrative penalties on the responsible person of the relevant administrative authority in charge of land.

PART SEVEN: LEGAL LIABILITY

Article 73: If land is illegally assigned through sale and purchase or by other means, the administrative authority in charge of land of the relevant people's government at or above the county level shall confiscate the illegal income. If agricultural land is converted into construction land without authorization in violation of the master land use plan, buildings and other facilities newly constructed on the land illegally assigned shall be demolished and removed within a specified time limit and the land shall be restored to its original condition. If the newly-constructed buildings and facilities on the illegally assigned land conform to the master land use plan, they shall be confiscated and an additional fine may be imposed. Administrative penalties shall be imposed on all directly responsible person in charge and on other directly liable persons. If a criminal offence has been committed, criminal liability shall be pursued according to law.

Article 74: If, in violation of this Law, arable land is occupied for the construction of kilns or tombs or unauthorized construction of buildings, sand extraction, quarrying, mining or soil removal is carried out on arable land which damages the conditions for plantation, or the development of land causes desertification or salinization of the land, the administrative authority in charge of land of the relevant people's government at or above the county level shall order rectification or rehabilitation of the land within a specified time limit, and, additionally, may impose a fine. If a criminal offence has been committed, criminal liability shall be pursued according to law.

Article 75: If, in violation of this Law, anyone refuses to perform their obligation to restore land, the administrative authority in charge of land of the relevant people's government at or above the county level shall order rectification within a specified time limit. If rectification is not carried out within the time limit, the administrative authority in charge of land of the people's government at or above the county level shall order the payment of a restoration fee, to be used solely for restoration of land, and, additionally, may impose a fine.

Article 76: If anyone illegally occupies land without permission or by obtaining approval by fraudulent means, the administrative authority in charge of land of the relevant people's government at or above the county level shall order the return of the land illegally occupied. If anyone converts agricultural land into construction land in violation of the master land use plan, any newly-constructed buildings and other facilities on the illegally occupied land shall be demolished and removed within a specified time limit and the land shall be restored to its original condition. If the newly-constructed buildings and facilities on the illegally occupied land conform to the master land use plan, they shall be confiscated, and, additionally, a fine may be imposed. Administrative penalties shall be imposed on the directly responsible person in charge of the work unit which occupies land illegally and on the all directly liable persons. If a criminal offence has been committed, criminal liability shall be pursued according to law.

If the area of land occupied exceeds the approved area, the area occupied in excess of the approved area shall be treated as illegally occupied land.

Article 77: If a rural resident illegally occupies land to construct a residence without approval or with approval obtained by fraudulent means, the administrative authority in charge of land of the relevant people's government at or above the county level shall order the return of the land illegally occupied and the demolition and removal of any newly-constructed premises on the illegally occupied land within a specified time limit.

If a standard prescribed by a province, autonomous region or municipality directly under the central government is exceeded, the land additionally occupied shall be treated as illegally occupied land.

Article 78: If a work unit or individual that does not have the authority to approve the requisition or use of land illegally approves the occupation of land, or if a work unit or individual illegally approves the occupation of land in excess of its limit of approval authority, or if a work unit or individual approves the use of land in violation of the usage specified in the master land use plan, or if a work unit or individual approves the occupation or requisition of land in violation of the procedures specified by law, the relevant approval documents shall be invalid and administrative penalties shall be imposed on the person and directly responsible for the illegal approval of the requisition or use of land, and on all other directly liable persons. If a criminal offence has been committed, criminal liability shall be pursued according to law. The land illegally approved or used shall be repossessed. If the persons involved refuse to return the land, the matter shall be treated as illegal occupation of land.

If the illegal approval of requisition or use of land causes loss to the parties concerned, liability for compensation shall be attributed according to law.

Article 79: If the requisition compensation and other relevant fees of the work unit whose land is requisitioned are seized or misappropriated and it amounts to a criminal offence, criminal liability shall be pursued according to law. If the seizure or misappropriation does not amount to a criminal offence, administrative penalties shall be imposed according to law.

Article 80: If State-owned leaseholds are recovered according to the law but the parties concerned refuse to deliver the land, or land is not returned upon the expiration of the term for temporary use, or State-owned land is used not in accordance with the approved usage, the administrative authority in charge of land of the relevant people's government at or above the county level shall order the land to be returned and shall impose a fine.

Article 81: If the leasehold owned by a peasants' collective has been granted, assigned or leased without authorization for non-agricultural construction, the administrative authority in charge of land of the relevant people's government at or above the county level shall order rectification within a specified time limit, confiscate the illegal income and, additionally, impose a fine.

Article 82: If registration of a change in the land is not carried out in accordance with this Law, the administrative authority in charge of land of the relevant people's government at or above the county level shall order registration to be carried out within a specified time limit.

Article 83: If, in accordance with this Law, newly-constructed buildings or other facilities on illegally occupied land are ordered to be demolished and removed within a specified time limit, the work unit or individual that owns the construction project must immediately cease construction and carry out demolition and removal. If the work unit or individual continues with the construction, the authority which issued the penalty decision shall have the authority to halt the construction. If the work unit or individual that owns the construction project is dissatisfied with the administrative penalty decision ordering the demolition and removal with a specified time limit, it may institute proceedings in the people's court within fifteen days from the date on which it received the demolition and removal order. If the work unit or individual has neither instituted proceedings nor carried out demolition and removal within the said time limit, the authority that issued the penalty decision shall apply to the people's court for enforcement. The costs of enforcement shall be borne by the violator.

Article 84: If the officials of the administrative authority in charge of land are derelict in their duties, abuse their functions and powers or practise graft and such dereliction of duty, abuse of functions and powers or graft amounts to a criminal offence, criminal liability shall be pursued according to law. If the dereliction of duty, abuse of functions and powers or graft does not amount to a criminal offence, administrative penalties shall be imposed according to law.

PART EIGHT: SUPPLEMENTARY PROVISIONS

Article 85: This Law applies to land used by Sino-foreign equity joint ventures, Sino-foreign co-operative joint ventures and wholly foreign-owned enterprises. If the law provides otherwise, such other provisions shall apply.

Article 86: This Law shall be implemented as of January 1, 1999.

SEVERAL ISSUES CONCERNING THE EXAMINATION, APPROVAL AND ADMINISTRATION OF EXPERIMENTAL FOREIGN-INVESTED CONCESSION PROJECTS CIRCULAR

To: Planning Commissions (Planning and Economic Commissions), Power Bureau and Communications Offices (Bureaux) of all provinces, autonomous regions, centrally-governed municipalities and municipalities with an independent development plan.

For a long time, infrastructure facilities and primary industries such as communications and energy have been the bottleneck of the national economic development of our country. To improve this situation, it is necessary to actively direct foreign investments, in line with the State's industrial policies, towards our infrastructure facilities and primary industries for urgent development. For this purpose, apart from the State's continued encouragement of foreign businessmen in the setting up and operation of infrastructure facilities and primary industrial projects in our country in the form of Sino-foreign equity joint ventures, Sino-foreign co-operative joint ventures and wholly foreign-owned enterprises, the State is intended to try out foreign invested infrastructure projects, from the experience of foreign countries, in the investment form of building-operation-transfer (generally known as "BOT"). In order to do a better job for the experiment, we hereby inform you of the following relevant matters:

1. Foreign invested concession projects referred to herein shall mean foreign invested infrastructure projects in the form of building operation transfer. The governmental department shall award, by way of a concession agreement and within the prescribed period, the project to the project company established for the concession project by the foreign company. The project company shall be responsible for the investment, financing, construction, operation and maintenance of the project. Upon expiration of the concession period, the project company shall transfer the facilities of the concession project to the governmental department without compensation.
2. During the concession period, the project company shall hold the ownership of the facilities of the concession project and the rights in respect of investment, financing, project design, construction, equipment procurement, operation and management of, and reasonable charging for, the concession project and shall undertake the obligations in respect of repair and maintenance of the facilities of the concession project. The governmental department shall have the right to supervise, inspect and audit the concession project and require the project company to make rectification and impose a penalty in accordance with the law in the event that the project company is found to have acted in violation of the provisions of the concession agreement.
3. To ensure the smooth implementation of concession projects in our country in the event that a project company suffers serious economic losses due to the change in our country's policies during the concession period, the project company shall be allowed to reasonably increase the charging standards or to extend the concession period. The State

shall guarantee the conversion of foreign exchange required for the project company for repaying principal and interest on loans and remitting bonuses out of China. However, the project company shall bear risks in respect of investment, financing, construction, procurement, operation and maintenance. The government shall not provide guarantee for any fixed returns on investments. Neither Chinese domestic financial institutions nor non-financial institutions in the country shall provide security for its financing.

4. Considering that setting up concession projects is a new task in our country, it is necessary to carry out the task in an active and steady manner. To avoid rushing, headlong into concession projects, it is necessary to carry out an experiment first and to extend such experiment gradually until experience is gained. During the experimental period, the area of experiment shall cover for the time being projects such as coal-fired power plants with a capacity of 2X300,000 kilowatts and above, hydraulic power plants with a capacity of less that 250,000 kilowatts, 30 to 80 kilometre highways of a high grade, separate bridges with a length of more that 1,000 meters, separate tunnels and urban water supply plants.

5. Selection of pilot concession projects shall start from the regional level up to the central level. In principle, such pilot concession projects shall be those projects that fall within the medium and long term plans of the State. An initial feasibility study report on the selected pilot project shall be prepared by the planning department of the province (district or municipality) of the place where the project is located, in conjunction with the department in charge of the industry in accordance with the current planning administrative system. The initial feasibility study report shall be examined and approved by the State Planning Commission upon preliminary examination by the department in charge of the industry. When necessary, the report shall be reported to the State Council for examination and approval upon preliminary examination by the State Planning Commission. Apart from particulars such as project details, engineering, technology and environmental protection, an initial feasibility study report on a concession project shall specifically describe the following particulars: analysis of market demand, total investment amount, fulfilment of external conditions, economic and financial analysis, initial charging standards, principles of price adjustment, term of concession, principles of risk sharing, associated facilities to be supplied by the government and obligations to be assumed by the government.

6. Upon approval of the initial feasibility study report on the pilot concession project, the local government shall be responsible for preparing documents on qualification pre-assessment and tender proposals so that foreign investor shall be selected by way of open tender. The State Planning Commission shall organize a tender appraisal committee comprising the department in charge of the industry, local government department as well as technical, economic and legal advisors, responsible for examination of tender proposals, pre-assessment of the qualifications of investors, tender appraisal, tender determination and awarding.

7. Provincial (district or municipal) government of the place where the pilot concession project is located shall assist the successful tenderer in applying for, on the strength of the tender winning approval document, handling procedures for approving the articles of association of the project company at the Ministry of Foreign Trade and Economic Co-operation, and procedures for registration with the administration for industry and commerce.

8. Upon approval of the concession agreement (when necessary, the State Planning Commission shall report such agreement to the State Council for approval), the State Planning Commission shall authorize provincial (district or municipal) government or the department of the industry to officially sign the concession agreement with the

project company, and such agreement shall take into effect from the date of signing.

9. For the purpose of smooth implementation of the experiment of concession projects, the State Planning Commission shall set up a permanent organization responsible for organizing, daily liaison, co-ordination, etc. in respect of the experiment of concession projects.

At present, the State Planning Commissions is taking the lead in formulating the Foreign Invested Concession Projects Tentative Provisions which will be promulgated for implementation upon approval by the State Council.

PRC, INVITATION AND SUBMISSION OF BIDS LAW

Ref no: 5000/99.08.30

(Promulgated on August 30, 1999 and effective as of January 1, 2000.)

PART ONE: GENERAL PROVISIONS

Article 1: This Law has been formulated to standardize bid invitation and bid submission activities, to protect the interests of the State, the public interest and the lawful rights and interests of the parties involved in bid invitation and bid submission activities, to increase economic benefits and to ensure project quality.

Article 2: This Law applies to bid invitation and bid submission activities conducted in the People's Republic of China.

Article 3: Bids must be invited for the following construction projects undertaken in the People's Republic of China, including surveying for, and design, construction and supervision of, the projects as well as the procurement of important equipment, materials, etc. for the construction:

(1) projects with a bearing upon the public interest and public safety such as large-scale infrastructure projects, public utility projects, etc.;

(2) projects which are entirely or partially funded by the investment of State-owned funds or financed by the State;

(3) projects using loans from international organizations or foreign governments, or aid funds.

The specific scope of and scale standards for the projects enumerated in the preceding paragraph shall be formulated by the State Council's development planning authority in concert with the other relevant authorities of the State Council and submitted for the approval of the State Council.

If laws or State Council regulations contain provisions on the scope of other projects which are subject to the invitation of bids, those provisions shall be complied with.

Article 4: No work unit or individual may divide a project which legally requires the invitation of bids into several small parts or otherwise avoid the invitation of bids.

Article 5: Bid invitation and bid submission activities shall abide by the principle of openness, fairness, impartiality and good faith.

Article 6: The bid invitation and bid submission activities for a project which legally requires the invitation of bids shall not be subject to territorial or departmental restrictions. No work unit or individual may illegally restrict or preclude the participation in bid submission by legal persons or other organizations from outside his or its own region or network and may not in any manner illegally interfere in the bid invitation and bid submission activities.

Article 7: Bid invitation and bid submission activities and the parties concerned shall be subject to lawfully implemented supervision.

The relevant administrative supervision authorities shall supervise bid invitation and bid submission activities in accordance with the law, and shall investigate and handle illegal acts committed during bid invitation and bid submission activities.

Regulations on the administrative supervision of bid invitation and bid submission activities and the specific division of authority among the relevant authorities shall be formulated by the State Council.

PART TWO: INVITATION OF BIDS

Article 8: A bid inviting party is a legal person or other organization which puts forward a project and invites bids therefor in accordance with the law.

Article 9: If relevant State regulations require that project examination and approval procedures be carried out for a certain project for which bids are to be invited, the examination and approval procedures shall be carried out and approval shall be obtained first.

The bid inviting party shall have the appropriate amount of funds, or have secured the source of funds, for conducting an invitation of bids, and the same shall be truthfully specified in the bid invitation documents.

Article 10: Invitations of bids are divided into public invitation of bids and private invitation of bids.

The term "public invitation of bids" refers to the method whereby the bid inviting party, through a bid invitation announcement, invites unspecified legal persons or other organizations to submit bids.

The term "private invitation of bids" refers to the method whereby the bid inviting party, through a bid invitation letter, invites specific legal persons or other organizations to submit bids.

Article 11: If public invitation of bids is not appropriate for a certain project which the development planning authority of the State Council has determined to be a key State project or which the people's government of the province, autonomous region or municipality directly under the central government has determined to be a key local project, a private invitation of bids may be conducted, subject to the approval of the development planning authority of the State Council or the people's government of the province, autonomous region or municipality directly under the central government.

Article 12: A bid inviting party has the right to appoint a bid invitation agency of its own choice to carry out bid invitation matters. No work unit or individual may in any way designate a bid invitation agency for the bid inviting party.

A bid inviting party which has the capability to prepare the bid invitation documents and organize the bid evaluation may carry out the bid invitation matters itself. No work unit or individual may coerce it into appointing a bid invitation agency to carry out the bid invitation matters.

A bid inviting party which carries out bid invitation matters itself for a project for which the invitation of bids is legally required shall report the same to the relevant administrative supervision authorities for the record.

Article 13: A bid invitation agency is a non-governmental intermediary organization which is established in accordance with the law and engages in the bid invitation agency business and provides related services.

A bid invitation agency shall meet the following conditions:

(1) have business premises and the appropriate amount of funds to engage in the bid invitation agency business;

(2) have the specialized capability necessary to prepare bid invitation documents and organize bid evaluations; and

(3) have a pool of experts in technology, economics, etc. meeting the conditions stipulated in the third paragraph of Article 37 hereof who may serve as candidates for a bid evaluation committee.

Article 14: The qualifications of bid invitation agencies engaging in the bid invitation agency business for construction projects shall be subject to recognition by the administrative authority in charge of construction of the State Council or of the people's government of the relevant province, autonomous region or municipality directly under the central government. The specific procedures shall be formulated by the administrative authority in charge of construction of the State Council in concert with the relevant State Council authorities. The competent authorities for recognizing the qualifications of bid invitation agencies engaging in other bid invitation agency business shall be specified by the State Council.

No superior-subordinate relationship or other relationship of shared interest may exist between a bid invitation agency and administrative authorities or other State authorities.

Article 15: A bid invitation agency shall carry out bid invitation matters within the scope of its appointment by the bid inviting party and shall abide by the provisions hereof concerning bid inviting parties.

Article 16: If the bid inviting party employs the public invitation of bids method, it shall issue a bid invitation announcement. The bid invitation announcement for a project for which the invitation of bids is legally required shall be issued in a State-designated newspaper or periodical, on a State-designated information network or in other State-designated media.

The bid invitation announcement shall specify such matters as the name and address of the bid inviting party, the nature, quantities, location and time of the project, the method of obtaining the bid invitation documents, etc.

Article 17: If the bid inviting party employs the private invitation of bids method, it shall send a bid invitation letter to at least three specific legal persons or other organizations which have the ability to handle the project and which have a good credit standing.

The bid invitation letter shall specify the matters stipulated in the second paragraph of Article 16 hereof.

Article 18: Depending on the requirements of the project, the bid inviting party may require, in the bid invitation announcement or the bid invitation letter, that potential bidders provide relevant documents certifying their qualifications and details of their business situation and may investigate the qualifications of potential bidders. If there are State regulations on the qualification requirements of bidders, such regulations shall be complied with.

A bid inviting party may not restrict or preclude potential bidders by specifying unreasonable conditions and may not discriminate against potential bidders.

Article 19: The bid inviting party shall prepare bid invitation documents in accordance with the special characteristics and requirements of the project. The bid invitation documents shall specify all substantive requirements and conditions, including the technical requirements for the project, the standards for the examination of the bidders' qualifications, bid price requirements, the bid evaluation standards, etc. and the principal terms of the contract to be executed.

If there are State regulations concerning the technology and standards for the project for which bids are invited, the bid inviting party shall include the corresponding requirements in the bid invitation documents in accordance with those regulations.

If the project for which bids are invited needs to be split up into phases and/or the construction period needs to be specified, the bid inviting party shall split up the project into reasonable phases and/or specify a reasonable construction period and specify the same in the bid invitation documents.

Article 20: The bid invitation documents may not require or specify a specific producer or supplier or contain other particulars which favour or preclude potential bidders.

Article 21: In light of the specific circumstances of the project for which bids are invited, the bid inviting party may organize an on-the-spot survey of the project for the potential bidders.

Article 22: The bid inviting party may not disclose to a third party the names or number of potential bidders which have received bid invitation documents or other bid invitation and bid submission details which could affect fair competition.

If the bid inviting party has set a reserve price, the confidentiality of the reserve price must be maintained.

Article 23: If the bid inviting party makes necessary clarifications or amendments to the bid invitation documents, it shall notify in writing all the parties that have received the bid invitation documents at least 15 days before the deadline for the submission of bidding documents specified in the bid invitation documents. The contents of the clarifications or amendments shall become an integral part of the bid invitation documents.

Article 24: The bid inviting party shall set a reasonable time necessary for the bidders to prepare their bid documents. However, for projects which legally require the invitation of bids, the time between the date on which the issue of the bid invitation documents commences and the deadline for the submission of bid documents by the bidders may not be less than 20 days.

PART THREE: SUBMISSION OF BIDS

Article 25: A bidder is a legal person or other organization that responds to an invitation of bids and participates in the bidding competition.

If a scientific research project for which bids are invited according to law permits individuals to participate in the bidding, the provisions of this Law concerning bidders shall apply to those individuals submitting bids.

Article 26: A bidder shall have the capability to undertake the project for which bids are invited. If relevant State regulations or the bid invitation documents specify requirements as to bidder qualifications, the bidders shall possess the required qualifications.

Article 27: A bidder shall prepare its bid documents in accordance with the requirements of the bid invitation documents. The bid documents shall respond to the substantive requirements and conditions put forward in the bid invitation documents.

If the project for which bids are invited is for construction work, the particulars of the bid documents shall include the rÈsumÈs and business achievements of the person in charge of the project and the principal technical personnel intended to appoint, and the machinery and equipment intended to use in completing the project, etc.

Article 28: The bidders shall deliver the bid documents to the bid submission address before the deadline for the submission of bid documents specified in the bid invitation documents. After receiving the bid documents, the bid inviting party shall sign for receipt and preserve the same, and may not open them. If there are fewer than three bidders, the bid inviting party shall invite bids anew in accordance with this Law.

The bid inviting party shall refuse to accept bid documents which are delivered after the deadline for the submission of bid documents specified in the bid invitation documents.

Article 29: Before the deadline for the submission of bid documents specified in the bid invitation documents passes, a bidder may supplement, amend or withdraw the bid documents it has submitted, and it shall notify the bid inviting party thereof in writing. The content of the supplementation or amendments shall become an integral part of the bid documents.

Article 30: If a bidder, on the basis of the actual circumstances of the project as specified in the bid invitation documents, intends to subcontract out some of the non-principal, non-key parts of the work after its bid is accepted, it shall specify the same in the bid documents.

Article 31: Two or more legal persons or other organizations may organize as a consortium and jointly submit a bid as a single bidder.

Each of the members of a consortium shall have the appropriate capability to undertake the project for which bids are invited. If relevant State regulations or the bid invitation documents specify requirements as to bidder qualifications, each of the members of the consortium shall possess the corresponding required qualifications. If the consortium is composed of work units that specialize in the same field, the qualification grade of the consortium shall be determined according to the qualification grade of the work unit with the lowest qualification grade.

The members of a consortium shall execute an agreement for joint submission of a bid, clearly specifying the work and responsibilities each member intends to undertake, and shall submit such agreement together with the bid documents to the bid inviting party. If the winning bid was submitted by a consortium, the members of the consortium shall jointly execute a contract with the bid inviting party and bear joint and several liability towards the bid inviting party for the project that they have won.

A bid inviting party may not coerce bidders into organizing a consortium to jointly submit a bid and may not restrict the competition among the bidders.

Article 32: Bidders may not collude on the bid price, may not preclude fair competition from other bidders or prejudice the lawful rights and interests of the bid inviting party or other bidders.

Bidders and the bid inviting party may not collude in the submission of bids in order to harm the interests of the State, the public interest or the lawful rights and interests of a third party.
Bidders are forbidden from bribing the bid inviting party or members of the bid evaluation committee in order to have their bid accepted.

Article 33: A bidder may not submit a below cost bid price in competing for a project, or submit its bid in the name of a third party or use other fraudulent means to have its bid accepted.

PART FOUR: OPENING OF BIDS, EVALUATION OF BIDS AND DETERMINATION OF THE WINNING BIDDER

Article 34: The bids shall be opened in public at the time of the deadline for submission of the bid documents as determined in the bid invitation documents. The bids shall be opened at the pre-determined place specified in the bid invitation documents.

Article 35: The opening of the bids shall be presided over by the bid inviting party, and all the bidders shall be invited to attend.

Article 36: When opening the bids, the bid inviting party or the representative chosen by him shall inspect the status of the seals on the bids; alternatively, the same may be inspected and notarized by a notarial institution appointed by the bid inviting party. After the seals have been confirmed to be intact, the working personnel shall break the seals in public and read out the names and bid prices of the bidders and other major particulars of the bid documents.

All bid documents received by the bid inviting party by the deadline for submission of bid documents as specified in the bid invitation documents shall have their seals broken and be read out in public at the time the bids are opened.

Minutes shall be kept of the bid opening procedures and be filed for future reference.

Article 37: Bid evaluation shall be the responsibility of a bid evaluation committee organized according to law by the bid inviting party.

If a project legally requires the invitation of bids, the bid evaluation committee shall be composed of the representative of the bid inviting party and relevant experts in technology, economics, etc. The number of members shall be an odd number of five or more, and the number of experts in technology and economics, etc. shall account for at least two-thirds of the total.

The experts referred to in the preceding paragraph shall have worked in their relevant fields for at least eight years and have a senior title or attained an equivalent professional level. They shall be selected by the bid inviting party from the list of experts provided by the relevant State Council authority or the relevant authority of the people's government of the province, autonomous region or municipality directly under the central government or from the list of experts in the relevant fields forming part of the bid invitation agency's pool of experts. For ordinary projects, the experts may be selected at random. For special projects, they may be determined directly by the bid inviting party directly.

Persons with a material interest in the bid inviting party may not sit on the bid evaluation committee for the relevant project. Those already sitting on the committee shall be replaced.

The list of members of the bid evaluation committee shall be kept confidential until the winning bidder has been determined.

Article 38: The bid inviting party shall take the steps necessary to ensure that strict confidentiality is maintained during the evaluation of the bids.

No work unit or individual may illegally intervene in or influence the course and/or result of the bid evaluation.

Article 39: The bid evaluation committee may require bidders to give the necessary clarification or explanation of those contents of the bid documents whose meaning is not clear. However, such clarification or explanation may not exceed the scope of the bid documents or change the substantive contents of the bid documents.

Article 40: The bid evaluation committee shall evaluate and compare the bid documents in accordance with the evaluation standards and methods determined in the bid invitation documents. If a reserve price has been set, reference shall be made thereto. After the bid evaluation committee has completed the evaluation, it shall submit a written bid evaluation report to the bid inviting party and recommend qualified candidates for the status of winning bidder.

The winning bidder shall be determined by the bid inviting party on the basis of the written bid evaluation report submitted, and the candidates for the status of winning bidder recommended, by the bid evaluation committee. Alternatively, the bid inviting party may authorize the bid evaluation committee to directly determine the winning bidder.

If the State Council has special regulations concerning the evaluation of bids for special projects, such regulations shall be complied with.

Article 41: The bid of the winning bidder shall meet the following conditions:

(1) it complies to the greatest possible extent with all of the overall evaluation standards specified in the bid invitation documents; and

(2) it satisfies the substantive requirements of the bid invitation documents and its bid price is the lowest among those evaluated, except for bid prices below cost.

Article 42: If, following evaluation, the bid evaluation committee considers none of the bids to meet the requirements of the bid invitation documents, it may reject all of the bids.
If all the bids for a project which legally requires the invitation of bids are rejected, the bid inviting party shall invite bids anew in accordance with this Law.

Article 43: Until the winning bidder has been determined, the bid inviting party may not hold negotiations with bidders on substantive contents such as bid prices, bid plans, etc.

Article 44: The members of the bid evaluation committee shall perform their duties in an objective and impartial manner, observe their professional ethics and bear personal liability for the evaluation opinions put forward by them.

The members of the bid evaluation committee may not have private contacts with bidders or accept property or other benefits from bidders.

The members of the bid evaluation committee and the relevant working personnel participating in the evaluation may not disclose details of the evaluation and comparison of the bid documents, details of the recommendation of candidates for the status of winning bidder and other relevant details of the bid evaluation.

Article 45: After the winning bidder has been determined, the bid inviting party shall issue a letter of acceptance to the winning bidder and simultaneously inform all the losing bidders of the result of the determination of the winning bidder.

The letter of acceptance shall be legally binding on the bid inviting party and the winning bidder. If the bid inviting party changes the result of the determination of the winning bidder, or the winning bidder renounces the project which it has won, after the letter of acceptance has been issued, it shall assume legal liability therefor according to law.

Article 46: The bid inviting party and the winning bidder shall conclude a written contract in accordance with the bid invitation documents and the winning bidder's bid documents within 30 days of the date of issuance of the letter of acceptance. The bid inviting party and the winning bidder may not subsequently conclude other agreements which contravene the substantive terms of the contract.

The winning bidder shall pay a performance bond if the bid invitation documents require the winning bidder to do so.

Article 47: For projects which legally requires the invitation of bids, the bid inviting party shall submit a written report on the invitation and submission of bids to the relevant administrative supervision authority within 15 days of the date of determination of the winning bidder.

Article 48: The winning bidder shall perform its obligations, and complete the project which it has won, in accordance with the contract. The winning bidder may not assign the project which it has won to a third party, or break up the project which it has won and subsequently assign the parts to third parties.

Subject to the provisions of the contract or the consent of the bid inviting party, the winning bidder may subcontract out the completion of some of the non-principal, non-key parts of the work for the project which it has won. The subcontractors shall possess the appropriate qualifications required and may not sub-subcontract its project.

The winning bidder shall be accountable to the bid inviting party for the subcontracted projects, and the subcontractors shall bear joint and several liability for the subcontracted projects.

PART FIVE: LEGAL LIABILITY

Article 49: If this Law is violated by failing to invite bids for a project for which bids must be invited, or by breaking up a project for which bids must be invited into several small parts or by otherwise avoiding the invitation of bids, the offender shall be ordered to rectify the situation within a specified time limit and may be subjected to a fine of not less than 0.5% and not more than 1% of the amount of the project contract. If the project is entirely or partially funded with State-owned funds, the implementation of the project or allocation of funds may be suspended. The persons directly in charge and other directly responsible personnel of the work unit shall be disciplined according to law.

Article 50: If a bid invitation agency violates this Law by disclosing details or materials which relate to the bid invitation and submission procedures and are subject to maintenance of confidentiality, or if it colludes with the bid inviting party or a bidder in order to harm the interests of the State, the public interest or the lawful rights and interests of a third party, it shall be fined not less than Rmb 50,000 and not more than Rmb 250,000, and the persons directly in charge and other directly responsible personnel of the work unit shall be fined not less than 5% and not more than 10% of the amount of the fine imposed on the work unit. In addition, the illegal income, if any, shall be confiscated. If the circumstances are serious, the agency's qualifications to act as bid invitation agent shall be suspended or revoked. If a criminal offence is constituted, criminal liability shall be pursued according to law. If loss is caused to others, liability for damages shall be assumed according to law.

If any of the acts mentioned in the preceding paragraph has an impact on the result of the determination of the winning bidder, the acceptance of the winning bidder's bid shall be void.

Article 51: If the bid inviting party imposes unreasonable conditions to restrict or preclude potential bidders or if it discriminates against potential bidders, or if it imposes on bidders a mandatory requirement to organize a consortium or if it restricts the competition among the bidders, it shall be ordered to rectify the situation and may be subjected to a fine of not less than Rmb 10,000 and not more than Rmb 50,000.

Article 52: If the party inviting bids for a project which legally requires the invitation of bids discloses to others the names or number of potential bidders which have received bid invitation documents or other bid invitation and bid submission details which could affect fair competition, or if it discloses the reserve price, it shall be given a warning and may additionally be subjected to a fine of not less than Rmb 10,000 and not more than Rmb 100,000. The persons directly in charge and other directly responsible personnel of the work unit shall be disciplined according to law. If a criminal offence is constituted, criminal liability shall be pursued according to law.

If any of the acts mentioned in the preceding has an impact on the result of the determination of the winning bidder, the acceptance of the winning bidder's bid shall be void.

Article 53: If a bidder colludes with one or more other bidders or with the bid inviting party in the submission of its bid, or if a bidder seeks to win the project by offering a bribe to the bid inviting party or one or more of the members of the bid evaluation committee, the acceptance of its bid shall be void, the bidder shall be fined not less than 0.5% and not more than 1% of the amount of the project which it won and the persons directly in charge and other directly responsible personnel of the work unit shall be fined not less than 5% and not more than 10% of the amount of the fine imposed on the work unit. In addition, the illegal income, if any, shall be confiscated. If the circumstances are serious, the bidder's bidding qualifications for projects which legally require the invitation of bids shall be suspended for one to two years and the same shall be publicly announced, or the administration for industry and commerce shall revoke its business licence. If a criminal offence is constituted, criminal liability shall be pursued according to law. If loss is caused to others, liability for damages shall be assumed according to law.

Article 54: If a bidder submits its bid in the name of a third party or uses other fraudulent means to have its bid accepted, the acceptance of the bid shall be void. If loss is caused to the bid inviting party, it shall assume liability for damages according to law. If a criminal offence is constituted, criminal liability shall be pursued according to law.

If a bidder for a project which legally requires the invitation of bids commits any of the acts mentioned in the preceding paragraph but the circumstances are not sufficient to constitute a criminal offence, it shall be fined not less than 0.5% and not more than 1% of the amount of the project which it won and the persons directly in charge and other directly responsible personnel of the work unit shall be fined not less than 5% and not more than 10% of the amount of the fine imposed on the work unit. In addition, the illegal income, if any, shall be confiscated. If the circumstances are serious, the bidder's bidding qualifications for projects which legally require the invitation of bids shall be suspended for one to three years and the same shall be publicly announced, or the administration for industry and commerce shall revoke its business licence.

Article 55: If the party inviting bids for a project which legally requires the invitation of bids violates this Law by holding negotiations with bidders on substantive contents such as bid prices, bid plans, etc., it shall be given a warning and the persons directly in charge and other directly responsible personnel of the work unit shall be disciplined according to law.

If any of the acts mentioned in the preceding has an impact on the result of the determination of the winning bidder, the acceptance of the winning bidder's bid shall be void.

Article 56: If a member of the bid evaluation committee accepts property or other benefits from a bidder, or if a member of the bid evaluation committee or relevant working personnel participating in the evaluation discloses to others details of the evaluation and comparison of the bid documents, the recommendation of candidates for the status of winning bidder or other relevant details of the bid evaluation, he shall be given a warning and the property accepted shall be confiscated, and he may additionally be subjected to a fine of not less than Rmb 3,000 and not more than Rmb 50,000. A member of the bid evaluation committee who has committed any of the aforementioned acts shall be stripped of his qualifications for membership of bid evaluation committee and may never again participate in the evaluation of bids for projects which legally require the invitation of bids. If a criminal offence is constituted, his criminal liability shall be pursued according to law.

Article 57: If the winning bidder determined by the bid inviting party was not among the candidates lawfully recommended by the bid evaluation committee, or if all the bids for a project which legally requires the invitation of bids have been rejected by the bid evaluation committee but the bid inviting party subsequently and on its own authority determines a bidder to be the winning bidder, the acceptance of the winning bidder's bid shall be void. The bid inviting party shall be ordered to rectify the situation and may be subjected to a fine of not less than 0.5% and not more than 1% of the amount of the project for which it determined the winning bidder. The persons directly in charge and other directly responsible personnel of the work unit shall be disciplined according to law.

Article 58: If the winning bidder assigns the project which it has won to a third party, or break ups the project which it has won and subsequently assign the parts to third parties, or violates this Law by subcontracting out some of the principal or key parts of the work for the project which it has won, or if a subcontractor sub-subcontracts its project, the assignment, subcontracting or sub-subcontracting shall be void and the winning bidder or the subcontractor, as the case may be, shall be fined not less than 0.5% and not more than 1% of the amount of the project assigned, subcontracted or sub-subcontracted. In addition, the illegal income, if any, shall be confiscated. The winning bidder or the subcontractor, as the case may be, may be ordered to suspend business and rectify the situation. If the circumstances are serious, its business licence shall be revoked by the administration for industry and commerce.

Article 59: If the bid inviting party and the winning bidder fail to conclude a contract in accordance with the bid invitation documents and the winning bidder's bid documents, or if the bid inviting party and the winning bidder conclude an agreement which contravenes the substantive terms of the contract, they shall be ordered to rectify the situation and may be subjected to a fine of not less than 0.5% and not more than 1% of the amount of the project won.

Article 60: If the winning bidder fails to perform the contract concluded with the bid inviting party, the performance bond shall not be refunded. If the losses caused to the bid inviting party exceed the amount of the performance bond, the winning bidder shall also compensate for the excess. If the winning bidder did not pay a performance bond, it shall be liable for compensation of the losses suffered by the bid inviting party.

If the winning bidder fails to perform its obligations in accordance with the contract concluded with the bid inviting party and the circumstances are serious, its bidding qualifications for projects which legally require the invitation of bids shall be suspended for two to five years and the same shall be publicly announced, or the administration for industry and commerce shall revoke its business licence.

The preceding two paragraphs shall not apply if the non-performance of the contract was due to force majeure.

Article 61: The decision to impose administrative penalties under this Part shall be made by the relevant administrative supervision authority designated by the State Council, except in instances where this Law has already designated the authority to impose the administrative penalty.

Article 62: If, in violation of this Law, any work unit restricts or precludes the participation in bid submission by legal persons or other organizations from outside its own region or network, or designates a bid invitation agency for the bid inviting party, or coerces a bid inviting party into appointing a bid invitation agency to carry out the bid invitation matters or otherwise intervenes in the bid invitation and bid submission activities, it shall be ordered to rectify the situation. The persons directly in charge and other directly responsible personnel of the work unit shall be given a warning and have a demerit or serious demerit recorded according to law; if the circumstances are serious, such persons shall be disciplined by being demoted, dismissed or expelled according to law.

If an individual abuses his office to commit any of the illegal acts mentioned above, his liability shall be pursued in accordance with the preceding paragraph.

Article 63: If working personnel of the State authority legally charged with the duty to carry out administrative supervision of bid invitation and submission activities commit favoritism, graft, abuse of official power or dereliction of duty, and the same constitutes a criminal offence, their criminal liability shall be pursued according to law. If no criminal offence is constituted, they shall be subjected to administrative action according to law.

Article 64: If the acceptance of the winning bidder's bid for a project which legally requires the invitation of bids is void due to violation of this Law, the winning bidder shall be determined anew from the remaining bidders in accordance with the conditions specified in this Law for determination of the winning bidder, or bids shall be invited anew in accordance with this Law.

PART SIX: SUPPLEMENTARY PROVISIONS

Article 65: If a bidder or another interested party considers bid invitation and submission procedures not to be in compliance with relevant provisions of this Law, it or he shall have the right to lodge an objection with the bid inviting party or to complain to the relevant administrative supervision authority according to law.

Article 66: Subject to relevant State regulations, the invitation of bids shall not be required for projects with special circumstances not suited to the invitation of bids, such as those which involve State security, State secrets or emergency rescue, the use of poverty relief funds as remuneration for people in poor areas given employment rather than outright aid, or the need to use peasant workers.

Article 67: Where bids are invited for a project using a loan from an international organization or foreign government or aid funds, and the lender or financier has different regulations in respect of the specific conditions and procedures for the invitation and submission of bids, its regulations may be applied, unless they are against the public interest of the People's Republic of China.

Article 68: This Law shall be implemented as of 1 January 2000.

ADMINISTRATION OF THE ASSIGNMENT FOR COMPENSATION OF HIGHWAY OPERATING RIGHTS PROCEDURES

Part One - General Provisions

Article 1: The *Administration of the Assignment for Compensation of Highway Operating Rights Procedures* (hereinafter the "Procedures") are formulated in accordance with current state laws and regulations and relevant state provisions in order to quicken the pace of highway construction, to open up channels for the funding of highway construction, to standardize the acts of assignment for compensation of highway operating rights (hereinafter the "assignment") and to protect the legal rights and interests of both the assignor and assignee investor.

Article 2: These Procedures apply to highways (here and hereinafter excluding national or regional political and military highways) built and managed by departments in charge of communications at every level nationwide.

Article 3: The assignment of highway operating rights shall comply with the current state industrial policy, be beneficial to the construction of China's highway network, realize the spirit of the highway construction plan and, on the condition that China's current laws, regulations and relevant provisions are abided by, proceed based on the principles of appropriate development and of giving preference to domestic investors.

Article 4: The Ministry of Communications is responsible for the supervision and management of the assignment of highway operating rights nationwide. The general offices (bureaus, committees) of communications of people's governments in every province, autonomous region and municipality directly under the Central Government (hereinafter "provincial-level departments in charge of communications") are in charge of the supervision and administration of the assignment of operating rights for highways within their jurisdiction.

PART TWO – DEFINITION OF HIGHWAYS OPERATING RIGHTS

Article 5: Highway operating rights are intangible assets depending on the tangible assets of the highways. Highway operating rights refer to the rights, approved by the people's governments at the provincial level or above, (i) to collect tolls for the passage of vehicles over highway facilities that have been completed and are operational and (ii) to operate service facilities within a designated area along highways whose construction was funded by departments of communications.

Article 6: The assignment of highway operating rights is the sort of concessions by provincial-level departments in charge of communications authorizing their subordinate highway operation companies (here and hereinafter the "assignor") to assign within a certain period, following approval and within the specified scope the operating rights for all or part of a highway to a unit, with legal person qualifications, within or outside of the provincial boundaries.

PART THREE – ORGANIZATION AND ADMINISTRATION OF THE ASSIGNMENT OF OPERATING RIGHTS

Article 7: The assignment of operating rights for national highways and highways constructed with funds from centrally administered surcharges on vehicle purchases or with funds from central public finance shall be reported by the provincial-level departments in charge of communications to the Ministry of Communications for examination and approval.

The assignment of operating rights for highways at the provincial level and below constructed with regular local fees, with funds from local public finance or through self-financing shall be reported by the provincial-level departments in charge of communications to the provincial-level people's government for examination and approval. The provincial-level departments in charge of communications is also responsible for reporting such assignment to the Ministry of Communications for the record.

Article 8: Where the Ministry of Communications has approved the assignment of operating rights for highways, it is responsible for doing the coordination work with the relevant State Council departments that are involved.

Where the Ministry of Communications and the provincial-level people's government have approved the assignment of operating rights for highways within their scope, the provincial-level departments in charge of communications are responsible for doing the coordination work with the relevant departments within the province that are involved.

PART FOUR – SCOPE OF THE ASSIGNMENT OF HIGHWAY OPERATING RIGHTS

Article 9: The specific content of the scope for the assignment of highway operating rights is: (i) the right to collect tolls for the passage of vehicles over highway facilities such as 40 km highway sections of at least four lanes and 500 metre long large-scale free-standing bridges or tunnels of at least four lanes and (ii) the right to operate within a designated area along highways service facilities such as catering, refuelling, vehicle maintenance, shops and advertising.

When assigning highway operating rights, either both the right to collect tolls for the passage of vehicles and the right to operate service facilities may be assigned or only the right to collect tolls for the passage of vehicles may be asigned.

Article 10: The procedures for the assignment to a foreign investor of operating rights for highways constructed with loans from international financial institutions or foreign governments which have not yet been fully repaid can only be carried out in accordance with the *Procedures* when consented to by the departments that originally approved the use of foreign loans and when approved by the foreign 'window' department in consultation with the foreign lending institution

Article 11: Of highway operating rights, the assignment of the right to collect tolls for the passage of vehicles shall in principle use the following criterion: the estimated period required to recover the investment plus a reasonable number of profitable years (a reasonable number of profitable years normally should not exceed 50% of the estimated period required to recover the investment), being not more than 30 years in total.

Of highway operating rights, the assignment of the right to operate service facilities shall be handled in accordance with relevant State regulations

PART FIVE – APPRAISAL OF THE ASSET VALUE OF THE HIGHWAY OPERATING RIGHTS

Article 12: In accordance with the *State Council, Administration of the Appraisal of State-owned Assets Procedures*, in the assignment of operating rights for national highways and highways constructed with funds from centrally administered surcharges on vehicle purchases or with funds from central public finance, the assignor shall via the provincial-level departments in charge of communications submit to the Ministry of Communications a request for an asset appraisal to be included in the plan. The State Administration for State-owned Assets shall approve the inclusion in the plan and confirm the appraisal results.

Article 13: In accordance with the *State Council, Administration of the Appraisal of State-owned*

Assets Procedures, in the assignment of operating rights for highways at the provincial level and below constructed with regular local fees, with funds from local public finance or through self-financing, the assignor shall submit to the provincial-level departments in charge of State-owned assets a request for an asset appraisal to be included in the plan. The provincial-level departments in charge of State-owned Assets shall approve the inclusion in the plan and confirm the appraisal results.

Article 14: The unit which undertakes to appraise the value of the assets of the highway operating rights must be an appraisal organization with qualifications approved by a State-owned assets administration at the provincial level or above (hereinafter "State-owned assets administration departments"). Given the particularity of highway operating rights, the assignor shall thoroughly investigate the organization which undertakes to appraise the highway operating rights. When necessary, an appraisal organization shall be assigned by the departments in charge of communications at the provincial level or above.

Article 15: The report requesting the appraisal of the assets of the highway operating rights shall be submitted by the assignor. The costs incurred as a result of such appraisal shall be borne by the party entrusting the assets appraisal.

Article 16: In determining the full replacement value of the assets of the highway operating rights, reference shall be made to common, international appraisal methods, viz. by adopting a combination of the 'current value of earnings' and the 'replacement cost' methods.

Article 17: The final accounts for the completion of the highway whose operating rights are being assigned are a commercial secret and may not be disclosed to the assignee. The highway operating rights assets appraisal report confirmed by the State-owned assets administration departments shall serve as proof of the transaction value of the assignment for compensation. The actual transaction value of the assignment of highway operating rights may not be lower than the value in the confirmed appraisal report.

Part Six - Examination and Approval Procedures for the Assignment of Highway Operating Rights

Article 18: When filing for the assignment of highway operating rights the assignor shall provide the following documents, materials and relevant supporting documents:

(1) The Feasibility Report for the assignment of the highway operating rights;

(2) An explanation of the economic strength of the assignee;

(3) The highway operating rights assignment agreement executed between the assignor and the assignee;

(4) A notice with the confirmed results, verified and approved by the State-owned assets administration departments, of the highway operating rights asset value appraisal;

(5) A proof of the assignee's creditworthiness provided by an intermediary organization such as a financial institution or an accounting firm;

(6) A duplicate of the assignee's legal person certificate;

(7) Other relevant documents and materials.

Article 19: Following an examination of the materials filed by the assignor for the assignment of highway operating rights, the provincial-level departments in charge of communications shall – in accordance with the limits of examination and approval authority as stipulated in Article 7 hereof – report such assignment to the Ministry of Communications or to the provincial-level people's government for examination and approval.

Article 20: The assignor and assignee shall execute a contract for the assignment of highway operating rights on the basis of the approval document of the assignment of the highway operating rights. The Parties shall send a duplicate of the contract to both the Ministry of Communications and the provincial-level people's government for the record.

Article 21: If the assignee in the assignment of the highway operating rights is a foreign investor, such investor, after having obtained the assignment approval documents, shall establish a foreign investment enterprise within the People's Republic of China, in accordance with the prescribed limits of examination and approval authority and procedures for foreign investment enterprises.

Article 22: No unit or department may assign highway operating rights without approval

PART SEVEN – USE OF EARNINGS FROM HIGHWAY OPERATING RIGHTS

Article 23: The income obtained by the assignor from the assigned highway operating rights shall first be used to repay the loan for the construction of the highway whose operating rights have been assigned and to develop new highway construction projects. No unit may use the earnings from the assigned highway operating rights for other projects not related to highway construction.

Article 24: The assignee is encouraged to directly invest the earnings from the highway operating rights into new construction highway projects in China.

Article 25: Following any assignment of operating rights for highways constructed with funds from centrally administered surcharges on vehicle purchases or with funds from central public finance, the original investment by the Central Government and the income shared in according to the invested amount remain the rights and interests of the Central Government and shall be held by a relevant Ministry of Communications entrusted investment organization. With the consent of the Ministry of Communications, such sums may continue to be invested in highway construction in the same region, or may be allocated as part of an overall plan by the Ministry of Communications for use in other highway construction projects.

SUPPLEMENTARY PROVISIONS

Article 26: Following the assignment of highway operating rights, the assignor may not recover the highway operating rights during the term of assignment. The assignee may not, for whatever reason, re-assign the highway operating rights to a third party.

Article 27: Without approval of the people's government at the provincial level or above, no additional tollbooths may be installed on the highway whose operating rights have been assigned.

Article 28: The assignee may not, for whatever reason, collect tolls for the passage of vehicles with fixtures carrying out emergency tasks, such as fire engines, hospital ambulances, public security garrison vehicles, emergency disaster relief transport vehicles, etc.

The collection of tolls from vehicles with People's Liberation Army license plates shall be handled in accordance with government regulations.

Article 29: State departments in charge of communications at all levels are authorized to supervise and curb any act of seizing or damaging highways and their ancillary facilities during the term of assignment of highway operating rights.

Article 30: The highway policy and management of highways whose operating rights' assignment has been approved shall be exercised by agencies and personnel of the departments in charge of communications at the provincial level or below. The required outlay shall come from the organization operating the highway operating rights. The amount to be paid shall follow the standard prescribed by the local government.

Article 31: The assignee shall, in accordance with relevant highway maintenance norms and standards promulgated by the Ministry of Communications carry out an effective maintenance to ensure that the highway facilities are in an optimal technical state. Upon expiry of the term of operation the assignee shall return the highway facilities intact to the assignor without compensation.

Article 32: Where previous relevant procedures regarding the assignment of highway operating rights do not agree with the *Procedures,* the latter shall be implemented.

Article 33: The interpretation of the *Procedures* is the responsibility of the Ministry of Communications.

(*translation: J. Roger DECAVELE*)

PRC, ADMINISTRATION OF URBAN REAL PROPERTY DEVELOPMENT TENTATIVE PROCEDURES

(Promulgated by the Ministry of Construction on January 23, 1995, and effective as of March 1, 1995.)

PART ONE: GENERAL PROVISIONS

Article 1: These Procedures are formulated in accordance with the PRC, Administration of Urban Real Property Law in order to strengthen the administration of, govern activities in, and safeguard the legal rights and interests of parties in real property development.

Article 2: Parties engaging in real property development and implementation of the administration of real property development within the area of State-owned land in urban planning areas shall abide by these Procedures.

Article 3: Real property development shall be carried out in conformity with State's industrial policies, plans for the national economy and plans for the development of society.

In real property development, urban planning must be strictly implemented, and overall plans, reasonable overall arrangements, comprehensive development and associated infrastructure construction carried out in accordance with the unified principles of economic, social and environmental benefits.

Article 4: The State Council's administrative department in charge of construction shall be responsible for the nationwide administration of real property development.

The administrative authorities in charge of construction in provinces, autonomous regions and centrally-governed municipalities shall be responsible for the administration of real property development within their administrative areas.

The People's Government administrative authorities in charge of construction or real property at the municipal and county level (hereinafter, "Authority in Charge") shall be responsible for the administration of real property development within their administrative areas.

PART TWO: REAL PROPERTY DEVELOPMENT PROJECTS

Article 5: Real property development projects shall be determined in accordance with urban planning, annual construction land use plans and market demands. Such projects shall be set up after approval.

Article 6: Prior to the assignment or allocation of leaseholds for land to be used for real property development projects, the Authority in Charge shall arrange for the relevant authorities to provide requirements for design plans for the project, time limits for development, construction of infrastructure facilities and ancillary structures, and compensation and resettlement in respect of demolition, and issue a "Proposal on Construction Requirements for a Real Property Development Project".

The Proposal on Construction Requirements for a Real Property Development Project shall include:

(1) the nature, scale and time limit for development of the project;

(2) planning control targets and requirements for design plans;

(3) requirements for the construction of infrastructure facilities and ancillary structures for public service;

(4) division of ownership after completion of construction of infrastructure facilities and public facilities;

(5) requirements for compensation and resettlement in respect of demolition required by the project; and

(6) method of operating the project, etc.

The Proposal on Construction Requirements for a Real Property Development Project shall be submitted to the authority responsible for administration of grants or allocations of land, and its contents shall form an essential part of the provisions of the contract for the grant of leaseholds or the approval document for the allocation of leaseholds.

Article 7: Real property development enterprises shall, within 15 days after signing a contract for the grant of leaseholds or receipt of an approval document for the allocation of leaseholds, file a record with the construction Authority in Charge and obtain a Handbook for a Real Property Development Project.

Article 8: Plans for compensation and resettlement in respect of demolition carried out by a real property development project must be made in accordance with the relevant provisions of the Administration of the Demolition and Removal of Urban Housing Regulations, and such plans may be implemented only after they have been approved.

Article 9: After a real property development project has been determined, application for determination of the location must be made to the urban planning Authority in Charge, and the urban planning Authority in Charge shall issue a Planning Permit for Land to be Used for Construction.

After a real property development enterprise has obtained a Planning Permit for Land to be Used for Construction, it shall organize surveys, plans and designs for the project in accordance with planning and design requirements.

Plans related to design plans for real property development projects must undergo application and approval procedures in accordance with relevant laws and regulations for administration of urban planning, and real property development enterprises shall apply to the urban planning Authority in Charge for issuance of a Construction Project Planning Permit.

After a Construction Project Planning Permit is obtained for a real property development project, application for work commencement may be made.

Article 10: Surveys, design plans and architectural plans for real property development projects shall be undertaken by appropriately qualified work units. Real property development enterprises shall sign written design plan contracts and architectural design contracts with design plan and architectural design work units.

Article 11: Normally, when a real property development project is under construction, construction of underground facilities within the area of the land occupied by the project shall be completed first.

Construction of ancillary infrastructure facilities outside the land occupied by the project shall be centrally organised by the construction administrative Authority in Charge in accordance with the regulations of the local People's Government. Actual construction plans shall be provided in the Proposal on Construction Requirements for a Real Property Development Project.

Article 12: Where leaseholds for real property development were obtained by grant, the purpose for which the land is developed and the time limits for commencing work and carrying our development must be as determined in the contract for grant of leaseholds. Where development work has not commenced in a year after the date specified in the grant contract, an idle land fee of up to 20% of the amount of the grant of leaseholds may be charged. Where development work has not commenced after two years, the leaseholds may be recovered without consideration, unless the delay has been caused as a result of force majeure, actions by the government or relevant government authorities, or works necessary to be done prior to the commencement of the development.

Where leaseholds for real property development were obtained by allocation and development did not begin within the specified time limit, the matter may be handled by reference to the above-mentioned provisions.

Article 13: Where a real property development enterprise develops real property in phases, the amount of investment for each phase shall be commensurate with the scale and total amount of investment of the project. Funds shall be invested according to schedule and in accordance with the contract for grant of leaseholds or the approval document for the allocation of leaseholds, and used for construction of the project.

Article 14: Real property development enterprises shall select appropriately qualified construction work units in accordance with regulations, and sign written contracts with such work units.

Article 15: The construction of a real property development project must conform to relevant State plans, construction technical standards and requirements, and be examined and accepted in accordance with the standards for examination and acceptance of quality.

Article 16: Comprehensive examination and acceptance shall be carried out upon completion of a real property development project. The real property development enterprise shall apply for comprehensive examination and acceptance to the Authority in Charge, and the Authority in Charge shall arrange for the relevant authorities to carry out comprehensive examination and acceptance within one month after receipt of such application. Where the project is found not to be up to standard, the project may not be delivered for use.

Comprehensive examination and acceptance shall take account of:

(1) whether or not planning requirements have been implemented;

(2) whether or not ancillary construction of infrastructure facilities and public service facilities have been completed;

(3) whether or not procedures for examination and acceptance of the quality of individual projects have been completed;

(4) whether or not plans for compensation and resettlement in respect of demolition have been implemented;

(5) whether or not property management has been implemented; and

(6) other matters.

Article 17: Real Property development enterprises shall assume liability for the quality of real property development projects.

Liability for quality between real property development enterprises and design and construction work units shall be determined in accordance with the provisions of relevant laws and regulations.

PART THREE: REAL PROPERTY DEVELOPMENT BUSINESS

Article 18: A real property development enterprise must comply with the provisions of Article 38 and 39 of the PRC, Administration of Urban Real Property Law when assigning leaseholds.

The assignee in a leasehold assignment shall file a record with the Authority in Charge within 15 days of carrying out registration procedures for change of leaseholds, and carry out relevant procedures, such as change in project developer, etc. on the strength of the leasehold assignment contract.

Where the assignee continues to carry out real property development, he must possess the requirements to engage in real property development.

Article 19: Leaseholds obtained pursuant to law may be used as value for equity investment, in accordance with relevant laws and regulations, in real property development equity or cooperative joint venture business.

The parties to an equity joint venture or cooperative joint venture shall lawfully establish a real property development enterprise after determining a project.

Article 20: When leaseholds are assigned and commodity premises are sold, written contracts shall be entered into by the parties.

Article 21: Prior to sales (including pre-sales) of commodity premises, real property development enterprises shall decide on property management work units and methods, and such work units and methods shall be included in the sales contracts for such commodity premises.

Article 22: Except for housing projects subject to preferential price ceiling by the State, prices for the assignment of leaseholds and sale of commodity premises shall be subject to charges on the market.

Real property development enterprises shall report actual transacted prices to the Authority in Charge within 15 days of the date of signing a contract for assignment of leaseholds or contract for the sale of commodity premises. Where commodity premises are pre-sold, a report of the actual transacted prices shall be made to the Authority in Charge within 15 days of the date of final settlement.

Where transacted prices are witheld or not actually reported, the Authority in Charge shall set an authentic appraised price and provide such price to the tax authority as the base for the calculation of taxable amount.

Article 23: Pre-sale of commodity premises by real property development enterprises shall conform to the relevant provisions of the Administration of the Pre-sale of Urban Commodity Buildings Procedures.

Article 24: Where a seller of a pre-sold commodity premise assigns the said real property development project, the original pre-sale contract for such commodity premise shall continue to be implemented by the assignee. A supplementary contract to the original contract for pre-sale of such commodity premise shall be entered into by the assignor, assignee and the purchaser of such commodity premise.

The assignor and assignee of a project shall, within 15 days of the date of signing a supplementary contract, file a record with the Authority in Charge and carry out relevant alteration procedures on the strength of such supplementary contract.

Article 25: After a real property development project is completed and delivered for use, procedures for registration of real property ownership shall be carried out for any real property retained by the real property development enterprise for its own use or for lease.

The purchaser of a commodity premise shall carry out procedures for registration of real property ownership within 30 days of the date of signing a sales contract. Purchasers of pre-sold commodity premises shall carry out procedures for registration of real property ownership within 30 days of the date of final settlement.

PART FOUR: REAL PROPERTY DEVELOPMENT ENTERPRISES

Article 26: "Real property development enterprises" shall mean economic organizations engaged in the development and operation of real property, including enterprises which are specialized in real property development and enterprises which run real property development as a sideline.

Article 27: Unless otherwise provided in law, establishment of a real property development enterprise shall require registration of such enterprise as a limited liability company or company limited by shares in accordance with the PRC, Company Law.

Previously formed real property development enterprises shall gradually be restructured into standardised companies in accordance with the relevant regulations of the State Council.

Article 28: The following requirements shall be met for establishing a real property development company:

(1) have a name and organizational structure in conformity with the registration as a company legal person;

(2) have fixed office premises appropriate to the requirements of real property development business;

(3) have registered capital of Rmb1 million or above, and working capital of no less than Rmb1 million;

(4) have four or more special technical personnel with professional certificates in real property and architectural engineering, and two or more personnel with certificates specially in charge of accounting; and

(5) other requirements as specified in laws and regulations.

The People's Government administrative Authorities in Charge of construction in provinces, autonomous regions and centrally-governed municipalities may formulate regulations in accordance with the actual circumstances in their areas concerning registered capital, working capital and special financial and technical personnel as long as the requirements thereof are not lower than the requirements set out in items 3 and 4 above.

Article 29: Within one month of obtaining a business licence, a real property development company shall file a record with the Authority in Charge of the place where the registry is located.

The following documents must be submitted for the record:

(1) a photocopy of the company's business licence (sealed by the registry);

(2) the articles of association of the company;

(3) the company's capital verification certificate;

(4) appointment documents and personal information on the legal representative and the general manager of the company;

(5) the credentials, appointment documents and employment contracts of professional financial and technical personnel; and

(6) other documents specified by the Authority in Charge.

Article 30: The Authority in charge shall issue a Certificate of the Quality Grading of a Real Property Development Enterprise to established companies that have completed procedures, and shall request the administrative Authority in Charge of industry and commerce to deal with companies which do not meet the requirements for establishment.

Article 31: The quality grading of a real property development enterprise shall be determined in accordance with the assets, special financial and technical personnel and track records in development business of such real property development enterprise.

The People's Government administrative Authorities in Charge of construction in provinces, autonomous regions and centrally-governed municipalities shall formulate standards for different grades of enterprises to undertake different scales of development projects in accordance with the requirements of the Ministry of Construction in combination with actual local circumstances.

Article 32: Real property development enterprises shall record the main items of each stage of implementation of real property development projects and the suggestions for examination, approval and handling of their development business activities made by the relevant government Authority in Charge in the Handbook for Real property Development Projects.

Real property development enterprises shall send the Handbooks for Real Property Development Projects to be examined by the Authority in Charge twice a year and in accordance with the implementation of each stage of the project.

PART FIVE: LEGAL LIABILITY

Article 33: When work begins without authorization in violation of the regulations of Article 9 hereof, penalties shall be imposed by the urban planning Authority in Charge in accordance with the relevant provisions of the PRC, Urban Planning Law.

Article 34: The Authority in Charge shall order a real property development enterprise to stop the following activities and may additionally impose a fine of up to 1% of the total investment in the project:

(1) a work unit without the appropriate qualifications has been appointed to undertake design tasks in violation of Article 10 hereof;

(2) a construction work unit without the appropriate qualifications has been appointed to undertake construction tasks in violation of Article 14 hereof.

Article 35: Where item 2 of Article 18 hereof is violated by failing to handle relevant procedures in respect of matters such as change of developer of a real property development project within a time limit, the Authority in Charge shall order rectification within a time limit and may additionally impose a fine of up to Rmb50,000.

Article 36: Where actual transacted prices are not truly reported in violation of Article 22 hereof, the Authority in Charge may impose a fine of up to Rmb200,000.

Article 37: The Authority in Charge shall issue a warning, order rectification within a time limit and may additionally impose a fine of up to Rmb20,000 where:

(1) the record is not filed within a time limit in violation of Article 29 hereof;

(2) a Certificate of the Quality Grading of a Real Property Development Enterprise is forged or altered; or

(3) a Handbook for a Real Property Development Project is not filled out truthfully or is not submitted for inspection within the specified time.

Article 38: Where the personnel of the Authority in Charge commit dereliction of duty, abuse their powers or give or receive bribes, their work units or the Authority in Charge at a higher level shall impose administrative penalties. Where a criminal offence is constituted, criminal liability shall be pursued according to law.

PART SIX: SUPPLEMENTARY

Article 39: Real property development on State-owned land outside urban planning areas shall be carried out by reference to these Procedures.

FOREIGN INVESTMENT INDUSTRIAL GUIDANCE CATALOGUE (REVISED)

Ref no. 2110/97.12.31(2)
(Promulgated by the State Planning Commission on 31 December, 1997 and effective as of 1 January, 1998.)

ENCOURAGED FOREIGN INVESTMENT INDUSTRIAL GUIDANCE CATALOGUE

1. Agriculture, Forestry, Animal Husbandry, Fishery and Related Industries

- Opening up and development of wasteland, barren hills and tidal flat (excluding those containing military installations), improvement of medium- and low-yield fields.
- Development of new, high-quality and high-yield varieties sugar, fruit trees, vegetables, flowers and plants, forage grass, etc.
- Serialized soilless cultivation of vegetables and flowers and plants.
- Forest planting and introduction of improved tree varieties.
- Breeding of good breeding stock and birds, and offspring seed for aquatics (not including precious and fine varieties unique to China).
- Breeding of famous, special and fine aquatic products.
- New varieties of effective and safe crude pesticides (that reach an insect and germ killing rate of 80 per cent or more and are safe to people, livestock and crops).
- High-concentration chemical fertilizers (potash fertilizers, phosphate fertilizers)
- Development of new agricultural film production and agricultural film products (fibre film, photodegradable film, multi-purpose film and raw materials).
- Raw antibiotics for animal use (including antibiotics, chemosynthesis)
- New products and new forms of anthelmintic, insecticides and anti-coccidiosis for animal use.
- Development of resources in respect of additives and feed proteins.
- New technologies and equipment for the storage, retention of freshness, drying and processing of grains, vegetables, fruits, meat and aquatic products.
- Chemical products for forestry, new technology for the comprehensive utilization of secondary wood, small wood, fuel wood and bamboo materials from forest areas, and new products from such utilization.
- Construction and operation of hubs for the comprehensive use of water resources (with the Chinese party holding the controlling shares or in the leading position).
- Manufacture of new technology water-saving irrigation equipment.
- Manufacture of new technology mechanical equipment and tools for agriculture.
- Projects for the remedy and construction of ecological environment.

2. **Light Industry**

- Design, processing and manufacturing of moulds for non-metallic articles.
- Paper pulp (with an annual production of 170,000 tons or more of wood pulp and construction of a related raw material base).
- Leather finishing and related new technology equipment.
- Production of no-mercury alkaline manganese secondary batteries and lithium ionic batteries.
- Production of special industrial sewing machines with high-technological content.
- Production of polyimide freshness-preserving film.
- Production of new and highly effective enzymic preparations.
- Production of compound and mono-isolate flavours.
- Research and popularization of technology for the application of freon substitutes.
- Processing of diacetate and tows for cigarette making.

3. **Textile Industry**

- Production of wood pulp for textile chemical fibre (with an annual production of 100,000 tons or more and construction of a related raw material base).
- Special textile products for industrial use.
- Printing, dyeing and post-treatment and processing of close-imitation fabric of chemical fibers and high-grade fabric materials.
- Production of auxiliaries, oils and dyes for textiles.

4. **Communications, Transportation, Post and Telecommunication Industries**

- Railway transport technology and equipment: design and manufacture of train locomotives, rolling stock and main parts and components; design and manufacture of line equipment; technology and equipment manufacture for high speed railways; manufacture communication signal equipment and monitoring equipment for transportation safety; manufacture of equipment and materials for electrified railways.
- Construction and operation of feeder railways, regional railways and their bridges, tunnels and ferry facilities (not allowed to be operated by wholly foreign-owned enterprises).
- Design and manufacture of new-modelled machinery and equipment for public roads and ports.
- Construction and operation of urban underground railways and light railways (with the Chinese party holding the controlling shares or in the leading position).
- Construction and operation of highways, independent bridges and tunnels.
- Construction and operation of public pier facilities to be used by ports (with the Chinese party holding the controlling shares or in the leading position).
- Construction and operation of civil airports (with the Chinese party holding the controlling shares or in the leading position).
- Manufacture of equipment for DCS/CDMA digital cellular portable communication systems.
- Manufacture of 2.5 GB/s or more synchronous optical and synchronous microwave digital transmission equipment.
- Manufacture of 2.5 GB/s optical telecommunications, wireless telecommunications and data telecommunications metering instruments.
- Manufacture of ATM exchange equipment.

5. **Coal Industry**

- Design and manufacture of equipment for coal extraction, transportation and screening.
- Coal extraction and screening (with the Chinese party holding the controlling shares or in the leading position for special and rare coal).
- Liquefied production of water slurry and coal.
- Comprehensive development and utilisation of coal
- Comprehensive development and utilization of fuel low-calorific value and associated resources.
- Coal pipe transportation
- Surveying and development of coal bed gas.

6. **Power Industry**

- Construction and operation of thermal power stations having a unit capacity of 300,000 kW or more.
- Construction and operation of hydro-power stations designated for generating power.
- Construction and operation of nuclear power stations (with the Chinese party holding the controlling shares or in the leading position).
- Construction and operation of thermal power stations using clean coal burning technology
- Construction and operation of power stations using new sources of energy (including solar, wind, magnetic, geothermal, tidal and biological energy, etc.).

7. **Ferrous Metallurgy**

- Super-high power electric furnaces of 50 tons and above (equipped with external refining and successive casting), and converter steel smelting of 50 tons and above.
- Stainless steel smelting.
- Production of cold-rolled silicon plates.
- Production of hot-rolled and cold-rolled stainless steel plates.
- Steel oil pipes.
- Processing and disposal of steel scrap.
- Extraction and dressing of iron ores and manganese.
- Production of direct reducing iron and reducing iron derived from melting.
- Extraction of high-aluminium alumina and hardpaste ore, and production of chamotte.
- Processing of needle coke, tamped coke and coal tar into downstream products.
- Production of dried coke.

8. **Non-ferrous Metal Industry**

- Production of monocrystalline silicon (with a diameter of 8 inches or over) and polycrystalline silicon.
- Production of hard alloys, tin compounds and antimony compounds.
- Production of non-ferrous metallic compound materials and new alloy materials.
- Copper, lead and zinc mining (not permitted to be operated by wholly foreign-owned enterprises).
- Aluminium mining (not permitted to be operated by wholly foreign-owned enterprises) and production of aluminium oxide of 300,000 tons or more per annum.
- Rare earth applications.

9. **Petroleum, Petrochemical and Chemical Industries**

- Production of ionic membrane for caustic soda use.
- Ethylene with an annual production of 600,000 tons and above (with the Chinese

party holding the controlling shares or in the leading position).

- Polyvinyl chloride resin (with the Chinese party holding the controlling shares or in the leading position).
- Comprehensive utilization of ethylene by-product C5-C9 products.
- Engineering plastic products and plastic alloys
- Ancillary raw materials for compound materials (bisphenol A, butadiene- styrene-vinylpyridine latex, pyridine, 4.4-diphenylmethane diisocianate and vulcabond toluence).
- Basic organic raw materials for the chemical industry: comprehensive utilization of benzene, methylbenzene and dimethylbenzene (para-, ortho- and meta-) derivatives.
- Production of compounded rubber (solution styrene butadiene rubber, isoprene rubber, isoamyl rubber, ethylene-propylene rubber, butadiene method chloroprene rubber, polyurethane rubber, acrylic rubber and chlorohydrin rubber).
- Production of fine chemical industry: new dyes (pigments), intermediates, catalysts, auxiliaries and oil additives; new technology; processing technology for the commercialization of dyes (pigments); high technology chemicals for electronics and paper-making industries; food additives, feed additives; leather chemicals, oil field auxiliaries, surfactants; water treatment agents, adhesives, inorganic fibres and inorganic powder stuffing.
- Production of chlorination method titanium white.
- Production of coal-based chemical products.
- Recycling of waste gas, waste liquids and waste residue.
- Production of purifying agents, catalytic agents and other auxiliaries for clearing gas emitted from the rear of vehicles.
- Development and application of new technology for upgrading the three-time oil extraction rate (with the Chinese party holding the controlling shares or in the leading position).
- Construction and operation of pipelines for transporting petroleum and gas, petroleum depots, docks designated for petroleum use (with the Chinese party holding the controlling shares or in the leading position).

10. Mechanical Industry

- Manufacture of high-power welding robots and efficient welding line equipment.
- Production of insulating materials (insulating grade F and H) and shaped insulators resistant to high temperatures.
- Manufacture of trackless extraction, loading and transportation equipment for use in mine pits; mechanical transmission dumpers for mine use with a capacity of 100 tons or more; movable crushers; wheel excavators with a capacity of 3,000 m3 / hour or more; loaders for mine use with a capacity of 5 m3 or more; whole-section tunnelers.
- Manufacture of multicolour offset machines designated for web and folio or paper of larger size.
- Manufacture of cleaning equipment for mechanical and electronic wells, and production of medicals.
- Manufacture of turbocompressors, mixing granulators forming part of complete sets of equipment with an annual output of 300,000 tons or more of synthetic ammonia, 480,000 tons or more of urea and 300,000 tons or more of ethylene (with the Chinese party holding the controlling shares or in the leading position).
- Manufacture of complete sets of equipment such as new-type looms, new-type paper-making (including pulp-making) equipment.

- Development and manufacture of precision on-line surveying instruments.
- Manufacture of new technology detection instruments for safety production and environmental protection.
- New components and materials for instruments (mainly new switches and functional materials for instruments such as intelligent sensors for instruments, connectors for instruments, flexible circuit boards, photoelectric switches, approach switches etc).
- Research, design and development centres for major and primary machinery, basic parts, major technological Installations.
- Ratio, serving hydraulic pressure technique, low-power air-driven controlled valves, filler hermetically sealed production.
- Production of precision dies, precision moulds, standard components for dies.
- Manufacture of urban sewage treatment equipment with a capacity of 250,000 tons or more per day, industrial wastewater membrane treatment equipment, upstream anaerobic fluidized bed equipment and other equipment for biological treatment of wastewater, equipment for the production of flyash bricks (5 to 10 tons/ year), waste plastics recycling equipment, desulfurization and denitration equipment for industrial boilers, large bag-type dust collectors resistant to high temperatures and acids.
- Manufacture of precise bearings and special bearings for various main engines.
- Manufacture of key parts and components for motor vehicles: brake assemblies, driving bridge assemblies, gearboxes, diesel fuel pumps, pistons (including piston rings), air valves, hydraulic tappets, axle bushes, superchargers, filters (triple filters), constant velocity universal joints, shock absorbers, seat angle adjusters, car locks, rear view mirrors, window openers, instrument combinations, lights, lamps, dashboards, lamps and bulbs, special high-strength fasteners.
- Manufacture of dies for motor vehicles and motorcycles (including stamp dies, injection moulds and extrusion moulds etc.) and jigs (welding jigs, inspection jigs etc.).
- Manufacture of cast and forged blanks for motor vehicles and motorcycles.
- Technology research, design and development centres for motor vehicles and motorcycles.
- Production of special vehicles such as special desert vehicles for the petroleum industry.
- Manufacture of key parts and components for motorcycles: carburettors, magnetos, starter motors, lamps, disk brakes.
- Manufacture of new technology equipment for on-line water quality surveying instruments.
- Manufacture of specially designed machinery and equipment for flood control and emergency.
- Manufacture of machinery for clearing damp land and removing silt.
- Production of complete sets of feed processing equipment of capacity 10 tons/ hour or more and their key parts.
- Design and manufacture of new instruments and equipment for oil extraction and development.

11. Electronics Industry

- Production of large-scale integrated circuits, whose line width is 0.35 micron or below.
- Production of new electronic components (including chip components) and electronic and electrical components.
- Production of photoelectric devices, sensitive components and transducers.
- Manufacture of large and medium-sized computers.

- Production of compatible digital televisions, high definition televisions (HDTV), digital magnetic tape recorders and players.
- Development of special materials for semiconductors and for use in photoelectronics.
- Manufacture of new display devices (panel display devices and display screens).
- Manufacture of systems for computer assisted design (3-dimensional CAD), computer assisted testing (CAT), computer assisted manufacturing (CAM) and computer assisted engineering (CAE) systems and other computer application systems.
- Manufacture of special equipment, instruments, tools and dies for use in electronics.
- Manufacture of instruments and equipment for the collection of hydrologic data.
- Manufacture of instruments and equipment for satellite communications systems.
- Manufacture of equipment for digital cross-connected .
- Manufacture of equipment for air traffic control systems (not permitted to be operated by wholly foreign-owned enterprises).
- Development and manufacture of high-capacity optical and magnetic disk storage units and their components.
- Development and manufacture of new printing devices (laser printers etc.).
- Manufacture of equipment for data communications multimedia systems.
- Production of monomode optical fibres.
- Manufacture of equipment for telecommunications systems designated for interconnection to networks.
- Manufacture of equipment for the new technology of the backup telecommunications networks.
- Manufacture of ISDN.

12. Construction Materials, Equipment and Other Articles from Non-Metallic Ores

- High-quality float glass production lines with a daily fusion capacity of 500 tons or more.
- High-grade sanitary ware production lines with an annual production capacity of 500,000 pieces or more, and their accessory hardware and plastic parts.
- New construction materials (wall materials, finishing materials, waterproof materials and heat insulation materials).
- Production lines of new drying process cement with a daily capacity of 4,000 tons or more of clinkers (restricted to the central and western regions)
- Facilities for the storage and transportation of bulk cement.
- Articles of glass fibers (through direct melting process) and glass-fibre reinforced plastic with an annual capacity of 10,000 tons or more.
- Inorganic non-metallic materials and manufactured products (quartz glass, artificial crystal).
- High-grade fire resistant refractories for glass, porcelain and glass-fibre furnaces.
- Deep processing technology and manufacture of equipment for of plate glass.
- Manufacture of tunnel excavators, and of underground excavation equipment for urban underground railways.
- Manufacture of special urban sanitary equipment.
- Manufacture of machinery and equipment for tree transplanting machinery.
- Manufacture of machinery and equipment for the trimming and repair of pavements.

13. Pharmaceutical Industry

- Crude chemicals pharmaceutical that are under Chinese patent protection or are granted administrative protection, special pharmaceutical intermediates required to be imported.
- Antipyretic and analgesic medicines produced by adopting new technology equipment.
- Vitamins: nicotinic acid.
- New anti-cancer drugs and new cardiovascular drugs.
- Pharmaceutical preparations: new agents and products made from new technologies such as the slow releasing, controlled releasing, target agents and skin absorbing.
- Amino acids: serine, tryptophan, histidine, etc.
- New types of pharmaceutical packaging materials, containers and advanced pharmaceutical manufacture equipment.
- New, highly efficient and economical contraceptives.
- New technology, new equipment and new instruments for product quality control of traditional Chinese medicines or changing the form or packaging of such medicines.
- New technology for the analysis of active components in traditional Chinese medicines and new processes and new equipment for their extraction.
- New pharmaceuticals produced with bio-engineering technology.
- Development and application of new adjutant.
- Production of reagents for diagnosis of hepatitis, AIDS, radiation immune, etc.

14. Medical Apparatus and Equipment Manufacturing Industry

- Medical x-ray units of 80 kW or more with small radiation dosage, which are equipped with intermediate frequency technology, computer-controlled technology and digital image processing technology.
- Electronic endoscopes.
- Catheters.

15. Aerospace and Aviation Industries

- Design and manufacture of civil aircraft (with the Chinese party holding the controlling shares or in the leading position).
- Manufacture of components and parts of civil aircraft.
- Design and manufacture of aviation engines (with the Chinese party holding the controlling shares or in the leading position).
- Manufacture of airborne aviation equipment.
- Manufacture of light gas turbines.
- Design and manufacture of civil satellites (with the Chinese party holding the controlling shares or in the leading position).
- Manufacture of satellite payloads (with the Chinese party holding the controlling shares or in the leading position).
- Manufacture of components and parts of civil satellites.
- Development of the application technology of civil satellites.
- Design and manufacture of civil carrier rocket (with the Chinese party holding the controlling shares or in the leading position).

16. New Industries

- Microelectronic technology.
- New materials.
- Bio-engineering technology (not including genetic engineering technology).
- Network technology for information and communications systems.

- Isotopic, radiation and laser technology.
- Technology for marine development and marine energy development.
- Technology for desalination and utilization of sea water.
- Development technology for energy conservation.
- Technology for the renewal and recycling of resources.
- Engineering and technology for the prevention, monitoring and control of environmental pollution.

17. Service Industry

- Information and consultancy on international economy, science and environmental protection.
- Maintenance and after-sales service of and for precision instruments and equipment.
- Construction of advanced new technology and new product development centres, and incubation of enterprises.

10. Projects whereby products are all for exportRestricted Foreign Investment Industrial Projects Catalogue

Category A

1. Light Industry

- Production of washing machines, refrigerators and freezers.
- Synthetic fatty alcohol, alcohol ether and ether sulphate.
- Production of compressors with an axle power of below 2 kW to be used by air-conditioners and refrigerators.

2. Textile Industry

- Chemical fibre silk noil yarn made from conventional sliced textile.
- Production of viscose staple fibres with a single-line capacity of below 20,000 tons/year.

3. Petroleum, Petrochemical and Chemical Industries

- Production of barium salt
- Construction of refineries with a capacity of below 5 million tons.
- Cross-ply tyres, re-treading old tyres (excluding meridian tyres) and production of low-performance industrial rubber parts.
- Production of sulphurized titanium white.

4. Machine-building Industry

- Manufacture of equipment for ordinary polyester filaments and staple fibers.
- Manufacture of diesel generator sets.
- Production of various ordinary abradants (including corundum and silicon carbide), grinding wheels of below 400 mm in diameter and artificial diamond saw sheets.
- Production of electric drills and grinders.
- Ordinary carbon steel welding rods.
- Standard ordinary-grade fasteners, small-sized and small to medium-sized ordinary bearings.
- Ordinary lead-acid batteries.
- Containers.
- Elevators.
- Aluminium alloy hubs.

5. Electronics Industry

- Satellite television receivers and their key components.
- Switchboard equipment to be used by digital programme-controlled bureaus and users.

6. Pharmaceutical Industry

- Production of chloramycetin, lincomycin, gentamycin, dihydrostreptomycin, amikacin, hydrochloric acid tetracycline, oxytetracyline, acetyle spiramycin, medemycin, kitasamycin, ilotycin, norfloxacinum, ciprofloxacin and ofloxacin.

- Production of analgin, aspirin, paracetamol, vitamin B1, vitamin B2 and vitamin B6.

7. **Manufacture of Medical Apparatus**
   - Production of middle- and low-grade B-type ultrasound scanners.

8. **Transport Service Industry**
   - Taxis (limited to vehicles purchased domestically).
   - Gas stations (limited to the construction and operation of gas stations ancillary to highways).

Category B

1. **Agriculture, Forestry, Animal Husbandry, Fishery and Related Industries**
   - Development and production of grain, cotton, oil seeds (with the Chinese party holding the controlling shares or in the leading position).
   - Processing and export of rough wood from precious varieties of trees (not permitted to be engaged in by wholly foreign-owned enterprises).
   - Fishing in coastal waters and inland waters (not permitted to be engaged in by wholly foreign-owned enterprises).
   - Planting and breeding of Chinese traditional and herbal medicines (not permitted to be engaged in by wholly foreign-owned enterprises).

2. **Light Industry**
   - Production of table salt, industrial salt.
   - Production of non-alcoholic beverages of foreign brands (including solid drinks).
   - Production of millet wine and colourless spirits of famous brands.
   - Processing of tobacco such as cigarettes, cigars and filter tips.
   - Processing and production of wet blue skins leather of swine, bovine animals and sheep or lambs.
   - Production of natural flavours.
   - Processing of fat.
   - Paper and paperboards.

3. **Textile Industry**
   - wool weaving, cotton weaving.
   - Raw silk, greige.
   - modified and highly delicate simulated chemical fibres, and special chemical fibres such as polyester and carbon fibres (not permitted to be engaged in by wholly foreign-owned enterprises).
   - fibre and non-fibre polyester, acrylic fibre and spandex (not permitted to be engaged in by wholly foreign-owned enterprises).

4. **Transport, Postal and Telecommunications Industries**
   - Construction and operation of trunk railway lines (with the Chinese party holding the controlling shares or in the leading position).
   - Transportation by water (with the Chinese party holding the controlling shares or in the leading position).
   - Transportation by motor vehicles across the national border (not permitted to be engaged in by wholly foreign-owned enterprises).
   - Transportation by air (with the Chinese party holding the controlling shares or in the leading position).
   - General aviation (with the Chinese party holding the controlling shares or in the leading position).

5. **Power Industry**

   - Construction and operation of normal coal-driven thermal power plants with a unit capacity of below 300,000 kW (with the exception of small-scale power grids, power plants located at remote and mountainous areas and power plants using low-quality coal or gangue).

6. **Non-ferrous Metal Industry (Not Permitted To Be Engaged In By Wholly Foreign-owned Enterprises)**

   - Copper processing, aluminium processing.
   - Mining, dressing, smelting and processing of precious metals (gold, silver and platinum family).
   - Mining of nonferrous metals such as tungsten, tin and antimony.
   - Surveying, mining, dressing, smelting and separation of rare earths.

7. **Petroleum, Petrochemical and Chemical Industries**

   - Sensitive materials (films, film rolls, PS plate, printing paper).
   - Extraction and processing of ludwigite.
   - Benzidine.
   - Ionic membrane caustic soda and organic chlorine series chemical products
   - Meridian tyres (with the Chinese party holding the controlling shares or in the leading position)
   - Raw materials for synthetic fibre: precision terephthalic acid, vinyl cyanide, caprolactam, nylon 66 salt, etc.

8. **Machine-building Industry**

   - Assembled vehicles (including all kinds of sedan cars, goods vehicles, passenger coaches, modified vehicles) and motorcycles (with the Chinese party holding the controlling shares or in the leading position).
   - Engines for motor vehicles and motorcycles (with the Chinese party holding the controlling shares or in the leading position)
   - Manufacture of air-conditioning compressors and electronically-controlled fuel injection systems, electronic brake anti-lock systems and safety air bags for motor vehicles, and other electronic equipment systems, electrical machinery and aluminium radiators for motor vehicles.
   - Overhaul and disassembly (refitting) of used motor vehicles, motorcycles and their engines.
   - Thermalelectrical equipment: manufacture of generating sets of 100,000 kW or more (power generators, steam turbines, boilers, auxiliary engines and control installations), gas turbine combined cycle power generating equipment, recirculating fluidized bed boilers, IGCC technology and equipment, and PFBC, desulfurization and denitration equipment (not permitted to be engaged in by wholly foreign-owned enterprises).
   - Hydroelectric power equipment: manufacture of hydroelectric generating sets with a runner of 5 metres or more in diameter (including hydroelectric auxiliary engines and control installations), large pumped-storage sets of 50,000 kW or more and large through-flow sets of 10,000 kW or more (not permitted to be engaged in by wholly foreign-owned enterprises).
   - Nuclear power sets: manufacture of sets of 600,000 kW or more (not permitted to be engaged in by wholly foreign-owned enterprises).
   - Equipment for the distribution and transformation of electricity: manufacture of large transformers, high-voltage switches, mutual inductors and cable equipment of 220 kV or more (not permitted to be engaged in by wholly foreign-owned enterprises).

- Caterpillar bulldozers with a horse-power below 320, below 3-cubic-metre wheeled loaders, below 50-ton mobile cranes (not permitted to be engaged in by wholly foreign-owned enterprises).
- Manufacture of sheet casting machines.
- Photocopiers and cameras.

9. Electronics Industry

- Colour televisions (including projector-typed televisions), colour kinescopes and glass bulbs.
- Photographic cameras (including photographic and video cameras in the same housing).
- Video recorders, magnetic heads, magnetic drums and mechanisms of video recorders.
- Portable communications systems (cellular systems, trunk systems, radio paging, radio telephony).
- Equipment for satellite navigation and positioning receivers and their key components (not permitted to be engaged in by wholly foreign-owned enterprises).
- Manufacture of equipment for VSAT system.
- Manufacture of equipment for below 2.5 GB/S optical synchronous digital series, 144 MB/S or below microwave telecommunications systems.

10. Construction Materials and Equipment and Other Articles from Non-Metallic Ores

- Exploration for and mining and processing of precious non-metallic ores such as diamonds and other natural gems (not permitted to be engaged in by wholly foreign-owned enterprises).

11. Pharmaceutical Industry

- Chinese traditional and herbal medicines, semi-finished and finished Chinese prepared medicines (with the exception of Chinese medicinal drinks and tablets prepared by traditional processing technology).
- Drug precursors: ephedrine, pseudo-ephedrine, ergometrine, ergonovine, lysergic acid, etc.
- Penicillin G.
- Production of addictive narcotics and psychoactive drugs (with the Chinese party holding the controlling shares or in the leading position).
- Hi-tech production of vaccine (vaccine against AIDS, vaccine against hepatitis C, vaccine for contraception purpose, with the Chinese party holding the controlling shares or in the leading position).
- Production of vaccine, antitoxin and toxoid (Bacille Calmette Guérin vaccine, and vaccine against poliomyelitis, DPT (diphtheria, pertussis and tetanus), measles, encephalitis B, epidemic cerebro-spinal meningitis, etc.) Under the State immunity planning.
- Production of vitamin C.
- Production of blood products.

12. Medical Apparatus and Equipment Manufacturing Industry

- Disposable syringes, infusers, blood transfusion devices and blood bags.
- Manufacture of large-scale medical equipment including CT, MRI and medical accelerators.

13. Ship-building Industry (with the Chinese Party Holding the Controlling Shares or in the Leading Position)

- Repair, design and manufacture of special vessels, high-performance vessels and vessels of 35,000 tons or more.
- Design and manufacture of marine diesel engines, auxiliary engines, wireless communications, navigation equipment and accessories.

14. **Domestic and Foreign Trade, Tourism, Real Property and Service Industries (Not Permitted to be Engaged in by Wholly Foreign-owned Enterprises)**

- Domestic commercial business (with the Chinese party holding the controlling shares or in the leading position).
- Foreign trade (with the Chinese party holding the controlling shares or in the leading position).
- Travel agencies.
- Co-operative running of schools (with the exception of elementary education).
- Medical institutions (with the Chinese party holding the controlling shares or in the leading position).
- Accounting, auditing, legal consultancy services, brokerage companies.
- Agency businesses (vessels, transportation of goods, futures, sales, advertising etc.).
- High-grade hotels, villas and high-grade office buildings and international convention and exhibition centres.
- Golf courses.
- Development of tracts of land.
- Large-scale tourist, cultural and recreational parks and artificial landscape.
- Construction and operation of State-level tourist areas.

15. **Financial and Related Services**

- Banks, financial companies, trust and investment companies.
- Insurance companies, insurance brokerage and agency companies.
- Securities companies, investment banks, merchant banks and fund management companies.
- Leasing financing.
- Foreign exchange brokerage.
- Financial, insurance and foreign exchange consultancy.
- Production, processing, wholesale and sale of gold, silver, gems and jewels.

16. **Miscellaneous**

- Printing industry, publishing and distribution business (with the Chinese party holding the controlling shares or in the leading position).
- Import and export merchandise inspection, appraisal and verification business (not permitted to be engaged in by wholly foreign-owned enterprises).
- Manufacture, publication and distribution of audio and video products, and electronic publications (with the Chinese party holding the controlling shares or in the leading position).

17. **Other Industries Which Are Restricted by the State or by International Treaties Concluded or Acceded to by China Prohibited Foreign Investment Industrial Projects Catalogue**

(A)

1. **Agriculture, Forestry, Animal Husbandry, Fishery and Related Industries**

- Wild plant and animal resources protected by the State.
- Precious, high-quality breeds that are rare in China (including high-quality genes from crop and plant cultivation, the animal husbandry industry and the aquatic product industry).
- Construction in respect of natural reserves for flora and fauna.
- Processing of green teas and special teas (famous tea, fermented black tea etc.).

2. **Light Industry**

- Ivory carving and processing of tiger bones.
- Handmade carpets.
- Bodiless lacquerware.
- Articles of pearl-like stone or hawksbill turtle shell.

- Delicate blue and white porcelain.
- Xuan paper and ingot-shaped ink tablets.

3. Power Industry and Urban Public Utilities

- Construction and operation of power grids.
- Construction and operation of urban water supply, drainage, coal .gas and heating pipe networks.

4. Extraction, Dressing and Processing in the Mining Industry

- Extraction, dressing, smelting and processing of radioactive minerals.

5. Petroleum, Petrochemical and Chemical Industries

- Mining and processing of boromagnesite.
- Mining and processing of celestite.

6. Pharmaceutical Industry

- Traditional Chinese medicine materials listed as of natural resources protected by the State (musk, liquorice root etc.).
- Traditional roasting technology for traditional Chinese herbal medicine to be prepared in small pieces for decoction, and traditional Chinese medicinal products prepared by means of secret Chinese recipes.

7. Transportation, Postal and Telecommunications Industries

- Operation and management of the postal service and telecommunications business.
- Control of air traffic.

8. Trading and Financial Industries

- Financial businesses derived from commodity futures, financial futures etc.

9. Broadcasting, Film and Television Industries

- Radio stations and television stations (bases), transmission stations and relay stations (bases) at all levels.
- Production, publication, distribution and release of radio and television programmes.
- Production, distribution and screening of films.
- Screening of videos.

10. Journalism

11. Armament Production Industry

12. Miscellaneous

- Projects which jeopardize the safety and efficient use of military facilities.
- Raw materials and processes which are carcinogenic, or cause deformity or mutation.
- Horse-race trackers and gambling.
- Sex-related services.

13. Other Industries Which Are Prohibited by the State or by International Treaties Concluded or Acceded to by China